Meaningful Action

CAMBRIDGE LANGUAGE TEACHING LIBRARY

A series covering central issues in language teaching and learning, by authors who have expert knowledge in their field.

For a complete list of titles please visit: www.cambridge.org/elt/cltl

A selection of recent titles in this series:

The Roles of Language in CLIL
Ana Llinares, Tom Morton and Rachel Whittaker

Materials Development in Language Teaching (Second Edition)
Edited by Brian Tomlinson

Values, Philosophies, and Beliefs in TESOL
Making a Statement
Graham Crookes

Listening in the Language Classroom
John Field

Lessons from Good Language Learners
Edited by Carol Griffiths

Teacher Language Awareness
Stephen Andrews

Language Teacher Supervision
A Case-Based Approach
Kathleen M. Bailey

Conversation
From Description to Pedagogy
Scott Thornbury and Diana Slade

The Experience of Language Teaching
Rose M. Senior

Learners' Stories
Difference and Diversity in Language Learning
Edited by Phil Benson and David Nunan

Task-Based Language Teaching
David Nunan

Rules, Patterns and Words
Grammar and Lexis in English Language Teaching
Dave Willis

Language Learning in Distance Education
Cynthia White

Group Dynamics in the Language Classroom
Zoltán Dörnyei and Tim Murphey

Testing for Language Teachers (Second Edition)
Arthur Hughes

Motivational Strategies in the Language Classroom
Zoltán Dörnyei

The Dynamics of the Language Classroom
Ian Tudor

Using Surveys in Language Programs
James Dean Brown

Approaches and Methods in Language Teaching (Second Edition)
Jack C. Richards and Theodore S. Rodgers

Teaching Languages to Young Learners
Lynne Cameron

Classroom Decision Making
Negotiation and Process Syllabuses in Practice
Edited by Michael P. Breen and Andrew Littlejohn

Establishing Self-Access
From Theory to Practice
David Gardner and Lindsay Miller

Collaborative Action Research for English Language Teachers
Anne Burns

Affect in Language Learning
Edited by Jane Arnold

Developments in English for Specific Purposes
A Multi-Disciplinary Approach
Tony Dudley-Evans and Maggie Jo St John

Language Learning in Intercultural Perspective
Approaches through Drama and Ethnography
Edited by Michael Byram and Michael Fleming

Meaningful Action
Earl Stevick's influence on language teaching

Edited by

Jane Arnold and Tim Murphey

CAMBRIDGE
UNIVERSITY PRESS

CAMBRIDGE UNIVERSITY PRESS
Cambridge, New York, Melbourne, Madrid, Cape Town,
Singapore, São Paulo, Delhi, Mexico City

Cambridge University Press
The Edinburgh Building, Cambridge CB2 8RU, UK

www.cambridge.org
Information on this title: www.cambridge.org/9781107610439

First published 2013

Printed and bound in the United Kingdom by the MPG Books Group

A catalogue record for this publication is available from the British Library

Library of Congress Cataloguing in Publication data
Meaningful Action: Earl Stevick's Influence on Language Teaching / Edited by
Jane Arnold and Tim Murphey.
    p. cm.—(Cambridge Language Teaching Library)
  Includes bibliographical references and index.
  ISBN 978-1-107-61043-9 (pbk.)
  1. Language and languages—Study and teaching. 2. Language teachers—
  Training of. I. Arnold, Jane, 1944- editor of compilation. II. Murphey,
  Tim. editor of compilation. III. Stevick, Earl W. honouree. P53.755M43
  2013 418.0071—dc23   2012042707

ISBN 978-1-107-61043-9 Paperback

Contents

Contents

Contributors

Jane Arnold, University of Seville, Spain

Heidi Byrnes, Georgetown University, USA

Christopher N. Candlin, Macquarie University, Sydney, Australia

Mark A. Clarke, University of Colorado, Denver, USA

Jonathan Crichton, University of South Australia, Australia

Zoltán Dörnyei, University of Nottingham, UK

Madeline Ehrman, US Foreign Service Institute (retired); Independent training consultant and facilitator

Donald Freeman, University of Michigan, USA

Carolyn Kristjánsson, Trinity Western University, Canada

Diane Larsen-Freeman, University of Michigan, USA

Alan Maley, Visiting Professor, Leeds Metropolitan University, UK

Tim Murphey, Kanda University of International Studies, Japan

David Nunan, Anaheim University / the University of Hong Kong

Rebecca Oxford, Professor Emerita, University of Maryland, USA, and Professor, Air University, United States Air Force

Herbert Puchta, Independent materials writer and educational consultant

Scott Thornbury, The New School, New York, USA

Adrian Underhill, Independent training consultant and facilitator, UK

Leo van Lier, Monterey Institute of International Studies, California, USA

Penny Ur, Oranim Academic College of Education, Israel

Acknowledgements

The authors and publishers acknowledge the following sources of copyright material and are grateful for the permissions granted. While every effort has been made, it has not always been possible to identify the sources of all the material used, or to trace all copyright holders. If any omissions are brought to our notice, we will be happy to include the appropriate acknowledgements on reprinting.

IGI Global for Figure 1.1 on p. 13 from 'Collaborating with a (Non) Collaborator: Interpersonal Dynamics and Constructions of Identity in Graduate Online Learning' by Carolyn Kristjánsson from *Interpersonal Relations and Social Patterns in Communication Technologies: Discourse Norms, Language Structures and Cultural Variables* by Jung-ran Park and Eileen Abels, published by IGI Global, 2010;

Figure 2.1 on p. 33 from 'Diseño, aplicación y análisis de un programa de enseñanza integral de español a un grupo de menores no acompañados' by Carmela Greciet, 2009;

Cengage Learning for the text on p. 183 from *Working with Teaching Methods 1E* by Earl Stevick, copyright © 1998, published by Heinle/ELT, a part of Cengage Learning, Inc. Reproduced by permission, www.cengage.com/permissions;

Routledge for the text on pp. 185–186 from 'SLA after the Social Turn: Where cognitivism and its alternatives stand' by Lourdes Ortega from *Alternative Approaches to Second Language Acquisition* edited by Dwight Atkinson, pages 177–178, published by Routledge, 2011;

The University of Texas Press for the text on p. 233 from *The Dialogic Imagination: Four Essays* by M. M. Bakhtin, edited by Michael Holquist, translated by Caryl Emerson and Michael Holquist, published by the University of Texas Press, copyright © 1981;

Copyright Clearance Center on behalf of System for the Ehrman and Leaver Learning Styles Model on pp. 266–269 adapted from *Cognitive styles in the service of language learning* by Madeline Ehrman and Betty Lou Leaver, System Journal, September 2003. Reproduced with permission;

Use of photo on p. 304 by permission of Earl Stevick and family.

Preface

Jane's voice: I have been fortunate to have maintained personal contact with Earl Stevick over many years. When I called to wish him a happy birthday in October 2010, while he was, as usual, speaking so wisely and well, it suddenly occurred to me that it would be a very worthwhile project to put together a volume which would be a tribute to his significant influence on the language teaching world.

Tim's voice: Jane mentioned her project to me and it seemed such a wonderful idea that I immediately offered to co-edit the book, sending a playful working title 'The Earl of Language Teaching: Stevick's Enduring Impact on the Profession'.

The idea grew and grew as many key professionals in the field joined us. We are indebted to them not only for their thought-provoking chapters, which themselves are examples of meaningful action, but also for their enthusiasm and support in many different ways. Our special thanks to Carolyn Kristjánsson, who has been in close contact with Earl and has worked with him in recent years, for preparing the Epilogue, *A Way with Words,* about Earl and his influence.

The sense of community created among the contributors is a clear validation of Earl's philosophy and teachings. This community was greatly facilitated by frequent email exchanges. Tim's computer counts 320 emails between Jane and himself in little over seven months, with more than a thousand involving all the contributors.

Comments and anecdotes about Earl made by language teaching professionals in many parts of the world can be found in the Appendix.

In the final stages of this book's preparation, the contributors were very sad to learn of the passing of our esteemed colleague, Leo van Lier. His light will continue to shine.

Introduction

A world of meaningful action

In this book we wish to explore the importance of meaningful action for language teaching and learning. Earl Stevick (1998: 20), using a phrase from Alfred Adler, pointed out that we all wish to feel we are 'an object of primary value in a world of meaningful action'. This is very important in a learning context because if we feel that we are valued and capable, that what we do has meaning and is relevant to our goals and needs, this will lead us to make a greater effort. Stevick recognized that meaningfulness occurs both inside ourselves and with others, and he stressed repeatedly the importance of researching and having a better understanding of what was happening 'inside and between the people in the classroom' (Stevick 1980: 4). The possibility of taking meaningful action relates to a whole range of terms, such as agency, self-determination, autonomy, investment, motivation, ideal and possible selves, self-confidence, self-esteem, risk-taking, resilience, socialization and belonging. Many of these are closely connected to Stevick's work and will be dealt with in these chapters.

According to Stevick, *meaning* 'refers to what difference participation in a given activity ... makes to an individual, relative to his or her entire range of drives and needs' (1976: 47). This would seem to match well with the idea of learning as 'a process of becoming a member of a certain community' characterized by 'knowing and doing' (Sfard 1998: 6) as opposed to the passive view of learning in which the mind is likened to a container, gradually being filled with knowledge.

Agency and depth in learning

Stevick's words suggest agency, the ability to take action, which can make life more meaningful. As he says, our 'world of meaningful action' is something which 'draws on the power figures in our lives, and on our peer groups, and on the more or less tightly integrated set of goals that we have adopted for ourselves' (1998: 22). Echoing much in Stevick's thinking, Duff (2012: 417) describes agency as referring to our capacity

1

to choose, control our lives and work towards self and social transformation. Several of the chapters in this book foreground agency as a key issue for both learners and teachers. In addition to the notion of control of one's behaviour, agency also takes in 'the ability to assign relevance and significance to things and events' (Lantolf and Thorne 2006: 143), that is, meaningfulness. Relevance is related to what Stevick refers to as depth, which he convincingly argues is central to learners' experience of the language. This is true since a '"world of meaningful action" is not a flat, two-dimensional thing like a map ... If what a student says makes little or no difference to him or her, it has little "depth"', but if the learning experience makes a difference, if it is deep, then it 'draws more energy from the learner's "world of meaningful action", and in turn it helps to shape that world' (Stevick 1998: 22).

While activities we use in the classroom for language teaching may be considered communicative or enjoyable, they do not necessarily involve depth and meaningfulness. Littlejohn (2008: 215–16) points out that 'fun' activities are not enough to truly engage learners over time and that 'conducive circumstances' – including locus of control (which is closely related to agency), a sense of value and purpose, the preservation of self-esteem and opportunities for feelings of success – are important for sustaining motivation. Factors like this bring depth, which, as Stevick (1998: 23) says, 'in a language course contributes to a sense of "primacy," at the same time as it enhances the meaningfulness of the action'.

Good learners will strive to make a foreign language more meaningful to themselves, but what is also important is that they strive to make *themselves* more meaningful to others through using the language. When learners can use the foreign language successfully in a communicative situation, the agency they experience can lead them to feel connected to other participants and to enjoy a sense of belonging to a new community.

Using initiative and interacting in a foreign language can be exciting for learners, and the feeling of achievement produced is highly motivating. A partial explanation for this comes from recent research in the field of neuroscience, which can help us to understand the importance of meaningfulness, agency and motivation in terms of the action of chemical neurotransmitters in the brain. Our brains release dopamine when we feel excitement, challenge and hope (Sapolsky 2009), and this release can be produced by awareness of having achieved something that is meaningful for us. However, it has also been shown that continued success alone does not automatically bring about this feeling of excitement. Rather, it seems we need to be challenged if we are to maintain the optimal level of excitement. What is most effective is when the challenges of a task match our skill level; at this point we enter a state of flow (Csikszentmihalyi 1990). Note that this does not mean we are always successful in a state of flow, but rather we are challenged to strive for something we deem meaningful, and this, in and of itself, is meaningful action. In such moments our dopamine levels are at their highest (Sapolsky 2005: 91).

Thus, in a view of language learning which is broader than that of merely depositing some linguistic knowledge into a container inside the learner's head, meaningful action and agency are essential ingredients. Pavlenko and Lantolf (2000: 169–79) argue that 'ultimate attainment in second language learning relies on one's agency ... Agency is crucial at the point where the individuals must not just start memorizing a dozen new words and expressions but have to decide on whether to initiate a long, painful, inexhaustive and, for some, never-ending process of self-translation.' We would add, however, that when depth, meaning and experiences of success are involved, the process may also be very gratifying.

Teaching under the Stevick influence

Earl Stevick's work has been an important reference for language teachers and researchers and has empowered and continues to empower teachers to act meaningfully in their own classes, to challenge the status quo and to think more deeply about what is happening 'inside and between' students in their classes. His reflections on the role of the teacher are illuminating: 'we should judge creativity in the classroom by what the teacher makes possible for the student to do, not just by what the teacher does' (Stevick 1980: 22). This way of conceptualizing teaching is in line with student-centred learning, relationship-based learning, and the focus on task-based learning. However, all of these options still depend upon a sensitive teacher realizing the importance of student agency and creating classrooms in which students are encouraged to support each other and feel free to give voice to their ideas. Being student-centred and relationship-based does not reduce the importance of the teacher who is 'the central and the most powerful figure in the classroom' (Stevick 1980: 15), and does not negate the fact that the teacher 'more than anyone else, sets the tone for the interpersonal atmosphere' (p. 168). For example, when a teacher is constantly evaluating students, especially in an insensitive manner, or when he or she leaves no room for students to participate in decision-making processes regarding their learning, it will be very difficult for them to maintain a sense of primacy, to see themselves as adequate, valued individuals. If, on the other hand, the students are part of the evaluation loop and can at times initiate it by engaging in evaluating themselves and in giving feedback to others, including the teacher, and if they are active participants in classroom decisions, then their sense of primacy will be strengthened.

Stevick acknowledged the importance of the teacher's role still further by proclaiming: 'It is the teacher's necessary contribution toward making this new and bewildering corner of the student's "world of meaningful action" into a stable, well-lighted place in which to work (or play!)' (1980: 18). In a similar vein, Wilga Rivers (1976: 96) wrote:

> The essence of language teaching is providing conditions for language learning – using the motivation which exists to increase our students' knowledge of the new language; we are limited only by our own caution, by our own hesitancy to do whatever our imagination suggests to us, to create situations in which students feel involved.

Good teaching, then, is more than a collection of techniques, useful though these may be. As Palmer (1998: 10–11) says, 'good teaching comes from the identity and integrity of the teacher ... Good teachers possess a capacity for connectedness. They are able to weave a complex web of connections among themselves, their subjects and their students so that students can learn to weave a world for themselves' – a meaningful world.

Beyond the classroom

At the meta-level, we need to ask if the structures that are created to foster education also foster meaningful action. Do our schools, curriculums, programmes and syllabi invite belonging, agency and meaningful action? For example, course designing, as Stevick (1998: 165–6) notes, generally involves asking these questions: 'WHAT is the course supposed to teach ...? FOR WHOM are we designing it ...? WHY are we designing it ...? HOW shall we go about it ...?' However, he adds another question: 'Is this course to serve any DEEPER AIMS ...?' He illustrates what he means by deeper aims with suggestions from Murphey (1998) which refer to learning experiences which can change your life and lead you to truly enjoy learning.

Without neglecting the language learning goals in our classes, we can also be concerned on some level, either directly or indirectly, with life goals. Stevick (1998: 172) mentions some options – 'activation of one's full powers ... developing skills at constructive interaction with others ... self-awareness' – which can enhance the language learning process, bringing more meaning to it. While his main focus here was on students and teachers and their activities in classrooms, it is clear that those responsible for language education on all levels can find ways to encourage teachers to help students to have more ownership of their learning and become agentive organizers of their own meaningful actions.

This volume in honour of Earl Stevick's enduring impact on the profession explores meaningful action in three domains: the relationship that learners have with themselves and with others, classroom activity and diverse frameworks supporting language learning.

References

Csikszentmihalyi, M. (1990) *Flow: The Psychology of Optimal Experience*, New York: Harper Perennial.

Duff, P. (2012) 'Identity, agency, and second language acquisition', in Gass, S. M. and Mackey, M. (eds.) *Handbook of Second Language Acquisition*, London: Routledge, pp. 410–26.

Lantolf, J. P. and Thorne, S. (2006) *Sociocultural Theory and the Genesis of Second Language Development*, Oxford: Oxford University Press.

Littlejohn, A. (2008) 'The tip of the iceberg: factors affecting learner motivation', *RELC Journal*, 39(2): 214–25.

Murphey, T. (1998) *Language Hungry*, Tokyo: MacMillan Languagehouse. New edn (2006) Innsbruck: Helbling Languages.

Palmer, P. J. (1998) *The Courage to Teach*, San Francisco: Jossey-Bass Publishers.

Pavlenko, A. and Lantolf, J. P. (2000) 'Second language learning as participation and the (re)construction of selves', in Lantolf, J. P. (ed.) *Sociocultural Theory and Second Language Learning*, Oxford: Oxford University Press, pp. 155–77.

Rivers, W. (1976) *Speaking in Many Tongues: Essays in Foreign Language Teaching*, Rowley, MA: Newbury House.

Sapolsky, R. (2005) *Monkeyluv: And Other Essays on Our Lives as Animals*, New York: Scribner.

Sapolsky, R. (2009) 'The uniqueness of humans: Stanford's Class Day Lecture', September 2009.

Sfard, A. (1998) 'On two metaphors for learning and the dangers of choosing just one', *Educational Researcher*, 27: 4–13.

Stevick, E. W. (1976) *Memory, Meaning and Method: Some Psychological Perspectives on Language Learning*, Boston: Heinle & Heinle.

Stevick, E. W. (1980) *Teaching Languages: A Way and Ways*, Rowley, MA: Newbury House.

Stevick, E. W. (1998) *Working with Teaching Methods: What's at Stake?*, Boston: Heinle & Heinle.

Part A

Meaning-making inside and between the people in the classroom

Earl Stevick (1980: 4) made an important point when he affirmed that success in language learning depends to a large extent on what goes on 'inside and between the people in the classroom'. This implies that taking into account the 'inside', the intrapersonal aspects of learners, can help us as teachers to make learning more meaningful and thus more effective, while the second aspect, the 'between', reminds us that often meaning is not made alone. Stevick stated that he came to understand that the most important part of what 'goes on' is 'the presence or absence of harmony – it is the parts working with, or against, one another' (1980: 5). Harmony may refer to whole-person learning where the body, mind and emotions of the learner work together, but it also includes in a very central way the need to establish a good atmosphere and productive relationships 'between the people' in the classroom. Stevick (1980: 22) refers to Becker's notion that as human beings we don't establish and maintain our own meaning by ourselves; we make meaning together.

The importance of the *other* in learning is essential. Vygotsky stressed that the intermental (between minds) comes before the intramental (within the individual): 'Any function in the child's cultural development appears twice, or on two planes; first it appears on the social plane, and then on the psychological plane, first it appears between people as an interpsychological category, and then within the child as an intrapsychological category' (Vygotsky 1981: 163). This process of internalization is usually the result of meaningful action, both socially and personally.

In language learning, opening a coursebook and doing a grammar exercise could be considered action. In language teaching, presenting the class with a detailed explanation of verb tenses could also be considered action. However, in both cases they would not necessarily be experienced as meaningful action. From his research Littlejohn (2008: 214)

7

finds that many learners 'appear to see their classes as mainly consisting of "exercises", free of any memorable content'. Even in a class based on communicative language teaching, activities may not seem relevant to learners. Something more, perhaps at times elusive, is needed to make what goes on in class meaningful action, something with depth, as Stevick might call it.

Action is, of course, about doing, but to facilitate meaningful action it can be helpful to start with an awareness of what goes on inside the learners, of matters such as their self-concept. As Dörnyei (2009: 11) states, self-concept traditionally refers to 'a summary of the individual's self-knowledge related to how the person views him/herself at present'. This can be influenced by the relationships that exist in the language classroom, where learners construct a sense of identity in relation to the new language. According to Norton (2000: 4), identity can be seen as our understanding of our relationship to the world, how we construct that relationship in time and space, and how we understand our possibilities for the future. Current views of identity related to language learning emphasize social as well as affective dimensions. Positive identity development co-occurs with increasing agency, which Ahearn (2001: 112) defines as the 'socioculturally mediated capacity to act'. When learners develop agency, they are stimulated to take control and to make informed choices, to invest more resources in their learning since they find personal relevance in the learning process and are led to participate more actively.

In Part A, while focusing at times on individual or 'inside' aspects, the chapters also foreground the relational aspects, the connections established 'between' members of a learning community.

Carolyn Kristjánsson discusses in Chapter 1 issues relating to identity, agency and options for development of *selfhood* through aspects such as interpersonal validation and humour in the language classroom. Drawing on data from a longitudinal study of a community-based language programme for adults, this chapter considers how meaning-making starts with an understanding of who we are in the classroom and how our sense of identity there is closely linked to frames of reference beyond. Learners are not merely receivers of information about language but social subjects who use it to create and sustain community. The role of the teacher in supporting learner initiative is essential here.

In Chapter 2 Jane Arnold points out the importance for language learning of affective factors, including beliefs. Learner beliefs have a great influence on learning since learners who are confident, who believe they have the ability to learn, will be more likely to take steps to gain greater control over their learning. This chapter presents research which shows how enhancing self-concept and self-confidence through meaningful self-esteem activities, teacher confirmation and the L2 Motivational Self System (Dörnyei 2009) can pave the way to greater investment by students in the learning process and thus better language learning.

Herbert Puchta in Chapter 3 brings in connections with neuroscience and educational theory to illuminate aspects of language learning, especially the need to engage the learner's brain. Drawing on work by neuroscientist James Zull, he shows how factors such as challenge, personal discovery and participation with others as co-creators of experience can lead to a greater sense of control in the learning situation. What Stevick referred to as 'depth' in learning is given support here by neurobiological evidence. Puchta also considers the relationship of learners with the material used and how for more efficient learning it is important to take into account the brain's need for relevance, positive emotion and creativity.

Scott Thornbury presents a model of cognition in Chapter 4 which is grounded in the holistic idea that language use (and, by extension, language learning) is interdependent on its contexts of use, including the very physical context of the language user's own body. Within this perspective, taking on a new language is seen both as a process of acquiring new mind–body mappings, and also as a socially constructed process, involving aligning oneself with members of the target speech community. Meaningful action is thereby both embodied and embedded in the social context. Echoing Stevick's call for harmony, a use-based, life-enhancing vision of language learning is invoked, whereby, as Thornbury says, mind, body and world are conjoined.

In Chapter 5 Christopher Candlin and Jonathan Crichton explore Trust as a central theme in Stevick's work, one which reveals his prescient awareness of its importance to language teaching and learning. To create the conditions for the classroom as a 'world of meaningful action', Trust depends on acknowledging those social and interactional conditions that are constantly in play and at risk in language learning. While students are central to this process, both students and teachers are involved in co-constructing Trust. The authors argue that 'Putting our Trust in the learner' carries profound implications for the practice of language teaching and propose a 'multi-perspectival' approach to researching and developing Trust-based awareness, curricula and practices.

The two remaining chapters of Part A deal with narratives, which are an important way to express personal meaning as they can help strengthen the sense of self and communicate the self to others. Shore (1996: 58) has expressed very effectively the significance of narratives, through which 'experience is literally talked into meaningfulness'.

Reading or listening to learners' narratives, we can observe learning and meaning-making in action.

In Chapter 6 Rebecca Oxford begins by discussing research and the types of language that learner narratives commonly use. She notes that in learner narratives, successful learners' self-descriptions often involve a combination of heightened motivation, emotional charge and a sense of competence. This combination creates a sense of flow and 'hot cognition'. She also shows how learner narratives frequently reveal fascinating, complex interactions between personal factors on the one hand and social dynamics, such as power and identity, on the other. The large range of emotions in learner narratives is another key theme. In addition, the chapter offers useful approaches and aids for narrative work by learners and suggests ways to appreciate, interpret and evaluate this versatile tool for language learning.

Learner stories can be of use to teachers in many ways. An obvious one is by helping us to understand our learners, but they can also contribute to enriching our practice and developing our agency and identity as teachers. One of the advancements in language teaching that has made possible a greater sense of agency has been the emergence of a learner-centred approach to curriculum development. David Nunan has been a leading figure in this movement, and in Chapter 7 he relates how his interest in learner-centredness became a key part of his professional life through his learners' stories, which have influenced his thinking and attitudes. For both research and pedagogy, he stresses the importance of stories in language learning and teaching, of listening to learners' voices.

References

Ahearn, L. (2001) 'Language and agency', *Annual Review of Anthropology*, 30: 109–29.

Dörnyei, Z. (2009) 'The L2 motivational self system', in Dörnyei, Z. and Ushioda, E. (eds.) *Motivation, Language Identity and the L2 Self*, Bristol: Multilingual Matters, pp. 9–42.

Littlejohn, A. (2008) 'The tip of the iceberg: factors affecting learner motivation', *RELC Journal*, 39(2): 214–25.

Norton, B. (2000) *Identity and Language Learning*, Harlow: Longman.

Shore, B. (1996) *Culture in Mind: Cognition, Culture and the Problem of Meaning*, Oxford: Oxford University Press.

Stevick, E. (1980) *Teaching Languages: A Way and Ways*, Rowley, MA: Newbury House.

Vygotsky, L. (1981) 'The development of higher forms of attention in childhood', in Wertsch, J. V. (ed.) *The Concept of Activity in Soviet Psychology*, Armonk, NY: M. E. Sharp, pp. 144–88.

1 Inside, between and beyond: agency and identity in language learning

Carolyn Kristjánsson

Introduction

One of Earl Stevick's enduring contributions to the field of language education is the insight that 'success depends less on materials, techniques, and linguistic analyses, and more on what goes on inside and between people in the classroom' (Stevick 1980: 44).[1] An important part of what does or does not go on has to do with relevance, in other words, the connection between something on the external dimension of human experience with something on the internal dimension of the student's appreciation of self (Stevick 1980: 119). Relevance breaks down if what happens does not make sense in terms of the learner's past, present or future realities (p. 118). The affairs of the classroom are thus firmly connected to the world beyond.

Conceptualizing the language learner in this way suggests not only a focus on the person, but a focus on that person as a 'person-in-the-world' (Lave and Wenger 1991: 5). It also encompasses matters of agency and identity (Miller 2010). In what follows, I explore this with reference to interaction in an adult immigrant language classroom along with connections to realities beyond it.

Agency

Second language acquisition researchers working within a sociocultural paradigm view the interrelated notions of agency, self and identity as being of importance in the learning of additional languages (van Lier 2010: ix). From a sociocultural perspective, agency is viewed as a person's capacity to act within the possibilities afforded by the social structures in which he or she is situated (van Lier 2008; Miller 2010). More specifically, as a context-related capacity:

> Agency refers to people's ability to make choices, take control, self-regulate, and thereby pursue their goals as individuals, leading, potentially, to personal or social transformation ... A sense of agency

---

[1] I wish to thank Bill Acton for helpful feedback on earlier drafts of this chapter.

11

enables people to imagine, take up, and perform new roles or identities (including those of proficient L2 speaker or multilingual) and to take concrete actions in pursuit of their goals. Agency can also enable people to actively resist certain behaviors, practices, or positionings, sometimes leading to oppositional stances and behaviors leading to other identities.

(Duff 2012: 417)

In addition to action or performance, agency is also understood to encompass the capability to ascribe relevance and significance to things and events, including agentive behaviour (Lantolf and Thorne 2006; van Lier 2008; Miller 2010). Miller connects the dots by suggesting that 'the capacity to act and ability to assign relevance and significance to such acts emerge as individuals are positioned as (potential) agents within ideologically defined spaces' (2010: 466). Put differently, the prevailing belief and value systems in any number of contexts, including political, social and institutional, shape conditions for interaction between people and come to bear on the significance that they ascribe to it. Explaining further, Miller contends that the constraints established by constructing a particular identity position at a given point also enable a person to act purposefully in that interactional space. Thus, 'recognizable subject positions such as "language learner" or "adult immigrant" or "small business owner" can enable individuals to act meaningfully and also resist and transform such positioning' (p. 468).

Identity

According to Ishiyama (1995a), meaningful action is motivated by a need for self-validation, that is the 'affirmation of one's sense of self, purpose in life, and meaningful personal existence in a given sociocultural context' (Ishiyama and Kitayama 1994: 168). It is a process often mediated in and through language (Ishiyama 1995b). In this view, self is represented as a multidimensional construct consisting of five elements: physical, or what I call *bodily self* (the body and physical aspects of being), *familial self* (family roles and relationships), *sociocultural self* (social and cultural roles and relationships outside the family context), *transcultural-existential self* (the existential aspect of self capable of relating to others at a level beyond the restrictions of sociocultural norms or externally imposed values) and *transpersonal self* (the spiritual or ego-transcending aspect of self) (Ishiyama 1995a). These interrelated dimensions are co-occurring, fluid and holistic. In related work I have suggested that the way in which an individual personally experiences or assigns significance to a particular dimension of self at any given time will draw on *physical, cognitive, affective* and/or *spiritual* awarenesses and capacities, some of which will be foregrounded more than others, depending on circumstances (Kristjánsson 2010).

From this perspective, identities are constructed and validated or invalidated around the five basic dimensions of self in various contexts of human existence. These contexts of existence can be conceptualized in terms of four overlapping domains: interpersonal *relationships, activities,* symbolic and practical objects or *things,* and *places* or landmarks (Ishiyama 1995a). As I have noted elsewhere (Kristjánsson 2010), the domains do not exist in a vacuum but are located within a constellation of *sociocultural structures* such as government, educational institutions, organized religion and kinship structures, to name a few. These encompass relations of power and are themselves situated in broader orientations towards the world which include, but are not limited to, cultural and ideological frames, represented by the term *worldviews.* Worldviews come to bear on how all aspects are understood and interpreted in constructing identities for self and positioning others at any given junction in time and space. This is depicted in the diagram of situated multidimensional identity in Figure 1.1.

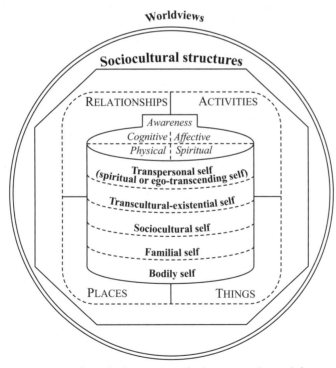

Figure 1.1   Situated multidimensional identity (adapted from Kristjánsson 2010)

What insights about relevance might such perspectives afford when applied to the investigation of interaction in a language classroom? More specifically, what might be learned about how practices within the classroom structure possibilities for engagement of self, and how might the related exercise of agency and constructions of identity be informed by broader frames of reference and perceptions of reality? I turn now to an example to address these questions.

An example

A few years ago, I conducted a study in a volunteer-run, community-based language programme that offered classes to adults who were newcomers to Canada. Classes were held two mornings a week, and an important feature of the programme was an activity known as 'What did you do on the weekend?' This took place during the first part of the first class each week when students at all levels were given an opportunity to talk about something they did or something that happened to them over the weekend. It was not uncommon for classes to spend up to 90 minutes, or 25% of the week's class time, engaged in this exercise, although there was no pressure on students to participate more than they were willing and topics were up to them. The purpose of the activity was to provide opportunities for learners to use English to talk about things that were going on in their lives outside of the classroom. These sessions were typically characterized by regular accounts of routine undertakings mixed with lighthearted moments of teasing and shared jokes; however, there were also times when students chose to disclose matters that were serious in nature.

One such instance occurred in an intermediate class of female students consisting of immigrant women and mothers of young international students, many alone with their children in Canada. The class was video recorded as part of a broader investigation and a transcription made of the interaction. On the day when this exchange took place, there were 14 Taiwanese and Korean women present along with the female Canadian-born teacher of German descent. The morning began with a Taiwanese student describing the death of a 33-year-old cousin from cancer. The next student told of her ageing father's spiritual experience in a hospital in Taiwan. A third student spoke of her husband's return to Korea for another three-month period and how her son had cried inconsolably at his departure. The fourth student, Juling, a Taiwanese woman, began by saying that she had been unwell over the weekend, linking her condition to interrelated physical and emotional causes. When the teacher suggested it was because she missed her husband who was in Taiwan, Juling rejected the explanation, countering with her own view that it was due to lack of friendship.

Juling: Last week I'm very sad because I feel uncomfortable. I have some runny nose ... and cough and I feel very lonely.
Teacher: Oh, you miss your husband.
Juling: No, because I came to here and haven't good friend (fights tears) and so I pray.

Amid offers of support and friendship from others in the class, Juling told how she had called an immigrant acquaintance who had initially experienced physical illness in Canada which she too linked to loneliness. Now that the acquaintance had friends, this was no longer a problem. Juling reported that the woman had given her advice on how to make friends, but that she felt she still did not know what to do and so she had prayed once again. She subsequently received phone calls from several friends who lived at a distance and neighbours dropped by for a visit. She interpreted these events as an answer to her prayer. The teacher responded empathetically:

Teacher: Good. I sometimes have lonely days, too. I think we all do ... Women need each other. We need to talk, and I know for lots of you it must be very hard.

This led to a declaration from Mi-Hye, the most senior Korean student, that Juling had good friends among those in the class and comments from others that Juling was not the only one to feel sad and lonely. Jinhee, another Korean student whose husband was in Korea, then initiated an account of her own recent experience, which turned into a humorous, yet serious, co-constructed commentary with the teacher and Mi-Hye each incorporating disclosures of their own.

Jinhee: Early morning I receive a call from my husband. Suddenly, why I cried? I don't know.
Teacher: Because you missed him! [General laughter]
Jinhee: I'm not missing him. Just a little. [General laughter; Jinhee laughs]
Teacher: [Acts as if phoning] But all of a sudden you hear his voice and then you really miss him!
Mi-Hye: My husband always with me, but I sometimes will cry too. [General laughter] Yeah, not husband! [General laughter]
Teacher: I miss my children now that they're married and don't live in my house. Sometimes I'm crying [gestures to show tears streaming down face] and my husband says, 'What's the matter?' [with mock teary voice] 'I miss C!' [General laughter]

15

> Jinhee: Sometimes my feeling is low. I am crying. My husband really worry about me. He say, 'Why you crying?' So I answer.
>
> Mi-Hye: 'I need you.' [Much general laughter]
>
> Teacher: 'I need you!' [More general laughter]
>
> Mi-Hye: 'Right now.'
>
> Teacher: 'Yeah, right now! Come home!'
>
> Jinhee: [Mimics her husband] 'I think you catch some cold?' I, 'Yes', but I'm not catch cold. [Laughs]
>
> Teacher: You just said you did.

Jinhee finished her account by stating that in contrast to when she was in Korea, in Canada she too sometimes experienced the feelings described by Juling. The teacher then turned to Juling and commented on the benefits of her disclosure. Two other students offered related contributions:

> Teacher: Juling, it is very good that you shared this with the class because now you know that we all have this.
>
> Yu-Jeong: Now I think it is time to test myself, to [be] strong.
>
> Teacher: Oh yeah ... It's a testing time.
>
> Yu-Jeong: [To Juling] Everyone is difficult, are difficult, live here.
>
> Yunjin: You have to stand alone ... we feel alone, lonely. Try to share, share together. [Gestures to include the class]

Juling responded by elaborating further on the cause of her loneliness: missing the Lunar New Year celebration in Taiwan. This sparked an exchange, initiated by Jinhee and supported by the teacher, regarding special holidays and the loneliness people feel when separated from loved ones at such times. At the end, the teacher again thanked Juling for her contribution. Juling responded with an apology, an action met with protests from the teacher and other students:

> Teacher: Don't be sorry!
>
> Various: Don't be sorry!
>
> Jinhee: Don't be sorry. [Gestures with hand to indicate 'no']
>
> Teacher: No, it's very good ... you feel better when you talk about it and you find out that others feel the same thing.

Yalin, a Taiwanese student, then offered to help Juling make contact with other Chinese in the church community to which she belonged. This was followed by additional comments of affirmation and support for Juling and a concluding observation by Jinhee that listening to Juling's story had caused those in the class to feel closer. The teacher concurred, bringing this part of the activity to an end.

Classroom practices and possibilities for self, agency and identity

Language teachers often place high value on communicative language use; however, what actually goes on in many classrooms falls short of the mark. In fact, studies across a broad spectrum of language classrooms have shown that interaction is frequently teacher led and dominated, often characterized by IRF (teacher initiation – student response – teacher feedback) (Sinclair and Coulthard 1975) or IRE (teacher initiation – student response – teacher evaluation) (Mehan 1979) sequences (Thornbury and Slade 2006; Waring 2009; Doherty 2010). By contrast, the interaction arising from the 'What did you do on the weekend?' (hereafter Weekend) activity is a complex multi-participant discussion that encompasses the exchanges of six students and a teacher, and resembles casual conversation.

Viewed through the lens of Systemic Functional Linguistics (SFL) (Halliday 1994), language is a resource for making several kinds of meaning simultaneously: meaning about the world, meaning about the message and interpersonal meaning about the roles and relationships of people. Casual conversation accomplishes all of the above; however, it is driven by interpersonal meanings (Eggins and Slade 1997: 6). This is encoded in a variety of ways that communicate attitudinal stance, including evaluative language and humorous devices. The latter facilitates the serious work of evaluative meaning-making while representing attitudes less explicitly. The former constructs an attitudinal profile of feelings, thoughts and behaviour along a continuum of negative to positive orientation. An analysis of interpersonal meaning provides a view of how people in conversation enact and construct their social identities, position and reposition conversation partners, and build alignments (Eggins and Slade 1997: 314; Thornbury and Slade 2006: 69). In short, it provides a linguistic snapshot of social action in a given context. It is therefore helpful to take a closer look at the use of evaluative language by participants in the Weekend interaction. For this purpose, I draw on the tools of Appraisal analysis, using the following categories (Eggins and Slade 1997: 125; Martin and White 2005: 42–68):

- AFFECT: speakers' expression of emotional states
  Guiding question: How do you feel about this?
- APPRECIATION: speakers' reaction to and evaluations of reality – concrete, abstract, material or semiotic things
  Guiding question: What do you think/know/understand/believe about this process/event/phenomenon?

17

- JUDGEMENT: speakers' judgements about behaviour or character
  – the ethics, morality or social values of people
  Guiding question: How do you judge this behaviour or this person's character?

The results of an Appraisal analysis of the transcript of interaction in the Weekend activity show that evaluative language is associated with the lived experiences of participants, that is, identity positionings and alignments related to the realities of women who are newcomers to Canada. More specifically, the interaction highlights their feelings in this regard and is characterized by the use of linguistic resources of AFFECT throughout. For example, Juling begins by framing her weekend experience in such terms (e.g. 'I'm *very sad*', 'I feel *uncomfortable*', 'I feel *very lonely*') and brings her initial account to a close by attributing the unexpected events of the weekend to an answer to the prayer born out of loneliness ('Because I prayed, "God, I'm *very lonely*"'). The teacher extends the scope of the discussion by noting her own experience of loneliness and generalizes it to others ('I sometimes have *lonely days* too. I think we all do'). Subsequent comments by Yunjin, Jinhee, Mi-Hye and Yu-Jeong incorporate comments that describe related feelings linked to their experiences as newcomers to Canada. While much of the interaction revolves around feelings of loneliness associated with this aspect of their lives, it ends on a positive affective note when Jinhee sums up the impact of hearing Juling's story ('we *feel more close*').

In addition to disclosing personal feelings, participants also communicate their perceptions of the circumstances and related behaviours of newcomers to Canada, drawing on linguistic resources of APPRECIATION and JUDGEMENT. For example, Juling's feeling of sadness is precipitated by the perception that she does not have a close friend ('I came to here and *haven't good friend*') while Yu-Jeong notes the difficulties faced by all ('Everyone is *difficult* ... live here'). From Yunjin's perspective, newcomers cannot look to others for support ('You have to *stand alone*'); however, within the class the situation is different. Whereas Juling positions herself as unable to make friends, Mi-Hye challenges this by observing that she has friends in the class ('You have *very good friends* here'). For her part, the teacher highlights the acceptability of Juling's disclosure ('it is *very good that you shared this* with the class because now you know that we all have this') and reframes her behaviour with reference to the general desirability of and need for women to support each other. When Juling apologizes for her tearful disclosure ('I'm *sorry*'), suggesting a perception of her behaviour as inappropriate for that setting, the teacher counters with an explicit statement of approval ('No, it's *very good*'), repeating her earlier statement that talking about difficulties is an antidote to feelings of isolation.

To summarize, the contributions of participants in the Weekend activity feature expressions of Appraisal linked to self or others within the context of personal stories and related comments regarding the experience of being newcomers to Canada. It is within the context of this overarching story that identity positions are constructed in the give and take of meaningful discourse action by overt naming or implication, including instances where positions are claimed (e.g. 'friendless newcomer'), resisted (e.g. 'lonely wife'), renegotiated (e.g. 'newcomer with good friends'), transformed (e.g. it's a time to be strong – i.e. 'strong women') and extended (e.g. all women (not just newcomers) need each other – 'mutually supportive women'). However, these discursively constructed positions can also be seen as grounded in broader, foundational, dimensions of self.

Ishiyama's (1995a) model of validation is based on the assumption that people are motivated to seek validation, that is affirmation, around the five dimensions of self. By linking the Appraisal analysis above to the broader categories of self and related validation domains derived from Ishiyama's work, we can gain an enhanced understanding of agency demonstrated in the Weekend activity. Table 1.1 illustrates this connection with Appraisal samples from the interaction which have been

Table 1.1 *Appraisal analysis and validation elements*

Appraisal	Appraisal category	Dimension of self	Validation domain
I feel very lonely. I haven't good friend.	Affect – Appreciation – (Judgement –)	Sociocultural self under/ invalidated	Relationships
I prayed, 'God I am very lonely.' ... He brought you some hope. Good. [He brought you some hope.]	Affect – Affect + Appreciation +	Transpersonal (spiritual) self validated	Relationships

(*cont.*)

Table 1.1 (cont.)

Appraisal	Appraisal category	Dimension of self	Validation domain
You have very good friends here. ... we all care about you.	Appreciation + (Judgement +) Affect +	Sociocultural self validated	Relationships
We all do [have lonely days]. Women need each other.	Affect – Appreciation +	Transcultural-existential self validated – all have similar needs	Relationships
I cried. I am not missing him [my husband]. Just a little bit.	Affect – Affect –	Familial self under/ invalidated	Relationships
In Taiwan ... every year I have this special dinner [Lunar New Year celebration], but this year I haven't.	Appreciation + Appreciation –	Sociocultural self under/ invalidated	Place/Thing/ Activity
It is very good that you shared this with the class.	Judgement +	Sociocultural self validated	Relationships

thematically analysed with reference to Ishiyama's categories. This level of analysis suggests that the evaluative comments made by participants can not only be understood as views related to particular lived experiences and perceptions of reality, but also be seen to indicate validation or invalidation of foundational dimensions of participants' sense of self. Although the Weekend interaction centres primarily upon identity positions related to the dimension of sociocultural self, the discussion also encompasses appeals made to the transpersonal, transcultural and familial self as illustrated. At the most basic level, positive polarity, i.e. an expression of positively oriented sentiment (+), generally signals validation of a dimension of self. Negative polarity, an expression of negatively oriented sentiment (–), generally signals invalidation. However, there are exceptions, as illustrated by the comment 'We all do [have lonely days]', where a statement of negative polarity signals empathy and thus serves as a means of validating Juling, the lonely student. The strong representation of relationships in the domain category underscores the importance of interpersonal interaction as a source of validation for participants at this time in their lives.

The link between the validated or invalidated sense of self and identity construction can be further illustrated in the development of Juling's account. Juling begins her contribution to the Weekend activity by positioning herself as someone who has been unwell. When the teacher seeks to define that condition further in terms of familial self and positions her as 'lonely wife', Juling resists. Instead, she claims the identity of 'friendless newcomer', an appeal to her sense of sociocultural self. She constructs this position with reference to three types of awareness: physical (cough, runny nose), emotional (very sad, very lonely) and cognitive (I don't know [how to get friends]). The state of invalidated sociocultural self causes her to pray, a recourse which invokes the dimension of transpersonal self and positions her as someone who claims a spiritual identity. This sense of self is subsequently validated when she perceives her prayer to be answered. In the rest of her account, she engages in identity construction related to the dimension of sociocultural self.

As illustrated above, expressions of evaluation in the Weekend activity can be linked to the validation or invalidation of self and related constructions of identity by participants. Validation can also be linked to the building of interpersonal alignment and group solidarity, to which I now turn, using 'interpersonal validation' as a cover term for validation or invalidation of self or others.

Interpersonal validation can be seen to occur at different levels; however, it is helpful to start by noting expressions of validation linked to patterns of negative and positive Appraisal. The Weekend interaction encodes multiple expressions of invalidation. These expressions can most easily be identified by noting patterns of negative polarity linked to personal pronouns, particularly first person singular. Juling, for example, is seen to take up a position of invalidation (e.g. 'I'm very sad', 'I feel very lonely'), as is Jinhee, although to a lesser extent ('I'm not missing him. Just a little bit'). The intensity of Juling's feelings is highlighted by her repeated use of intensifying devices (e.g. *very sad*, *very lonely*) as opposed to Jinhee's use of mitigating devices (e.g. *a little bit*).

At the simplest level, the next step in tracing interpersonal validation is to identify positive polarity in comments made by one participant in response to the expressions of invalidation by another. These comments are frequently, although not necessarily, identified by the second person pronoun explicitly stated or implied as the Appraised item. For example, in the Weekend interaction, the focus is primarily on Juling whose disclosure of invalidation becomes a springboard for validating interaction directed specifically towards her. On this basis there is evidence of Juling being validated by other participants, including Mi-Hye ('You have very good friends here') and the teacher (e.g. 'We all care about you').

However, while Juling is the primary focus of the exchange, in the process of responding to her, interactants offer statements of validation pertaining to themselves or others in the group. This takes place, for example, through supportive evaluative remarks whereby they align themselves with Juling and her comments or the related comments by others (e.g. Yunjin: 'Everyone is sometimes feeling sad'; Mi-Hye: 'I sometimes will cry too'), extend the topic by interjecting a new angle (e.g. Teacher: 'Women need each other') or prolong or append to the discussion (e.g. Yu-Jeong: 'Now I think it is time to test myself, to [be] strong'). As the discussion unfolds, validating remarks become multi-targeted and carry embedded expressions of interpersonal validation at various levels, when, for example, Speaker C's alignment with Speaker B suggests alignment with and support of Speaker A whom Speaker B has validated (e.g. Jinhee's account of the call from her husband in follow-up to and alignment with Yunjin's comments ('Everyone is sometimes feeling sad … not only you') spoken to Juling). The Appraisal-based enactment of interpersonal validation and building of interpersonal alignment and solidarity profiled in the Weekend interaction is depicted in Figure 1.2.

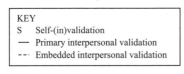

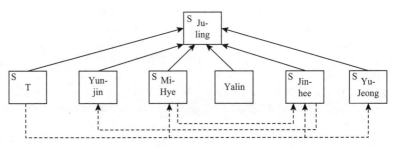

Figure 1.2   Profile of interpersonal validation and interpersonal alignment

Humour also features prominently in the interaction, and like the evaluative language of Appraisal, has the interpersonal function of negotiating attitudes and alignments and thus represents agentive behaviour. It is significant because it enables the serious work of evaluative meaning-making to proceed while representing attitudes less directly (Eggins and Slade 1997: 116). In this interaction, humour is invoked to signal alignment and support of Jinhee's initial position (feelings of sadness not linked to missing her husband) along with the revised position (missing him a little) while enabling Jinhee, Mi-Hye and the teacher to address potentially sensitive topics of personal significance (depression, loneliness) in the collaborative construction of Jinhee's story. The humorous framing also enables Jinhee to simultaneously position herself as a strong woman (pretending to have a cold so her husband would not worry) while admitting that circumstances are different in reality, a position underscored by the teacher's response ('You just said you did').

Finally, whereas traditional classroom talk is characterized by IRE or IRF sequences in which the teacher takes the initiative, students respond and the teacher provides evaluation or feedback, the Weekend interaction reveals a different pattern. In this case, the interaction is characterized by multiple sequences of student initiation – teacher response, in some cases followed by student evaluation or feedback. An example of this sequence can be seen in the opening lines of Juling's account:

Juling: Last week I'm very sad because I feel uncomfortable ...
Teacher: Oh, you miss your husband.
Juling: No, because I came to here and haven't good friend ...

This is also evident in the opening lines of Jinhee's story.

Jinhee: Early morning ... Suddenly, why I cried? I don't know.
Teacher: Because you missed him!
Jinhee: I'm not missing him. Just a little.

Additional examples of student initiation – teacher response can be seen throughout the Weekend interaction. For example, when Yu-Jeong offers her first contribution, the teacher echoes her statement affirmingly:

Yu-Jeong: Now I think it is time to test myself, to [be] strong.
Teacher: Oh yeah ... It's a testing time.

This pattern is also visible in the co-construction of Jinhee's story as the teacher highlights Mi-Hye's initiatives, deliberately contributing to the humorous tone, and offers a supportive comment in response to Jinhee's disclosure:

Mi-Hye: 'I need you.'
Teacher: 'I need you!'
Mi-Hye: 'Right now.'
Teacher: 'Yeah, right now! Come home!'
Jinhee: [Mimics her husband] ... I, 'Yes,' but I'm not catch cold.
Teacher: You just said you did.

Overall, the teacher takes a prominent role in the Weekend interaction, evidenced by turn-taking after every one or two student contributions with only two exceptions. However, her responses function primarily to support initiatives taken by students and enable the ongoing development of the Weekend interaction. Although she is a prominent presence in the discussion, she does not dominate it. Her moves enact a pattern of collaborative use of power in the development of the conversation and construct a much more symmetrical relationship between participants than is evident in typical classroom talk.

Discussion

How do practices surrounding the Weekend activity structure possibilities for engagement of self, and how might the exercise of agency and constructions of identity be informed by broader frames of reference and perceptions of reality? To begin with, the Weekend activity positions learners as social subjects rather than subjects of language learning. Students are not presented with predetermined social realities around which to practise language. Instead, the open-ended nature of the activity invites stakeholders to create meanings around the social realities of their choice. Participants are positioned as members of a community who have matters of interest to share with each other. Validating responses from other participants affirm them in this capacity. Language is first of all a resource for meaningful action, a medium for communicating matters of relevance. The perception of the discussion as authentic social interaction on the part of stakeholders is demonstrated in that the declarations of friendship and offers of support made in the context of this exchange transcend the boundaries of the activity and the classroom. Three weeks later during the Weekend activity, various students commented on the time spent with their children at an art club that had been started in Juling's home. The club had been facilitated by Yalin, who arranged for an art teacher through her contacts. In addition, Juling reported having spent an afternoon with Yu-Jeong and her children at the park. The discursive agency

24

demonstrated in the earlier Weekend activity had led to demonstrations of social agency beyond the classroom which subsequently became the topic of further discussion in the classroom.

Stevick (1998) introduces the terms *control* and *initiative* in the context of his broader discussion of opportunities for meaningful action in the language classroom (see van Lier, this volume). One element of control is the structuring of classroom activity (Stevick 1998: 32). Initiative refers to decisions about who speaks, what they say and when they say it, choices along a range of possibilities provided by whoever exercises control (p. 33). According to Stevick, 'when a student displays initiative ... he [or she] is beginning to play an active, central, self-validating role in a "world of meaningful action"' (p. 34). While Stevick does not use the term agency, van Lier (2008) links Stevick's discussion to the construct, suggesting that initiative can be empirically tied to learner agency by studying learner contributions in the context of classroom interaction (p. 174). Based on this standard, there is much evidence of learner agency in the Weekend interaction examined above, including evidence of validation. However, if agency is viewed as a context-dependent construct, the picture is incomplete if one considers student moves only. To complement van Lier's position, I suggest that *control* can be empirically tied to teacher agency by investigating the co-occurring teacher contributions in the context of classroom interaction. A review of the Weekend interaction indicates that while the structure of the activity creates space for learner agency by positioning students as social subjects, the way in which the teacher supports learner initiatives facilitates their investment in it.

Investment, according to Stevick, means making a choice that leaves one committed, and it can be associated with the notion of *yield*, which refers to the response one person receives from another as the result of an investment (Stevick 1998: 51). As Stevick sees it, 'The quality of "yield" that one gets in return for a particular act of "investment" has a powerful effect on one's readiness to "invest" further' (p. 51). Norton Peirce (1995) also draws on the construct of investment, linking it to human agency, social identity and power, to illuminate the relationship of learners to the target language and their varying desires to learn and use it. She takes the position that power, created in the context of interpersonal and intergroup relations, comes to bear on the possibilities for learner investment. With the potential to be collaborative or coercive, 'relations of power can serve to enable or constrain the range of identities that language learners can negotiate in their classrooms and communities' (Norton 2000: 9). Her understanding complements and extends that of Stevick, providing additional insights into the way in which a teacher exercises control and the related possibilities for initiative and investment on the part of learners. In the classroom interaction examined here, the teacher's enactment of collaborative power relations plays an important role in structuring space for the negotiation of identities that are meaningful and relevant to learners in the context of the Weekend activity and beyond.

But what broader frames of reference might inform the teacher's action in the classroom? Bucholtz and Hall (2005) define identity in terms that recognize the interconnectedness of individual-level agentive actions with institutional-level ideological structures. Although formal language education has often failed to accommodate important aspects of learner identity (Morgan 2002), the use of the Weekend activity suggests a different perspective in this context, a community-based programme sponsored by a church. At an institutional level, lead administrators characterize the institution and the programme as agents of social change: 'The church has to take a lead in actively embracing cultures and ethnic people that are coming ... breaking down the cultural and communication barriers.' In practical terms this is described as 'us[ing] English as a Second Language as a way of developing a better community ... a greater understanding and cooperation between people'. In light of these comments, it would seem that the pedagogical space in the classroom studied here is informed by ideologically defined space at the institutional level whereby those responsible for the programme seek to reverse exclusion. Rather than representing programme participants simply as language clients, institutional discourse positions students as members of the community, people who have the right not just to speak, but also to be heard.

Conclusion

According to Stevick (1980: 118–19), relevance in the classroom lies in the connection between something on the internal dimension of a student's appreciation of self with something on the external dimension of his or her relationships with other people and the outside world. Insofar as relevance has to do with perceptions of self, it can be linked to identity. Insofar as it involves interaction with others and the outside world, it can be linked to agency. Williams and Burden (1997: 44) observe that education is concerned with 'making learning experiences meaningful and relevant to the individual, with developing and growing as a whole person ... It must be underpinned by a set of beliefs about the kind of society that we are trying to construct and the kinds of explicit and implicit messages that will best convey those beliefs.' A thoughtful look at what goes on inside and between people in the classroom will reveal much about beliefs related to meaningful action and identity on the part of stakeholders – not only in the immediate learning environment, but also in society beyond.

References

Bucholtz M. and Hall, K. (2005) 'Identity and interaction: a sociocultural linguistic approach', *Discourse Studies*, 7(4/5): 585–614.

Doherty, C. (2010) 'Doing business: knowledges in the internationalised business lecture', *Higher Education Research and Development*, 29(3): 245–58.

Duff, P. (2012) 'Identity, agency, and second language acquisition', in Gass, S. M. and Mackey, M. (eds.) *Handbook of Second Language Acquisition*, London: Routledge, pp. 410–26.

Eggins, S. and Slade, D. (1997) *Analysing Casual Conversation*, London: Continuum.

Halliday, M. (1994) *An Introduction to Functional Grammar*, 2nd edn, London: Edward Arnold.

Ishiyama, F. I. (1995a) 'Use of validationgram in counseling: exploring sources of self-validation and impact of personal transition', *Canadian Journal of Counselling*, 29(2): 134–46.

Ishiyama, F. I. (1995b) 'Culturally dislocated clients: self-validation and cultural conflict issues and counseling implications', *Canadian Journal of Counselling*, 29(3): 262–75.

Ishiyama, F. I. and Kitiyama, A. (1994) 'Overwork and career-centered self-validation among the Japanese: psychosocial issues and counseling implications', *International Journal for the Advancement of Counselling*, 17(3): 167–82.

Kristjánsson, C. (2010) 'Collaborating with a (non)collaborator: interpersonal dynamics and constructions of identity in graduate online learning', in Park, J. R. and Abels, E. (eds.) *Interpersonal Relations and Social Patterns in Communication Technologies: Discourse Norms, Language Structures and Cultural Variables*, Hershey, PA: IGI Global, pp. 305–27.

Lantolf, J. and Thorne, S. (2006) *Sociocultural Theory and the Genesis of Second Language Development*, Oxford: Oxford University Press.

Lave, J. and Wenger, E. (1991) *Situated Learning: Legitimate Peripheral Participation*, Cambridge: Cambridge University Press.

Martin, J. R. and White, P. R. R. (2005) *The Language of Evaluation: Appraisal in English*, New York: Palgrave Macmillan.

Mehan, H. (1979) *Learning Lessons: Social Organization in the Classroom*, Cambridge, MA: Harvard University Press.

Miller, E. (2010) 'Agency in the making: adult immigrants' accounts of language learning and work', *TESOL Quarterly*, 44(3): 465–87.

Morgan, B. (2002) 'Critical practice in community-based ESL programs: a Canadian perspective', *Journal of Language, Identity, and Education*, 1(2): 141–62.

Norton, B. (2000) *Identity and Language Learning*, Harlow: Longman.

Norton Peirce, B. (1995) 'Social identity, investment, and language learning', *TESOL Quarterly*, 29(1): 9–31.

Sinclair, J. and Coulthard, R. (1975) *Towards an Analysis of Discourse,* London: Oxford University Press.

Stevick, E. (1980) *Teaching Languages: A Way and Ways,* Boston, MA: Heinle & Heinle.

Stevick, E. (1998) *Working with Teaching Methods: What's at Stake?,* Boston, MA: Heinle & Heinle.

Thornbury, S. and Slade, D. (2006) *Conversation: From Description to Pedagogy,* Cambridge: Cambridge University Press.

van Lier, L. (2008) 'Agency in the classroom', in Lantolf, J. and Poehner, M. (eds.) *Sociocultural Theory and the Teaching of Second Languages,* London: Equinox, pp. 163–86.

van Lier, L. (2010) 'Foreword: agency, self and identity in language learning', in O'Rourke, B. and Carson, L. (eds.) *Language Learner Autonomy: Policy, Curriculum, Classroom,* Oxford: Peter Lang, pp. ix–xviii.

Waring, H. (2009) 'Moving out of IRF (Initiation-Response-Feedback): a single case analysis', *Language Learning,* **59**(4): 796–824.

Williams, H. and Burden, R. (1997) *Psychology for Language Teachers,* Cambridge: Cambridge University Press.

2 Self issues and motivated behaviour in language learning

Jane Arnold

Introduction

Cognitive ability is, of course, related to achievement in second or foreign language learning, but from both anecdotal and research sources we know that it is neither sufficient nor necessarily the most important factor. Stern (1983: 386) affirmed that 'the affective component contributes at least as much and often more to language learning than the cognitive skills'. Similarly, it is no secret that in providing for a happy ending to the language learning story, there is much more involved than the use of the latest methods or gadgets. Affective factors are vital characters in the story. Earl Stevick (1980: 4) gave us a useful framework for organizing these factors when he referred to success in language learning as being determined to a large extent by what goes on *inside* and *between* the people who are involved in the learning/teaching process. We can take the *inside*, then, as the learner's internal characteristics, such as motivation, anxiety or self-esteem, and the *between* as the relational aspects connecting learners or learners and teacher.

In this chapter we will focus on aspects of both the *inside* and the *between* and will explore specifically the importance of issues related to the self for language learning. We will see how research in three self-related areas in language learning – self-esteem, teacher confirmation and the L2 Motivational Self System – indicates that attention to these areas can provide useful support for language learning. As Mercer (2011: 1) says, 'Teachers often experience first-hand how learner behaviours and attitudes are driven by their sense of self and how this can vary across individuals in ways that are complex and often difficult to predict.' When dealing with self-related issues, it is, of course, essential to keep in mind the fact that the sense of self is greatly influenced by the individual's relations with others.

Language is closely connected with one's identity, one's 'subjective view of self' (Edwards 2009: 2). In many ways, language and self are intertwined. Williams (1994: 77) pointed out that 'language belongs to a person's whole social being; it is part of one's identity and is used to convey this identity to other people. The learning of a foreign language involves far more than simply learning skills, or a system of rules, or a grammar; it involves an alteration in self-image.' To a much greater degree than with other subjects, when learners in a foreign language classroom have to speak, their self-image is on the line. Trying to convey one's ideas in an imperfect linguistic vehicle can cause anxiety and lead to a refusal to take the risks involved in speaking, thus greatly limiting the learning process. When discussing second language acquisition, Norton and McKinney (2011: 73) point out that 'every time learners speak, they are negotiating and renegotiating a sense of self in relation to the larger social world'. Kristjánsson (this volume) shows options for developing selfhood in the world of the classroom.

One's self-image or self-concept is related to beliefs about oneself, especially in a specific domain. Beliefs are not the same as reality, but they can condition behaviour as if they were. In all aspects of life, what we do is influenced by what we believe, even though these mental constructs may be no more than our conviction about something and may not represent reality at all.

Puchta (1999: 66) stresses the importance of beliefs for learning; they are 'strong perceptual filters. They serve as explanations for what has happened and they give us a basis for future behaviour.' In the language learning process, beliefs may be about the language (we may believe it to be difficult, easy, useful, ugly, etc.) or the process of language learning (we may consider it is impossible to learn a language well unless we study in a country where it is spoken, or we may think that we have to study grammar rules to learn it). However, often the most important belief is about oneself (that one is not good at learning languages or that one is making progress and can learn). A student who believes he can't learn the language is right. He can't unless he changes this belief. Concern with learner beliefs about the self is very relevant as 'the overwhelming conclusion from both research and theory is that the perceptions one has of self significantly affect attitudes, behaviours, evaluations, and cognitive processes. In classroom research the concept an individual has of self also plays an important role' (McCroskey et al. 1977: 269). If students have a low self-concept regarding language learning, this takes energy away from the learning task at hand since they have to deal with feelings of inadequacy, and this will keep them from investing the necessary effort to make progress. When no progress is made, this reinforces the belief that they are not capable of learning the language. Mercer (2011: 2) summarizes the far-reaching influence of learner self-beliefs, which 'form the psychological basis that connects together and underlies learners' interpretation of their experiences, their current behaviours, motivations, affective reactions and future goals'.

Fortunately, since beliefs are not fixed and not directly connected to reality, they can be changed, even if this is not a simple matter. As they are formed through experience, learners' negative beliefs about their abilities to learn a language created from unsuccessful contact with the language in the past can be influenced positively if they are in a learning environment where a 'can-do' climate is created. Stevick (1976: 43) reminds us how, with Suggestopedia, Lozanov stressed the importance of *desuggesting* limitations from previous experiences and suggesting positive options for the current learning situation and how instruction can be carried out 'in such a way that students will draw for themselves a new set of unconscious or even conscious conclusions that will open up to them possibilities far beyond what they had even dreamed of before' (Stevick 1998: 148). Teachers can communicate to their students that they expect them to do well and will provide them with any help they need to do so.

One influential aspect of beliefs related to language learning is self-efficacy. When Oxford and Shearin (1994) revised diverse motivational models, self-efficacy was seen to have a significant impact on motivation in language learning. Basically, self-efficacy can be defined as 'one's judgment of how well one can execute courses of action required to deal with prospective situations', and it has been found that 'L2 learners with established goals and a sense of self-efficacy will focus on learning tasks, persist at them, and develop strategies to complete tasks successfully so they can meet their goals' (Oxford and Shearin 1994: 21). This is closely related to Dörnyei's (2001: 56) definition of self-confidence, which 'refers to the belief that a person has the ability to produce results, accomplish goals or perform tasks competently'. An enhanced self-concept, then, can give learners a greater sense of being able to take control of their learning and of willingness to invest more energy in the process: a greater sense of agency.

MacIntyre (2002: 63) stresses the role of our emotions in motivation: 'given the pervasiveness of emotions, their role in energizing behaviour, and their flexibility over time, it is clear that emotion forms a key part of the motivational system'; he adds that 'the difference between the engaged and unengaged learner lies in the emotions experienced during language learning'. This may be explained on the neurobiological level because of the importance of emotion and feeling in the self as, according to Damasio (2010: 109), 'their machinery is used in the building of the self'.

I would now like to look at three specific areas that relate to the self, and to emotions and motivation in language learning.

Self-esteem

While self-concept – what we observe when we look inside – is of a basically cognitive nature, self-esteem is our affective, evaluative processing of what we observe about ourselves, how we feel about it. Writing in the early years of work on self-esteem, Coopersmith (1967: 4–5) defined it thus:

> By self-esteem we refer to the evaluation which the individual makes and customarily maintains with regard to himself; it expresses an attitude of approval or disapproval, and indicates the extent to which the individual believes himself to be capable, significant, successful, and worthy. In short, self-esteem is a personal judgment of worthiness that is expressed in the attitudes the individual holds toward himself.

Robert Reasoner, founder of the International Council for Self-Esteem, has written convincingly about the importance of self-esteem for learning and has developed practical applications for the classroom. He stresses that work with self-esteem in education is not about empty praise and creating unrealistic expectations but rather about developing commitment and responsibility and helping students to reach their potential (1982). His model of five components to be dealt with in the learning situation – Security, Identity, Belonging, Purpose and Competence – has been adapted to the ELT context (de Andrés and Arnold 2009; Arnold and de Andrés 2010).

Considering self-esteem in the classroom is never a case of not demanding the best of our students, but we will not get the best from them if there is affective interference in their cognitive processing. Self-esteem, as Dweck (2000: 4) says, 'is a positive way of experiencing yourself when you are fully engaged and are using your abilities to the utmost in pursuit of something you value'. Concern with a balanced view of self-worth from which it is easier to carry out learning tasks has proved to be an important element in educational contexts. Speaking specifically of language learning, Richard-Amato (2009) notes that good learners tend to have higher self-esteem. We can expect that learners who are confident in their abilities to learn the language will be more motivated. Thus, in any activity that is as motivation-dependent as language learning, we cannot afford to ignore self-esteem.

Research has shown the usefulness of using self-esteem activities in language classrooms to improve both learner self-esteem and performance in the second language. In one study with young learners of English in Argentina, a collaborative active research project was carried out, and both of the classroom teachers involved in the project found that the programme of self-esteem activities for teaching English implemented by the researcher had improved not only interpersonal skills but also academic performance in oral and reading skills (de Andrés 2007: 51).

An adaptation of this study (Greciet 2009) was done in Spain at a vocational school with a small group of 'unaccompanied minors', adolescent sub-Saharan immigrants who were alone in the country and thus in a very difficult psycho-social situation. Activities to support self-esteem were introduced in their Spanish as a second language class and were found to be very useful in developing willingness to communicate, which has been shown to facilitate communication and language learning (MacIntyre et al. 1998). The attitude of these students towards their language learning improved, and particularly interesting were the changes in self-concept evidenced in a projective test, which involved drawings of themselves at the beginning and the end of the intervention. Drawings are often used to complete data collected with subjects who, because of age or lack of adequate language skills, are not able to express highly developed ideas, here about how they see themselves. In the case of one learner, 'Ya Ya', the two psychologists who analysed the drawings (Figure 2.1) noted very important changes in the second drawing made after the intervention using self-esteem activities in the language classes: the smiling face, open arms, feet on solid ground, and the incorporation of plants all reflect a more positive self-concept.

Figure 2.1   Drawings at the beginning and the end of the intervention (Greciet 2009)

While considerations relating to self-esteem are important in any language class, they can be even more so in special situations, such as with dyslexic language learners who are prone to losing motivation easily and to having low self-esteem. Csizér et al. (2010: 484) recommend that when working with these students, teachers create a classroom oriented towards success since 'experiencing success is a prerequisite for improving the generally low self-esteem of students with dyslexia and it enhances language learning attitudes, which are important in influencing motivated behavior'. Similarly, Schleppegrell (1987) pointed out that with older language learners, fear of failure may be greater than for younger students, and so teachers need to be especially concerned with increasing their self-confidence by designing activities which are oriented towards learner success. (See de Andrés and Arnold 2009 for activities of this nature.). The need for success-orientation is supported by data from neuropsychological research which indicates the importance of positive affect on cognition and how task success can facilitate it (Ashby et al. 1999). Littlejohn (2008: 219) explains how 'feelings of success fuel motivation, as achievement enhances self-image and confidence in an upward spiral in which increased levels of achievement enhance motivation which in turn leads to further increases in achievement'.

Using language learning activities which foster self-esteem is one way to change limiting beliefs that learners may have. A related way to enhance learners' self-concept is through teacher confirmation.

Teacher confirmation

Research done on the concept of teacher confirmation in the area of communication studies (Ellis 2000) and extended to the context of language learning (León 2005) strongly emphasizes the role of the teacher in fomenting a positive self-concept in learners and points to ways to do so. Kathleen Ellis (2000: 266) defines teacher confirmation as 'the transactional process by which teachers communicate to students that they are endorsed, recognized and acknowledged as valuable, significant individuals', and she stresses how important this is in helping them to establish their identities and significance as human beings. In her research she found that there is 'a large, significant indirect effect of teacher confirmation on cognitive learning', and she recommends working with teacher confirmation within three groups of factors: '(a) teachers' responses to students' questions, (b) demonstrating interest in students and in their learning, and (c) teacher style' (p. 246).

Stevick (1998: 23) stresses that, in addition to a world of meaningful action where relevant learning occurs, we also want to promote 'a feeling of primacy, or at least strength, within that world. Hence the need for attention from the teacher.' Teacher confirmation can contribute to establishing this sense of primacy and preparing the way for meaningful action in the learning experience.

Using questionnaires and interviews in a study with a large population of secondary school students of English in Spain, León (2005) established a teacher confirmation scale which lists specific confirming behaviours on the part of language teachers. The most frequent examples students gave can be grouped in the following areas: the teacher congratulates students verbally and non-verbally when they do something well, conveys to students confidence in their possibilities with encouraging comments, pays attention to what students say, makes eye contact and smiles at them, shows interest in answering students' questions, shows interest in students as persons. Behaviour of this nature reinforces the positive self-concept of learners and encourages them to participate more actively in the learning tasks and thus smoothes the road to language learning.

In further research on teacher confirmation in the EFL context (Piñol 2007), secondary school students completed a questionnaire with items relating to the language learning process. The teachers were then given an explanation of teacher confirmation and asked to consciously incorporate behaviours listed on Leon's (2005) teacher confirmation scale in their classes. With no other variations in the class content, after six weeks the questionnaires were again completed by students and on several significant items positive responses had almost doubled (see Table 2.1).

Table 2.1 *Student responses before and after the incorporation by teachers of specific confirming behaviour in the classroom (Piñol 2007)*

	Before	After
I feel comfortable speaking English	26%	46%
In class I express myself freely	26%	52%
English is interesting for me	18%	37%

One important pedagogical implication from this study is that teacher confirmation is something that can easily be incorporated by teachers into their classroom behaviour, and when it is, it can lead to significantly greater motivation on the part of students. This would imply the usefulness of inclusion of work with profiles of confirming and non-confirming teacher behaviour in pre-service and in-service teacher training.

In light of research of this nature, we would do well to take into consideration the importance of helping students to believe in themselves and their ability to learn, which can undoubtedly influence their motivation and their academic progress. The two studies mentioned above were carried out with adolescent learners, a group whose self-concept may be very vulnerable. As Fontana (1988: 277) says, 'adolescents are often prey to insecurity. While they search for identity, they are never sure that the people they are becoming will prove acceptable in the adult world. Thus, although they may seem unimpressed now by parents and teachers, the support and good opinion of such people is still vital to them.' Given the need for interaction, language learning is a very relational experience, and teachers can do much to establish good relationships with students in order to facilitate learning.

When considering the importance of teacher confirmation, last but not least is the reciprocal nature of the process. León (2008) found that when students feel recognized and worthwhile, their behaviour is likely to be of the type that makes the teacher feel acknowledged and more motivated as well.

The L2 Motivational Self System

Both teachers and researchers stress the importance of motivation. In fact, classroom teachers often use motivation as a catch-all term to provide an explanation for students' results: a poor student (*He has no motivation*), a good student (*She is really motivated*). Gardner and Lambert (1972) noted that, when dealing with individual variation in learners' achievement, aptitude was often less important than motivation. Similarly, in one of his rare comments about teaching, Chomsky (1988: 181) pointed out the truly vital nature of motivation: 'The truth of the matter is that about 99 per cent of teaching is making the students feel interested in the material.'

There have been many complex and elegant definitions of motivation, but the basic idea can generally be reduced to the state of wanting to do something enough to put out the effort necessary to achieve it. There tends to be a mixture of the cognitive (setting goals) and the affective (mobilizing the energy to reach them).

Among the most interesting recent developments in language motivation studies is the proposal by Dörnyei (2009) of the L2 Motivational Self System which, while maintaining roots in previous work, broadens and enriches the field of L2 motivation research and theory with concepts from psychology such as the 'possible selves'. Markus and Nurius (1986: 954) described the concept of possible selves: 'individuals' ideas of what they might become, what they would like to become and what they are afraid of becoming. They provide the essential link between self-concept and motivation.' In relation to this, Markus and Ruvolo (1989: 213) discuss the notion of the ideal self, the self that we would like to be, and its relevance for achievement: 'imagining one's own actions through the construction of elaborated possible selves achieving the desired goal may directly facilitate the translation of goals into intentions and instrumental actions'. In a language learning context, if our ideal self speaks the second language, this can motivate us to learn it. Here there is, then, a double task for the teacher: to ensure that the ability to speak the language is seen as attractive by the students and to make it seem possible by encouraging students and explaining that if they are willing to work, they can reach their goals.

Dörnyei and Ushioda (2011: 83–4) emphasize, however, that these future self-guides do not motivate automatically. They summarize several conditions seen to be necessary for the motivating capacity of future self-guides to be triggered. For example, the learner needs to have a developed future self which is specific and vivid enough to evoke a motivational response, and future self-guides should be seen as possible and realistic and be regularly activated.

From the perspective of possible selves, the role of the teacher in determining language learning motivation is crucial. Markus and Nurius (1986: 955–6) explain that 'possible selves are views of the self that often have not been verified or confirmed by social experience; they comprise the self-knowledge that is the most vulnerable and responsive to changes in the environment'. Thus, a student's possible ideal self as a speaker of the target language may be in a fragile state. As our range of possible selves depends significantly on others to preserve and reinforce them, the teacher can have a great influence on students' conceptions of their possible selves as regards their language learning and in this way on their motivation. As Parker Palmer (1998: 6) puts it, 'teachers possess the power to create conditions that can help students learn a great deal – or keep them from learning much at all'. A success-oriented teaching style can provide anchoring for learners' ideal language learner selves, just as excessive and abrasive criticism in the classroom can lead to a negative self-evaluation of their possibilities and to strong demotivation.

One thing that makes the possible selves theory so interesting is that, as Dörnyei (2009: 15) points out, these possible selves 'involve images and senses, approximating what people actually experience when they are engaged in motivated or goal-directed behaviour', and he affirms that 'it is the experiential element that makes possible selves "larger" than any combination of goal-related constructs'. Markus and Ruvolo (1989: 211) state 'a goal will have an impact on behaviour to the extent than an individual can personalise it by building a bridge of self-representations between one's current state and one's desired or hoped for state'. There is, then, an opportunity for teachers to lead students towards more motivated behaviour by strengthening their images of themselves in the future as successful speakers of the language.

Using mental imagery to improve performance has been shown to be effective in a number of areas, including language learning. Brown (1991: 86) offers an interesting option for changing limiting beliefs which he calls the visualization game. One of the aspects of language learning that students generally find difficult is communicating with native speakers in the target language, so he recommends telling students to see themselves in their mind's eye talking fluently to people in the language, imagining fully all the details of the situation. In this way, he says, when they are in a real conversation, they will in a sense have been there before. This technique of mental rehearsal has been used very successfully in many competitive sports, and often it has been proven to be as effective or even more so than actual practice. It is also commonly used by musicians and people in a wide variety of other professions. One reason it works is that in mental rehearsal we can see ourselves doing the task well, which can influence our beliefs about our ability to do so. Seeing ourselves as successful can increase our confidence and thus our ability to perform better. Furthermore, there is evidence that actual activity and mental experiencing of the activity involve the same neurological patterns. Kosslyn et al. (2002: 342) state that 'mental images are in many respects surrogates for percepts ... Visual mental imagery and visual perception activate about two-thirds of the same brain areas.'

Dörnyei's (2009: 29) L2 Motivational Self System includes three main dimensions: (1) *ideal L2 self*, 'if the person we would like to become speaks an L2, the *"ideal L2 self"* is a powerful motivator to learn the L2 because of the desire to reduce the discrepancy between our actual and ideal selves', (2) *ought-to L2 self*, 'the attributes that one believes one ought to possess to meet expectations and to *avoid* possible negative outcomes' and (3) *L2 learning experience*, 'which concerns situated, "executive" motives related to the immediate learning environment and experience (the impact of the teacher, the curriculum, the peer group, the experience of success)'. Along with the guiding function of the ideal self towards what we would like to achieve, he also mentions the feared self which guides us away from what we want to avoid.

In his work with therapy, Carl Rogers (1965) considered that the discrepancy between the real self (existing in the present but not fully expressed by the individual) and ideal self (seen as not real and out of reach) would lead to dysfunction. However, in the context of language learning, when dealing with the ideal self, it is a case of helping the learners to release limiting beliefs about their ability and to stimulate the desire to learn the language and plan how best to do so. The two theories define 'ideal self' differently. For Rogers, the idea is to avoid beliefs in an exaggerated, unhealthy ideal that is impossible to attain, whereas in the L2 self model (Dörnyei 2009), it is a matter of giving up limiting beliefs in order to attain an ideal that can in fact be reached with effort and positive attitudes.

Possible selves motivation is influenced by several factors. Norman and Aron (2003: 501) have proposed that 'one's motivation to attain a particular possible self depends at least in part on that possible self's: (a) availability, (b) accessibility, and (c) perceived control over the attainment/avoidance of that possible self'. This is particularly interesting for the language learning context because it points to the possibility of enhancing an ideal L2 self by making it more available and accessible; suggestions for doing so have been put forth (Arnold et al. 2007), and research has been carried out in different learning situations.

Self-relevant imagery in L2 classroom and research contexts

A six-step strategic plan for developing self-relevant imagery to support the L2 Motivational Self System has been developed by Dörnyei (2009: 33–8). Taking into account the necessary conditions mentioned earlier, he suggests the following components:

1. Creating the vision. This involves helping learners to develop a vision of their ideal L2 self.
2. Strengthening the vision. Creative imagery work can be used to make learners' ideal L2 self images more elaborate and vivid.
3. Substantiating the vision. For the self images to support motivation effectively, they must be seen to be realistic. This involves reality checks and consideration of possible obstacles.
4. Keeping the vision alive. In the classroom many activities such as warmers, films, music and cultural events related to the target language can provide ideal L2 self-reminders.
5. Operationalizing the vision. Effective self-guides need to be accompanied by action plans for reaching the desired end-state, including work with goal-setting but also factors of a methodological nature such as study plans and appropriate types of instruction.
6. Counterbalancing the vision. Students can be reminded of possible limitations if they don't know foreign languages.

Ways to work with self-relevant imagery in classroom activities can be found in Hadfield and Dörnyei (2013). There is growing evidence from research that work of this nature can be an effective way to facilitate the language learning process.

In a major study with Chinese learners of English, Magid found that his intervention, using imagery and related goal-setting activities, showed 'that it is possible to enhance L2 learners' vision of their Ideal L2 self through visualisation training' (Magid 2011: 281). The qualitative data from his study is very illuminating. He found learners were able to develop a stronger ideal L2 self, as can be seen in this statement from 'Kurt': 'My imagination of how I can use English in the future became better ... Now I can imagine things in a more detailed way.' 'Karen' felt more protected from feelings of failure in the learning process: 'Before when I would fail, I would become depressed. Now I build a positive picture in my mind which motivates me to work and gives me hope. I learned to build a picture in my mind.' Another important factor was greater self-confidence. 'Robin' commented that 'listening to the positive situations gave me confidence in my English which I now feel all the time' (Magid 2011: 200, 205, 210).

Unlike some theories which do not provide teachers with specific and effective ways to develop learner motivation, the Ideal L2 Motivational Self System 'is an educator-friendly approach in that there is a potential to increase the language learners' motivation by changing their future self-guides' (Magid 2011: 117). This idea was the focus of a study (Fernández 2011) with Spanish learners of English on the tertiary level. An intervention was designed to develop and strengthen the ideal L2 self, first of all by using spoken comments while projecting from the computer visual images relating to aspects of possible experiences in which knowing English would be important for these students (travelling in English-speaking countries, communicating with speakers of English, living abroad, using English in work contexts and so forth). Then in later sessions with visualization exercises, students were encouraged to create mental images of themselves using English successfully in different contexts, and between sessions they were asked to try to return to these images on their own. In a final questionnaire 80% of the students reported doing so, and 94% said the visualization sessions had made them feel more motivated towards English. Among the reasons they gave were: 'I felt good and want to keep learning English to be able to achieve all that I was imagining'; 'Every day I imagine myself speaking English well and working as a teacher. I feel very happy and have more confidence in myself'; 'imagining specific situations in which I was able to speak English well encourages me to work hard to learn to speak well'.

In another study, Mackay (forthcoming) explored the effectiveness of Dörnyei's proposal of the L2 Motivational Self System in the classroom context. This entailed the design and implementation of an intervention to translate self theories into practical classroom activities based on Hadfield and Dörnyei (2013) and the subsequent analysis of implications for learners' self-concept, motivation and engagement with the target language. For one activity used in the study, the area of the future L2 self, specifically the *ought-to* and *feared* L2 selves, was introduced through visual stimuli. Students were then asked to read and compare fictional case studies of learners with diverse types and levels of motivation. By discussing which of the fictional learners they identified with most and why, the students became more aware of their own motivational profiles. Then a guided visualization was done to help them imagine positive future L2 selves and this was then discussed in groups. As a follow-up activity, each learner further elaborated in written form their 'vision' of their future L2 self. From the interview data in her study, there is clear evidence that work with the ideal L2 self can be very beneficial for learners who feel demotivated.

Conclusion

Stevick (1980: 24) defended a type of education which doesn't fail 'to call forth the student's full powers'. Kalaja and Barcelos (2006: 2) have pointed out that one problem with current research on beliefs and second language acquisition is that it frequently considers beliefs 'as stable mental representations that are fixed a-priori constructs' when actually they are 'emergent and dynamic ... they change and evolve as we experience the world' (Barcelos and Kalaja 2006: 233). As we have seen, Lozanov emphasized the importance of learning to deal with limiting beliefs, and one of the advantages of work with self-esteem, teacher confirmation and the L2 Motivational Self System is that these limiting beliefs can be changed, and this can greatly empower students. Furthermore, when learners feel supported and see themselves successfully using the language, they can also come to imagine themselves more as a part of the community that speaks the language. As Norton and McKinney (2011: 76) explain, learners' imagined communities 'include future relationships that exist only in the learners' imagination ... These imagined communities are no less real than the ones in which learners have daily engagements'; they affirm that these communities might have great impact on learners' identities and their willingness to invest effort in the learning process.

Meaning-making inside and between the people in the classroom

Research such as that mentioned in this chapter shows that self-related issues in the foreign language classroom are very significant and that teachers can play an important role by not only providing their learners with the necessary linguistic input for learning the language but also ensuring that through attention to these issues, the learning process is most effective.

References

Arnold, J. and de Andrés, V. (2010) 'Cultivating confidence', *English Teaching Professional*, **26**: 4–6.

Arnold, J., Puchta, H. and Rinvolucri, M. (2007) *Imagine That: Mental Imagery in the EFL Classroom*, Innsbruck: Helbling Languages.

Ashby, F. G., Isen, A. M. and Turken, A. U. (1999) 'A neuropsychologial theory of positive affect and its influence on cognition', *Psychological Review*, 106(3): 529–50.

Barcelos, A. M. F. and Kalaja, P. (2006) 'Conclusion: exploring possibilities for future research on beliefs about SLA', in Kalaja, P. and Barcelos, A. M. (eds.) *Beliefs about SLA: New Research Approaches*, New York: Springer, pp. 231–40.

Brown, D. (1991) *Breaking the Language Barrier*, Yarmouth: Intercultural Press.

Chomsky, N. (1988) *Language and Problems of Knowledge*, Cambridge, MA: MIT Press.

Coopersmith, S. (1967) *The Antecedents of Self-Esteem*, San Francisco: Freeman and Co.

Csizér, K., Kormos, J. and Sarkadi, A. (2010) 'The dynamics of language learning attitudes and motivation: lessons from an interview study of dyslexic learners', *The Modern Language Journal*, 94(3): 470–87.

Damasio, A. (2010) *Self Comes to Mind: Constructing the Conscious Brain*, New York: Pantheon Books.

de Andrés, V. (2007) 'Self-esteem and language learning: breaking the ice', in Rubio, F. (ed.) *Self-Esteem and Foreign Language Learning*, Newcastle: Cambridge Scholars Press, pp. 30–55.

de Andrés, V. and Arnold, J. (2009) *Seeds of Confidence: Self-Esteem Activities for the EFL Classroom*, Innsbruck: Helbling Languages.

Dörnyei, Z. (2001) *Teaching and Researching Motivation*, Harlow: Pearson Education.

Dörnyei, Z. (2009) 'The L2 motivational self system', in Dörnyei, Z. and Ushioda, E. (eds.) *Motivation, Language Identity and the L2 Self*, Bristol: Multilingual Matters, pp. 9–42.

Dörnyei, Z. and Ushioda, E. (2011) *Teaching and Researching Motivation*, 2nd edn, Harlow: Pearson Education.

Dweck, C. (2000) *Self-Theories: Their Role in Motivation, Personality and Development*, Philadelphia: Psychology Press.

Edwards, J. (2009) *Language and Identity*, Cambridge: Cambridge University Press.

Ellis, K. (2000) 'Perceived teacher confirmation: the development and validation of an instrument and two studies of the relationship to cognitive and affective learning', *Human Communication Research*, 26(2): 264–91.

Fernández, G. (2011) 'Activación y refuerzo del yo ideal y sus efectos en la motivación para el aprendizaje de inglés como L2', unpublished research, University of Seville.

Fontana, D. (1988) *Psychology for Teachers*, Basingstoke: Palgrave Macmillan.

Gardner, R. C. and Lambert, W. (1972) *Attitudes and Motivation in Second Language Learning*, Rowley, MA: Newbury House.

Greciet, C. (2009) 'Diseño, aplicación y análisis de un programa de enseñanza integral de español a un grupo de menores no acompañados', unpublished MA thesis, Universidad Internacional Menéndez Pelayo, Santander.

Hadfield, J. and Dörnyei. Z. (2013) *From Theory to Practice: Motivation and the Ideal Language Self*, London: Longman.

Kalaja, P. and Barcelos, A. M. F. (2006) *Beliefs about SLA: New Research Approaches*, New York: Springer.

Kosslyn, S. M., Cacioppo, J. T., Davidson, R. J., Hugdahl, K., Lovallo, W. R., Spiegel, D. and Rose, R. (2002) 'Bridging psychology and biology: the analysis of individuals in groups', *American Psychologist*, 57(5): 341–51.

León, I. (2005) 'La confirmación del profesor de inglés percibida por el alumno en Educación Secundaria', unpublished MA thesis, University of Seville.

León, I. (2008) 'La confirmación y la desconfirmación en el aula de inglés en educación secundaria: un estudio de su reciprocidad', unpublished PhD dissertation, University of Seville.

Littlejohn, A. (2008) 'The tip of the iceberg: factors affecting learner motivation', *RELC Journal*, 39(2): 214–25.

MacIntyre, P. D. (2002) 'Motivation, anxiety and emotion in second language acquisition', in Robinson, P. (ed.) *Individual Differences in Second Language Acquisition*, Amsterdam: John Benjamins, pp. 45–68.

MacIntyre, P., Clément, R., Dörnyei, Z. and Noels, K. (1998) 'Conceptualizing willingness to communicate in a L2: a situational model of L2 confidence and affiliation', *The Modern Language Journal*, 82: 545–62.

Mackay, J. (forthcoming) 'An Ideal L2 Self intervention: implications for self-concept, motivation and engagement with the target language', PhD dissertation, University of Barcelona.

Magid, M. (2011) 'A validation and application of the L2 Motivational Self System among Chinese Learners of English', unpublished doctoral dissertation, University of Nottingham.

Markus, H. R. and Nurius, P. (1986) 'Possible selves', *American Psychologist*, 41: 954–69.

Markus, H. R. and Ruvolo, A. (1989) 'Possible selves: personalized representations of goals', in Pervin, L. A. (ed.) *Goal Concepts in Personality and Social Psychology*, Hillsdale, NJ: Lawrence Erlbaum, pp. 211–41.

McCroskey, J. C., Daly, J. A., Richmond, V. P. and Falcione, R. L. (1977) 'Studies of the relationship between communication apprehension and self-esteem', *Human Communication Research*, 3(3): 269–77.

Mercer, S. (2011) *Towards an Understanding of Language Learner Self-Concept*, Heidelberg: Springer.

Norman, C. and Aron, A. (2003) 'Aspects of possible self that predict motivation to achieve or avoid it', *Journal of Experimental Social Psychology*, 39: 500–7.

Norton, B. and McKinney, C. (2011) 'An identity approach to second language acquisition', in Atkinson, D. (ed.) *Alternative Approaches to Second Language Acquisition*, London: Routledge, pp. 73–94.

Oxford, R. and Shearin, J. (1994) 'Language learning motivation: expanding the theoretical framework', *Modern Language Journal*, 78: 12–28.

Palmer, P. J. (1998) *The Courage to Teach*, San Francisco: Jossey-Bass Publishers.

Piñol, J. (2007) 'La influencia de la confirmación del profesor en el aprendizaje de inglés en la Educación Secundaria Obligatoria', unpublished MA thesis, University of Seville.

Puchta, H. (1999) 'Beyond materials, techniques and linguistic analyses: the role of motivation, beliefs and identity', plenary paper presented at the 33rd Annual International IATEFL Conference, Edinburgh, 28 March–1 April.

Reasoner, R. (1982) *Building Self-Esteem in Secondary Schools*, Palo Alto, CA: Consulting Psychologists Press.

Richard-Amato, P. (2009) *Making It Happen: From Interactive to Participatory Language Teaching – Evolving Theory and Practice*, Harlow: Pearson ESL.

Rogers, C. (1965) *Client-Centered Therapy*, Boston: Houghton Mifflin.

Schleppegrell, M. (1987) *The Older Language Learner*, ERIC Digest (ED287313), Washington, DC: ERIC Clearinghouse on Languages and Linguistics.

Stern, H. H. (1983) *Fundamental Concepts of Language Teaching*, Oxford: Oxford University Press.

Stevick, E. W. (1976) *Memory, Meaning and Method: Some Psychological Perspectives on Language Learning*, Boston: Heinle & Heinle.

Stevick, E. W. (1980) *Teaching Languages: A Way and Ways*, Rowley, MA: Newbury House.

Stevick, E. W. (1998) *Working with Teaching Methods: What's at Stake?*, Boston: Heine & Heinle.

Williams, M. (1994) 'Motivation in foreign and second language learning: an interactive perspective', *Educational and Child Psychology*, 11: 77–84.

3 Engaging adult learners: what ELT can learn from neuroscience and educational theory

Herbert Puchta

Introduction

In his seminal work, *Memory, Meaning and Method*, Earl Stevick stresses the 'power and the pervasive role of emotional factors' in the foreign language learning process while pointing out that 'just how these emotional factors influence the process of memory is still the subject of some discussion' (Stevick 1996: 7). In this chapter, I draw on some new findings from neurobiology and educational theory to discuss the role of positive and negative emotions in engaging adult students in the foreign language learning process. I also refer to some key insights from those areas into the impact that emotional processes have on memory.

When adults talk about their foreign language learning experiences, they frequently mention that being able to communicate in a foreign language gives them pleasure. We can assume that part of this rewarding activity is the ability to understand and formulate complex thought in that language, to use it as a means of expressing creativity and to develop the ability to understand what others say. At least some students might also enjoy using the foreign language as a gateway that provides access into cultural contexts and helps them develop interpersonal skills through a process called empathy (Stevick 1996: 144), that is, the ability to put themselves in someone else's shoes, or see the world through his or her eyes.

The opposite can also happen. Being a learner of a foreign language, especially during the early stages of the learning process, can be a frustrating experience. Paul, a former colleague of mine – a highly respected maths teacher with a deep interest in political science, very well read, and an eloquent and entertaining communicator in his mother tongue – mentioned his frustrating experiences with learning Spanish as a foreign language:

> It's alright as long as I am in one of those typical travelling situations, when I order a meal, check in at an airport or something like that. But as soon as I want to have a real conversation with someone things become so tedious. Then small talk is not enough – but what do you do when small talk is all you have? As soon as people start talking

> about more interesting things, I can first of all hardly follow what
> they are saying, and even when I can … by the time I've worked out a
> sentence that doesn't even get close to what I really wanted to say, the
> conversation has moved on, and I'm lost. That's when I start feeling
> like an idiot!

What Paul is saying here is probably not unusual for quite a few adult
learners who are used to expressing themselves eloquently in their
mother tongue, and who, in the earlier stages of learning a foreign language, find themselves incapable of taking part in an intellectual conversation in that language. The outcome of such experiences can lead to
feelings of frustration, to the development of limiting beliefs about one's
own ability to learn a foreign language, and to negative self-fulfilling
prophecies (see Arnold, this volume, and Puchta 1999).

In this chapter I am going to discuss some recent and very intri-
guing findings from neurosciences (neurobiology in particular), and the
important lessons that I think we as language teachers can learn from
those findings. Neuroscience is an area that has over the last few years
offered us fascinating views into how the human brain works, many of
which seem promising enough to lead to significant changes in educational methodology. Neurobiological findings – the work of James E.
Zull (2002, 2011) in particular – help us to understand better the nature
of our students' learning successes (and also their failures) and at the
same time give us concrete pointers that can lead to the enrichment of
our teaching. The major benefits in our field, as I will explain below, are
the resulting insights into the ways in which beliefs and emotions have a
major impact on the success or otherwise of the learning process.

In his ground-breaking work, Zull discusses neuroscientific investiga-
tions into the workings of the brain and shows how emotions and learning are influenced by how the biological brain interacts with our senses
and the physical world. A number of the findings he elaborates on are
immediately applicable to the foreign language class, and intimately tied
up with the question of whether or not a student is fully engaged in the
learning process. A few of these findings may seem familiar to the experienced teacher; for example, they may be 'what we have always felt'–
that is, confirmation of ways of teaching used by successful teachers. For
less experienced teachers, the findings can be very useful pointers in a
positive direction.

Knowledge is physical

Learning is a physical-chemical process, and whenever we learn something new, some change happens in our brain. 'Our brains are physical

maps of reality, and the existing neuronal networks are replicas of the physical form of objects in the world, those objects and events that make up our concrete experience' (Zull 2002: 92). The brain's networks are made of physical, tangible matter, formed from many millions of neurons (nerve cells) and networks of neurons, which meet at tiny gaps known as synapses. A synapse is 'bridged' by new knowledge, and each time that particular bit of knowledge is revisited, the bridge between the neurons becomes stronger. The bridges that were formed in childhood, hence used over and over again, are the strongest of all, which is why we tend to retain our earlier memories while we forget more recent ones.

It is the neuronal networks in the brain that are used to store information. As Zull (2002: 98) points out, 'there is a neuronal network in the brain for everything we know'. This means that when our students learn a new word, this word is remembered and represented in their brains within a neuronal network – and when they learn a new tense, that learning leads to the formation of another whole new neuronal network. There are networks for understanding grammar, for sentence creation and indeed for basically anything that makes up language. Such networks can get connected with other networks. But we do not use our neuronal networks only for information retrieval; we use them when we integrate information with what we already know in order to create new knowledge, and we use the new facts we have learned by building more neuronal networks.

Hence, as far as current science allows us to believe, learning inevitably builds on our prior knowledge, and so teaching that fails to take into consideration what the students already know does not lead to effective learning. What seems to be happening in many classrooms, however, is that teachers don't see what could be called the 'neuronal value' of the students' prior knowledge. I suspect that the reason for that lies in the phenomenon that prior knowledge often appears to be incomplete and full of errors or wrong conclusions about the system of the language and so on. It seems that some teachers will therefore not build on the students' prior knowledge, and this in turn means that the learning process may well be seriously hampered. Zull (2002: 94) stresses that there is no point in trying to 'banish wrong ideas by simply stating they are wrong' and points out that taking them seriously and building on them is a precondition for students finally getting it right, which at the same time has a positive effect on memory (p. 124).

Learning is brain change

The human brain is *not* a container or a structure that simply stores information. Likewise, students do not, at a later stage, simply retrieve from their brain knowledge they have stored as outcomes of their learning processes. Neuroscience clearly shows us that the process of learning affects the brain directly and physically, by literally changing the brain's structure while learning is taking place. In fact we can say that there is no learning without physical change in the brain. At the root of the physical changes that take place when the brain learns, there are chemical processes which lead to the more efficient bridging of synapses and the growth of neuronal networks. The more the brain changes through such neural activity, the more our students will remember, the more they will learn and the more the brain itself will develop.

The question, then, for us as teachers is what we can do to facilitate the building of neuronal networks in our students' brains.

Practice makes perfect – or does it?

Not surprisingly, practice is one of the keys to changing the brain; there is in fact a saying that 'Neurons that fire together, wire together.' In other words, it could be assumed that the more our students practise, for example, a certain grammar structure, the better for their language learning and the development of their brain. However, we have to be cautious about such beliefs, as not all kinds of practice lead to long-lasting learning effects. In fact, practice can actually achieve the opposite if it does not offer enough sensory stimulation (Zull 2002: 152). Sensory input is central to any kind of learning; however, if the input becomes monotonous and dull, our students will stop taking notice, just as we tend to notice less and less any sensory input from an aspect of our environment that has remained more or less the same over a period of time.

Some friends of mine live in an amazing house in the Brazilian rainforest, almost at the edge of a waterfall. It is an amazing experience for any visitor to their place to walk out on the balcony and be surrounded by hummingbirds, and the sound of the waterfall is dramatic and real. But what is astonishing about the sound, too, is to notice how my perception of it changes from 'very loud' to 'less noticeable' within a period of only a couple of weeks. The brain has a tendency to blank out after some time sensory stimuli that it does not regard as relevant – the sound of the waterfall becomes less relevant after some time, and so we seem to notice it less on a conscious level. For the very same reason, if, for example, our students do not see a certain grammar structure as being relevant to them, they might, especially when doing mechanical practice, stop noticing its aspects, and hence there is likely to be less learning.

The role of emotions

Changes in the brain depend on the release of certain chemicals, and the outcome of this process can lead to feelings of joy and happiness. How does this happen? And can we as teachers influence in any way the production of those chemicals that contribute to learning in our students' brains? Zull's research suggests that we can. He stresses that the brain changes physically when we learn and he states that the change is most extensive and powerful when emotion is part of the learning, which seems to strongly support Stevick's observation about the importance of 'depth' in the foreign language learning process (see, e.g., Stevick 1996: 132–8): 'The chemicals of emotion, such as adrenalin, serotonin, and dopamine, act by modification of synapses; and modification of synapses are the very root of learning ... In some cases, such change does not occur at all unless the emotion chemicals and structures in the brain are engaged' (Zull 2003: 2).

As mentioned in Chapter 1, Stevick focuses on the importance of relevance, that is, the connection we make between something we perceive outside ourselves and something within us. When we regard something as relevant to us, that connection is made and our body responds by releasing chemicals that result in a positive feeling. So in the case of learning being perceived as relevant, we feel positive about our new acquisition of language: this feeling is a tangible reward for making progress. Apropos of 'making progress', Zull (2002: 61 and 2011: 149) argues that there may be a connection between the release of dopamine and action, both physical and mental. According to this argument, students enjoy the learning process because what is inherent in the process itself is movement (metaphorically speaking). This happens, for example, when we get engaged in a process that starts when we are faced with a challenge and finishes at the point when we manage to solve a puzzle. Zull also stresses that the drive to keep reading a good book or watching a film comes from 'anticipated movement', that is, our wish to witness things happening, and he adds that 'Success is progress towards a goal, and nothing succeeds like success. This could be one of the most important aspects of intrinsic motivation. Achievement itself is rewarding, and that may simply be because it is recognized as movement' (Zull 2002: 62).

Studies show that both physical and mental movement are such powerful learning tools because it is through action that we discover 'the hidden images in our own brain' (Zull 2011: 149). In other words, thinking actively – when we do things such as writing down our thoughts about something, talking aloud to ourselves, engaging in a discussion with someone, taking our time to silently reflect on something that engages us, or playing around in our mind with knowledge we have just acquired – can help us integrate recently acquired knowledge with prior knowledge, discover new aspects about something we already know, or develop a deeper understanding of a concept. This explains the phenomenon I have observed, that we understand complex matters better through the process of explaining it to others. As a teacher trainer, for example, I have occasionally noticed that showing a group of teacher trainees a teaching strategy they have not come across before and sharing my ideas about it with them have helped me to develop my own ideas and thoughts much more clearly and deeply. Neurobiological research gives us reason to believe that such phenomena are not uncommon.

Ownership

Another key element of learner engagement is discovery. Children discover things serendipitously, through random processes. In contrast, those adults who have developed their thinking skills well and are used to thinking in a systematic and targeted fashion tend to believe that all thinking is a planned and plannable activity – but this is not the case. In fact, discovering new things depends to a certain extent on random thinking, on 'thinking outside the box', on daring to think differently and engaging in experimental thought, or simply starting to reflect on something, 'seeing it from different angles', waiting for the moment when we make connections that help us create new meaning. Learning that takes place through personal discovery lasts longer and is more enjoyable for students (releasing, as it does, more of the reward chemicals into the body). This kind of learning is so powerful, too, as it creates a sense of ownership in the learner.

As Thornbury (2005: 63) stresses in his discussion of developing students' speaking skills, ownership is of significant importance in learning a foreign language as 'learning a skill is not simply a behaviour (like practice) or a mental process (like restructuring) … Central to the notion of a transfer of control is the idea that aspects of the skill are appropriated. Appropriation has connotations of taking over the ownership of something, of "making something one's own".'

Seen from a neuroscientific point of view, ownership is a key outcome of learning processes. When we discover something new, when we develop an idea that we feel is ours and become aware that we are the creators of that idea, we begin to have a sense of ownership of our creation. This helps us develop our thinking skills, in that the process of becoming aware of our ownership means that we engage in metacognition, and hence we improve our ability to think about thinking.

Teaching as an art

Zull (2003) likens teaching to art. In his discussion of art he stresses two aspects that are important: we are recipients of art (when we go to a museum, look at paintings in a gallery, listen to a concert, watch a dance performance, read a novel), or we can become artists ourselves. As recipients of a piece of art we can – when we are lucky enough – become emotionally engaged. We experience this when the book we read, the piece of music we listen to, the show we watch 'speaks to us'. In other words, we become emotionally engaged through our reception of a piece of art and it follows that we form a lasting memory.

The same is true of the foreign language learning process, as Stevick stresses. He talks about the fact that most of the sensory impressions our brain gets exposed to are not remembered, and he underlines personal relevance and 'depth' as key factors for retrieving information: 'the "deeper" the source of a sentence within the student's personality, the more lasting value it has for learning the language' (Stevick 1996: 196).

Not only do the neurobiological findings quoted so far support this argument, but they also show that when students get engaged in a personal and deep way, their brain will learn by doing far more than just 'remembering' input. The new input will make connections with prior knowledge, and chances are that the process of integration will lead to the development of new knowledge, insight and understanding.

It makes perfect sense to assume not only that the perception of art leads to emotional processes, but also that the creation of art probably triggers even more emotions. That must be the case, as it means a deeper involvement from the person who creates it: 'since creativity is based on the decisions made by the creator, the reward system kicks in when we are in control and inventing things that we have thought of ourselves. Freedom and ownership are part and parcel of the neurochemistry of arts' (Zull 2003: 2).

It is not difficult to see the importance of these neuroscientific findings to the foreign language learning process. One thing we can say straightaway is that as far as reception is concerned we need to find texts that 'speak' to our students in terms of being relevant and accessible to them. When they do, our students' brains will start releasing the chemicals that create feelings of joy and happiness. It is important to note that the creation of those feelings does not necessarily have to come from the content of the text (at least not during the early stages of the foreign language learning process); they might, for example, come from the brain's own reward system when students make progress in understanding L2 texts. Whatever their origin, these feelings of success will in turn help to create neuronal networks that lead to longer-lasting retrieval of the language our students are exposed to.

Such neuronal activity will also enable them to learn to use the foreign language better and more flexibly. The pleasurable feelings will encourage them to reflect on the language they are learning, and so help them develop their own competence and confidence. Hence, when it comes to the process of the students' production of the foreign language, this requires us as teachers to engage our students in activities where they themselves can develop feelings of becoming 'artists' or 'creators' of language. If, as their foreign language emerges, they sense those very positive emotions of freedom and ownership in the way an artist does when creating a picture or composing a piece of music, they will learn much more successfully, and their learning will have longer-lasting effects.

The choice of texts for adult learners

Over the last three decades, ELT has seen a radical change as far as the texts used in the foreign language class are concerned. This has happened partly because the communicative approach has gained more ground over structuralist teaching concepts, and that has led to querying the usefulness of what used to be the staple diet of ELT. Coursebooks used to offer lots of texts (*What am I doing now? – I am standing in front of the board*) that were artificial and pragmatically meaningless (see Widdowson 1998).

The trend these days is moving in the opposite direction. We are finding more dialogues that are modelled on what people say in real-life situations, and genres of texts are used that are perceived to be more relevant for adult learners because they are authentic. The move towards more 'real' language and text genres has also gained enormous momentum because of the influence of corpus linguistics and the very useful snippets of information it makes available to coursebook writers and curriculum planners alike. Research into spoken English has given us an in-depth perception of what people are really likely to say in certain situations, and has also helped us to get a more accurate picture of language in actual use (see, e.g., the ground-breaking research of Carter and McCarthy 2006).

One of the outcomes is that we are now finding more 'real English' in coursebooks, and it seems that teaching materials for the adult classroom are at the forefront of this development. The reason for this is obvious: for many adult students, proficiency in English is a tool they need to develop in order to be successful professionally, and many of them need to achieve international language certificates to enter university or to qualify for a certain position in their professional lives. The growing influence of standardized tests has brought about a need for internationally recognized levels of competence (such as those laid out in the *Common European Framework of Languages*; see The Council of Europe 2001) and a trend towards more 'real' texts.

There seems to be a belief among coursebook authors that teaching materials for adults need to be serious in order for adult learners to take them seriously. At the same time, it is not uncommon to hear teachers comment on a lack of lighter content in current coursebooks. Medgyes (2002), for example, carefully analyses ELT materials and notices that they are lacking in humour. He stresses that including more humour, among other things, eases tension in the classroom, strengthens motivation, has a positive effect on the group dynamics and helps foster the students' creativity.

The search for 'serious' content that is perceived to be relevant for adults often leads to texts or text genres that students might be very happy to read or listen to in their mother tongue. However, in order for students to decode such texts successfully, they often need complex conceptual, contextual and cultural knowledge and understanding on top of their knowledge of the language and relevant reading or listening skills. If their foreign language level is still rather low, this can just be too much for them to handle. Widdowson (1998: 711) maintains:

> I would ... argue against using authentic language in the classroom, on the fairly reasonable grounds that it is actually impossible to do so. The language cannot be authentic because the classroom cannot provide the contextual conditions for it to be authenticated by the learners. The authenticity or reality of language use in its normal pragmatic functioning depends on its being localized within a particular discourse community. Listeners can only authenticate it as discourse if they are insiders. But learners are outsiders, by definition, not members of user communities. So the language that is authentic for native speaker users cannot possibly be authentic for learners.

In support of that view, Widdowson (1998: 712) adds: 'This objection is so obvious that it seems odd that the authenticity argument should ever be taken seriously.' Whereas this seems an extreme position because it does not differentiate as to whether the learners referred to are, say, students at elementary or lower intermediate level, or maybe students at university preparing for an international exam at C2 level, classroom experience shows that what one could call 'pedagogical overload' may indeed lead to frustrating emotional experiences that achieve the opposite of what was intended.

As Perry (2006: 26) stresses, adult learners, as well as younger ones, have deeply ingrained in their brains a powerful reflex called the 'fear response'. We feel that reflex in moments of existential threat such as hunger, pain or danger – and quite frequently the classroom equivalent, shame. At that point, all our mind can focus on is whatever we need in order to get out of the unpleasant situation. Under such circumstances, there is no way that the human mind is going to be open to new information; novelty is seen only as a further threat, and even though the threat situations in the classroom are very different from those our brains are wired to recognize, that situation is no exception.

De Andrés and Arnold (2008: 19) point out the importance of establishing rules and routines for the development of a sense of security in the classroom so learners know what is expected of them and feel safe. Speaking from the perspective of neuroscience, Perry (2006: 27) states that 'When the learner feels safe, curiosity lives. When we are safe and the world around us is familiar, we crave novelty. Conversely, when the world around us is too new, we crave familiarity. In such situations, we are more easily overwhelmed, distressed, frustrated. Therefore we want familiar, comforting and safe things.' These explanations seem more than plausible. Although a good teacher can engender a sense of security in a class, the use of a text that bears scant relevance to the lives of the students for whom it is intended is likely to have a counterproductive effect on their progress. Why then, when it comes to creating and choosing texts for the foreign language class, do we not look for more familiar, comforting and safe things?

Development of cognitive tools

An interesting theory about the development of the human mind comes from educational philosopher Kieran Egan. It may further explain why a feeling of safety is such an important precondition for learning, and it may guide us towards an understanding of what kinds of texts would be more relevant to our adult students – especially in the early stages of their foreign language learning – than those that we currently find in coursebooks and many language classrooms.

Egan (1997) postulates that a person's intellectual growth happens naturally, through the acquisition of certain intellectual qualities (he calls them 'developments') deeply rooted in our cultural history. In order for an individual's intellect to grow appropriately, the development of certain 'cognitive tools' is essential. Here is a very basic summary of his ideas, which could serve as a basis for understanding how the human mind develops from childhood to adult years.

Table 3.1 *A summary of a person's intellectual development (Egan 1997)*

Intellectual developments	Short description	Cognitive tools
Mythic understanding (is typically developed in primary school years)	Understanding of the world is based on binary opposites (good–evil; happy–sad; tiny–huge). No clear borderline between reality and imagination – story-thinking!	Understanding stories; narrating; images and imaginative thinking; metaphor; categorizing; rhyme, rhythm and pattern; humour; small talk ('gossip'); engagement with the natural world
Romantic understanding (developed during adolescence)	Growing interest in reality and its limits; rational thinking starts developing; longing for ideal qualities (love, courage, genius, creativity, etc.); identification with models (heroes and heroines); an interest in the exotic, mysterious and what is far away from one's own life situation	Fascination with extremes; association with heroes; sense of wonder and excitement; cumulating knowledge; development of the 'literary eye' – understanding and making flow charts, bar charts, lists, graphs, etc.
Philosophic understanding (developed during the pre-university years)	Developing an interest in theory and theories; wanting to understand how the world works and what the exceptions are; metacognition (thinking about thinking) develops; pattern detection; ordering knowledge into schemata	Growing sense of abstract reality; a sense of agency; understanding general ideas and their anomalies; search for authority and truth; meta-narrative understanding (aiming to explain the world by combining facts, events, beliefs and ideas plus our emotions towards them into general constructs)
Ironic understanding (the ideas of the intellectually fully developed adult mind)	A sophisticated state of mind and thinking that allows the free choice and use of the various layers of understanding developed previously (mythic, romantic and philosophic); enjoys and is open to self-contradiction	Ability to appreciate and utilize irony; aware of a range of different forms of understanding and perspectives; able to discern the value of these forms practically, aesthetically and relating to specific circumstances

Table 3.2 *The cognitive functions of four areas of the cerebral cortex (Zull 2002: 18)*

Kieran Egan: key cognitive functions	James Zull: brain regions involved
Mythic layer: gathering information	Sensory cortex
Romantic layer: making meaning of information	Integrative cortex near the sensory cortex
Philosophic layer: creating new ideas from meanings created	Integrative cortex at the front
Ironic layer: acting on the ideas developed	Motor cortex

It would appear that the growing intellectual requirements needed to develop the various cognitive tools listed in Egan's theory each have a clear correspondence with the cognitive functions of four areas of the cerebral cortex, as defined by Zull (2002: 18).

Relevance

I remember well what happened a few years ago when I started learning Italian as a foreign language. A few months into the learning process, a friend gave me a simplified reader – a lightweight romance, not something I'd normally read. And yet I devoured the story and derived considerable satisfaction from being able to understand it, which on reflection was quite a surprise to me. There is no way I would have kept on reading the same kind of story in my mother tongue – I would most probably have put it aside in half a minute. Why did I not do that with the reader? Why did I actually enjoy the activity? Let's turn again to our two models discussed above. Understanding demanding texts is impossible without fairly sophisticated language knowledge and skills. But my Italian was at elementary level. So – with the higher intellectual echelons of ironic understanding and philosophic thinking sadly inaccessible to me at the elementary level of my target language – one explanation for the pleasure I got out of understanding a rather pedestrian text might be the 'sense of movement' gained from understanding the text. Another seems to be connected to a kind of 'regression' into the cognitive frame of a far less developed stage of mind – a stage of mind that was accessible to me without breaking the flow of reading in L2. This explanation seems to be in line with what Egan says about the adult (ironic) thinkers: although clearly capable of sophisticated understanding and thinking, they still have available within their portfolio of cognitive tools those that belong to the previous layers of understanding (mythic, romantic and philosophical), and they can enjoy using those if they choose to do so.

When learning a foreign language, even the developed adult thinker needs security. Following what we have discussed earlier, that security is unlikely to come from reading and listening processes that require sophisticated ways of thinking and understanding, at least during the first few years of the learning process. As Schmidt et al. (1996: 55) have – not surprisingly! – found, humans are motivated to 'engage in activities that they enjoy and that do not arouse anxiety'. Paul, quoted at the beginning of this chapter, suffers from the fact that in the foreign language he is learning there is no way he can express his normal degree of sophistication of thinking. It seems that he would be well advised to be patient. His passion, political science, will remain inaccessible for him for some time in the foreign language; much time, patience and investment (see Norton Peirce 1995) will be required until he can at last take part in discussions relating to his favourite intellectual pursuit.

The models presented above, however, seem to give us clear indications of how we can make foreign language learning more enjoyable for adult students during those phases of 'restricted' accessibility – keeping in mind that the sensation of joy seems to facilitate cognitive engagement. So what we need – until more sophisticated content becomes accessible to students and can be expressed confidently by them – is lighter content, more closely akin to texts that the students choose to read for their own recreation. Support for such an argument also comes from a study on 'flow theory' in foreign language learning carried out by Egbert (2004). The term 'flow' (Csikszentmihalyi 1994) is used to describe a state of experience that is characterized by intense focus and leads to excellence in the performance of a task. Egbert (2003: 504) stresses the importance of 'focused attention' in supporting flow experiences and quotes a study carried out by McQuillan and Conde (1996) that comes to the conclusion that 'most of the texts that supported flow were those that participants had read for their own enjoyment, ones in which they had interest, and those in narrative form, partly because it was easier to focus on these texts'.

Adult students can be absolutely thrilled when they are able to understand texts – no matter that the content is well below what they are normally used to reading and listening to in their L1. Let's take as an example Catherine, whose mother tongue is English and who is a brilliant intellectual with a highly sophisticated linguistic mind. She says that she remembers tackling the Pitman's version in shorthand of *Three Men in a Boat*, a book written in the ponderously humorous style fashionable about a hundred years ago. As she laboriously worked her way into the text, she found herself almost weeping with laughter at jokes she would normally have dismissed as boring – and 40 years later, she still remembers that learning experience with great pleasure.

A look at the cognitive tools list above might help us find content likely to be seen as more relevant by our learners themselves. For a change, why not use humour, strong emotional contrasts, inspiring stories about real-life heroes and heroines, and texts about the extreme, the absurd, and the weird and wonderful, at least at the earlier stages of the learning process?

Freedom and ownership

These days, writing programmes for adult learners frequently follow a systematic syllabus based on principles of genre writing. In this approach, students are trained to write using various kinds of real-life text genres. Examples include invitations to a social gathering, emails, various kinds of letters, complaints, discursive text-types, etc. This kind of writing is often regarded as highly relevant and important by teachers and students alike, especially if students are preparing for international exams. However, as important as the different genres of texts are, this type of writing alone might not be enough if we want to take seriously what neurosciences tell us about the workings of the brain.

We have discussed previously that the brain needs positive emotions, experiences of success and a sense of freedom and ownership in order to be fully engaged in the learning process. However, important as the writing of 'real' text may indeed be, emotional engagement will most probably not arise in a majority of learners from the kind of writing mentioned. It seems equally important to engage our students in spontaneous, personal, free or creative writing tasks, as these are more likely to create that sense of freedom and ownership that neuroscientific research stresses as so important. This is not a suggestion to replace one (genre-based) method with the other (creative writing), but rather an advocacy for using both. What is not yet clear, however, is whereabouts within the learning process the study of genre-based writing and of creative writing should best be located – if indeed there is any ideal place in that process for either of them.

We have seen previously that we can create neuronal networks successfully when learning builds on what we already know. The students' prior knowledge is concrete, and though it may be incomplete, that is, full of linguistic errors and gaps, it is extremely important. Zull (2002: 109) suggests that 'writing assignments are helpful in discovering the prior knowledge of students'. Following on from that, it would be interesting to see the results of a balanced approach to writing whereby students write freely, spontaneously and creatively at the beginning of a new teaching phase (be that a unit in a coursebook or a theme-based project). If the teacher then looks at the students' writing with a non-judgemental attitude, that could lead to important insights which might in turn give guidance on how to carry on with the teaching. As Zull (2002: 109) states, 'Prior knowledge is a gift to the teacher; it tells us where and how to start.'

In a teaching model of this type, the more 'technical' genre-based writing would happen at a later stage, towards the end of a teaching phase, and it would go far beyond a mere model-based development of various text genres. The focus would be on the development of specific skill strategies in a process-oriented way, considering what we know about how the brain learns best, by leading students through a cycle of stages. In such an approach, students would be involved in *gaining experience* at writing certain text genres, *reflecting* on the quality of their writing (guided by the teacher), *developing* new ideas based on the knowledge gained in the reflection phase, and finally *testing* their strategic know-how in a new writing task.

To come back to what has been stressed previously about the need for texts to be accessible, relevant and emotionally involving, there are strong arguments for an equivalent model to develop the students' genre-specific writing. Accessibility in the receptive area would correlate with mastering writing sub-skills (how to brainstorm, draft, edit, etc.) in the productive domain; relevance would equal manageability (which requires language competence, skills and discourse strategies), and emotional involvement in the productive process is a direct outcome of freedom and ownership – the more students can tell the story they want to tell, the more depths their writing process will be drawing on.

Conclusion

As Egbert (2003: 505) notices, 'enjoyment' and 'playfulness' are terms that 'scholars do not usually apply to the experience of or research on classroom language learning'. There seems, however, to be enough evidence from both neuroscientific research and educational theory to support an approach that advocates the use of 'lighter' texts in adult classrooms – at least in the earlier stages of learning – that help students get more readily into 'flow states' when they read or listen in the language they are learning, because they will find them easier to enjoy. Likewise, it seems we are well advised to activate adult students' prior knowledge more systematically and regularly than is currently done in most classrooms. Spontaneous speaking and especially writing activities will help to create those important feelings of 'freedom and ownership' with the students, and make it possible for teachers to use the language produced as evidence of the students' prior knowledge so that they can make more informed choices on the *what* and the *how* of their teaching. Such an approach might also lead not only to better academic results on the students' side, but to more fun in the classrooms – and consequently an increased level of job satisfaction for the teacher.

References

Carter, R. and McCarthy, M. (2006) *Cambridge Grammar of English: A Comprehensive Guide – Spoken and Written English Grammar and Usage*, Cambridge: Cambridge University Press.

Csikszentmihalyi, M. (1994) 'Interest and the quality of experience in classrooms', *European Journal of Psychology of Education*, 9: 251–70.

de Andrés, V. and Arnold, J. (2008) *Seeds of Confidence: Self-Esteem Activities for the EFL Classroom*, Innsbruck: Helbling Languages.

Egan, K. (1997) *The Educated Mind: How Cognitive Tools Shape Our Understanding*, Chicago: University of Chicago Press.

Egbert, J. (2003) 'A study of flow theory in the foreign language classroom', *The Modern Language Journal*, 87(4): 499–518.

McQuillan, J. and Conde, G. (1996) 'The conditions of flow in reading: two studies of optimal experience', *Reading Psychology: An International Quarterly*, 17: 109–35.

Medgyes, P. (2002) *Laughing Matters: Humour in the Language Classroom*, Cambridge: Cambridge University Press.

Norton Peirce, B. (1995) 'Social identity, investment and language learning', *TESOL Quarterly*, 29(1): 9–31.

Perry, B. D. (2006) 'Fear and learning: trauma-related factors in the adult education process', in Johnson, S. and Taylor, K. (eds.) *The Neuroscience of Adult Education: New Directions for Adult and Continuing Education*, San Francisco: Jossey-Bass, pp. 21–7.

Puchta, H. (1999) 'Beyond materials, techniques and linguistic analyses: the role of motivation, beliefs and identity', plenary paper presented at the 33rd Annual International IATEFL Conference, Edinburgh, 28 March–1 April.

Schmidt, R., Boraie, D. and Kassabgy, O. (1996) 'Foreign language motivation: internal structure and external connections', in Oxford, R. (ed.)

Language Learning Motivation: Pathways to the New Century, Manoa: University of Hawai'i Press, pp. 9–56.

Stevick, E. W. (1996) *Memory, Meaning and Method: A View of Language Teaching*, 2nd edn, Boston: Heinle & Heinle.

The Council of Europe (2001) *Common European Framework of Reference for Languages*, Cambridge: Cambridge University Press.

Thornbury, S. (2005) *How to Teach Speaking*, Harlow: Pearson Longman.

Widdowson, H. G. (1998) 'Context, community and authentic language', *TESOL Quarterly*, **32**(4): 705–16.

Zull, J. E. (2002) *The Art of Changing the Brain: Enriching the Practice of Teaching by Exploring the Biology of Learning*, Sterling VA: Stylus Publishing.

Zull, J. E. (2003) 'Arts, neuroscience and learning', *New Horizons for Learning: News from the Neurosciences*. Available online at http://education.jhu.edu/newhorizons/Neurosciences/articles/Arts-neurosciences-and-learning (accessed August 2011).

Zull, J. E. (2011) *From Brain to Mind: Using Neuroscience to Guide Change in Education*, Sterling, VA: Stylus Publishing.

4 The learning body

Scott Thornbury

> Hands, do what you're bid:
> Bring the balloon of the mind
> That bellies and drags in the wind
> Into its narrow shed.

(W. B. Yeats)

Introduction

The humanist tradition has provided a useful corrective to the view that learning, whether of languages or of anything else, is primarily an intellectual endeavour. As Williams and Burden (1997: 30) note, 'Humanism provides an added dimension ... in that it emphasises the development of the whole person rather than focusing solely upon the development and employment of cognitive skills', the whole person being understood as including 'the individual's thoughts, feelings and emotions'. If the strictly mentalist, Cartesian view could be paraphrased as 'I think, therefore I learn', the humanist view is more 'I think, feel and desire, therefore I learn.'

The humanist concern for the *person*, however, does not (or should not) ignore the *people*. The dual focus of language learning, both on the (inner) person and on the people (in the room), is well captured in Stevick's oft-cited assertion that 'success depends less on materials, techniques, and linguistic analyses, and more on what goes on inside and between the people in the classroom' (1980: 4). In so doing, he invokes 'a world of meaningful action' within which the learning experience is situated.

In this chapter I want to extend this line of thought by arguing that language – and hence both language use and language learning – is both embodied by, and physically embedded in its contexts of use, and that what happens between people and within them is all part of a seamless process, by which the learning mind extends far beyond its 'narrow shed'. Or, as Churchill et al. (2010: 237) put it, 'brains are in bodies, bodies are in the world, and meaningful action in these worlds is in large part socially constructed and conducted'.

The theoretical model which I shall adopt is a dynamical systems-based, ecologically oriented one, generally known now as situated cognition, which takes the position that 'human cognitive processes are inherently social, interactive, personal, biological, and neurological, which is to say that a variety of systems develop and depend on one another in complex ways' (Clancey 2009: 11). Proponents of situated cognition, such as Robbins and Aydede (2009: 3), take three distinct but interrelated positions:

> First, cognition depends not just on the brain but also on the body (the embodiment thesis). Second, cognitive activity routinely exploits structure in the natural and social environment (the embedding thesis). Third, the boundaries of cognition extend beyond the boundaries of individual organisms (the extension thesis).

Using this three-part model to structure my argument, I hope to show how language is profoundly implicated in these embodying, embedding and extending processes, and, moreover, that language learning is enhanced – even, in Stevick's terms, *harmonized* – when the situated nature of language use (at all three levels) is fully engaged.

Embodied

In what sense, then, is language use – and, by extension, language learning – *embodied*? Cognitive linguistics takes as its starting point the premise that language, far from being an abstract and isolated system operating according to its own laws, is 'rooted in human experience of the physical world' (Lee 2001: 48) and is a reflection, therefore, of 'the human perceptual system and human understanding of the spatial-physical-social world we inhabit' (Tyler 2008: 459). One example of this is the way that *kinesthetic image schemata*, derived from how we physically experience space and motion, not only underpin our understanding of spatial relations but extend to the way we construe other, more abstract phenomena. Take this extract from a newspaper article, for example:

> English is on the up at the moment, an up that is probably unprecedented in world history. But world history is full of languages that have dominated for a long time, yet there aren't too many of them around now.
>
> (Interview with Nicholas Ostler, *Guardian Weekly*, 12.11.2010)

The short text includes two prototypical examples of what Mark Johnson (1987: 100) calls 'the experiential embodied nature of human rationality': (1) *English is on the up* and (2) *history is full of languages*.

The use of the word *up* to connote increase, in the sense that MORE IS UP, emerges – according to Johnson (1987: xiv) – 'from a tendency to employ an UP-DOWN orientation in picking out meaningful structures of our experience. We grasp the structure of verticality repeatedly in thousands of perceptions and activities we experience every day, such as perceiving a tree, our felt sense of standing upright, the activity of climbing stairs.' Likewise, the idea that history is a container, and hence can be 'full of languages', is an extension of our own embodied sense of physical containment. According to Johnson, 'our encounter with containment and boundedness is one of the most pervasive features of our bodily experience' (1987: 21).

Cognitive linguists argue that such experientially based 'image schemata' are integral to meaning and to rationality – and, of course, to language. The way that language is structured, used and learned is largely determined by the fact that, as Johnson puts it, 'the body is in the mind' (1987: xxxviii).

One well-documented manifestation of this is the choice of particles for phrasal verbs. We *fill up* the tank, the future is *looking up* and children both *grow up* and are *brought up*. Likewise, notions of boundedness and containment are intrinsic, not only to the semantics of the noun phrase in many languages (witness countable and uncountable nouns), but also to verb aspect.

On the assumption that bringing such relationships to conscious awareness may facilitate learning, a number of researchers (e.g. Kövesces and Szabó 1996) have investigated the mnemonic potential of unpacking the image schemata and conceptual frameworks that 'motivate' common idioms and phrasal verbs. Lindstromberg and Boers have extended this line of experimentation to include actual physical movement in the learning of certain verbs of movement. Drawing on research into L1 vocabulary learning, which shows that 'acting out word meanings helps school-age children to increase their L1 vocabularies' (Lindstromberg and Boers 2005: 243), their research demonstrated that when learners were asked to enact or mime a 'manner-of-movement' verb (such as *hurl*, *pounce* or *sway*), better retention resulted than if they were asked only to explain it. Enactment also appeared to prime learners to understand not only the literal but the figurative meanings of these verbs. Moreover, simply watching someone else enact the meaning of these verbs was equally effective, bearing out research in the field of cognitive neurophysiology 'which suggests that simply watching the performance of an action may trigger imagery that is purely motoric' (p. 244).

Research into the embodied nature of language use and of language learning would seem to validate Stevick's (1996: 132) arguments in support of Asher's (1996) Total Physical Response (TPR) methodology, i.e. that 'it encourages – indeed, practically forces – multi sensory involvement and resulting multi sensory images ... It meets in an integrated way needs that are physical and social as well as cognitive.'

Embedded

That language is *embedded* in its contexts of use is hardly news: it dates
back at least to Malinowski and his claim that language becomes intel-
ligible only when it is placed within its 'context of situation'. Learning
'how to mean' in a language, therefore, means mapping a semantic system on to a social one. Indeed, as Halliday (1978: 120) puts it, 'the
linguistic system is a part of the social system. Neither can be learnt
without the other.' Cognitive scientists, too, have contributed insights
into how language is processed in its contexts of use: 'Language processing is not something that happens just in the individual brain of a
speaker or a listener. In many circumstances, the proper analysis of language processing is at the level of the organisms and the environment in
which they are situated' (Spivey and Richardson 2009: 396).

In a very broad sense, then, the 'embeddedness' principle is now
taken for granted, and for some time second language teaching methodologies have invoked the socially situated nature of language use,
both in defining the goals of language learning and in formulating its
pedagogical practices.

More recently, however, second language learning has experienced
what has been called 'a social turn' (Block 2003). This has been largely
driven by the increasing popularization of sociocognitive accounts
of language learning (e.g. Batstone 2010), which in turn share common ground with sociocultural learning theory (Lantolf 2000; Lantolf
and Thorne 2006), as well as with theories of language socialization
(Kramsch 2002) and identity formation (Norton 2000; Kramsch
2009). What these various schools of thought share is an allegiance
to a socially situated view of learning, where language acquisition is
no longer regarded as a purely internal and cognitive process. Indeed,
Ellis (2008: 536) notes that one researcher goes so far as to suggest that
the language acquisition device 'is located in the interaction that takes
place between speakers rather than inside their heads. That is acquisition occurs *in* rather than as *a result of* interaction.' The net effect of
these 'new social perspectives' is that, according to Ortega (2009: 217),
'additional language learning is not only shaped by the social context in
which it happens; it is bound inextricably to such context'.

Central to this paradigm shift is a transition from one metaphor of language learning to another: from *acquisition* to *participation* (Sfard 1998).
According to the participation metaphor, language learning is construed,
not as a process of *getting*, but as one of *becoming* – of becoming a
member of a particular discourse community. Rather than being simply
a cognitive process, learning is a social practice and, as such, 'involves
the whole person; it implies not only a relation to specific activities, but a

relation to social communities – it implies becoming a full participant, a member, a kind of person' (Lave and Wenger 1991: 53).

Crucially implicated in this process of becoming a participant is language: 'Learning to become a legitimate participant in a community involves learning how to talk (and be silent) in the manner of full participants' (Lave and Wenger: 105). Talk is also the means by which knowledge is jointly constructed – 'the process by which experience becomes knowledge' (Halliday 1993: 94) – and, since knowledge construction is central to learning, it follows that talk mediates learning. As van Lier (1996: 171) puts it, 'Learning takes place when the new is embedded in the familiar ... Conversational interaction naturally links the known to the new.'

From this perspective, teaching-learning is, as Mercer (1995: 84) terms it, a *long conversation*, 'in the sense that the talk generates its own context and continuity, so that the knowledge that is created carries with it echoes of the conversations in which it was generated'. As an example, Mercer offers this extract of talk from a science class, in which two boys have been set the task of devising a categorization system for seashells:

DANIEL:	I can't think of a way to separate these two [*indicating two shells*]. I've got to separate some of these.
TEACHER:	What's an obvious difference between them?
DANIEL:	They are cones.
GRAHAM:	They are pointed?
TEACHER:	All right. That would ... [*long pause*] So you could separate those two but it wouldn't be a question that applies to those [*indicating two other shells*]. Is there one difference between those two that is also a way you could group those?
DANIEL:	Well, that's pointed ... [*indicates one shell*].
TEACHER:	um.
DANIEL:	... and that one isn't.
	[*And later, after the teacher has left ...*]
DANIEL:	What was the last one we asked before this one?
GRAHAM:	'Is it patterned?'

DANIEL: No. Because these [*indicating shells*] are
                 coiled and then we said ...
GRAHAM: 'Is it pointed?'

(Mercer 1995: 69)

Mercer uses this extract to show how meaning-making is embedded both in its physical context (e.g. the objects that they are manipulating) but also in the jointly constructed history of the boys' and the teacher's earlier talk. Together they create a shared communicative space – what Mercer elsewhere (2000) calls an 'intermental development zone', which is continuously reconstituted as the conversation evolves. 'Common knowledge and understanding is the product of their interaction' (Mercer 2000: 172). Put another way, cognition is distributed in language-mediated activity.

There is more to the interaction, of course, than language. What we are missing from the transcription of the conversation between the two schoolboys and their teacher is an account of the way that other, non-linguistic, systems, such as actions, gesture (including pointing), gaze and body language, are all mutually supportive and, thereby, majorly implicated in the joint construction of knowledge. The quality of joint attention, in particular, where the participants are oriented to the same objects in the environment, through gaze, gesture, as well as talk, is considered to be 'central to the organization of human language and intersubjectivity' (Goodwin 2007: 57).

In order to track these other modes of meaning, a number of researchers, coming from an ethnographic tradition and drawing on sociocognitive theory, have been conducting fine-grained analyses of talk-in-action. Developing Goffman's notion of 'footing', Goodwin (2007: 69), for example, demonstrates that, 'in face-to-face human interaction parties organize their bodies in concert with each other in ways that establish a public, shared focus of visual and cognitive attention'. Extrapolating from an activity sequence in which a father helps his daughter with her homework, he argues that the observed processes of mutual alignment, embodied action and shared attention are fundamental to processes of education and apprenticeship.

Similarly, Atkinson (2010: 611) explores the way that learning – and in this case, second language learning – is a socially situated, adaptive behaviour, a process 'of continuously and progressively fitting oneself to one's environment, often with the help of guides'. Atkinson proposes what he calls 'the alignment principle': 'Learning is more discovering how to align with the world than extracting knowledge from it' (2010: 610). To demonstrate how this might be realized in practice, he traces, in minute detail, the interaction a Japanese schoolgirl has with her aunt, an English teacher, as they work through a homework exercise together: an intricate meshing of language, gesture, gaze and laughter, inseparable from the experience of learning itself.

A complexity theory, or dynamic systems view (Larsen-Freeman and Cameron 2008a; Ellis and Larsen-Freeman 2009), has further enriched our understanding of the interconnected and interdependent nature of learning ecologies. According to this view, learner and context are inextricably connected, each adapting to the other in a dynamic way, such that 'linguistic knowledge is not *given* but adaptively *achieved* by the individual in the environment ... What this means is that meaning is not located in the brain, in the body, in the environment or in a particular linguistic form: it is a function of the global state of the system, and it emerges in the interaction' (Larsen-Freeman and Cameron 2008a: 109).

To capture both these embedded and these emergent properties of language learning, van Lier (2004: 81) uses, as an analogy, the self-organizing nature of learning how to play a game, such as football, where the rules emerge out of both the activity of playing and the shared experience of having seen others play, until a point is reached where 'the rules of the game become learnable, in an interaction between bottom-up discovery, and top-down instruction, within the social context of playing the game'.

The way that – through socially mediated practice – 'the rules ... become learnable' is sometimes captured in the self-reports of language learners themselves. Schmidt and Frota (1986), for example, used a variety of means, including a journal, to track the combination of formal instruction and out-of-class use that the subject (R) experienced as he gained proficiency in Brazilian Portuguese. The rules became learnable once they were instantiated in their contexts of use. At one point, for example, R recounts a breakthrough moment:

> I've reached a new take-off point ... The main thing that's happened is that I'm suddenly hearing things I never heard before, including things mentioned in class ... I can't believe that what I notice isn't crucial for what I can do.

> (Schmidt and Frota 1986: 280–1)

The researchers hypothesized that 'R learned and used what he was taught if he subsequently heard it and if he *noticed* it' (p. 279, emphasis in original).

Although this study was originally situated firmly within a cognitive paradigm, which highlighted the internal, attentional processes – including noticing – that are hypothesized to cause language acquisition, the above account is also consistent with an ecological perspective, that is, one that argues that learning involves 'aligning one's resources with situational demands and shaping the environment to match the language resources one brings' (Canagarajah 2007: 933).

Irrespective of the theory we adopt, we can think of learning, and of language learning in particular, as a process that is both external and internal to the learner. It is external in the sense that it is embedded in the social processes that both historically and at the present moment shape the emerging conversation. It is internal in the sense that the 'script' of this conversation constitutes the learner's linguistic memory as it were: an individualized, but socially constructed, grammar and lexicon that is available for consultation and deployment as the learner moves beyond the classroom into situations of authentic language use.

Extended

The notion, outlined so far, that cognition – and hence learning – is both embodied and embedded is relatively uncontroversial. But, as Robbins and Aydede (2009: 8) comment, 'the same cannot be so easily said ... of the claim that cognition is *extended* – the claim that the boundaries of cognitive systems lie outside the envelope of individual organisms, encompassing features of the physical and social environment'. And yet many cognitive processes, such as computation, memorization and even conversation, typically involve a productive loop between the biological brain and external environmental structures, whether physical, social or technological.

Clark (2011: 81), for example, identifies key ways in which 'body and world come to share the problem-solving load with the biological brain', one being 'the use of "deictic pointers" and active sensing routines that retrieve information from worldly sources just in time for problem-solving use'. And Spivey and Richardson (2009) describe experiments in which conversational partners perform the kind of communicative tasks familiar to second language classrooms, such as instructing one another how to build a model out of Lego blocks. These show that conversants are sensitive to one another's eye movements, and that the resulting patterns play a functional role in comprehension, leading to the conclusion that 'in conversation, the degree to which a listener follows a speaker's gaze around the world is an indicator of their understanding' (2009: 396).

An anecdote of Leo van Lier's nicely captures the way that body and world are jointly implicated in language development when he describes how his three-year-old son, who had been brought up speaking Spanish in Peru, uses the available semiotic tools in a supermarket to formulate his first words in English:

> One day he was being wheeled through the local supermarket, sitting in front of the shopping cart in which so far the only item was a box of Rice Krispies. At that point he spotted another cart coming down the

aisle, and this cart has also just a box of Rice Krispies in it. Noting this coincidence, M produced his first utterance in English: 'Look! This on this!'

(van Lier 2002: 146)

Van Lier notes that the situation 'afforded' Marcus with an opportunity to connect signs (Rice Krispies packets) and signifying devices (gesture and language) and audience (his father).

Words are used, but these words function only in conjunction with gestures (a pointing finger), gaze, and the parts of the physical surroundings staked out. The whole scene can be referred to as semiotic action, and in this semiotic action language emerges and becomes a constitutive part. So, speaking is always a part of a context of meaning-producing actions, interlocutors, objects, and relations among all these. In other words, language emerges as an embodied and situated activity.

(van Lier 2002: 146)

A highly sophisticated attempt to explore the nature of this activity is the Speechome project (Roy 2009), in which a single child's first language acquisition is tracked from birth, using state-of-the-art video- and audio-recording equipment to identify patterns of interaction and joint activity – including reference to objects and people in the physical environment – between the child and his caregivers. Fine-grained computational analysis of these complex vectors of situated activity, resulting in 'word births', are being used to model machine language learning systems. One implication of this massive study is that transcripts of parent–child speech alone do not predict the onset of word learning, but that the 'whole picture' – including gaze, 'body language' and voice quality – needs to be taken into account. Moreover, the physical and social world is not just the background or context for language acquisition, but a key player, forming part of a coupled system, such that language and context are inextricably connected. As Atkinson (2002: 538) puts it: 'Certainly, at critical points in development, language may seem to "come inside" – but if one end of language, so to speak, is embedded in cognitive space, the other end is just as strongly embedded in social space.'

One means by which language extends into social space is by means of gesture. Gesture studies (see McCafferty and Stam 2008 for a review) have identified a number of functions of gesture, including the observation that speakers gesture when they are having difficulties in speech production or when searching for lexical items. This underscores the fact that gesture seems to facilitate thinking, and, by extension, learning. We have already seen (with regard to learning verbs of movement) how gesture, by physically embodying cognitive structures, serves in the learning of their associated linguistic representations. This is but one manifestation of the way 'we think with our hands'. As Lantolf and Thorne (2006: 95) put it, gestures are 'material carriers of thinking': they serve a self-regulatory function by means of which speakers manage their internal thought processes. This self-regulatory function accounts for the fact that gesturing seems to occur even when there is no explicit communicative need for it, such as when speaking on the phone, or to oneself. Moreover, as Clark (2011: 123) notes, gesturing increases with task difficulty and 'when reasoning about a problem rather than merely describing the problem'. This cognitive function of gesture would seem to be significantly implicated in learning. Gullberg (2008: 293) hypothesizes that, by gesturing, 'speakers unload cognition onto an external representation, thereby liberating processing resources which can be re-assigned to memorization, planning, or other working-memory intense operations'. As evidence, Gullberg cites studies that show that 'children who receive gestural input with vocabulary explanations retain significantly more items than those who do not. Importantly, children who also reproduce the gestures themselves perform even better than children who do not even if they have had gestural input' (2008: 292).

Moreover, and consistent with Atkinson's 'alignment principle' mentioned above, the teacher's own 'body language' can play an important role in offering the learner 'legitimate peripheral participation' (Lave and Wenger 1991) in the target learning community. Quinlisk (2008: 39), for example, refers to 'a huge body of research that associates teachers' non-verbal immediacy cues with increases in affective, cognitive, and behavioural learning outcomes in various settings'. While supporting evidence from second language classrooms is scant, Sime (2008: 274) reports a study of second language learners' perceptions of teachers' gestures, which, among other findings, suggests that, in one classroom at least, 'a developed sense of intersubjectivity seems to exist, where both learners and teacher share a common set of gestural meanings that are regularly deployed during interaction. This seems to facilitate communication and give learners a sense of stability: they know what to expect after an answer and how to make sure that their input is right or valued.'

The role played by both gesture and posture in socializing learners has, of course, always been understood, at least intuitively, by teachers. The admonition 'Don't slouch' reflects an understanding of the fact that the physical presentation of self is a semiotic system in its own right – what the French sociologist Pierre Bourdieu calls *hexis*, or what is popularly known as 'body language', that is, the expressive use of gesture, posture and gait. Bourdieu (1991: 86) asserts that 'language is a body technique, and specifically linguistic, especially phonetic, competence is a dimension of bodily hexis in which one's whole relation to the social world, and one's whole socially informed relation to the world, are expressed'. Thus, the way we 'perform' our gender, age, ethnicity, social and cultural affiliations, and so on is not confined simply to lexical and grammatical choices but is encoded in our accent, our intonation, our gestures, the way we sit, stand and walk – that is to say they are all part of a single continuum. As Block (2010: 48) reminds us, 'it is worth bearing in mind how communicative resources are physically embodied; i.e. they are the evolving products of the human body's interactions in physical and social spaces over a lifetime'.

Language learners transitioning from their home language culture to another one often experience the dislocation associated with new 'hexical' choices. In a first-person account of acquiring English in the United States, Eva Hoffman (1989: 146), Polish by birth, writes:

> My mother says I am becoming 'English'. This hurts me, because I know she means I'm becoming cold. I'm no colder than I've ever been, but I'm learning to be less demonstrative. I learn this from a teacher who, after contemplating the gesticulations with which I help myself to describe the digestive system of a frog, tells me to 'sit on my hands and then try talking'. I learn my new reserve from people who take a step back when we talk, because I'm standing too close, crowding them.

Later in this account (p. 245), Hoffman describes the successful transition into her second language hexis in vividly physical terms:

> For a long time, it was difficult to speak these most intimate phrases, hard to make English – that language of will and abstraction – shape itself into the tonalities of love ... But now the language has entered my body, has incorporated itself in the softest tissue of my being.

Conclusion

To sum up, then: the view of cognition, and hence of learning, that I have outlined above argues that cognition is *situated*, and that it is situated in at least three senses – i.e. that it is physically embodied, that it is embedded in its situational context, and that its reach extends beyond the biological brain. Applied to classroom second language learning, this is a view that would seem to support Stevick's claim that what is important is less the materials, techniques and linguistic analyses, and more what goes on both within and between the people in the room – with an added emphasis on the fact that what goes on *between* the people in the room includes not only their language, but also all the paralinguistic features of their interactivity.

According to this ecological view, the 'small culture' (Holliday 1999) of the language classroom constitutes a kind of contextually sensitive and communal 'mind' that has its own emergent properties and is capable of self-organized and socially mediated learning. Such a view affirms Breen's (1985: 149) claim that 'the language I learn in a classroom is a communal product derived through a jointly constructed process'. That is to say, what is learned has less to do with what constitutes 'input' – in mechanistic input–output terms – than what already exists in terms of locally situated and communally owned affordances. 'When we are active in a setting,' writes van Lier (2002: 150), 'affordances are created by our activity and the surrounding world'.

What this means for teachers is that the classroom dynamic should, ideally, be structured in such a way that the resources that the participants bring to the endeavour – their experiences, feelings, knowledge (both linguistic and non-linguistic) – are maximally exploited for opportunities for authentic language use, as in the 'Weekend activity' (Kristjánsson, this volume). In answering the question 'If language is intrinsically embodied and embedded, then what does that mean for its acquisition?', Churchill et al. (2010: 249) argue that, 'if language is learned for worldly use, the learning process itself must be use-based'. And they add (p. 249):

> in this view, language learning is not primarily about squirreling away abstract linguistic competence in an isolated cognitive space ... Rather, language learning is a process of building meaningful ways of participating in socio-material worlds – of constructing flexible, reliable, and therefore survival-enhancing repertoires of ecosocial participation.

The notion of 'ecosocial participation' would seem to capture, retrospectively, features of what have been referred to as humanistic methodologies – particularly Counselling Language Learning, with its emphasis on small-group and learner-generated conversations, but also Total Physical Response, which exploits the physical nature of the classroom ecology. Indeed, the argument for the embodied nature of language strongly supports a role for incorporating the kinesthetic and gestural aspects of communication in language learning. In an account of her own learning and teaching of French, Alice Kaplan (1993: 134–5) provides a graphic example of how this might be achieved:

[Teaching] is physical, shockingly physical ... Occasionally I divide our bodies in half, our left side speaking English, our right side speaking French so we can feel the difference in our posture, our hands, our muscles. Our English side slouches, while our French side is crisp and pointed. In English we gesture downwards with one hand, in French our entire arm is in a constant upward movement. With our French side, we shake imaginary dirt from our hand with a repeated flick of the wrist, to show we are impressed, scandalized, amused. This is interesting, to be double like this with them, and funny enough for comfort.

Acknowledgement of the physical and situated aspects of language learning raises interesting questions as to the viability and efficacy of distance – and specifically online – learning. Some writers, such as Brumfit (2001: 125), are sceptical: 'The Internet cannot be a substitute for the holistic understanding that comes from direct meetings with individuals; knowledge transfer cannot be a substitute for seeing, smelling, hearing and walking through unfamiliar settings.' On the other hand, there is increasing recognition of the fact that online environments are in themselves holistic ecosystems with the potential to embed powerful language learning affordances. Gee (2007: 73), for example, describes the ways in which video games 'encourage and recruit situated, experiential, and embodied forms of learning and thinking'. They do this because in order to make sense of the semiotics of the game, whether in the form of numbers, symbols, words or whole texts, the player must integrate them into his or her developing understanding of the virtual world he or she is helping to construct and negotiate. 'Every potentially meaningful sign ... is a particular sort of invitation to embodied action' (Gee 2007: 83). Likewise, Thorne et al. (2009: 815), reviewing recent research into the behaviour of internet-based interest groups, and of online gaming, argue that 'what occurs online, and often outside of instructed educational settings, involves extended periods of language socialization, adaptation, and creative semiotic work that illustrate vibrant communicative practices'. Finally, the growing accessibility of smartphones and tablets suggests that the situatedness of language learning need no longer be confined to the immediate environment, nor even the local community, and that the concept of 'the porous classroom', where learners can both access data and communicate with other speakers with little or no effort or cost, is fast becoming a reality.

In terms of classroom research, a situated view of language learning argues for thicker descriptions of classroom interaction than those that capture only the verbal exchanges. The fine-grained studies of instructor–learner interaction by Churchill et al. (2010) and Atkinson (2010) that include photographic data along with descriptions of gesture and posture offer a useful model for the kind of research that goes some way to meeting the requirements that Larsen-Freeman and Cameron (2008b: 204) propose, whereby, from a complex systems perspective, the researcher 'cannot separate the learner or the learning from context in order to measure or explain them'.

Finally, from the perspective of teacher education, a situated view of learning argues for the importance of sensitizing trainee teachers to the importance, not just of psychological variables, but of context variables, starting from the physical classroom space and moving out, to include social, cultural and political factors as part of a concentric continuum. At the same time, the learners' contributions, both individual and collaborative, need to be foregrounded in a pedagogy that exploits the learning opportunities offered by the people in the room, and their common humanity. As Atkinson (2002: 537) puts it, 'If language is in the world at the same time as it is in the head, then we need to account for its integrated existence, rather than adopt positions that reduce the life – the humanity – out of language.'

Putting the life back into language – and into language learning – by 'harmonizing' the learning experience so that mind and body are working in unison within a 'world of meaningful action' is a project integral to Earl Stevick's life and work. This chapter represents an attempt to continue moving that project forward.

References

Asher, J. (1996) *Learning Another Language through Actions: The Complete Teacher's Guidebook*, 5th edn, Los Gatos, CA: Sky Oaks Productions.

Atkinson, D. (2002) 'Towards a sociocognitive approach to second language acquisition', *The Modern Language Journal*, 86: 525–45.

Atkinson D. (2010) 'Extended, embodied cognition and second language acquisition', *Applied Linguistics*, 31: 599–622.

Batstone, R. (ed.) (2010) *Sociocognitive Perspectives on Language Use and Language Learning*, Oxford: Oxford University Press.

Block, D. (2003) *The Social Turn in Second language Acquisition*, Edinburgh: Edinburgh University Press.

Block, D. (2010) 'Engaging with human sociality: thoughts on communication and embodiment', *Applied Linguistics Review*, 1(1): 45–56.

Bourdieu, P. (1991) *Language and Symbolic Power*, Cambridge: Polity Press.

Breen, M. P. (1985) 'The social context for language learning: a neglected situation?', *Studies in Second Language Acquisition*, 7: 135–58.

Brumfit, C. (2001) *Individual Freedom in Language Teaching*, Oxford: Oxford University Press.

Canagarajah, S. (2007) 'Lingua franca English, multilingual communities, and language acquisition', *The Modern Language Journal*, **91**: 923–39.

Churchill, E., Okada, H., Nishino, T. and Atkinson, D. (2010) 'Symbiotic gesture and the sociocognitive visibility of grammar in second language acquisition', *The Modern Language Journal*, **94**: 234–53.

Clancey, W. J. (2009) 'Scientific antecedents of situated cognition', in Robbins, P. and Aydede, M. (eds.) *The Cambridge Handbook of Situated Cognition*, Cambridge: Cambridge University Press, pp. 11–34.

Clark, A. (2011) *Supersizing the Mind: Embodiment, Action, and Cognitive Extension*, Oxford: Oxford University Press.

Ellis, N. and Larsen-Freeman, D. (eds.) (2009) *Language as a Complex Adaptive System*, Oxford: Wiley-Blackwell.

Ellis, R. (2008) *The Study of Second Language Acquisition*, 2nd edn, Oxford: Oxford University Press.

Gee, J. P. (2007) *What Video Games Have to Teach Us about Learning and Literacy*, New York: Palgrave Macmillan.

Goodwin, C. (2007) 'Participation, stance and affect in the organization of activities', *Discourse & Society*, **18**: 53–73.

Gullberg, M. (2008) 'Gestures and second language acquisition', in Robinson, P. and Ellis, N. (eds.) *Handbook of Cognitive Linguistics and Second Language Acquisition*, Abingdon: Routledge, pp. 276–305.

Halliday, M. A. K. (1978) *Language as Social Semiotic: The Social Interpretation of Language and Meaning*, London: Edward Arnold.

Halliday, M. A. K. (1993) 'Towards a language-based theory of learning', *Linguistics and Education*, **5**: 93–116.

Hoffman, E. (1989) *Lost in Translation*, London: Vintage Books.

Holliday, A. (1999) 'Small cultures', *Applied Linguistics*, **20**: 237–64.

Johnson, M. (1987) *The Body in the Mind: The Bodily Basis of Meaning, Imagination, and Reason*, Chicago: Chicago University Press.

Kaplan, A. (1993) *French Lessons*, Chicago: University of Chicago Press.

Kövesces, Z. and Szabó, P. (1996) 'Idioms: a view from cognitive semantics', *Applied Linguistics*, **17**: 326–55.

Kramsch, C. (ed.) (2002) *Language Acquisition and Language Socialization: Ecological Perspectives*, London: Continuum.

Kramsch, C. (2009) *The Multilingual Subject*, Oxford: Oxford University Press.

Lantolf, J. P. (ed.) (2000) *Sociocultural Theory and Second Language Learning*, Oxford: Oxford University Press.

Lantolf, J. P. and Thorne, S. (eds.) (2006) *Sociocultural Theory and the Genesis of Second Language Development*, Oxford: Oxford University Press.

Larsen-Freeman, D. and Cameron, L. (2008a) *Complex Systems and Applied Linguistics*, Oxford: Oxford University Press.

Larsen-Freeman, D. and Cameron, L. (2008b) 'Research methodology on language development from a complex systems perspective', *The Modern Language Journal*, **92**: 200–13.

Lave, J. and Wenger, E. (1991) *Situated Learning: Legitimate Peripheral Participation*, Cambridge: Cambridge University Press.

Lee, D. (2001) *Cognitive Linguistics: An Introduction*, Oxford: Oxford University Press.

Lindstromberg, S. and Boers, F. (2005) 'From movement to metaphor with manner-of-movement verbs', *Applied Linguistics*, **26**: 241–61.

McCafferty, S. G. and Stam, G. (eds.) (2008) *Gesture: Second Language Acquisition and Classroom Research*, New York: Routledge.

Mercer, N. (1995) *The Guided Construction of Knowledge: Talk amongst Teachers and Learners*, Clevedon: Multilingual Matters.

Mercer, N. (2000) *Words and Minds: How We Use Language to Think Together*, London: Routledge.

Norton, B. (2000) *Identity and Language Learning: Gender, Ethnicity and Educational Change*, Harlow: Longman.

Ortega, L. (2009) *Understanding Second Language Acquisition*, London: Hodder Education.

Quinlisk, C. C. (2008) 'Nonverbal communication, gesture, and second language classrooms: a review', in McCafferty, S. G. and Stam, G. (eds.) *Gesture: Second Language Acquisition and Classroom Research*, New York: Routledge, pp. 25–44.

Robbins, P. and Aydede, M. (2009) 'A short primer on situated cognition', in Robbins, P. and Aydede, M. (eds.) *The Cambridge Handbook of Situated Cognition*, Cambridge: Cambridge University Press, pp. 3–10.

Roy, D. (2009) 'New horizons in the study of child language acquisition', invited Keynote Paper, Proceedings of Interspeech 2009, Brighton, UK. Available online at http://web.media.mit.edu/~dkroy/papers/pdf/Roy_interspeech_keynote.pdf (accessed 13 June 2011).

Schmidt, R. and Frota, S. (1986) 'Developing basic conversational ability in a second language: a case study of the adult learner of Portuguese', in Day, R. (ed.) *Talking to Learn: Conversation in Second Language Acquisition*, Rowley, MA: Newbury House, pp. 237–326.

Sfard, A. (1998) 'On two metaphors for learning and the dangers of choosing just one', *Educational Researcher*, **27**: 4–13.

Sime, D. (2008) '"Because of her gesture, it's very easy to understand": learners' perceptions of teachers' gestures in the foreign language class', in McCafferty, S. G. and Stam, G. (eds.) *Gesture: Second Language Acquisition and Classroom Research*, New York: Routledge, pp. 259–79.

Spivey, M. and Richardson, D. (2009) 'Language processing: embodied and embedded', in Robbins, P. and Aydede, M. (eds.) *The Cambridge Handbook of Situated Cognition*, Cambridge: Cambridge University Press, pp. 382–400.

Stevick, E. W. (1980) *Teaching Languages: A Way and Ways*, Rowley, MA: Newbury House.

Stevick, E. W. (1996) *Memory, Meaning and Method: A View of Language Teaching*, 2nd edn, Boston: Heinle & Heinle.

Thorne, S. L., Black, R. and Sykes, J. M. (2009) 'Second language use, socialization, and learning in internet interest communities and online gaming', *The Modern Language Journal*, 93: 802–21.

Tyler, A. (2008) 'Cognitive linguistics and second language instruction', in Robinson, P. and Ellis, N. (eds.) *Handbook of Cognitive Linguistics and Second Language Acquisition*, Abingdon: Routledge, pp. 456–88.

van Lier, L. (1996) *Interaction in the Language Curriculum: Awareness, Autonomy and Authenticity*, Harlow: Longman.

van Lier, L. (2002) 'An ecological-semiotic perspective on language and linguistics', in Kramsch, C. (ed.) *Language Acquisition and Language Socialization: Ecological Perspectives*, London: Continuum, pp. 140–64.

van Lier, L. (2004) *The Ecology and Semiotics of Language Learning: A Sociocultural Perspective*, Boston: Kluwer Academic.

Williams, M. and Burden, R. (1997) *Psychology for Language Teachers: A Social Constructivist Approach*, Cambridge: Cambridge University Press.

5 Putting our Trust in the learner

Christopher N. Candlin and Jonathan Crichton

Introduction

In his inspirational book *Memory, Meaning and Method* (1976), Earl Stevick directed our attention to many matters concerning language learning which have engraved themselves onto the hearts and minds of a whole spectrum of language teachers, and through them, on their learners. His focus on language teaching has always been couched in terms of principle, not just of models of practice, urging dialogue with teachers and especially with learners in whom he placed his Trust as cognitive, human and social beings at the centre of his inquiry.

Stevick's focus on the learner may appear at first map-like, outlining a territory, offering landmarks for the reader/practitioner: on the nature of learner contributions and success; the importance of metacognitive knowledge and learner beliefs; how learners construct themselves, their fellow learners and their teachers; how learners' worlds and discourses outside the classroom impinge upon their construction of, and participation in, the worlds and discourses *within* the classroom. One of the key messages in Stevick's work is that meaning is not static; it does not exist a priori (like a map or list of facts), but rather it is interpreted through the lens of students' experiences, and 'a world of meaningful action' is created which differs from one student to another. The depth of meaning that a piece of information has for a student depends on its relevance to the student's previous experiences. As Stevick writes, this word of meaningful action in the classroom

> is not a flat, two-dimensional thing like a map. Its structure has many dimensions, and some of its parts are much further from the surface than others. If what a student says makes little or no difference to him, it has little 'depth', in this sense. But some things that he says, or hears, or reads, make a difference to him in many ways. This kind of experience is relatively 'deep'. It draws more energy from his 'world of meaningful action', and in turn it helps to shape that world. (1980: 9)

In addition to this 'inside the learner' focus is his emphasis on the interactional order constructed mutually between teachers and students. There are many such examples in his writings, such as his reference to factors likely to build Trust or destroy it (Stevick 1976: 95–9). The unifying element of these factors is mutually agreed communication. In other words, Trust is built when the speakers have agreed on the purpose of communication, the actions that they need to take and the intentions that they need to get across when they talk. Indeed, there is a passage in that 1976 book which is entitled 'Interpersonal Trust', and which, in our view, has not received the acknowledgement it deserves. For us it is the interactional engendering of Trust that goes to the heart of Stevick's philosophy: it speaks to the interrelationship of teachers and learners, the building of confidence in mutual learning of the group, and the enhancement of the conditions for communication, what he calls 'Voice in Community'. Such a focus on Trust is both an inspiring example of Stevick's foresight and a challenge for current research and practice. For example, see Murphey's (this volume) use of student newsletters in the class, which cite students' words from their journals, trusting and implying that students will and can learn from each others' contributions. For a discussion of recent work on Trust, see Bachmann and Zaheer (2006) and on discourses of Trust, see Candlin and Crichton (2012a).

In summary, Stevick's position, and our own, is that language learning and teaching, like language use, is always a social, cultural and personal act. It is governed by varying degrees of mutual Trust where teachers and learners can feel freer to make communicative choices driven by their own individual investments of understanding, energy, motivation and commitment.

Stevick's emphasis on Trust

When we explore Stevick's work, especially through his two key books (1976 and 1980), we discern this awareness of the central importance of Trust, understood as contingent on interaction in context in the classroom. It shines through his concern for estimating the nature and extent of learner contributions to language learning. If we want our learners to speak in class in front of their peers, this will be much easier if an atmosphere of Trust has been established. Here, as Mercer (2000) and Candlin and Mercer (2000) argue, following Wertsch (1991), such a context is more than something locational or textual; it is, rather, *dynamic*, a product of people's thinking, a careful construction by the teacher of a community of shared understanding with learners. Stevick (1980: 7–8) emphasizes the importance of interaction and the relational aspects of language learning: 'a language class is one arena in which a number of private universes intersect one another. Each person is at the center of his or her own universe of perceptions and values, and each is affected by what the others do.' In a context like this, Trust is a central concern.

This explicit focus on Trust is clearly also present in *Memory, Meaning and Method*, where he foregrounds Trust as being of 'primal importance' and speaks of the importance of 'building an atmosphere of mutual trust', together with becoming critically aware of the 'variables that tend to build trust or destroy it' (Stevick 1976: 183–5) because, in his words, people need to (p. 184)

> feel relatively secure with those around them before they will say what is really on their minds ... only after a group figures out what its members have on their minds can it figure out what it wants to do; and there is no point in trying to decide how to use the time, energy, and other resources of a group until its goals have become clear.

He also underscores there are risks associated with the loss or absence of conditions of Trust, for 'each person exposes for public scrutiny and public testing – possibly for intolerable undermining – the one thing that he or she needs most, which is the self-evaluation that he or she has so laboriously fashioned. This means that the stakes in any social encounter are incredibly high' (Stevick 1980: 7).

This emphasis on the language classroom as a context in which the interactional and intersubjective conditions for building and sustaining Trust are constantly in play and at stake carries with it the implication that the learner's performance is being continuously evaluated not only from 'outside' but also 'internally'. From outside, 'we find ourselves in the power of the person who is imposing the new information and evaluating our mastery of it', which can endanger the learners' sense of 'primacy in a world of meaningful action' (Stevick 1980: 10). From inside, Stevick (p. 11) distinguishes in a manner reminiscent of Goffman (1959), the student's *'critical self'* from the *'performing self'*. The critical self may work in ways counterproductive 'for a situation that demands learning and performing' and can lead to intrapersonal conflict for the student and interpersonal conflict for the student and teacher. If a student is asked to speak in class, but the 'critical self' keeps him or her from doing so in a reasonable amount of time or at all, conflict may arise.

There are two further and related dimensions to this focal concern with context which we may derive from Stevick's work that could serve as a guide for current and future action. The first is appreciating the *crucial* and *problematic* nature of some learning sites (Candlin 1987; Auerbach 1995), where participants' identities, face, abilities, etc. are placed on the line. The language learning classroom can be one such site. A second dimension is that of the occurrence of *critical moments* in such sites where Trust and its conditions are particularly at stake. What we have in mind here are those instances where the topics and actions of communication touch most closely on the personalities and ideologies of the participants in a manner which might require them to reveal those ideological, social and even political positionings, through their choices of, and responses to, language. In a classroom such moments might involve the correction of a student, or the handling by the teacher of unexpected reactions to stereotypical attitudes thought by the teacher to be innocuous, or overly direct responses by students to what are conceived as racially motivated slurs. The interaction management of such moments critically engages with issues of Trust.

Learners as central in the discursive accomplishment of Trust

Much of what we discuss above on Earl Stevick's emphasis on Trust has at its heart issues concerning learner identity, and the extent to which learning in general and language acquisition in particular can be separated from the context of that learning and that acquisition.

In one type of research on second language acquisition, the learner is conceived of as an individual with various personal attributes which are – on the face of it – divorced from context. Alternatively, the individual is defined as a member of a group whose context ('female outworker from Sri Lanka', 'young upwardly mobile male language learner from Hong Kong') offers little scope for individual agency. An alternative position, and one which is now especially relevant in communities with considerable ethnic and linguistic diversity, for example in Australia, is to assert that such deterministic theories have little explanatory and critical adequacy, based as they are on small, largely homogeneous populations in often privileged learning circumstances. In this alternative position, such personality traits are held not to exhaust the identity of the person and not to be fixed but dynamic, changing over time and space. In this view, the social group labels serve to *mask*, rather than to reveal differentiation (see Bourdieu 1991), making little if any connection to the socially and historically constituted relationships of power that serve to create, or deny, opportunities for learners to speak, to interact and to learn.

It is not just a matter of undertaking an analysis of the social bases for language learning *within* the classroom, and the construction of learners as *people*; it is necessary to 'reconceptualise the learner' (Norton 2000) and to display how the opportunities for learning may be constrained by inequalities of power at home, in the workplace and in the community at large (see also Norton 2001). Seen this way, language learning is not just a skill but a complex social practice, closely related to how we define and place our Trust in particular learner identities. Learning to communicate in another language is not only a matter of becoming a better and more autonomous language learner; it has to do with making the link between learning and the achievement of access to rights and goods, to social and economic advantages. The road towards understanding learner identities and learner contributions begins with asking the right critical questions about context – e.g. in what contexts do I not have a voice due to lack of language, due to my gender, ethnicity, nationality or class? – and how both identities and contributions are constructed and valued in the contexts of language learning and language use. What then turns out to be crucial is the interplay between communication as both a socially and a cognitively strategic act where communication exists as a way of asserting identity and as a way of getting things done. It means, too, that we need to grasp that the constructs of *self* and *person* are frequently contested among learners and within each individual, that an individual learner's uses of language can serve both as evidence of solidarity with others and, at times, as a means of resistant struggle against institutions and their social practices. What is at stake here is Trust in both the 'external' and 'internal' senses highlighted by Stevick. Learners after all do not act out their language learning lives as if caged in some hermetically sealed communicative compartments. Stevick brings into play themes associated with Trust and confidence which imbue this sense of struggle, yet still seeks to establish some harmony between tolerance and authority, as here with a particular focus on students:

> Each of us must allow the other some of this uniqueness, and that is what I mean by 'tolerance'. Tolerance allows the pieces of the puzzle, the students in a classroom, the people in society, to fly off, each in its own direction. Authority, the coercive kind certainly, but also the noncoercive kind ... is a force that draws the pieces back together. But what will the pattern be, the pattern toward which these pieces will be drawn? This brings us back to the issue of 'what kind of mystery?' The artificial, synthetic, man-made kind of mystery stifles 'uniqueness' – tells a person what to see, and how to label what he sees, and how to run it through his mind. In choosing which man-made mystery to follow, the miracle worker acts for the person, and that is the end of 'freedom'. All of this brings to mind three other terms – Gattegno's – where he speaks of 'independence', 'autonomy', and 'responsibility'.
>
> (Stevick 1980: 287)

If it is time to listen as Stevick recommends to the voices of learners as individual persons, it is also important, as we have been emphasizing, to do so not only from their own individualistic perspective, but in interaction with others. In the messy practices, sites and moments of the classroom, and in the opaque social and institutional worlds beyond, learners as selves, persons and actors and their associated discourses are co-constructed in interaction with others. We cannot easily talk of *a* learner's contributions since learners are always in themselves plural, and their contributions to learning similarly differentiated and heterogeneous. What needs to be stressed are the social and affective conditions surrounding the making of these contributions. Classrooms, like other learning environments, are challenging, risky and at time intra- and interpersonally dangerous places, and thus, as Stevick highlights, the importance of the building of Trust as a counterpoint to such risk and danger. He deals with the concepts and conditions entailed by Trust and identifies the learner's 'security' as both crucial and dependent on the teacher's 'faith' and 'understanding'. He writes:

> If we, in our zeal to be 'humanistic', become too 'learner-centered' with regard to 'control', we undermine the learner's most basic need, which is for security. We may find that we have imposed our own half-baked anarchy on the class. Absence of structure, or of focus on the teacher, may well be all right in certain kinds of psychological training, but not in our classrooms. In a task-oriented group like a language class, the student's place is at the center of a space which the teacher has structured, with room for him to grow into. In this kind of relationship, there are two essentials for the teacher: faith that the student will in fact grow into that space and understanding of where the student is in that space at any given moment. When both these ingredients are present, there is the possibility of true 'humanism' in teaching.
>
> (Stevick 1980: 33)

The consequences for the teachers' 'professional vision' (Goodwin, 1994), of this teacher and learner interaction and their co-responsibility are that, while the student is 'central' in the role of learner, student and teacher are co-implicated in the 'world of meaningful action', in which, for example, the relationship between learner 'initiative' and teacher 'control' is not decided by the teacher or a particular methodology 'in advance'. Rather, it depends on both interpersonal and instrumental judgements by the teacher (and learner), exercising what Schön (1987) refers to as 'discretionary freedom', backed by professional judgement of the conditions pertaining in the interaction at hand and the particular perceptions, goals, relationships and histories of those involved (Stevick 1980: 16ff.). Such conditions always incur both talk and action. Stevick draws on the construct of *community* where his vision of the classroom is of a shared world of interaction geared towards learning and premised on Trust in which:

> all members – 'teachers' as well as 'students' – see that if any one of them is to get ahead, he or she must depend on the other. People who perceive themselves to be in such relationships tend to act in ways that are consistent with that perception. Then, as realities come to be not only experienced individually but also shared, learning becomes more profound for students and teachers alike.
>
> (Stevick 1976: 186)

Through navigating the discourses of negotiating and making meaning (Breen 1998, 2001), it is not only language and learning that are negotiated, but also institutional structures and practices that are consolidated or challenged. These processes are realized by all manner of semiotic means reflecting and reinforcing their significances to the actors involved. At the same time, as Auerbach (2000) emphasizes, students are enabled to shape and express their own 'voices'. In such a community, as Stevick writes:

> a student can in several senses find her 'voice' ... She is more likely to use her larynx for purposes other than mimicry ... and more important, her unique presence will be felt by those around her, and her personality will express itself in what she says. If the teacher's own ideas about how he ought to act are not too rigid, he too may come to have a voice in this kind of community.
>
> (Stevick 1976: 187)

To achieve and sustain such a unifying 'world of meaningful action', Trust is indispensable. Creating meaningful action depends on respecting the learners' views so that Trust can be created, that is, discursively accomplished. Given this, the question arises as to how the conditions for creating a world of meaningful action in learning and teaching are to be explored through a programme of research so as to better inform curriculum development and action. Such a programme will require a considerable broadening of the nature of, and relationship among, research planning, curriculum development and learning, and teaching action. It will need to acknowledge and harmonize in a coherent and educationally salient programme the analysis of Trust from the different perspectives of learners and teachers, the interactions among them, the social, textual and semiotic resources that they bring, and an appreciation of relevant institutional and historical affordances, risks and constraints.

We would argue that such a programme agenda, targeting research in and on practice (Schön 1983), requires what we refer to as a 'multi-perspectival' approach (Crichton 2010; Candlin and Crichton 2011, 2012b) that includes textual and semiotic analyses of discursive performances of Trust on site; interpretive, ethnographic and grounded studies of Trust-bearing learning and teaching practices; accumulated accounts of expertise by ratified members of the communities of practice in question together with first-hand accounts of interpretations of Trusting experiences by participating members.

Such an approach is represented in Figure 5.1. This Venn diagram attempts to capture the diversity and dynamic variability of influences on the formation of Trust. We propose that to the left side, the analyst/ action researcher in dialogue, coordination and research with the participants/students decides the relevant weighting of the different influences on the learners' lives. It is important for the development of Trust

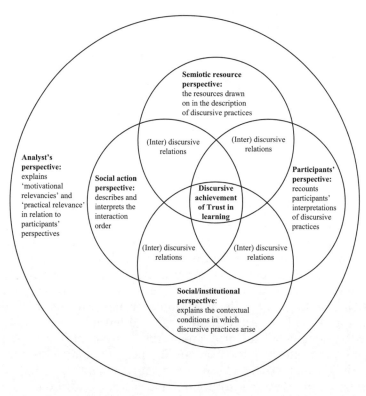

Figure 5.1   Framing a multi-perspectival programme of rescrach to underpin teaching/learning and curriculum design

that these emerge from collaborative engagement between the analyst and the participants. An example of this might be action logging and newslettering (Murphey, this volume) in which students' voices form a significant role in mediating teacher decisions upon curriculum and syllabus.

Participants are here understood to include, potentially, researchers, teachers, students and other legitimate members, brought together in configurations of the roles of analysts and participants, with the modes of collaboration depending on their relationship to, and engagement in, the research and practice agenda. Each of the overlapping circles represents a distinctive but mutually implicating analytical perspective, all of which are relevant to the investigation of the discursive achievement of Trust at a particular learning and teaching site. The *mutuality* of these perspectives is indicated by their convergence at the centre of the circles. The different perspectives foreground descriptive, interpretive and explanatory modes of analysis that may be brought to bear in the investigation. The overlaps between them highlight the *interdiscursive* nature of research and practice that seeks to combine these perspectives in the exploration of Trust at a particular site. Entry points to the analysis and to the research and teaching programme will vary in relation to particular sites in question and the relevant focal themes (Roberts and Sarangi 2005) that govern the experiences of participants, say issues surrounding enhancing learning autonomy, or building Trust, and to the particular research questions that are being addressed. What is important is that no one perspective is prime, and all perspectives are necessary and mutually informing.

Implications for curriculum design of 'putting our Trust in the learner'

Stevick's emphasis on the concepts and conditions entailed by Trust and their implications can be related to curriculum design, and he identifies the learner's 'security' as crucially dependent on what we are calling 'putting our Trust in the learner'.

To set such a statement into its curriculum context, an account of alternative paradigms for curriculum development, stimulated by the impetus to negotiated teaching initially provided by Barnes (1976), can be found in the concept of *'experiential learning'* as used by Viljo Kohonen and his colleagues at Tampere University in Finland (Kohonen 2001; Kohonen et al. 2001) (see also Candlin 2001, 2003). Kohonen and his colleagues argue that learning and teaching curricula have traditionally oriented themselves towards one of three paradigmatic models:

positivistic, constructivist and critical (see Figure 5.2). Similar distinctions have been drawn in relation to language education in earlier work on communicative curricula (Breen and Candlin 1981; Candlin 1984), and, more recently, in the context of re-emphasizing the contributions of learners to the language learning process (Breen 2000). Much of van Lier's work (1996, 2000, 2001) provides a similar analysis of these competing models, arguing that any curriculum which is responsive to context and is socially constructed necessarily highlights the hermeneutic and the interactive.

These paradigms suggest particular stances towards teaching and learning in the classroom, the roles of teachers and learners, the privileging of particular kinds of interaction and, indirectly, can serve as criteria for establishing the yardsticks by which classroom performance of both teachers and learners is to be measured and evaluated. They have, thus, quite significant practical relevance and consequences. As an example, we focus on one issue currently of pervasive concern in discussions of language teaching and learning, namely that of *autonomy*.

As authors writing on this topic argue (see Benson and Voller 1997; Little et al. 2003; Benson 2011), autonomy is both a construct and an action plan. It is also a process rather than some objective which once achieved requires no further encouragement or development. It is not just to be construed as some private, *independent* exercise of individualism. Autonomy is essentially *interdependent*, both in its manner of achievement and in the exercise of its potential in relation to language learning in the classroom and in the world outside the institution. In short, it is collaborative, co-constructed and critically needs to be deployed when challenges to learning and to communicative competence arise. Above all, it is dependent on the exercise of Trust in and between the participants concerned. A learner who does not feel Trust is much less likely to engage in autonomous behaviour.

Autonomy sits easily within a constructivist-critical curriculum paradigm, and in a real sense may be seen as one measure of the success of such a curriculum. Autonomy, rights and ownership are all overlapping co-constructing concepts that also imply a certain responsibility to collaborate. In the spirit of this interdependence, it is important

Positivistic:	context-free
Constructivist:	created hermeneutically
Critical:	socially constructed, dialogic and ecological

Figure 5.2   Three orientations towards curriculum design

to emphasize that learner autonomy and learner 'ownership' need not, and in any given *institutional* context cannot, imply the withdrawal of teacher responsibility for helping to create the contexts and conditions for learning, any more than teacher 'ownership' completely eclipses the learner. The emphasis on co-construction characteristic of the constructivist-critical paradigm explicitly enjoins *co*-ownership, which can be recognized and promoted by teacher recognition of the learner's modes of conceptualizing his or her world, within the classroom and outside. Where such a commitment to co-ownership is innovative is where it sets the contributions of teacher and learner in a dynamic, creative and interdependent relationship. The challenge for the curriculum, in terms of both design and delivery, is to so structure the process that these ownerships are held in a creative and productive tension, achieving balance.

Seen this way, a constructivist-critical curriculum is clearly more than a language curriculum; rather, it is a curriculum for social life where language learning is not simply a skill but a complex social and real-world practice in the manner outlined by Bourdieu (1982), closely bound up with learner identities, opportunities, facilitations and constraints. We may say, then, that language learning is not autonomous in any independent sense, but interdependently engaged with the demands of the social world.

For curriculum, design and delivery, this presents some unaccustomed challenges. If it is time to listen more to the voices of the learners as individual selves and as representative persons, then even more so is this true of teachers. How far does the curriculum serve to develop this interdependent autonomy among teachers? After all, they are partners, co-owners in the process. How well does the curriculum in design and delivery enable teachers to adjust and accommodate to this perhaps unaccustomed set of roles? What new skills and, perhaps even more importantly, what new mindsets, are required? After all, shifting curriculum paradigms can bring considerable personal challenges to teachers. Most immediately, proclaiming interdependent autonomy as a mutual goal of teachers and learners compels participants to recognize that in the sites, practices and moments of this critical and transformative classroom they are continually involved in processes of contestation for position and validation as well as in collaboration. So just as teachers need to cultivate Trust among students by engaging them in the meaningful action of negotiating instruction and learning, administrators need to cultivate Trust among teachers by engaging them in the meaningful action of curriculum review and renewal, with a strong voice of their own – both of which entail interdependent autonomy and discursive participation (see Crichton 2012).

These processes are characteristically mediated through discourse and interaction (Breen 2000). Accordingly, for autonomy to be achieved, participants, especially learners, need to be enabled and Trusted to communicate about the curriculum, especially its delivery, but also, indirectly perhaps, its design. Enabling language learners to reach that necessary discursive participation is perhaps the greatest challenge an autonomy-focused language learning curriculum has to face.

Moreover, the emphasis on autonomy as a goal for a constructivist-critical curriculum carries with it a particular research implication; if achieving autonomy is an interdependent process, then, as we argue earlier in this chapter, what is required to monitor the process are research models which are essentially formative, multi-perspectival and integrative of different sets of data. Above all, we need models whose data and findings can influence the direction of the curriculum, and which can suggest appropriate actions to its actors. In short, it needs a model which engages different research tools within an overall programme of action research (Stenhouse 1975; Breen and Candlin 1981; Burns 1999, 2010).

Such action research is targeted at *change*, whether in terms of attitude and belief, of pedagogic goals, of classroom practice or of post-instructional activity outside the institution. Why might such an approach to classroom- and setting-specific curriculum research be appropriate in the context of developing a constructivist-critical language learning and teaching curriculum imbued by Stevick's writings? Principally, because it would make explicit and recordable the links between practices – what participants do – and the discourses in which these practices are realized – how these practices are reflected in interaction and coded in language and communication. It would involve the study of how participants perform using all manner of semiotic means, but also the study of how they account for their actions seen through the perspective of their own reflective narratives of experience. In the manner outlined by Cicourel (1992), it would locate the communicative activities of participants within the institution, against the broader social, historical and structural framework of the current organizational and societal conditions within which the institution is placed and draws its *raison d'être*, as well as the organizational and social conditions that teaching and learning practices anticipate for learners in their lives beyond the institution. Any responsiveness to the need for change is not restricted to curriculum content and pedagogic practice; it extends to the redefining of learner and teacher roles in the direction of *both* participants increasingly becoming critically reflective practitioners in language learning and teaching.

How can such an action-research-based, autonomous curriculum be achieved? First, by constructing all pedagogy as a process of problem-raising in which teaching is seen as a *researchable* activity. In practical terms, it implies a change in mindset in which issues, questions, even disturbances in the classroom process are weighed in terms of their potential significance for adjustments to the teaching-learning process, and, where significant enough, to the overall curriculum guidelines. The *first* of four principles, then, for achieving a research-based curriculum intent on practice is to *make the research and the practice problem-based.*

Now of course, judgement as to significance is the key; no teacher can regard her or his actions as continually researchable in terms of relevance. However, unless there is some corporate or group sharing of these issues of potential relevance, backed up by informal teacher accounts, the basis for curriculum adjustment and development towards autonomy will be constrained. Accordingly, the *second* principle for achievement has to be the *deriving of an agenda for research from discussion and critical reflection.* Such an agenda cannot simply be wished for; it depends on creating a Trusting climate in the curriculum process where critical reflection becomes a typical mode of teacher behaviour. It needs to occur at all stages of the pedagogic process: in the design of tasks ensuring that they contain elements for learner and teacher consideration of the effectiveness and appropriateness of the tasks, in the monitoring of the process of the tasks and in the evaluation of task outcomes. For this to happen, the *third* principle needs to be invoked; that of *capitalizing on teachers' skills, interests and involvement, and, equally, convincing and enabling learners to take part in this reflective research process.* This collaboration in planning, executing and evaluating pedagogic activity is not just reflective teaching and learning, it *is* research. Indeed, as we have argued earlier, such research lies at the heart of the constructivist-critical curriculum.

Finally, the *fourth* key principle is that of *establishing an interdisciplinary, multi-perspectived research, teaching and curriculum development agenda* of the kind we have outlined above, where a range of methodologies associated with distinctive, yet mutually influencing, perspectives are combined so as to provide a rich and grounded explanation of those issues, challenges and problems that arise. Such a principle allows ample scope for individual and group research initiatives within an action-research-based programme centred on exploring learning events. Such research initiatives would include descriptions of learner language, small-scale or corpus-based; evaluations of learner motivation in relation to particular task-types and task modes; interactional analyses of learner–learner and teacher–learner engagements in particular pedagogic practices, for example, say, the posing and addressing of questions and responses; studies of teachers' (and learners') beliefs about language teaching and learning and the relationship between these beliefs and performance; utilization and usability studies of particular learning resources; performances of learners under particular task conditions; assessments of learner potential in relation to novel communicative demands; experimental studies of learner communicative competence, for example, say, in relation to responses to grammaticality or lexicality; longitudinal studies of post-instructional language behaviour of learners outside the classroom framework, etc.

Ultimately, as is always the case, everything hangs on the professional development of teacher researchers necessary to enable them to undertake this action research, the provision of expert support, the identifying of teaching with research, and the need to facilitate the research programme with effective resources. As we have argued, at the root of all such endeavour, and the premise and condition of such an undertaking, remains 'Putting our Trust in the learner'.

References

Auerbach, E. R. (1995) 'The politics of the ESL classroom: issues of power in pedagogical choices', in Tollefson, J. W. (ed.) *Power and Inequality in Language Education*, Cambridge: Cambridge University Press, pp. 9–33.

Auerbach, E. R. (2000) 'Creating participatory learning communities: paradoxes and possibilities', in Hall, J. K. and Eggington, W. G. (eds.) *Sociopolitics of English Language Teaching*, Clevedon: Multilingual Matters, pp. 143–64.

Bachmann, R. and Zaheer, A. (eds.) (2006) *Handbook of Trust Research*, Northhampton, MA: Edward Elgar.

Barnes, D. (1976) *From Communication to Curriculum*, Harmondsworth: Penguin.

Benson, P. (2011) *Teaching and Researching Autonomy in Language Learning*, 2nd edn, London: Pearson.

Benson, P. and Voller, P. (eds.) (1997) *Autonomy and Independence on Language Learning*, London: Longman.

Bourdieu, P. (1982) *Ce que Parler Veut Dire: L'economie des Echanges Linguistiques*, Paris: Fayard.

Bourdieu, P. (1991) *Language and Symbolic Power*, Cambridge: Polity.

Breen, M. P. (1998) 'Navigating the discourse: on what is learned in the language classroom', *Proceedings of the 1997 RELC Seminar*, Singapore: RELC. (Reproduced in Candlin, C. N. and Mercer, N. (eds.) (2000) *English Language Teaching in its Social Context*, London: Routledge.)

Breen, M. P. (ed.) (2000) *Learner Contributions to Language Learning: New Directions in Research*, London: Longman.

Breen, M. P. (2001) 'Introduction: conceptualization, affect and action in context', in Breen, M. P. (ed.) *Learner Contributions to Language Learning: New Directions in Research*, London: Longman, pp. 1–11.

Breen M. P. and Candlin, C. N. (1981) 'The essentials of a communicative curriculum in language teaching', *Applied Linguistics*, 1(2): 89–112.

Burns, A. (1999) *Collaborative Action Research for English Language Teachers*, Cambridge: Cambridge University Press.

Burns, A. (2010) *Doing Action Research in English Language Teaching: A Guide for Practitioners*, New York: Routledge.

Candlin, C. N. (1984) 'Syllabus design as a critical process', *Language, Learning & Communication*, 3(2): 129–45.

Candlin, C. N. (1987). 'Explaining moments of conflict in discourse', in Steele, R. and Threadgold, T. (eds.), *Language Topics: Essays in Honour of Michael Halliday*, Vol. II, Amsterdam and Philadelphia: John Benjamins, pp. 413–29.

Candlin, C. N. (2001) 'General Editor's preface', in Kohonen, V., Jaatinen, R., Kaikkonen, P. and Lehtovaara, J. (eds.) *Experiential Learning in Foreign Language Education*, London: Longman, pp. xi–xvii.

Candlin, C. N. (2003) *Learner Autonomy: From Concept to Curriculum – Developing a Research-Based Curriculum for Learner Autonomy*, Tokyo: Kanda University of International Studies (mimeo).

Candlin, C. N. and Crichton, J. (2011) 'Introduction', in Candlin, C. N. and Crichton, J. (eds.) *Discourses of Deficit*, Basingstoke: Palgrave Macmillan, pp. 1–22.

Candlin, C. N. and Crichton, J. (eds.) (2012a) *Discourses of Trust*, Basingstoke: Palgrave Macmillan.

Candlin, C. N. and Crichton, J. (2012b) 'From ontology to methodology: exploring the discursive landscape of trust', in Candlin, C. N. and Crichton, J. (eds.) *Discourses of Trust*, Basingstoke: Palgrave Macmillan, pp. 1–21.

Candlin, C. N. and Mercer, N. (eds.) (2000) *English Language Teaching in its Social Context*, London: Routledge.

Cicourel, A. (1992) 'The interpenetration of communicative contexts: examples from medical encounters', in Duranti, A. and Goodwin, C. (eds.) *Rethinking Context: Language as an Interactive Phenomenon*, Cambridge: Cambridge University Press, pp. 291–310.

Crichton, J. (2010) *The Discourse of Commercialization*, Basingstoke: Palgrave Macmillan.

Crichton, J. (2012) '"Will there be flowers shoved at me?": a study in organisational trust, moral order and professional integrity', in Candlin, C. N. and Crichton, J. (eds.) *Discourses of Trust*, Basingstoke: Palgrave Macmillan, pp. 131–46.

Goffman, E. (1959) *The Presentation of Self in Everyday Life*, New York: Doubleday Anchor.

Goodwin, C. (1994) 'Professional vision', *American Anthropologist*, 96(3): 606–33. doi:10.1525/aa.1994.96.3.02a00100.

Kohonen, V. (2001) 'Towards experiential foreign language education', in Kohonen, V., Jaatinen, R., Kaikkonen, P. and Lehtovaara, J. (eds.) *Experiential Learning in Foreign Language Education*, London: Longman, pp. 8–59.

Kohonen, V., Jaatinen, R., Kaikkonen, P. and Lehtovaara, J. (eds.) (2001) *Experiential Learning in Foreign Language Education*, London: Longman.

Little, D., Ridley, J. and Ushioda, E. (2003) *Learner Autonomy in the Foreign Language Classroom: Teacher, Learner, Curriculum and Assessment*, Dublin: Authentik.

Mercer, N. (2000) *Words and Minds*, London: Routledge.

Norton, B. (2000) *Identity and Language Learning: Gender, Ethnicity and Educational Change*, Harlow: Pearson Education.

Norton, B. (2001) 'Non-participation, imagined communities, and the language classroom', in Breen, M. (ed.) *Learner Contributions to Language Learning: New Directions in Research*, London: Pearson Education, pp. 159–71.

Roberts, C., and Sarangi, S. (2005) 'Theme-oriented analysis of medical encounters', *Medical Education*, 39: 632–40.

Schön, D. (1983) *The Reflective Practitioner: How Professionals Think in Action*, New York: Basic Books.

Schön, D. (1987) 'Changing patterns in inquiry in work and living', *Journal of the Royal Society of Arts Proceedings*, 135(5367): 225–31.

Stenhouse, L. (1975) *An Introduction to Curriculum Research and Development*, London: Heinemann.

Stevick, E. W. (1976) *Memory, Meaning and Method: Some Psychological Perspectives on Language Learning*, Rowley, MA: Newbury House.

Stevick, E. W. (1980) *Teaching Languages: A Way and Ways*, Rowley, MA: Newbury House.

van Lier, L. (1996) *Interaction in the Language Curriculum: Awareness, Autonomy and Authenticity*, London: Longman.

van Lier, L. (2000) 'From input to affordance: social-interactive learning from an ecological perspective', in Lantolf, J. (ed.) *Sociocultural Theory and Second Language Learning*, Oxford: Oxford University Press, pp. 245–60.

van Lier, L. (2001) 'Constraints and resources in classroom talk: issues of equality and symmetry', in Candlin, C. N. and Mercer, N. (eds.) *English Language Teaching in its Social Context*, London: Routledge, pp. 90–107. (Originally published in *Learning Foreign and Second Languages*, Modern Language Association of America.)

Wertsch, J. V. (1991) *Voices of the Mind: A Sociocultural Approach to Mediated Action*, Cambridge, MA: Harvard University Press.

6   Understanding language learner narratives

Rebecca L. Oxford

> We are always telling stories; our lives are surrounded by our stories
> and those of other people. We see everything that happens to us in
> terms of these stories, as we sometimes try to lead our lives as if we
> were recounting them.
>
> (Jean-Paul Sartre, *Les Mots*)

Introduction

In this chapter I explore language learner narratives in four ways.[1]
Specifically, I explain the context of general narrative research and
the relationship between narrative and story, identify general types of
language learner narratives, note important themes in existing learner
narratives and highlight useful ways to interpret new learner narratives. These interpretive tools are using empathy, accepting subjectivity, seeking emergent themes through grounded theory, noticing triple
re-storying, interpreting aesthetically, treating the narrative as a case,
expecting complexity, looking for influences, drawing trajectories, and
checking and evaluating the narrative.

The general context of narrative research

Narrative is pervasive. 'We dream in narrative, daydream in narrative, remember, anticipate, hope, despair, plan, revise, criticize, gossip,
learn, hate and love by narrative' (Hardy 1968: 5). Life itself can be
viewed as a narrative containing many smaller narratives (Moen 2006).
People without narratives do not exist, according to Polkinghorne
(1988). Narrative and story are often used as synonyms, and their ety-
mologies reveal that these terms have a double meaning of telling and

---

[1] This chapter is partly based on a keynote presentation I made in October
2009 for the 23rd Biennial Congress of the Deutsche Gesellschaft für
Fremdsprachenforschung (German Association for Foreign Language Research)
and the 600th anniversary of Leipzig University. A much longer article, also drawing on the keynote address but with many features different from this chapter, was
published in 2011 in the *Zeitschrift für Fremdsprachenforschung*, **22**(2): 221–41.

knowing (Harper 2010). Because narrative is 'the primary scheme by which human existence is rendered meaningful' (Polkinghorne 1988: 1), we interpretively construct and organize our own social realities and personal theories by selecting which details to notice, remember and emphasize (Ochs 1997; Bruner 1998). Participation in narrative practices – telling and responding to stories – can create identities and bring coherence and healing to lives (Mehl-Madrona 2010). Narrative inquiry is 'an ethnographic approach to eliciting understandings' (Pavlenko 2002: 213) through stories.

I gratefully dedicate this chapter to Earl Stevick, whose example and works inspired me and others to cross borders and to study deeply the narratives of language learners. Stevick's humanistic, caring and creative orientation is captured in his books, *Teaching Languages: A Way and Ways* (1981), *Success with Foreign Languages: Seven Who Achieved It and What Worked for Them* (1989), *Memory, Meaning and Method: A View of Language Teaching* (1996) and *Working with Teaching Methods: What's at Stake?* (1998). Of these books, all of which were professionally influential to me, the one most relevant to learner narratives was *Success with Foreign Languages*, as indicated below.

Categories of language learner narratives

Language learners' stories 'have always been there, buried under curriculum and classroom routines, demonstrating how learners try to make sense of their own language learning and connect it to their sociocultural contexts' (Chik 2005: 1). Three major categories of language learner narratives are histories, diaries/journals and case studies.

Histories

Language learner histories, autobiographical narratives created by learners who look back over a considerable time (retrospective narratives), are the first major category of language learner narratives. In addition to containing prose, these histories can contain poetry (see Oxford 1996), songs, photographs, drawings, videos and other media. Three groups of histories are identifiable.

The first group consists of learner histories that include not just the learners' interpretation but also interpretation by a researcher or teacher. For example, in Stevick's (1989) interview-based book, *Success with Foreign Languages*, successful language learners described their varied, creative learning experiences, with comments by Stevick. They commented on their own changing educational contexts – the classroom, the job setting and living abroad. The book showed that language learning occurs throughout a lifetime, not merely during formal schooling. In addition, the seven learners' stories alluded to interpersonal relationships, links between language and culture, specific learning strategies and broad learning preferences. In addition to talking about their successes, some of the interviewees also discussed an occasional sense of failure or discouragement in learning languages. Many of my studies (for instance, Oxford 1996; Oxford et al. 1998; Oxford et al. 2005) presented excerpts from learner essays and identified key themes, such as emotions, demotivation, attitudes, style conflicts, cultural influences and beliefs about education. Like Stevick, I provided not only the learners' interpretations but also my own.

In the second group of learner histories, the learner is both the author and the interpreter. Well-known examples are the book-length autobiographies of Rodriguez (1983/2004), Hong Kingston (1989), Hoffman (1990) and Lvovich (1997). The authors of these works are particularly insightful about their own experiences.

The third group of language learner histories consists of edited volumes that contain learners' stories and their own interpretations, with additional background material (but not interpretation) by the editors. Examples are *Reflections on Multiliterate Lives* (Belcher and Connor 2001) and *Tongue-Tied: The Lives of Multilingual Children in Public Education* (Santa Ana 2004).

Diaries/journals

In learner diaries, also known as journals, learners record on a regular basis numerous aspects of their learning processes. Learner diaries can be free-form or guided in some way by the teacher or researcher. Guided or directed diaries are often useful for understanding students' learning strategies. Certain learner diaries intensively reflect on the learner's interactions with native speakers, allowing the learner to take on the identity of 'researcher' (Norton 2000). When a learner diary or journal receives a regular response from the teacher and a dialogue is formed, this is called a *dialogue journal* (Peyton and Reed 1990). Some learner diaries are composed by teachers or researchers who are learning another language. These diaries include themes such as competitiveness, anxiety, gender, power, age, relationships with teachers, learning styles and strategies, culture and multilingualism (see Rivers 1979; Bailey 1983; Schmidt and Frota 1986; Campbell 1996; Bell 1997; Schulz and Elliott 2000; Carson and Longhini 2002).

Meaning-making inside and between the people in the classroom

Case studies

Sometimes a learner history or diary is part of a *case study*, in which the researcher deeply examines one or more cases – individual(s), group(s) or situation(s) – deliberately 'bounded' by relevant criteria, such as time, importance, space, context, role or function (Stake 1995; Yin 2003). Examples including a single case are Schmidt and Frota (1986), Spack (1997), Nam and Oxford (1998), Halbach (2000), Lam (2000), and Stakhnevich (2005). Examples including more than one case are Oxford et al. (2007) and Oxford et al. (2011). Many case studies are purely narrative, though case studies can also include pictures and statistics. Typically a case study includes a discussion of key themes and closes with what has been learned. It can be exploratory, explanatory or descriptive (Yin 2003).

Important themes in language learner narratives

In interpretations of learner narratives, the themes emerge from the narratives themselves rather than being imposed by the researcher. Sometimes emergent themes relate to theories already in the literature. I will point out some themes from my own narrative research and that of others: flow and hot cognition, complexity, emotion and identity. These are only some of the many themes in learner narratives.

Flow and hot cognition

Successful language learners often describe passion about learning for its own sake (intrinsic motivation), teamed with a sense of competence while performing challenging tasks. This reflects *flow* in learning (Csíkszentmihalyi 2008). It also embodies *hot cognition* (Pintrich et al. 1993; Oxford et al. 2011), that is, emotionally rich, motivated learning that brings heightened cognition. Here are some examples. As a teenager, Youfu wrote letters from his rural home in China's Yunnan province to ask questions of English-grammar experts at universities a thousand miles away. He joyfully received detailed answers and immediately applied the new grammatical information during extensive weekend interactions with English-speaking foreigners who regularly visited the nearby temple (Oxford et al. 2011). After Greg, a newly arrived American in Spain, decided to ignore his gnawing anxiety in order to throw himself into using Spanish consistently, miraculous changes occurred: he was able to understand far more, quickly became much more fluent, moved in with Spanish friends and was happy to feel socially accepted almost everywhere (Oxford 1996). Yaru, a young

Chinese woman, had been told that her English pronunciation was poor. Nevertheless, she suddenly intuited that if she communicated well in English, the visiting evaluator who was observing her English teacher would think the teacher was successful. Out of compassion for the teacher, Yaru took the first opportunity to stand and – in a flash of competence, pleasure and excitement – spoke at length in perfectly understandable English. This event saved the teacher and permanently rejuvenated Yaru's faith in her own language ability (Oxford et al. 2007).

Complexity

Learners who live in different cultures often describe complex, contradictory feelings in themselves and competing influences in their environments. Transplanted people become used to 'transcreation and transculturation' and learn 'to exist in constant confusion, to be a hybrid, in constant change' (Stavans 2002: 9). Sometimes they experience large-scale restructurings of their beliefs, attitudes, identity or cognition. For instance, Grete (described by Oxford et al. 2011) escaped with her parents from Nazi Germany as a Jewish refugee to China. In China she refused to respond to her parents in German, which for her carried a bitter political and emotional stigma. She eagerly learned Chinese and French (the lingua franca of her immigrant community) 'from the inside out', readily adapting and freely using her extroverted thirst for communication with people in the new multicultural setting. As a holistic, auditory learner she easily 'slipped into the new sounds'. Grete's chaotic linguistic and cultural cognitions self-organized to generate creative, new, complex understandings, yet she remained negative towards German, her native language. Only much later, after moving to an English-speaking country and encountering a German professor who talked to her about literature, did she have a major attitudinal change about German, finally accepting it as worthwhile and regaining a missing piece of her identity. The interaction of chaos and complexity in language learning was first explored by Larsen-Freeman (1997).

Emotion

Language learning, especially across cultures, is a 'profoundly unsettling psychological proposition' (Guiora 1983: 8). Cognitive developmental psychologist Piaget (1981: 3) described all learning as involving 'states of pleasure, disappointment, eagerness, as well as feelings of fatigue, effort, boredom', and MacIntyre (2002: 61) stated 'emotion ... pervades all of our activities'. Emotions are powerful motivators for cognition (Damasio 1994; Le Doux 1998). Like narrative therapy (White 2007), learner narratives often unite emotionally fragmented elements. Some learner narratives (e.g. Mori 1997) tend towards bleak emotions, others (e.g. Hales 2010) reflect ebullience, and many, like that of Shannon, reflect a dynamic balance. In Shannon's narrative about going to Korea to learn Korean and teach English (Oxford et al. 2011), she wrote about receiving a piece of fruit offered by an unknown farmer and about being deeply grateful for this unexpected kindness. She happily experienced generosity from her Korean host mother and playfulness with her Korean 'siblings', who helped bridge cultural and linguistic gaps. However, Shannon initially struggled with shame over her rudimentary knowledge of the language and over being naked in a communal Korean bath-house. Ultimately she felt that her Korean experience was a wonderful 'rebirth' and an expansion of identity.

In contrast, acculturation was painful for Rodriguez (1983/2004), a Mexican-American who was nervous when his parents awkwardly tried to speak English and felt alienated from his cultural background when interacting in middle-class American culture. He was not Mexican any longer, but he was not fully American either. He bitterly viewed himself as 'a comic victim of two cultures' (Rodriguez 1983/2004: 5). Unlike Rodriguez, Stavans (2002: 9), a Latino Jew, emphasized the positive hybrid identity of Latinos, who 'have chosen to consciously embrace an ambiguous, labyrinthine identity as a cultural signature'.

Identity

Learner narratives, like autobiographies in general, elucidate the learner's shifting identities and anchor them in time (Eakin 2008). Learning an additional language is 'a constant process of self-discovery, self-invention, and identity negotiation' (Stakhnevich 2005: 230). Sometimes learners consciously manage their identity through resistance or opposition (Canagarajah 1993; Valdes 2001), acceptance (Stavans 2002) or creation of counter-stories to contradict society's imposed image of their identity (Norton 2000). New or expanded personal identities are born through 'physically and symbolically cross[ing] the border ... between one way of being and another and perceiv[ing] themselves as someone other than who they were before' (Pavlenko and Lantolf 2000: 174). Below are some specific instances of identity understanding and identity management.

Lvovich's (1997) autobiography, *The Multilingual Self*, distinguished between the ideal self and the real self. As an adolescent in the former Soviet Union, Lvovich feverishly studied French and developed her 'ideal self' in French. Later in the United States, she struggled to build an American identity while learning English. She realized that her former 'ideal French self' was built on fantasies, and her 'American self' was part of her 'real life' in the United States. This comparison is reminiscent of humanistic psychologist Carl Rogers' (1965) contrast between the ideal self and the person's real self. (This is different from Dörnyei's (2009) interpretation of the ideal self.)

In Norton's poststructuralist view (2000), identity refers to how a person understands his or her relationship with others and with social power (see also Rosenwald and Ochberg 1992; Bell 2002). An individual's needs for recognition, affiliation and safety generate conflicting desires, making identity a site of struggle. Learner narratives that portray cultural and linguistic border-crossings – see Morales and Morales (1986), Kaplan (1993), Angélil-Carter (1997), Lim (1997) and Pavlenko (2001a, 2001b) and studies already mentioned – often reflect power, resistance, opposition, counter-stories and identity transformation. Stakhnevich (2005: 221–3), a Russian-born college teacher learning Spanish as a third language by immersion in Mexico, described herself as temporarily powerless: 'invisible', 'mute and deaf', 'at the abyss of no-language', at the mercy of three languages 'fused together into one powerful multi-being with a mind of its own'. Based on interviews, portfolios and participant observations, Norton (2000) presented some immigrants' lack of power and others' ability to manage their identities through salvaging elements of social power.

Approaches and aids

In dealing with language learner narratives, helpful approaches and aids include the following: use empathy, accept subjectivity, seek emergent themes, notice triple re-storying, interpret aesthetically, treat the narrative as a case, expect complexity, look for influences, draw trajectories, and check and evaluate the narrative.

Use empathy

Empathy, involving taking another's perspective, is crucial for eliciting and interpreting learner-narrative data. For instance, to elicit a narrative, the empathetic teacher or researcher uses welcoming, personal questions to invite learners to tell in-depth stories about their thoughts, feelings and experiences (Josselson and Lieblich 1995). Taking another's perspective demands humility, discernment and responsibility (Oliver 1996).

Meaning-making inside and between the people in the classroom

Accept subjectivity

Although the empirical validity of learner narratives is occasionally questioned due to factors of memory or face-saving, most experts argue that learner narratives are not intended to reflect microscopic accuracy of events but to capture perceptions of experiences and feelings with personal, subjective authenticity (Connelly and Clandinin 1999).

Seek emergent themes through grounded theory

An important tool is *grounded theory*, in which interpretive themes (theory or explanation) arise from the data (Corbin and Strauss 2007). The *open-coding stage* identifies or codes the phenomena (e.g. people, events, cognitions, emotions, motivations, identities or transformations) and categorizes them into themes. In open coding, the researcher continually compares the specific data points in the narrative with the emergent themes (constant comparison) and keeps adjusting or renaming the themes as necessary. The *axial-coding stage* links information across themes to identify the overall context, actions, sequence and outcomes. The *selective coding* stage, if used, involves choosing a main theme and relating the other themes to it. By examining the data multiple times with different coding processes, the researcher arrives at an explanation.

Notice triple re-storying

Narrative inquiry requires 'an analytic examination of the underlying insights and assumptions' of a story (Bell 2002: 208). In my view, language learner narratives involve 'triple re-storying'. When individuals learn a language, they cross an internal (and possibly a physical) border and thus re-story their own lives ('self-translation', Pavlenko and Lantolf 2000). When learners tell their language learning stories, they filter, organize and structure information, emphasizing some things and not others; this is the second re-storying. When a researcher – or the learner himself or herself – further analyses and interprets the story, he or she makes additional connections in what I call the 'third re-storying'. Re-storying is part of the ongoing, human search for meaning and understanding.

Interpret aesthetically

Aesthetic interpretations can add new perspectives. For instance, explore the narrative as a musical work with different instruments, movements, harmony and dissonance. For instance, Grete, described earlier, felt harmony in learning Chinese and French as a child in China, but for many years she experienced only dissonance about German, her native language, until her university professor led her back to that language (Oxford et al. 2011). I imagine various instruments, such as the flute, the violin, the bass and the cymbals, accenting this language learner's life story.

Additionally, plot the multiple voices (Bakhtin 1986) in the narrative: voices of learner in the past and the present and voices of others in the story (Wortham 2001). For example, Yaru's narrative, mentioned earlier (Oxford et al. 2007), could readily be analysed in terms of supportive and unsupportive voices from the past and present, including her own voice and the voices of others.

View the narrative as a painting by identifying a focal point, determining the balance, examining the shades and tints of feeling, recognizing movement or stasis, and identifying characters and scenes. As an example, the autobiography of Lvovich (1997) or Hoffman (1990) could be interpreted as a series of visual images depicting experiences as a learner in different countries and showing people, scenes and colours relevant to various life stages.

Treat the narrative as a case

This means to consider the narrative as a bounded case (see earlier) and as only one data source among several (triangulation). Ask questions such as 'Who, what, when, where, why, how, and with what outcome?' However, avoid reducing people or stories to a mere handful of variables. 'If you try to chop stories up and [merely] categorize the pieces you will lose sight of the continuity in each ... unfolding life and the complex interrelatedness of ... experiences' (Aoki 2008: 16).

Expect complexity

Do not expect a classical plot with a clear rise, turning point and resolution, although this might occur. Consider the story as a complex system, and pinpoint chaos or unpredictability, interrelationships and change. Also recognize that each story has multiple levels: immediate speech act, the self in an episode or frame, socially scripted relationships, cultural influences, told stories and untold stories (Fisher-Yoshida and Wasserman 2006).

Look for influences

Draw a daisy with a large centre representing the main issue or event and two layers of petals, a top layer and a second layer showing below. On the top-layered petals, note the most powerful influences in the story. On the second layer of petals, write down secondary influences (Fisher-Yoshida and Wasserman 2006).

Cultural values might be among the influences. Many narratives from Western learners reflect cultural values of logic, individualism, personal achievement and self-esteem, while many East Asian narratives reflect cultural values of ambivalence, self-criticism, acceptance of contradiction and strong group ties (Heine 2007; Miller et al. 2007).

Draw trajectories

Draw trajectories or action lines for people that reflect shifts in identities, attitudes, beliefs, events and interactions. Alternatively, draw the general path of the story and interpret the meanings of events and comments based on this path (Fisher-Yoshida and Wasserman 2006).

Check and evaluate the narrative

To be ethical, check the interpretations of any learner narrative with the relevant learner for validation and for feedback and revision if needed (Josselson 1996). Evaluate the narrative for emotional authenticity (Ellis and Bochner 2000) as well as story integrity, timing and causality (Connelly and Clandinin 1999).

Also consider the relevance of the narrative. In 'naturalistic generalization' or 'receptive generalization', the reader or listener has a vicarious experience through the narrative and decides whether the story is personally relevant (Smaling 2003). A contributor to Belcher and Connor's (2001) volume noted that his experiences, while somewhat exotic, were typical enough to cause other people to relate and understand.

Conclusion

Language learner narratives, the stories language learners tell, are important to facilitate a deeper understanding of second and foreign language learning and of learners themselves. Having analysed hundreds of language learner narratives from my own students and those of other teachers, I found that I could more readily provide language instruction that more effectively addressed learners' cognitive, affective, cultural and communicative needs. My concern for and understanding and appreciation of learners was deepened every time I heard or read a learner's story. Similarly, Tim Murphey described reading at least a thousand of his students' learner narratives in order to grasp their needs, interests and concerns (Willis 2011). Such serious involvement with learner narratives is likely to dramatically improve teaching practices by helping teachers discern the most fruitful methods and contexts for different types of learners.

Moreover, professionals who offer teacher development courses and write language textbooks need to pay attention to the learners' perspectives and experiences. Their work can be truly meaningful only if the learner is a central focus. Learner narratives offer these professionals an important resource.

In addition to the above benefits offered by learner narratives, the learners themselves obtain important advantages as they tell their stories. In my own studies, learners often made comments about how much they discovered by sharing their stories. Here are some examples: 'I found out more about who I am by talking about my learning experiences.' 'Discussing my language learning helped me understand the journey I have been on for years.' 'Thanks for asking about my life as a learner; you are the first one who ever did! This will help me greatly in the future.'

Language learners also gain from reading or hearing others learners' stories. For instance, my advanced ESL students benefited from discovering the learning experiences, learning strategies and interpersonal dynamics mentioned by other students whose stories they read in works by Bailey (1983), Lvovich (1997), Norton (2000), Carson and Longhini (2002), Oxford et al (2005) and others. My students were also relieved to know that even the very best language learners, such as those in Stevick's (1989) book or in my studies (especially Oxford 1996; Oxford et al. 2007), sometimes experienced difficulties and yet never gave up their quest to become proficient. From reading learner narratives, my students recognized that language learning involves the mind, the heart and the tongue and that the term 'courageous' aptly describes the process and those engaged in it. Encountering the stories of students who came before can inspire current students to keep on going even at the hardest times. Learning from other students through their narratives is similar to learning from near peer role models (see Murphey, this volume).

These are key reasons why learner narratives are important. Let us invite learners to tell their stories, and when they do so, let us pay close attention. We learn from learners, just as they learn from us.

References

Angélil-Carter, S. (1997) 'Second language acquisition of spoken and written English: acquiring the skeptron', *TESOL Quarterly*, **31**: 263–87.
Aoki, N. (2008) 'Teacher stories to improve theories of learner/teacher autonomy', *Independence*, **43**: 15–17.

Meaning-making inside and between the people in the classroom

Bailey, K. M. (1983) 'Competitiveness and anxiety in adult second language learning: looking at and through the diary studies', in Seliger, H. W. and Long, M. H. (eds.) *Classroom Oriented Research in Second Language Acquisition*, Rowley, MA: Newbury House, pp. 67–102.

Bakhtin, M. (1986) *Speech Genres and Other Late Essays*, ed. Emerson, C. and Holquist, M., Austin: University of Texas Press.

Belcher, D. and Connor, U. (eds.) (2001) *Reflections on Multiliterate Lives*, Clevedon, UK: Multilingual Matters.

Bell, J. S. (1997) *Literacy, Culture, and Identity*, New York: Peter Lang.

Bell, J. S. (2002) 'Narrative inquiry: more than just telling stories', *TESOL Quarterly*, 36: 207–13.

Bruner, J. (1998) 'Narrative and metanarrative in the construction of self', in Ferrari, M. D. and Sternberg, R. J. (eds.) *Self-Awareness: Its Nature and Development*, New York: Guilford, pp. 308–31.

Campbell, C. C. (1996) 'Socializing with the teachers and prior language learning experience: a diary study', in Bailey, K. M. and Nunan D. (eds.) *Voices from the Language Classroom: Qualitative Research on Language Education*, New York: Cambridge University Press, pp. 201–23.

Canagarajah, S. (1993) 'Critical ethnography of a Sri Lankan classroom: ambiguities in opposition to reproduction through ESOL', *TESOL Quarterly*, 27: 601–26.

Carson, J. G. and Longhini, A. (2002) 'Focusing on learning styles and strategies: a diary study in an immersion setting', *Language Learning*, 52: 401–38.

Chik, A. (2005) 'From individual differences to learner individuality and identity', paper presented in the Symposium of the AILA Scientific Commission on Learner Autonomy in Language Learning, 14th World Congress of Applied Linguistics, Madison, WI 25 July 2005.

Connelly, F. M. and Clandinin, D. J. (1999) 'Narrative inquiry', in Keeves, J. P. and Lakomski, G. (eds.) *Issues in Educational Research*, New York: Pergamon, pp. 132–40.

Corbin, J. and Strauss, A. (2007) *Basics of Qualitative Research: Techniques and Procedures for Developing Grounded Theory*, 3rd edn, Thousand Oaks, CA: Sage.

Csíkszentmihályi, M. (2008) *Flow: The Psychology of Optimal Experience*, New York: Harper.

Damasio, A. (1994) *Descartes' Error: Emotion, Reason, and the Human Brain*, New York: Penguin Putnam.

Dörnyei, Z. (2009) 'The L2 motivational self-system', in Dörnyei, Z. and Ushioda, E. (eds.) *Motivation, Identity, and the L2 Self*, Clevedon: Multilingual Matters, pp. 9–42.

Eakin, P. A. (2008) *Living Autobiographically: How We Create Identity in Narrative*, Cornell, NY: Cornell University Press.

Ellis, C. and Bochner, A. P. (2000) 'Autoethnography, personal narrative, reflexivity: researcher as subject', in Denzin, N. K. and Lincoln, Y. S. (eds.) *Handbook of Qualitative Research*, 2nd edn, Thousand Oaks, CA: Sage, pp. 733–68.

Fisher-Yoshida, B. and Wasserman, I. (2006) 'Moral conflict and engaging alternative perspectives', in Deutsch, M., Coleman, P. T. and Marcus, C. (eds.) *The Handbook of Conflict Resolution: Theory and Practice*, 2nd edn, San Francisco: John Wiley, pp. 560–81.

Guiora, A. Z. (1983) 'Introduction: an epistemology for the language sciences', *Language Learning*, 33: 6–11.

Halbach, A. (2000) 'Finding out about students' learning strategies by looking at their diaries: a case study', *System*, 28: 85–96.

Hales, D. (2010) *La Bella Lingua: My Love Affair with Italian, the World's Most Enchanting Language*, New York: Broadway.

Hardy, B. (1968) 'Toward a poetics of fiction', *Novel*, 2: 5–14.

Harper, D. (2010) 'Narrative, narration, story', Online Etymology Dictionary. Available online at http://www.etymonline.com (accessed 12 July 2011).

Heine, S. J. (2007) 'Culture and motivation: what motivates people to act in the ways that they do?', in Kitayama, S. and Cohen, D. (eds.) *Handbook of Cultural Psychology*, New York: Guilford, pp. 714–35.

Hoffman, E. (1990) *Lost in Translation*, Harmondsworth, UK: Penguin.

Hong Kingston, M. (1989) *The Woman Warrior: Memoirs of a Girlhood among Ghosts*, New York: Vintage.

Josselson, R. (ed.) (1996) *Ethics and Process in the Narrative Study of Lives*, Newbury Park, CA: Sage.

Josselson, R. and Lieblich, A. (eds.) (1995) *Interpreting Experience*, Thousand Oaks, CA: Sage.

Kaplan, A. (1993) *French Lessons: A Memoir*, Chicago: University of Chicago Press.

Lam, W. S. E. (2000) 'Second language literacy and the design of the self: a case study of a teenager writing on the Internet', *TESOL Quarterly*, 34: 457–82.

Larsen-Freeman, D. (1997) 'Chaos / complexity science and second language acquisition', *Applied Linguistics*, 18: 141–65.

Le Doux, J. (1998) *The Emotional Brain: The Mysterious Underpinnings of Emotional Life*, New York: Simon & Schuster.

Lim, S. G. (1997) *Among the White Moon Faces: An Asian-American Memoir of Homelands*, New York: Feminist Press at CUNY.

Lvovich, N. (1997) *The Multilingual Self: An Inquiry into Language Learning*, Hillsdale, NJ: Lawrence Erlbaum.

MacIntyre, P. D. (2002) 'Motivation, anxiety, and emotion in second language acquisition', in Robinson, P. (ed.) *Individual Differences and Instructed Language Learning*, Amsterdam: John Benjamins, pp. 45–68.

Mehl-Madrona, L. (2010) *Healing the Mind with the Power of Story*, Rochester, VT: Bear & Co.

Miller, P. J., Fung, H. and Koven, M. (2007) 'Narrative reverberations: how participation in narrative practices co-creates persons and cultures', in Kitayama, S. and Cohen, D. (eds.) *Handbook of Cultural Psychology*, New York: Guilford, pp. 595–614.

Moen, T. (2006) 'Reflections on the narrative research approach', *International Journal of Qualitative Methodology*, 5, Article 5. Available online at http://www.ualberta.ca/~iiqm/backissues/5_4/html/moen.htm (accessed 15 March 2011).

Morales, A. L. and Morales, R. (1986) *Getting Home Alive*, Ann Arbor, MI: Firebrand Books.

Mori, K. (1997) *Polite Lies: On Being a Woman Caught between Cultures*, New York: Henry Holt.

Nam, C. and Oxford, R. (1998) 'Portrait of a future teacher: case study of learning styles, strategies, and language disabilities', *System*, **26**: 52–72.

Norton, B. (2000) *Identity and Language Learning: Gender, Ethnicity, and Educational Change*, London: Longman / Pearson Education.

Ochs, E. (1997) 'Narrative', in van Dijk, T. (ed.) *Discourse as Structure and Process*, Thousand Oaks, CA: Sage, pp. 185–207.

Oliver, C. (1996) 'Systemic eloquence', *Human Systems: The Journal of Systems Consultation and Management*, **7**: 247–64.

Oxford, R. L. (1996) 'When emotion meets (meta)cognition in language learning histories', in Moeller, A. (ed.) *The Teaching of Culture and Language in the Second Language Classroom: Focus on the Learner*, special issue of *International Journal of Educational Research*, **23**: 581–94.

Oxford, R. L., with Daniels, S., Wei, M. and Richter, E. (2011) 'Emotions and hot cognition in second and foreign language (L2) learning', paper presented at the annual meeting of the American Association of Applied Linguistics, Chicago, IL, 26–29 March 2011.

Oxford, R. L., Massey, K. R. and Anand, S. (2005) 'Transforming teacher-student style relationships: toward a more welcoming and diverse classroom discourse', in Holten, C. and Frodesen, J. (eds.) *The Power of Discourse in Language Learning and Teaching*, Boston: Heinle & Heinle, pp. 249–66.

Oxford, R. L., Meng, Y., Zhou, Y., Sung, J. and Jain, R. (2007) 'Uses of adversity: moving beyond L2 learning crises', in Barfield, A. and Brown, S. (eds.) *Reconstructing Autonomy in Language Education: Inquiry and Innovation*, London: Palgrave Macmillan, pp. 131–42.

Oxford, R. L., Tomlinson, S., Barcelos, A., Harrington, C., Lavine, R., Saleh, A. and Longhini, A. (1998) 'Clashing metaphors about classroom teachers: toward a systematic typology for the language teaching field', *System*, **26**: 3–51.

Pavlenko, A. (2001a) 'Language learning memoirs as a gendered genre', *Applied Linguistics*, **22**: 213–40.

Pavlenko, A. (2001b) '"In the world of tradition, I was unimagined": negotiation of identities in cross-cultural autobiographies', *The International Journal of Bilingualism*, **5**: 317–44.

Pavlenko, A. (2002) 'Narrative study: whose story is it, anyway?', *TESOL Quarterly*, **36**: 213–18.

Pavlenko, A. and Lantolf, J. (2000) 'Second language learning as participation and the (re)construction of selves', in Lantolf, J. P. (ed.) *Sociocultural Theory and Second Language Learning*, New York: Oxford University Press, pp. 155–77.

Peyton, J. and Reed, L. (1990) *Dialogue Journal Writing with Nonnative English Speakers: A Handbook for Teachers*, Alexandria, VA: Teachers of English to Speakers of Other Languages.

Piaget, J. (1981) *Intelligence and Affectivity: Their Relationship During Child Development*, Palo Alto: Annual Reviews.

Pintrich, P. R., Marx, R. W. and Boyle, R. A. (1993) 'Beyond cold conceptual change: the role of motivational beliefs and contextual factors in the process of contextual change', *Review of Educational Research*, **63**: 167–99.

Polkinghorne, D. E. (1988) *Narrative Knowing and the Human Sciences*, Albany, NY: SUNY Press.

Rivers, W. M. (1979) 'Learning a sixth language: an adult learner's daily diary', *Canadian Modern Language Review*, **36**: 67–82.

Rodriguez, R. (1983/2004) *Hunger of Memory*, New York: Dial / Random House.

Rogers, C. R. (1965) *Client-Centered Therapy*, Boston: Houghton Mifflin.

Rosenwald, G. and Ochberg, R. (eds.) (1992) *Storied Lives: The Cultural Politics of Self-Understanding*, New Haven: Yale University Press.

Santa Ana, O. (2004) *Tongue-Tied: The Lives of Multilingual Children in Public Education*, Lanham, MA: Rowman and Littlefield.

Schmidt, R. W. and Frota, S. N. (1986) 'Developing basic conversational ability in a second language: a case study of an adult learner of Portuguese', in Day, R. R. (ed.) *Talking to Learn: Conversation in Second Language Acquisition*, Rowley, MA: Newbury House, pp. 237–326.

Schulz, R. A. and Elliott, P. (2000) 'Learning Spanish as an older adult', *Hispania*, **83**: 1207–19.

Smaling, A. (2003) 'Inductive, analogical, and communicative generalization', *International Journal of Qualitative Methods*, **2**, Article 5. Available online at http://www.ualberta.ca/~iiqm/backissues/2_1/html/smaling.html (accessed 3 April 2011).

Spack, R. (1997) 'The acquisition of academic literacy in a second language: a longitudinal case study', *Written Communication*, **14**: 3–62.

Stake, R. E. (1995) *The Art of Case Study Research*, Thousand Oaks, CA: Sage.

Stakhnevich, J. (2005) 'Third language acquisition in immersion: a case study of a bilingual immigrant learner', *Critical Inquiry in Language Studies*, **2**: 215–32.

Stavans, I. (2002) *On Borrowed Words*, New York: Penguin.

Stevick, E. W. (1981) *Teaching Languages: A Way and Ways*, Rowley, MA: Newbury House.

Stevick, E. W. (1989) *Success with Foreign Languages: Seven Who Achieved It and What Worked for Them*, London: Prentice Hall.

Stevick, E. W. (1996) *Memory, Meaning, and Method: A View of Language Teaching*, 2nd edn, Boston: Heinle & Heinle.

Stevick, E. W. (1998) *Working with Teaching Methods: What's at Stake?*, Boston: Heinle ELT.

Valdes, G. (2001) *Learning and Not Learning English: Latino Students in American Schools*, New York: Teachers College Press.

White, M. (2007) *Maps of Narrative Practice*, New York: W. W. Norton.

Willis, R. (2011) 'Interview with Tim Murphey, Parts 1 and 2', *ELT News*. Available online at http://www.eltnews.com/features/interviews/2011/04/interview_with_tim_murphey_1-2.html (accessed 6 April 2011).

Wortham, S. (2001) *Narratives in Action: A Strategy for Research and Analysis*, New York: Teachers College Press.

Yin, R. K. (2003) *Case Study Research: Design and Methods*, 3rd edn, Thousand Oaks, CA: Sage.

7 Listening to and learning from our learners

David Nunan

> Education is the kindling of a flame, not the filling of a vessel.
>
> (Socrates)
>
> Education is an admirable thing, but it is well to remember from time to time that nothing worth learning can be taught.
>
> (Oscar Wilde)
>
> Education is what is left when everything that has been taught is forgotten.
>
> (James Bryant)

Introduction

I have a deep and abiding interest in the lives of learners. In fact, during the 1970s and 1980s, I built my teaching practice on learners' perceptions, attitudes, beliefs and ideas as revealed through their stories. It was through listening to my learners and trying to understand and interpret the learning process from their point of view that I came to embrace the concept of learner-centredness. In a book I wrote back in the 1980s, entitled *The Learner-Centred Curriculum*, I made the point that in terms of planning, implementation and evaluation, a learner-centred curriculum will contain elements similar to what many good teachers have always done (in fact, the concept of learner-centredness goes back a long way – all the way back to Socrates):

> the key difference between learner-centred and traditional curriculum development is that, in the former, the curriculum is a collaborative effort between teachers and learners, since learners are closely involved in the decision-making process regarding the content of the curriculum and how it is taught ... This change in orientation has major practical implications for the entire curriculum process, since a negotiated curriculum cannot be introduced and managed in the same way as one which is prescribed by the teacher or teaching institution.
>
> (Nunan 1988: 2)

Meaning-making inside and between the people in the classroom

There is also a long-standing tradition in general education that places the learners and their experiences squarely at the centre of the learning process. This is the experiential learning tradition, which has diverse origins, drawing on Dewey's educational progressivism, Lewin's work in social psychology, Piaget's work in child language development, Kelley's cognitive theory of education and the work of Maslow and Rogers in the field of humanistic psychology.

My favourite contributions to the literature on experiential learning in the field of language education are the book by Legutke and Thomas (1991), and a chapter by Kohonen (1992). This is what Kohonen has to say:

> In experiential learning, immediate personal experience is seen as the focal point for learning, giving 'life, texture, and subjective personal meaning to abstract concepts and at the same time providing a concrete, publicly shared reference point for testing the implications and validity of ideas created during the learning process' (Kolb 1984: 21). But experience also needs to be processed consciously by reflecting on it. Learning is thus seen as a cyclic process integrating immediate experience, reflection, abstract conceptualization, and action.
>
> (Kohonen 1992: 14)

A great deal has been said and written about the use of narratives in educational research ('We seem to have no other way of describing "lived" time save in the form of a narrative'; Bruner 2004: 692). In this chapter, I want to revisit my professional development as a teacher through the eyes of my students. I will recount stories from several learners taken from different periods in my professional life – the first from many years ago in Australia, the final one of more recent vintage in Hong Kong. I believe that all of them carry powerful implications for language pedagogy and research, and in a later section of the chapter, I shall spell out the implications of the stories for language learning and teaching. These mesh with other collections of learners' stories including Earl Stevick's (1989) detailed account of seven individuals who achieved success with foreign language learning and what worked for them, as well as the accounts in three edited collections I worked on (Benson and Nunan 2002; Benson and Nunan 2004; Nunan and Choi 2010).

The learners whose stories make up the bulk of this chapter come from disparate backgrounds, are learning in quite different contexts and have different attitudes, approaches and motivations in learning language. However, their stories play out a number of themes that tie in to and support experiential learning and learner-centred education.

Learners' stories

Here are stories from six learners: Jalil, Alice, Grace, Rebecca, Sandy and Gloria.[1]

Jalil

Jalil comes in to my professional life in the early 1970s. He is serious and studious. His first language is Arabic and his second is French. Since migrating to Australia, he has devoted himself to mastering English with an intensity that I have rarely observed in second language learners, although at this time I am a relative newcomer to the field, and therefore my experience is rather limited.

In academic circles, behaviourism has been well and truly brought into disrepute. However, in language teaching, behaviourist-based audio-lingualism, the method I was trained in, is still going strong. The corner-stone of the method is the formation of sound linguistic habits through repetition and substitution drills. The explanation of grammatical rules is eschewed. For me, this is a good thing because my knowledge of English grammar could be written on a postage stamp. I am therefore rendered speechless on the first day of class when Jalil approaches me during the morning break and rather diffidently asks, 'Teacher David, Sir – first conditional, second conditional. What is difference?' Making a speedy recovery, I reply, 'Oh, that's Book 3. We're not there yet.'

At the end of class I ransack the bookshelf in the teachers' room and slip a dog-eared copy of Thomson and Martinet's *Practical English Grammar* into my bag. It's to be my constant companion for the rest of the year. (Many years later, I'm amazed to see that it's still in print, and, if Amazon.com is to be believed, still selling well.)

The multilevel text used in the school is audiolingual to the core with a few idiosyncratic features added in. One of these is a series of hand gestures that accompany the drill of the day. When drilling the simple past, you're supposed to make statements in the present progressive: *I'm walking to the door.* (Actually you're not – you're rooted to the floor at the front of the room.) You accompany the utterance by flinging your right arm backwards over your shoulder as though you're patting your back. The students are supposed to reply *Yesterday, I walked to the door.*

---

[1] These are all pseudonyms, apart from Rebecca, who gave permission for her name to be used. The Asian learners had adopted Western names, as is commonly the case, and I have therefore used Western pseudonyms for them.

It isn't too long before I'm heartily sick of this way of teaching. The arm-flailing routine and rote drilling are boring, and seem to have little effect on the ability of students to communicate in English outside of the classroom. This strikes me forcibly one day when we we've been practising the question pattern:

Is this   pen(s)?

Are these   your   book(s)?

                                                  pencil(s)?

As teacher, I'm supposed to do the usual hand-flapping and parroting: '*Is this your pen? –* (pause) *book*'. The students are meant to parrot back, '*Is this your book?*', '*Pencils.*' '*Are these your pencils?*' And so on ad nauseum.

In order to make the exercise a little more meaningful, I pass a small cloth bag around the class and ask students to drop a personal object into it. They then take turns extracting an object, and going around the class asking '*Is this your watch?*' – or *pen*, or *bracelet* – until the owner had been identified. Not a particularly revolutionary technique, I have to admit, but it was an advance on the unimaginative drills and the students seem to enjoy it. Within a few minutes they are engaged in the task, intoning '*Is this your ...?*' and '*Are these your...?*' effortlessly and fluently.

At the end of the class, I walk over to the parking lot at the rear of the school. Jalil walks with me, no doubt waiting for an opportunity to interrogate me on the intricacies of gerund and infinitive constructions. When I take a set of keys from my pocket and unlock the door to a rather shabby Toyota, his eyes light up. Like the other students, he is used to seeing me arrive and depart from class on my bicycle. He looks at the car, he looks at me, his eyes grow ever bigger, and he says, 'Teacher car?'

I groan. 'Jalil, what have we been practising for the last hour? "Is this your car?", "Is this your car?", "Is this your car?" And, no it isn't my car. It's a friend's. I'm dropping it off at the garage for him.'

Driving away from the school, depressed, a nagging question plays on my mind.

Why is it that Jalil is incapable of deploying in the real world structures that he can manipulate in class with minimal effort? How is it that he seems incapable of converting grammatical knowledge he has ingested from goodness-knows how many grammar books into an ability to use that knowledge to communicate?

Years later, I tell this story to the second language acquisition researcher Malcolm Johnston. Malcolm counters with the story of

Cengiz, one of the informants in his own research. One day, Cengiz confronts Johnston with the following puzzle:

> Before I came here (as an immigrant to Australia) I was knowing all
> the English language tense(s): present tense, past tense, present perfect
> tense, perfect tense, future tense, future in the past. Everything! I was
> knowing, I am knowing now. I just asked one day, er, the boss – I
> said to him 'How you knowing this tense?, for example "go". How
> can you use this word? Past tense? Present tense? The other tense?'
> He just looked me like that. He told me 'I don't know Cengiz.' This
> is Australian people. I am Turkish people. I am knowing. He doesn't
> know. Can you explain this?

Remembering Jalil, I have a great deal of sympathy with Cengiz's boss. Johnston comments:

> Cengiz's question is easy enough to answer: although their formal
> or explicit knowledge of the rules of the mother tongue may be quite
> limited, native speakers like his Australian boss possess an extensive
> and complex tacit or subconscious grammatical knowledge – so
> complex, in fact, that no formal grammar yet written has succeeded in
> capturing it. This is the pat explanation that most linguists would like
> to give to such an enquiry. Just because we can sidestep the question
> in this way, however, does not mean that we should dismiss it. In fact,
> Cengiz's plea stirs up a hornet's nest of issues for the language teacher
> and deserves very serious consideration.
>
> (Johnston 1987: 91)

Alice and Grace

Alice and Grace are identical twins. They enter my classroom a year or two after the departure of Jalil. I'm at a point where I'm thoroughly tired of audiolingualism which, despite rapidly evolving notions of 'language' and 'language learning', still holds most of the teaching profession in thrall. In my case, and in the case of some of my younger colleagues, it does not. We attempt to escape the dominant audiolingual methodology of the day by getting learners involved in learning through doing – through using language, seeing it as a tool for communicating rather than as a body of content to be internalized through mimicry and memorization. We get them involved in role plays and simulations; we have them listen to conversations that we'd recorded in the street. In short, we've invented communicative language teaching for ourselves without knowing it.

In order to bring our students along with us, we're careful to explain the rationale for what we're doing, and we monitor what our students think of these new ideas. Since my encounter with Jalil, I've tried to take my pedagogical bearings from my students. I'm fascinated by the stories they bring me from inside and outside of the classroom, so it's natural for me to get the students' perspectives on these new ways of learning.

However, for many weeks, I find it impossible to get much out of Alice and Grace – my two painfully shy identical twins who go everywhere together and who are reticent and withdrawn. One day, one of the twins is absent – I've no idea which one it is – but I seize the opportunity to start a conversation. After class I approach the one twin who is present and ask – 'So, how are you enjoying the English class?' Terrified, she leaps from her seat and heads for the door. 'Where are you going?', I call after her.

'To ask my sister,' she replies. Later in the course, one of the girls – I think it was Grace – does develop the confidence to respond to my questions. One day, having completed a role play that I feel has gone well, I ask the girl what she thought of it. She shakes her head. 'No like role play.' 'What about your sister?', I ask. 'She no like role play.'

I go home that evening in a state of depression for two reasons. In the first place, my attempts to incorporate a more communicative approach into my classroom is meeting with only marginal success. On the other hand, my attempts at teaching grammar don't seem to be particularly successful either. We had spent a lot of class time practising negation in the context of likes and dislikes – *He likes … I don't like … She likes … You don't like … We like … He doesn't like … They like … She doesn't like …* My students are great at manipulating the forms in class, but then in communication, they use forms they'd certainly never learned from me. No teacher nor any textbook that I'd ever come across taught *No like this* or *No like that*. However, I noticed students all around me using this and other forms that they had never been taught. Mismatches and asymmetries between teaching and learning were all around me, and yet I'd never really paid this any attention – nor was it anything that I'd ever been taught when I was training to be a teacher. In fact, I was taught that if learners made errors, then I must be doing something wrong. And that is the lesson I get from Alice and Grace – I'm not doing it right. There has to be another way.

Rebecca

Rebecca's story is somewhat different from the stories of the other learners in this chapter. In the first place, she is learning a language other than English. In the second place, she has a rather different relationship to me. My relationship to the other learners is that of teacher-to-student. In this case it's parent-to-child. Rebecca is my younger daughter.

Rebecca lives in Hong Kong, where she has resided since she was six. Her first foray into foreign language learning occurred in primary school when, at her own request, she enrolled in an after-school programme to learn French. As far as I can remember, she acquired very little French – largely, I suspect because 45 minutes a week is hardly adequate to make measurable progress in any foreign language. However, the experience was enjoyable, and it did create a positive mindset towards the learning of other languages.

After primary school, she attended a high school that required all students to study Putonghua (Mandarin Chinese) along with a European language. There Rebecca elects to study Spanish. Although the Hong Kong government strongly encourages locals to learn Putonghua, it is not widely spoken and remains, in effect, a foreign language.

There is no doubt that Rebecca is a 'good' language learner. She picked up, and maintains, passable conversational Cantonese even though, as a post-secondary school student, she has spent most of the last six years in the United States. She did this without formal study, but by hanging out with a peer group which included a number of native speakers of Cantonese.

One day, I return from a speaking tour to Latin America to find Rebecca sitting at the dining table doing her homework. She is in her first semester of junior high. Scattered about the table are her schoolbooks, including her Chinese and Spanish textbooks. I have to say that like most of her peer group, she's a reluctant homework doer. There are far more attractive things to do after school than declining Spanish verbs.

'So,' I say. 'How was school?'

'OK,' she replies, and sighs. School and schoolwork are not her favourite conversational topics.

'What homework are you doing?'

'Chinese and Spanish.'

'So tell me – what's your favourite language?' As she's living and learning in a Chinese milieu, I expect her to say 'Putonghua' but instead she replies 'Spanish'.

I'm a little surprised. 'Why is that?'

She pauses, smiles, and says, 'Because I love my teacher. And she loves me.'

'But you have no need for Spanish, do you?'

At that she sighs and says, 'Dad, I do Maths, Science, History, Geography, Drama and Art. I have no use for any of that stuff either. That's what school is all about. But Spanish is fun. My teacher makes it fun. We'll play games in Spanish. And I really love studying grammar. In Putonghua classes, we just sit and listen to the teacher, and do hours of stupid drills.'

117

I suspect that this is not the whole story, and a few evenings later at a parent/teacher evening I recount the story to Mrs Painter, the Spanish teacher. She laughs and tells me about her philosophy, which is rooted in experiential learning and is extremely learner-centred.

> At dinner parties, when people ask me what I do, I tell them I'm a teacher. When they ask me what I teach, I tell them 'children'. For me, languages are just a vehicle for the development of the whole individual. It's more than just an intellectual exercise. I'm concerned with the kids' emotional, physical, and social development as well. Sure – we have a textbook, but I use that just as a shell or a framework. I draw on what the kids bring to the learning process. As far as possible, I build my lessons on their interests and experiences. I also try to ensure that the learning experiences are developmentally appropriate. Lots of textbooks are either too babyish or too adult for the kids.

Earl Stevick (1971: vii) said much the same in the introduction to one of his early books, 'language study is inevitably a total human experience; writers and teachers ought therefore to act as though it is'.

Sandy

In the 1990s my colleague Phil Benson and I carried out a longitudinal study into the learning histories of 60 undergraduate students at the University of Hong Kong. These detailed narrative accounts provided fascinating insights into the differences and diversity among what on the surface appeared to be a pretty homogeneous group of learners. In fact a book we published, which drew partly on our insights as well as those of other contributors working in the same tradition, was entitled *Learners' Stories: Difference and Diversity in Language Learning*.

One of our informants was Sandy. Sandy was a smart, first-year student, and, unlike Alice and Grace, she wasn't at all shy. When asked to compare and contrast her experiences of learning English at high school with university, she said:

> When I was in secondary school, I seldom asked questions. The reason was that the teacher always tried to explain the stuff as detailed as possible, leaving no queries among students. Only the most curious student will ask questions. This method is well-known as the spoon-feeding education system in which we are fed with piles of notes and textbooks. On the other hand, students (especially some dumb one like me) only care about getting results good enough to enter a university. Students gradually become examination oriented. Eventually less and less students care about acquiring knowledge, which should be the aim of education. But in universities, things

are totally different. Lecturers only give a brief talk on the topics, leave a huge area for students to explore by themselves. This means that spoon-feed system no longer exists. Students cannot rely on the knowledge acquired in lectures.

When asked to spell out the actual strategies used by her high school teacher, she answered:

> I learn English in school by, just by doing some exercises on the class or homework. And when we prepare for the exam, we just do all the past paper and that's all, no special learning ... We have different approach if we have different teachers, some teacher will take primary (elementary) school approach. She will let you read a text and then tell you to underline some difficult words and then you have to jot them in a book and we did not like this way because we are not babies, for some teachers they will just give you ... we have a textbook and then she will tell us to do the exercise inside that.

When probed on whether she liked learning that way, she replied, 'No'. She laughs and continues, 'because we don't know what we are doing. In fact, I'm in, I was in the same school as Trudy (another of our informants) and all more less the same. Drills everyday, no fun at all.'

At this point, Trudy, who has been listening in adds, 'No fun at all, yes. Yeah, I am at the same school as Sandy. Even in English lesson, we don't speak English.'

Gloria

Gloria was another of the informants in the Hong Kong University study. I'm going to reproduce her story in some detail. It takes the form of what is known as a condensed narrative. These narratives were the heart of our research.

Informants were given the choice of narrating their language learning histories in either English or Chinese – whichever language they felt comfortable in. These were then translated and transcribed. The result was a lengthy account running to many pages that had to be condensed in some way. To do this, we followed a five-step procedure recommended by Lieblich et al. (1998: 62–3).

1. Read the material several times until a pattern emerges ... There are aspects of the life story to which you might wish to pay special attention, but their significance depends on the entire story and its contents. Such aspects are, for example, the opening of the story, or evaluations ... of the parts of the story that appear in the text.
2. Put your initial and global impressions of the case into writing.

3. Decide on special foci of content or themes that you want to follow in the story as it evolves from beginning to end.
4. Using coloured markers ... mark the various themes in the story, reading separately and repeatedly for each one.
5. Follow each theme throughout the story and note your conclusion. Be aware of where a theme appears for the first and last times, the transitions between the themes, the context for each one, and their relative salience in the text.

Here is Gloria's condensed narrative.

I first encountered English in kindergarten. I really don't remember if I ever heard it before then. I remember that the first thing we learned was the alphabet – A, B, C, A is for apple, that kind of thing. It was nothing special, just one more subject. But I didn't think it was a very important subject.

I don't remember whether my primary school was supposed to be Chinese- or English-medium. I don't think it was ever said. All subjects were taught in Chinese, even English. The main focus of the lessons was vocabulary, and simple conversations. Hello, I'm Gloria. Who are you? – that sort of thing. I remember that it was pretty boring. We had a book and had to follow along as the teacher read. Now and then, he'd ask us to spell words. Most of the time in primary school was spent copying stuff out. It didn't matter what the subject was. In English class, the teacher would give you a sentence and tell you to write it out several times.

I had no contact with English at all out of class, unless you consider doing English homework as contact. Extra-curricular activities after school were mainly sports. There was nothing in English.

When I got to years 5 and 6, I still didn't think that English was very important. We prepared for the Academic Aptitude Test, but the emphasis was on Chinese and Mathematics. We didn't have any special preparation for English or extra homework, so I didn't think that it was important. I remember that the focus in class was on grammar – memorizing tenses and that sort of thing.

After primary school, I went to an English-medium secondary school. In the beginning, what that meant was that for many subjects the textbook was in English. In class, the teachers spoke Chinese because their job was to make sure we understood, and the best way to do that was through Chinese.

Although we had a School English Society, my friends and I never thought of joining it on our own initiative. We thought more about

---

what sports we would play when we joined the Sports Club. English wasn't an activity that you could use or have fun with, it was a subject that you had to study and learn.

When I started in high school, I had more contact with English because it was an English-medium school and the teacher more or less had to speak English. Then my view of English began to change. I began to see that in addition to being a subject to be studied, it could also be used as a tool to study other subjects. For example, I studied History, and classes were conducted in English, so English became more important. In most classes the teachers used a mixture of Cantonese and English – probably fifty-fifty. There was a lot of switching between languages. Some people say this is bad, but the main thing is that the teachers use language that we can understand. What's the point of teaching a perfect lesson in English if we can't understand? So, Chinese played an important part, even in English class.

In senior high school, the most important influence was the public examinations and preparing for them. English was now more important than other subjects because I needed it to learn the other subjects. Also, the English exams were different. In the past, you only had to know grammar and vocabulary, but now you needed a much deeper understanding because you were tested on listening and speaking. The public exams completely dominated my life because my future depended on getting good results, and getting good results required good English. Everything we did was based on the exams. What it tested, we learned!

But I also started to see the importance of English out of class. I realized that I needed the language if I wanted to communicate with other people. When I was young, it never occurred to me that I would talk with a foreigner in English. The teacher also stressed the importance of using English out of class. She encouraged us to watch English television and subscribe to English language newspapers. But I hardly ever did these things; I was too lazy. I couldn't see how they would help me pass the public examination. English was important because of the exams. Sometimes I would read a newspaper if it was required for an assignment, but that's all.

Then in form seven, I had an experience that changed my attitude. I took a summer job at Philips and because it was on Hong Kong Island, I came into contact with a lot of foreigners. I was the only one in the store who could speak much English at all, and it made me feel superior. But speaking with foreigners made me realize my deficiencies. I sometimes had to get them to repeat three or four time before I could understand. And I noticed that the English that foreigners spoke was different from the English that Chinese people spoke. This experience made me realize that I really did need to learn English more wholeheartedly, that I would have a need to communicate with other people one day and that English is really very important.

Now that I'm at university, I think of English in a very different way from when I was in school. I don't have the pressure of an English exam hanging over me, and I use English, not because I have to take an exam, but because it's the medium of communication. Many of my lecturers are foreigners, so if I talk to them I have to use English. You have to write, speak and think in English. It's part of daily life. Also, if you're good at English you feel superior, and other people look at you as though you're superior. One of the differences between English and other subjects such as Geography is that I don't look at people who are good at Geography as that smart, necessarily, but I think of someone who is fluent in English as very smart.[2]

Discussion

What can we make of these learners stories? What insights do they provide into the language learning process? As I read and reread the stories, seven insights began to emerge. I have framed these as hypotheses to be contested again in other contexts and pedagogical realities.

Hypothesis 1. Learning will be enhanced if the curriculum and teaching methods are developmentally appropriate.

Rebecca's teacher, Mrs Painter, made the point that when teaching younger learners, it is important to hit the 'sweet spot' in order to optimize the effectiveness of instruction. In other words, it is important to use materials which are age appropriate and to expect students to learn something only when they're ready. Her success with Rebecca and with other learners underlines the importance of this point.

Hypothesis 2. Learning will be enhanced if you pay attention to all of the learners' needs: physical, emotional, social, creative and cognitive.

Not so long ago, I was doing a workshop with a group of secondary school teachers in Brazil. During a coffee break, several of the teachers

---

[2] First reproduced in Nunan and Bailey (2009).

expressed the fact that they were dispirited with their work. 'Our students can't see the point of learning English,' one of them said. I recounted Rebecca's story. After the break, we brainstormed some of the educational benefits of learning another language – any language – and they came to the conclusion that it was difficult to find a more suitable subject for the education of the whole learner. The trick, of course, was to help the learners see the point: to help them make connections between their language lessons and their physical, emotional, social, creative and cognitive development.

Hypothesis 3. Learning will be enhanced if the curriculum acknowledges that the relationship between teaching and learning is asymmetrical.

As we saw in the cases of Jalil, Alice and Grace (as well as Malcolm Johnston's informant, Cengiz), learners do not learn what teachers teach in a linear, additive fashion. Their stories reflect the fact that language acquisition is complex, organic and inherently unstable.

From his research, Johnston drew several conclusions: first, learners do behave systematically, and therefore it is important to try to understand what they are doing in their own terms. Second, learners' ideas of what is 'basic' are quite different from our own. Third, learners go about language learning in an active, constructive way: they do not just attempt to copy the native speaker.

> It is quite possible for a learner and a teacher to be working at cross purposes without either party being aware of it: while the teacher is attempting to drum one concept into the learner's head ... the learner may be utilizing the teaching material in quite a different way.
>
> (Johnston 1987: 101)

Hypothesis 4. Learning will be enhanced if the three key curriculum components, the syllabus, learning experiences and assessment, are in harmony.

Sandy and Gloria, two research informants in Benson and Nunan (2002) research, point out the demotivating effect of examination-oriented instruction.

Hypothesis 5. Learning will be enhanced if learners are given opportunities to contribute their own ideas, experiences and feelings to the learning process.

Rebecca's teacher, Mrs Painter, engaged her learners by using the learning tasks in the set textbook as frameworks or templates into which learners were able to pour their own ideas, experiences and feelings, and to make their own unique contributions to their learning processes.

Hypothesis 6. Learning will be enhanced if there is a focus on learning processes as well as the language content.

The twins, Alice and Grace rejected my attempts at closing the gap between the world of the classroom and the world beyond the classroom through role plays, simulations and the like because they couldn't see the point. They had been socialized into believing that drilling and memorization lay at the heart of language learning. However, by focusing on learning processes as well as language content, and by encouraging a reflective attitude on their part, I was able to get them to see the point, and eventually to embrace my early attempts at communicative language teaching.

Hypothesis 7. Learning will be enhanced if learners are given opportunities for authentic communication.

Again, the two informants in the Hong Kong University study talk about how demotivating it is to be subjected to relentless rote drilling. Gloria also spoke of the transformative effect of having opportunities for authentic communication outside of the language classroom.

Conclusion

In this chapter, I have attempted to make a case for the importance of listening to and learning from our learners. Like Stevick, 'I fear whoever … focuses more on teaching language than on teaching people' (1996: 249). From my earliest days as a teacher, I have sought to take my pedagogical bearings from my learners, and I hope that this contribution gives a flavour of how this came about, and how, by listening to my learners' voices, I was forced to the realization that to be an effective teacher, I had to 'lead from behind'. Through them, I came to appreciate the asymmetry between teaching and learning, and to see that often, while I was busily focusing on one thing, my learners were focusing on something else.

I hope that the chapter also presents a respectable case for the importance of storytelling in research. Many years ago, I came across the following statement from the British educator Lawrence Stenhouse, and it has stuck with me ever since.

> There is a need to capture in the presentation of the research the texture of reality which makes judgment possible for an audience. This cannot be achieved in the reduced, attenuated accounts of events which support quantification. The contrast is between the breakdown of questionnaire responses of 472 married women respondents who have had affairs with men other than their husbands and the novel

Madame Bovary. The novel relies heavily on that appeal to judgment which is appraisal of credibility in the light of the reader's experience. (Stenhouse 1982: 11)

References

Benson, P. and Nunan, D. (eds.) (2002) *The Experience of Language Learning*, special issue of *The Hong Kong Journal of Applied Linguistics*, 7(2).

Benson, P. and Nunan, D. (eds.) (2004) *Learners' Stories: Difference and Diversity in Language Learning*, Cambridge: Cambridge University Press.

Bruner, J. (2004) 'Life as narrative', *Social Research*, 71(3): 691–710.

Johnston, M. (1987) 'The case of -ing for the beginning learner', *Prospect*, 3(1): 91–102.

Kohonen, V. (1992) 'Experiential language learning: second language learning as cooperative learner education', in Nunan, D. (ed.) *Collaborative Language Learning and Teaching*, Cambridge: Cambridge University Press.

Kolb, D. (1984) *Experiential Learning: Experience as the Source of Learning and Development*, Englewood Cliffs, NJ: Prentice-Hall.

Legutke, M. and Thomas, H. (1991) *Process and Experience in the Language Classroom*, London: Longman.

Lieblich, A., Tuval-Mashiach, R. and Zilber, T. (1998) *Narrative Research: Reading, Analysis and Interpretation*, Thousand Oaks CA: Sage Publications.

Nunan, D. (1988) *The Learner-Centred Curriculum*, Cambridge: Cambridge University Press.

Nunan, D. and Bailey, K. (2009) *Exploring Second Language Classroom Research*, Boston: Heinle/Cengage.

Nunan, D. and Choi, J. (eds.) (2010) *Language and Culture: Reflective Narratives and the Emergence of Identity*, New York: Routledge.

Stenhouse, L. (1982) 'The problems of standards in case study research', in Bartlett, L., Kemmis, S. and Gillard, G. (eds.) *Perspectives on Case Study 2: The Quasi-Historical Approach*, Geelong Vic.: Deakin University Press.

Stevick, E. W. (1971) *Adapting and Writing Language Lessons*, Washington, DC: Foreign Service Institute.

Stevick, E. W. (1989) *Success with Foreign Languages*, Hemel Hempstead, UK: Prentice-Hall.

Stevick, E. W. (1996) *Memory, Meaning and Method: A View of Language Teaching*, 2nd edn, Boston: Heinle & Heinle.

Part B

Meaningful classroom activity

Our ultimate goal as language teachers is for our students to make meaning in our classrooms. The challenge for teachers is, of course, how to help them to do that most effectively. A key response to that challenge is constructing meaningful action in the language class. Kristjánsson (this volume) makes the important point that 'Language is first of all a medium for communicating matters of relevance.' From a Vygotskyan perspective, working with communication activities in the classroom would involve much more than speaking with grammatically correct sentences or giving information since, as Brooks and Donato (1994: 273) say, 'through speaking, individuals maintain their individuality and create a shared social world'.

In the classroom, experiences that connect to learners' lives and give them a greater sense of agency, of capacity to act, will inevitably have a better chance of turning linguistic information into productive acquisition of the language. The benefits of this type of classroom, however, are not only related to acquiring greater knowledge of the language. Engaging in meaningful learning where learners invest something of themselves can lead to self-growth and to individuals becoming more responsible participants in society. How can we encourage this? Fundamentally, teachers can create more meaningful classrooms through their interactions and relationships with learners and through the types of learning interventions they plan. Stevick (1976: 122) writes: 'There is a point at which the teacher's whole personality makes an impact ... where the teacher may try to supply missing motivation', but he adds there is also a point at which 'technique comes into its own, both for minimizing frustration and confusion, and for avoiding a feeling of stagnation in class activity'. He argues for 'DEEPER AIMS in addition to the teaching of language', something that might '"change your life" as contrasted with only "add to your language abilities"' (Stevick 1998: 166).

Meaningfulness is a concern not only of learners, but also of teachers. In a meaningful classroom the teacher is also learning. As Underhill says (1999: 140–1), 'my learning is about the group and its members including myself, now, moment by moment ... Perhaps I even set a limit on the learning my students can do during a lesson by the amount of learning I am doing alongside them and at the same time.' Objectives for language teaching have become greatly diversified. In one formulation '*being* is just as important as *doing*; a good language teacher *knows* and does but most essentially *is*' (Arnold and Brown 1999: 4). This means that we still need our knowledge of 'materials, techniques and linguistic analyses' (Stevick 1980: 4) but that there are other skills, related to Underhill's (this volume) description of facilitation, that can make the difference between unproductive activity and meaningful action.

In this part we will be exploring some of the 'Ways' of working in the classroom with techniques, activities and methodological options to turn the learning space into a 'world of meaningful action' where effective language learning occurs.

An extremely significant part of getting control of a new language is related to the successful acquisition of vocabulary. In Chapter 8 Penny Ur presents a research-based perspective on the importance of memory for language learning and specifically for vocabulary acquisition. Several aspects, including depth of processing, are discussed, and Ur suggests important implications for both teachers in the classroom and coursebook writers.

Teachers' agency has a direct and strong influence on their effectiveness in facilitating learning, and having more tools can lead to a greater sense of agency. Alan Maley, in Chapter 9, takes a look at practices common to a wide variety of methodological options available for teachers, from Grammar Translation to Dogme. While not all of these are used extensively now, Maley shows how practices characteristic of these methods, both traditional and modern, can be used in ways that engage today's language learners. He also encourages teachers to develop community in the classroom and to help learners find relevance in their learning by giving them a voice and exercising choice at appropriate levels.

Communicative approaches to language teaching have been with us for decades, but Communicative Language Teaching (CLT) has been associated with quite different models in the classroom. In Chapter 10, Zoltán Dörnyei discusses the traditional views of CLT and goes on to propose the Principled Communicative Approach (PCA), which integrates both a focus on form and a greater awareness of psychological aspects of language learning. He stresses the importance of finding the optimal balance between explicit and implicit learning. In the chapter he develops seven guiding principles of the approach based on information from research on instructed language learning.

Tim Murphey, in Chapter 11, brings to life 'adapting', a key concept in Stevick's work. Normally we speak of adapting to learners' zones of proximal development (ZPDs). However, Murphey illustrates how we, both students and teachers, have variable capacities to adapt and thus have zones of proximal adjusting (ZPAs). Through mediating activities in the classroom, such as shadowing, action logs and videoing, we can adjust to the ZPDs of others and develop our ZPAs. He also looks at the dialectic fusion, argued for by Vygotsky and Bahktin, of some apparent opposites: self and other, autonomy and community, and inside and between. He ends by looking briefly at the ZPA in the field of second language acquisition and, given the frequent bandwagon shifts that Stevick mentioned, Ortega's (2011) proposal for epistemological diversity is presented as a useful option.

In Chapter 12 Diane Larsen-Freeman discusses what Stevick terms 'technemes', which refer to the very small changes in a classroom activity that can renew its meaningfulness for students. This can be especially useful in classes with students of mixed levels since these changes can keep more advanced learners engaged and give slower learners more practice. Rather than 'repetition', Larsen-Freeman suggests using the term 'iteration', which is the act of repeating that results in a change to a procedure or system. Technemes also encourage students to adapt their resources to deal with the variation in an activity. The combination of iteration and adaptation make technemes a powerful tool to use in the classroom.

Adrian Underhill, in Chapter 13, illustrates a clear option for bringing greater meaningfulness and self-regulation through the atmosphere created in the classroom by the teacher who has developed certain qualities of the skill of facilitation. Many practical suggestions are given for deepening learning on what he terms the learner's 'Inner Workbench'. If the actors in the language learning process are to take more control of their own learning, it will help if what they do in the classroom is engaging and relevant for them, and Inner Workbench activities can add relevance.

References

Arnold, J. and Brown, D. (1999) 'A map of the terrain', in Arnold, J. (ed.) *Affect in Language Learning*, Cambridge: Cambridge University Press, pp. 1–24.
Brooks, F. B. and Donato, R. (1994) 'Vygotskyan approaches to understanding foreign language learner discourse during communicative tasks', *Hispania*, 77(2): 262–74.

Ortega, L. (2011) 'SLA after the social turn: where cognitivism and its alternatives stand', in Atkinson, D. (ed.) *Alternative Approaches to Second Language Acquisition*, London: Routledge, pp. 167–80.

Stevick, E. W. (1976) *Memory, Meaning, and Method: Some Psychological Perspectives on Language Learning*, Boston, MA: Heinle & Heinle.

Stevick, E. W. (1980) *Teaching Languages: A Way and Ways*, Rowley, MA: Newbury House.

Stevick, E. W. (1998) *Working with Teaching Methods: What's at Stake?*, Boston, MA: Heinle & Heinle.

Underhill, A. (1999) 'Facilitation in language teaching', in Arnold, J. (ed.) *Affect in Language Learning*, Cambridge: Cambridge University Press, pp. 125–41.

8 Memory and vocabulary acquisition

Penny Ur

In the first part of *Memory, Meaning and Method* (1976), Earl Stevick discussed a number of research studies into the way memory works in general, relating particularly to verbal memory (pp. 11–32). Since the book was written, a substantial amount of further research has been carried out on various aspects of vocabulary learning and memorization. In this chapter I shall look at selected studies that relate to topics in this area that appear in Stevick's book, discuss briefly some of the theoretical and practical issues they raise, and suggest practical applications to classroom teaching and materials design.

The topics are:

1. Memory traces
2. Retrieval-based vocabulary review
3. Learning words within semantic sets
4. Massed and distributed learning
5. Depth of processing

Memory traces

In early research on animal memory, it was shown that rats seemed to have a vague memory of previous learning, which – if it was not too long ago – helped them relearn the same target behaviour later (Stevick 1976). This led to a generalized theory about 'memory traces': the idea that even if we cannot consciously recall a particular experience or piece of information, and think we have forgotten it, a 'trace' remains in our memory which can be activated later and facilitates learning when the original stimulus is re-encountered.

It is interesting that hypotheses about memory traces and gradual learning have influenced language acquisition research very little, perhaps because of their rather vague and unquantifiable nature. In a typical research study on vocabulary learning, a group of learners is asked to learn a particular set of items under experimental conditions and is then tested to find out how well they have learned the target material, as contrasted with a control group (e.g. Tinkham 1997 and Mondria 2003, both mentioned later in this chapter). Sometimes there are both immediate and delayed post-tests, but in any case the results are quantified in terms of what the learners can demonstrate that they know in terms of accurate recognition or recall. Normally, no attempt is made to find out whether partial learning (leaving 'traces') has taken place.

An exception is a case study on the acquisition of vocabulary through reading, carried out by Pigada and Schmitt (2006). Most studies of incidental vocabulary learning in the course of extensive reading show a rather low rate of acquisition relative to the amount read (Laufer 2003). Pigada and Schmitt set out to show that if partial learning is taken into account, perhaps the rate is not as low as has been assumed. A student read a text that included a number of new words in the target language (French), and was then tested in an in-depth interview that aimed to elicit gains in knowledge of spelling, meaning and grammatical behaviour of the target words. It was found that he in fact made substantial partial gains in his vocabulary: for example, he could say what the grammatical collocation of a word was even if he could not remember its exact meaning. But most tests are not sensitive to such knowledge.

Practical implications

The following scenario is familiar to teachers. You ask a student to tell you what a word means, or how to express something in English; they can't do it; you tell them the answer and they make a gesture of frustration and say something like 'Oh yes, of course, now I remember.' They aren't just putting on an act: this reaction is a useful indication that they had the 'trace' in their memory and recognized the item the moment you activated it. Next time they are more likely to remember it on their own.

This means that practice exercises that largely 'give away' the right answer may be very helpful. An example is dictations where you provide the target word without the vowels and tell students the meaning: all they have to do is insert the vowels. They might not have been able to recall or even identify the meaning of the word on their own: but with the support of part of the spelling plus the meaning, they could get it, and learning is reinforced without the feeling of failure that results from a scenario like the one described above. Similarly, the teacher can begin to say the word and just ask the student to complete it; or give a hint like 'it rhymes with ...'.

A second practical implication has to do with awareness, rather than with actual procedures. Teachers need to be aware that even if students fail to get a passing grade on a test on specific language items, *this does not necessarily mean that they do not know them at all*. It just means that they do not know them well enough to pass the test; or, more specifically, that they do not know the particular aspect of linguistic knowledge that was being tested. Students also need to be aware of the same principle: failing a test does not demonstrate ignorance; it more probably demonstrates partial learning that needs to be completed and enriched.

Such awareness can lead to enhanced self-image and better motivation on the part of students who fail tests; and it can help teachers to take a longer-term view of learner progress.

Retrieval-based vocabulary review

A number of experiments on memory are based on the learning of a set of lexical items – either L1 or L2 – under different test conditions (Stevick 1976: 11–32). The learners are later asked to recall as many of the items as they can, and conclusions are drawn as to which conditions facilitate learning better. Such studies are only indirectly relevant to vocabulary teaching, since it is the meanings and uses of the items as much as the actual forms that we want our students to remember; nevertheless, they can provide interesting insights.

Some early research of this kind showed that attempts to actively retrieve the list of items learned, as a preliminary to testing, resulted in better recall (Darley and Murdock 1971, cited in Stevick 1976). This may seem like a simple confirmation of two fairly well-established assumptions within language learning: that you need multiple encounters with a lexical item in order for it to be permanently acquired (Zahar et al. 2001) and that practice, within a skill-learning model of language learning,[1] improves performance (Dekeyser 2007). But it is not quite so simple. The significant part of this particular hypothesis is that not all kinds of practice are equally productive of improvement in memory of lexis. Requiring learners actively to recall, or retrieve, previously learned items is significantly more effective than simply providing for re-encounters of the written or spoken items in meaningful contexts.

---

[1] Dekeyser and others suggest that language in formal learning contexts is learnt largely as a skill, similarly to the way we learn to play a musical instrument, drive a car, etc. The learner hears or reads a verbal description of the target behaviour ('declarative stage'), performs it according to this description repeatedly, thus transferring the declarative into tacit, proceduralized knowledge (proceduralization stage), and can eventually perform automatically, without needing to recall the verbalized description at all (automatization stage). Practice is therefore the repeated rehearsal of the behaviour (in the present context, the meaningful practice of a linguistic item or construction), which leads eventually to automatization.

133

Meaningful classroom activity

This hypothesis has been confirmed by more recent studies. Karpicke and Roediger (2008) showed that students who did repeated tests demanding retrieval of previously taught target items learned the items better than those who did only review exercises where the target items were provided together with exercises that required students to engage with them. Similarly, a study by Pastötter et al. (2011) indicated that retrieval exercises done during initial learning help retention.

It seems that repeatedly making the effort to recall target items from memory oils the retrieval channel, as it were, and makes it easier and faster to use. But this is true, of course, only if the learner *can* successfully retrieve the target items. Demanding unsupported recall of new items from students who have as yet only minimal 'traces' of their form and meaning, as in the scenario described at the beginning of the previous section, is likely to result in failure and no added learning – unless and until the teacher re-teaches the item.

Practical implications

Retrieval activities therefore need to be carefully timed so that the material is in fact still 'retrievable' when they are done. In practice, this means challenging students to recall vocabulary fairly soon after we have taught it for the first time, or after we have already reviewed it two or three times in previous lessons.

An example of an activity which does this is 'recall and share'. A set of ten or so recently taught vocabulary items is written up on the board. Students are not allowed to copy these down at this point but asked to 'photograph' them mentally: the teacher warns them that they are then going to need to try to recall them on their own. The items are then hidden or deleted, and the students challenged to write them down. They do this first individually: then they join in pairs or small groups to check meanings and spellings of the target items. Finally, the teacher reveals the items again so that students can check their answers.

Tests are normally seen as an assessment tool, but they can, as in the Karpicke and Roediger (2008) research referred to above, be used to enhance learning. If this is its main purpose, then the test has to be administered only after we have thoroughly taught and reviewed the target items and are fairly sure that the students will manage to recall them successfully.

Learning words in semantic sets

Research studies on learning lists of isolated lexical items commonly show that subjects help themselves remember such items by linking them to others through some semantic link (Stevick 1976: 18–22): *blue* helps them remember *red*, for example, because the two words belong to a similar category (Talmi and Moscovitch 2004).

This has led to an assumption that we should therefore teach new words in semantic sets: a set of animals, for example, or a set of parts of the body. But the research shows clearly that teaching new words as members of a semantic set does *not* lead to good learning. In a study described by Tinkham (1997), subjects were asked to learn nonsense-words which had been arbitrarily assigned meanings. One list was given meanings that all related to one semantic category (*sweater, shirt, jacket*, etc.); another was given mixed meanings (*frog, car, rain*, etc.). Subjects consistently remembered the second list better. Similar results were obtained in later studies by Waring (1998), Erten and Tekin (2008) and Papathanasiou (2009). It seems that if all the items are new, the fact that their meanings are linked leads to confusion and tends to slow down the memorization process. By the same token, one would expect that teaching pairs of opposites or pairs of synonyms or homonyms together would also be counterproductive.

How can these two findings be reconciled? The answer is that whether or not semantic links between words are useful for learning depends on the degree to which some or all of the members of the set are already mastered and available for retrieval in the learner's memory. If the learner has already come across items in the past and can retrieve them, then these can be used a) as a basis for learning other words that are semantically linked to them (within the same semantic category, for example, or a hyponym or superordinate) or b) as a basis for review and consolidation through the use of semantic links[2] (see examples below). But if *all* the items are new, it is better not to introduce them all together as a set, but to teach each in its own meaningful context, as an item in its own right.

Practical implications

The first obvious implication is that we should not load our students with a whole lot of new words taken from a single semantic area in one lesson. Some elementary coursebooks expect us to do this: if we are working with such materials we may therefore need to adapt extensively – omit some items and add others that are linked thematically, but not part of the same semantic set. However, we *can* make use of words our students already know in order to teach semantically linked

---

[2] For more on the importance of basing learning of new items on previous knowledge, see Puchta, this volume, pp. 45–61.

new ones. For example, if they have already learned the word *transparent* we might use it to explain the word *opaque*; however, we should probably not introduce both *transparent* and *opaque* together. Similarly, if they already know the words *cow*, *horse*, *mouse*, we can use these in the teaching of another animal, such as *sheep*, or in teaching the superordinate *animal*.

Semantic relations between previously taught words that need consolidation can also be used for interesting and varied practice exercises. For example, a set of words that are all animals can be written up on the board in a circle and students asked to link any two of them in a sentence, perhaps comparing them (*a tiger is bigger than a rabbit*) or expressing some kind of relationship (*a tiger can eat a rabbit*): each link is shown on the board by a line joining the two items. Or sets of four semantically linked words can be provided, for example *pasta*, *an egg*, *chocolate*, *chicken*, and the students challenged to say which is the 'odd one out' (there does not have to be any one 'right' answer: any of the items can be identified as the odd one out provided the students can give a convincing justification for their choice).

Massed and distributed learning

The evidence from research is that distributed learning is more effective than massed: a phenomenon which was discussed by Stevick (1976: 28) and has been extensively researched since (Baddeley 1997; Donovan and Radosevich 1999, *inter alia*). In other words, students will learn new vocabulary items better if they engage with them in, say, three 5-minute sessions, separated by a time-gap during which their attention is on other things, than if they engage with them for the whole of one 15-minute session. If the interval between sessions is too long, however, this benefit is lost: a very long time-gap between first and second encounters may mean that the original item has been forgotten and needs to be re-taught.

The question arises as to what is the optimum time-gap to be left between encounters? This question is no nearer being answered than it was in the 1970s; it appears to depend very much on the number and difficulty of the items to be memorized, and on the individual learner.

The principle, however, is to run a review of new items as long after the previous encounter as the students can remember them: the longer the gap, provided this condition is observed, the better. As with many other aspects of teaching, exactly how long such a gap is will depend on the teacher's professional judgement rather than on any research-based mathematical formula.

This principle logically leads to another generally accepted one: that of *expanding rehearsal* (Baddeley 1997). The first time we review a new item has to be fairly soon after it has been learned; thereafter gaps in review sessions can be successively lengthened as the learner remembers the item for longer and longer, until we reach the point at which it appears to be well established in his or her long-term memory.

The studies on massed and distributed learning in research on human memory can be linked to the research on vocabulary learning in second language acquisition, according to which multiple encounters with a new item are necessary for successful mastery. Exactly how many such encounters are needed is a matter for debate: certainly less than 8 is probably insufficient (Horst et al. 1998), and some researchers have put the optimum number as high as 16 (Zahar et al. 2001). Again, the number will depend on our own professional judgement, based on the difficulty of the item and our students' level and ability. Other factors may also play a part: there is, for example, some evidence that 'emotive' items are more easily learned than 'neutral' ones (Talmi and Moscovitch 2004); and the interest-value of the item to a particular student will also make a difference (see 'Depth of processing' below).

The bottom line, however, is the necessity for repeated and distributed vocabulary review of any newly learned items, regardless of whether these are learned incidentally through reading or intentionally in focused vocabulary-expansion procedures.

Practical implications

In spite of the fairly well-known assumptions about the retention of vocabulary described above, coursebooks typically do not provide the requisite number of re-encounters of newly learned vocabulary, nor do they tend to observe the principles of distributed learning or expanding rehearsal. Typically, a coursebook will present a list of vocabulary items to be learned at the end of a text where they appeared, and will also give a review exercise or test at the end of the unit. But from then on until the end of the course, there is unlikely to be any further focused review of these items. Hopefully, however, this will change in the future: now that most books have digital supplements and supporting websites with virtually unlimited space, there is far more potential for cumulative review of previously learned vocabulary.

In most cases, however, the onus is on us, the teachers, to initiate classroom or homework activities that provide the requisite number of re-encounters at acceptable intervals. Such activities can be based on re-reading or discussion of the text which was the source of the items, or on simple activities that do not demand extensive preparation or expensive materials (Ur 2012). At the end of the lesson during which new items have been taught, we might, for example, run the 'recall and share' activity described earlier. Subsequent reviews can be as simple as asking students to recall, later in the course, all the words we learned from a text, and reminding them of the ones they had forgotten; translation dictations (for monolingual classes whose language you know), where you say the item in the mother tongue, students write it down in English, or vice versa; guessing games based on definition, mime or pictures; requiring students to write a story that contextualizes a set of new items. Suggestions for such activities can be found in Ur (2012).

I am not suggesting that we attempt to teach a systematic programme of 10 to 16 carefully timed sessions of vocabulary review of all the items that we teach! However, we should make sure that our students get many more opportunities to review vocabulary than are normally provided in our coursebooks, and that such review activities, which need not take up a lot of time, are a regular feature of most of our lessons.

Depth of processing

Another research-based assumption about vocabulary learning is that a vocabulary item which students have learned or reviewed through processes involving careful thought about its form, meaning and use will be learned better than one that has merely been read aloud, translated or repeated. Craik and Lockhart (1972) suggested that such *depth of processing* is a significant factor affecting memory: material that has been more deeply thought about during the initial learning is more likely to be well remembered. Later studies of word learning supported this hypothesis (Craik and Tulving 1975) and is clearly something that Stevick himself strongly believed (1976: 41–4).

Within language-acquisition studies, a relevant concept here is that of *noticing* (Schmidt 1990). Schmidt maintains that we do not normally learn new language items or grammatical features unless we are aware of them: there is no such thing as 'subliminal' learning. Depth of processing would seem to be an extension of this: the more extensively we notice and attend to a feature, the better we are likely to learn it.

The *task involvement* hypothesis is a specific application of the principle of depth of processing developed by Laufer and Hulstijn (2001) in the context of second language vocabulary acquisition. Task involvement comprises *need* (the learner is motivated to find out the meaning of the target item), *search* (the learner actively searches for it, in a dictionary or by asking a teacher) and *evaluation* (the learner checks how the item compares with other similar ones and where it would be appropriately used in preference to others). A later study by Kim (2008) confirmed that task involvement, as defined above, was a significant factor in enhancing the retention of new vocabulary.

The teaching implication would seem to be that we should make sure our students process newly learned vocabulary as deeply as possible. But it is not quite so simple. Mondria (2003) checked out the effects of various similar strategies involving depth of processing on the learning of new vocabulary. One group of learners was asked to infer meanings of words from context, verify their inferences from a glossary and then memorize the words. Another group was provided with the meanings and simply asked to spend time memorizing them. The results when students were tested were very similar: no significant difference was found between the groups. The question therefore arises as to why time should be spent on inferencing and looking up words in a glossary if you get the same learning results without going to all that trouble? It seems that the factor which was most influential in producing successful learning was time spent on deliberate learning – the memorization stage – rather than on inferencing or searching in a glossary.

Similarly, Keating (2008), who tried out the task involvement hypothesis with a group of learners, found that although task involvement did indeed lead to better learning, the effect was much lessened or even neutralized when the amount of time invested was taken into account.

Practical implications

There seems no doubt that thoughtful processing of the meanings and forms of new items produces better learning. The question for the teacher is one of pedagogical efficiency: the ratio of learning outcomes to investment of time and effort. How can we ensure that vocabulary learning procedures exploit the time and effort available to produce optimum learning?

The answer seems to me to lie in the timing and goals of the vocabulary processing we are demanding from students.

Notice that in many 'deep processing' vocabulary-learning procedures – as in those described above – a substantial proportion of the time is spent *not knowing* what the item means. Typically, learners are asked first to find out the meanings of target items on their own – by inferencing, for example (e.g. Mondria 2003), or by puzzling out descriptions or definitions or hints provided by the teacher (e.g. Nation 2008: 20), or by looking them up in a dictionary (e.g. Laufer and Hulstjin 2001). During much of the time spent on such procedures, the learners do not in fact yet know the meanings of the words, and even when they find them they risk 'discovering' the wrong ones. This seems to me to be an

139

inefficient – sometimes even counterproductive – use of classroom time and student effort.

I would suggest that it would be more sensible to explain the meaning of the item frankly to the students from the start, at the same time as we present its written and spoken form, and *then* proceed to tasks which involve deep processing. Such tasks will, in this case, be designed on the basis that students already know the form and meaning of the word, and need to engage with it in different ways in order to make it more memorable. Activities might involve, for example, comparing the meaning of the target item with that of other ones previously learned; or deciding whether it is appropriate for different contexts; or brainstorming other items that might collocate with it; or comparing it with an L1 translation and discussing the differences; or retrieval activities such as the 'recall and share' one described earlier.

I am not implying that there is never any value in inferencing, understanding definitions or looking up vocabulary in the dictionary. These are, of course, important reading and learning strategies, and our students need to know how to use them when they encounter unknown lexis in a text. They are also important for self-study: in the absence of a teacher, learners needs to be able to use them in order to learn new vocabulary on their own. My claim is rather that in a teacher-led classroom situation where the main aim is vocabulary acquisition, they do not provide efficient and learning-rich deep processing of new items, and may be largely a waste of time.

Finally, as the Mondria (2003) research makes clear, deep processing is not enough. It is also important to allow time for students simply to study the new vocabulary and deliberately try to memorize it.

Conclusion

Much of the research on memory discussed by Stevick in *Memory, Meaning and Method* is still relevant today, and has been confirmed by later studies. It has been enriched in recent years by studies focusing particularly on memorization of second language vocabulary.

There is, however, a need for practitioners to relate critically to the research literature: not all of it can be applied directly to the second language classroom. This may be because there are sometimes apparent contradictions in research results which need to be disentangled; an example is the research on the learning of semantic sets described above. Or it may be because of pedagogical constraints, as in issues associated with depth of processing in vocabulary learning.

The problem of how, when and how much the results of research studies in cognitive psychology in general and language acquisition in particular can be applied to classroom teaching was the basis for much of Stevick's writing and continues to provide a major challenge for practitioners, researchers and theoreticians alike. This chapter has attempted to provide some possible 'bridges' between research, theory and practice relating to how well, and why, learners retain lexical items in memory.

References

Baddeley, A. (1997) *Human Memory*, Hove: Psychology Press.

Craik, F. I. M. and Lockhart, R. S. (1972) 'Levels of processing: a framework for memory research', *Journal of Verbal Learning and Verbal Behaviour*, **11**(6): 671–84.

Craik, F. I. M. and Tulving, E. (1975) 'Depth of processing and the retention of words in episodic memory', *Journal of Experimental Psychology*, **104**(3): 268–94.

Darley, C. F. and Murdock, B. M. (1971) 'Effects of prior free recall testing on final recall and definition', *Journal of Experimental Psychology*, **91**: 66–73.

Dekeyser, R. M. (2007) 'Situating the concept of practice', in Dekeyser, R. M. (ed.) *Practice in a Second Language: Perspectives from Applied Linguistics and Cognitive Psychology*, Cambridge: Cambridge University Press, pp. 1–18.

Donovan, J. J. and Radosevich, D. J. (1999) 'A meta-analytic review of the distribution of practice effect', *Journal of Applied Psychology*, **84**: 795–805.

Erten, I. H. and Tekin, M. (2008) 'Effects on vocabulary acquisition of presenting new words in semantic sets versus semantically unrelated sets', *System*, **36**(3): 407–22.

Horst, M., Cobb, T. and Meara, P. (1998) 'Beyond a clockwork orange: acquiring second language vocabulary through reading', *Reading in a Foreign Language*, **11**: 207–23.

Karpicke, J. and Roediger, H. L. (2008) 'The critical importance of retrieval for learning', *Science*, **319**: 966–8.

Keating , G. T. (2008) 'Task effectiveness and word learning in a second language: the involvement load hypothesis on trial', *Language Teaching Research*, **12**(3): 365–86.

Kim, Y. (2008) 'The role of task-induced involvement and learner proficiency in L2 vocabulary acquisition', *Language Learning*, **58**(2): 285–325.

Laufer, B. (2003) 'Vocabulary acquisition in a second language: do learners really acquire most vocabulary by reading? Some empirical evidence', *Canadian Modern Language Review*, **59**(4): 567–87.

Laufer, B. and Hulstijn, J. (2001) 'Incidental vocabulary acquisition in a second language: the construct of task-induced involvement', *Applied Linguistics*, **22**(1): 1–26.

Mondria, J.-A. (2003) 'The effects of inferring, verifying and memorizing on the retention of L2 word meanings', *Studies in Second Language Acquisition*, **25**(4): 473–99.

Nation, I. S. P. (2008) *Teaching Vocabulary*, Boston: Heinle Cengage.

Papathanasiou, E. (2009) 'An investigation of two ways of presenting vocabulary', *ELT Journal*, **63**(4): 313–22.

Pastötter, B., Schicker, S., Niedernhuber, J. and Bäuml, K.-H. (2011) 'Retrieval during learning facilitates subsequent memory encoding', *Journal of Experimental Psychology: Learning, Memory, and Cognition*, **37**(2): 281–97.

Pigada, M. and Schmitt, N. (2006) 'Vocabulary acquisition from extensive reading: a case study', *Reading in a Foreign Language*, **18**(1): 1–28.

Schmidt, R. (1990) 'The role of consciousness in SLL', *Applied Linguistics*, **11**: 129–58.

Stevick, E. W. (1976) *Memory, Meaning and Method: Some Psychological Perspectives on Language Learning*, Boston: Heinle & Heinle.

Talmi, D. and Moscovitch, M. (2004) 'Can semantic relatedness explain the enhancement of memory for emotional words?', *Memory and Cognition*, **32**(5): 742–51.

Tinkham, T. (1997) 'The effects of semantic and thematic clustering in the learning of second language vocabulary', *Second Language Research*, **13**(2): 138–63.

Ur, P. (2012) *Vocabulary Activities*, Cambridge: Cambridge University Press.

Waring, R. (1998) 'The negative effect of learning words in semantic sets: a replication', *System*, **2**(2): 261–74.

Zahar, R., Cobb, T. and Spada, N. (2001) 'Acquiring vocabulary through reading: effects of frequency and contextual richness', *Canadian Modern Language Review*, **57**(4): 544–72.

9 Winnowing the past: towards a principled eclecticism

Alan Maley

Introduction

In this chapter I shall examine three periods in language learning history: (1) the distant past, with its traditional practices of translation, repetition, rote memorization, reading aloud, etc. – all widely condemned with little or no empirical justification, (2) the more recent past: The Silent Way, Community Language Learning, Suggestopedia, Total Physical Response and the Natural Approach, and (3) the present: Dogme, Task-Based Learning, Cooperative Learning, and Content and Language Integrated Learning.

For each of the approaches examined, I shall attempt to draw out key features and principles which, if combined appropriately in a local context, could form the basis for a principled eclecticism accessible to teachers at the chalk face. I conclude that it is how teaching is done, rather than what is done, which is central to successful learning.

Preliminaries

Stevick once offered a riddle which posed the conundrum of the best method.

> In the field of language teaching, Method A is the logical contradiction of Method B: if the assumptions from which A claims to be derived are correct, then B cannot work, and vice versa. Yet one colleague is getting excellent results with A and another is getting comparable results with B. How is this possible?
>
> (Stevick 1976: 104–5)

The recent history of English Language Teaching has been characterized by a sometimes fevered search for the Holy Grail of the best or most effective method (Maley 2005, 2006). Latterly, this has been combined with a compulsion to collect, analyse and evaluate data through research. In fact, research has become a major enterprise in its own right, linked to, yet still separate from, the daily teaching enterprise. In *Memory, Meaning and Method*, Stevick sets out two opposing views on the value of research for language teaching. On the one hand, there is 'a belief that past failures have been due to insufficient knowledge, and that therefore we need to know more'. On the other, there is 'the assumption that past failures – and successes – have come from the degree of wisdom with which we have handled what we have known at the time' (Stevick 1976: 105). This notion, that we need not only continue the accumulation of data from research, but also winnow out the wisdom from what we already know, lies at the heart of this chapter.

In his seminal article 'There is no best method – why?', Prabhu (1990) provides a useful critical examination of the concept of method. His conclusion is that it is not so much 'method' itself which needs our attention but rather the intuitive know-how of teachers based on long experience. It is this which provides them with a basis of largely tacit and unformulated principles and practices with which to deal, moment by moment, with the unfolding unpredictability which characterizes classroom teaching. This he calls 'the teacher's sense of plausibility'. His concern, then, is to find ways of helping teachers to recognize, reflect upon and value their 'sense of plausibility' as an essential element in their professional growth.

Schumann (1999: 39) adds a convincing reason from neuroscience about why there can be no best method for teaching languages: all our brains are different and a 'method which fails to target efficiently a learner's neural circuits to subserve the skill being taught will not be the right method for that brain' even though it may be 'perfectly appropriate for another individual's brain'.

In a later article, 'Teaching is at most hoping for the best', Prabhu (1998) further explores the nature of classroom learning and concludes that the essential unpredictability of classroom encounters means that, while we may hope that students will learn something, just *what* they will learn is beyond our control. This chimes with Allwright's (1984) article, 'Why don't learners learn what teachers teach?'

Related to these preliminary reflections are the following four core facts about any classroom event. According to Norman Whitney (personal communication) 'any classroom event is unpredictable, unrepeatable, unobservable in all its details, especially what is going on inside learners, and has unforeseeable, long-term consequences, not all of them purely pedagogical'.

We can now draw some preliminary conclusions from these loosely related strands of reflection:

- There is a need for a healthy scepticism towards the claims of any single methodological 'solution'.
- The contexts of learning are so diverse that no single method will ever be adequate to deal with them all.

- Academic research alone is not enough to get a full understanding of what goes on inside the learning black box.
- We need to focus on the principles which underlie the many, sometimes only superficially different, methodological approaches (Kumaravadivelu 2003; Meddings and Thornbury 2009). This is indeed what Stevick himself was attempting in *Memory, Meaning and Method*. In short, we need to consider, as he did, what he called a 'psychodynamic interpretation of what happens in language classes ... intra- or interpersonal action' or 'what goes on inside and between folks' (Stevick 1976: 119) as this can greatly influence the effectiveness of any methodological approach.

Traditional practices

In this section I propose to examine briefly a set of practices which are commonly branded 'traditional' and regarded as both outmoded and unproductive. They include translation, repetition (especially drilling), rote memorization, reading aloud, choral repetition, dictation, teaching based on grammar rules and use of the L1. Such practices are features of more than one approach, of course, but I have chosen to deal with them as a set of interrelated practices rather than as manifestations of any particular method.

Such 'traditional' procedures have been pedagogically taboo for so long now that they are commonly dismissed without further thought or proof (Cook 2010). They are generally considered to be boring, artificially contrived (unnatural), top-down and teacher-centred, and unproductive, with no transfer from what is learned to what is needed for use. While it is not my purpose to defend them here, it does seem worth examining them a little more carefully than we commonly do. We need also to bear in mind that what teachers actually do in classrooms may be at variance with what experts lay down as desirable practice. And if such practices do, in fact, survive behind the closed doors of many a classroom, there may be good reasons for that survival.

Translation has long been the victim of a monolingual approach to foreign language learning (Howatt and Widdowson 2004). There are signs however, of a resurgence of interest in it. Cook (2010) makes a carefully argued case for its reassessment. He points out that no serious research has been done to justify its virtual exclusion from current L2 teaching practice. He suggests that the use of translation in teaching challenges the conceptualization of language teaching based on monolingualism, native speakerism, naturalism and absolutism which emerged in the early years of the twentieth century and which has survived unexamined ever since. He points to the close association of this monolingual model with the growth of vested interests in publishing, examinations, private language schools and universities in metropolitan countries, and the whole apparatus of teacher certification based on this model where the use of translation might represent a threat.

Clearly, if teachers do not share a language with their students, translation will not be an option, but when teachers do share students' L1 and are able to work with it, it can stimulate 'noticing' (Schmidt 1990), open up interesting discussions and lead to understanding of the way both the L1 and the L2 function. It can also provide natural contexts for sensitizing students to the range of possible ways of expressing a given content and can be a powerful tool for developing both grammatical and lexical growth (Duff 1989; Grellet 1991).

Turning to **Repetition**, which is also habitually branded as demotivating, Kramsch (2009) points out that there are positive aspects of the practice which can support learning. Clearly, successful language learning cannot be accomplished without repetition. Tannen (1989) considered that actually repetition is something that is at the heart of language. Rarely does anyone learn a language item after a single exposure. It is odd then that repetition should have earned such a bad name. This may be in large part due to its close association with pattern drills and dreary, mindless exercises. But repetition can be done in many different ways, and even pattern drills can be made both more interesting and more meaningful (see Helgesen 2006). Repetition can also be achieved surreptitiously in rehearsed performance (Maley 1999), by reconstruction tasks (Duff and Maley 2007), by variations in dictation procedures (Davis and Rinvolucri 1988) and by delayed repetition, the internal repetition in the inner voice of a sound, word or sentence before saying it externally and audibly (Underhill 2005).

Choral repetition is widely regarded as anathema to 'modern' views of language learning. There are, however, ways of managing choral repetition as performance (Maley 1999; Lutzker 2007) which involve students in deep processing of the text, intense reflection on the ways it needs to be spoken for the best effect and bonding with fellow students to form a learning community. Various forms of voice and drama exercises can also help students to arrive at an apprehension of the text from the inside (Maley 2000).

Rote memorization has also been characterized as a sterile and demotivating activity, leading to the accumulation of language items not then available for subsequent 'natural' use. How true is this, in fact? Much depends on what is memorized, how it is memorized and for what purpose. To ask students to commit bland, uninteresting texts to memory is clearly unproductive. By contrast, memorizing texts with high salience, such as songs, poems, jokes, advertising slogans, can be both enjoyable and relevant, leaving the material readily available for incorporating in future 'real' communication (Bilborough 2011). To ask students to learn core vocabulary at the outset as a pre-requisite for subsequent learning may, in fact, prove very motivating (Meara 2009). So, in and of itself, rote memorization cannot simply be dismissed.

Another hardy survivor is **Dictation**, which nonetheless gets a bad press. Davis and Rinvolucri (1988) showed decisively how dictation could be adapted to produce high learning payoffs. Their book offers teachers 74 different ways of doing dictation, most of which are highly 'communicative' and engaging.

Reading aloud is often tarred with the brush of boredom. Once again, much depends on what is being read, who is reading it and for what purpose. Clearly, the typical mechanical reading around the class by students may well be counterproductive, unless it has been rehearsed. And reading aloud from a written text is only distantly related to fluent, unrehearsed speech. However, there are powerful reasons for incorporating reading aloud by the teacher, provided it is expressively and accurately done. For one thing, it offers the students a phonological model in the meaningful context of a story or a poem. It also gives students a role model in the pursuit of reading: 'If this is interesting for the teacher, maybe it is interesting for me too.' Finally, it offers students a highly memorable, aesthetic experience of the language they are learning.

Grammar, rule-based teaching is similarly the target of criticism for 'modern' approaches to learning. Clearly, the heavy, deductive, rule-first approach which characterized much traditional teaching is unlikely to appeal to many students. Yet even this kind of teaching does appeal to certain kinds of learner. There is, too, a case to be made for the conscious learning of the rules system for everyone (Walter 2011), and Dörnyei (this volume) speaks of the need to join explicit and implicit learning approaches. Nation (2009) advises that teaching should be divided into four strands with each given roughly *equal* importance: meaning-focused input; meaning-focused output; *language-focused learning* and fluency development. So there is certainly a role for deliberate, conscious learning of grammar (and other parts of the language system).

Finally, and perhaps most perplexingly, the **use of the students' L1** has been virtually banned in many approaches in recent decades. Using the L1 was believed to interfere with the formation of direct connections and the development of an autonomous system for the L2. This view has been increasingly challenged in recent years, most notably by Cook (2001), Deller and Rinvolucri (2002), Butzkamm and Caldwell (2009), Kramsch (2009) and Cook (2010). They point out how almost inevitably the L2 is linked with the L1, especially in the years after the L1 is well established. Using it can save time, avoid confusion and ambiguity, as well as aid discussion and understanding. It can also reduce feelings of stress and inadequacy, and promote feelings of group solidarity and identity. There is little or no evidence that, if used judiciously, it necessarily slows acquisition. And learners tend to refer back and forth between their L1 and L2 anyway, regardless of what applied linguists may say.

The evolution of a purely monolingual model certainly provides part of the explanation, leading, as mentioned above, to the growth of strong commercial, academic and political vested interests in maintaining it.

Uncovering principles in traditional practices

I have tried to show how this constellation of traditional practices might have more to contribute to the language learning process than has been allowed by the applied linguistics establishment. Clearly, however, this would depend on certain conditions being met. It is from these conditions that we can derive some of the key principles I wish to uncover. It will be convenient here to divide these into the *what*, the *why* and the *how* of any given procedure or practice. Let us then look at aspects of the traditional practices discussed above in terms of these three factors.

The what

This refers to the actual, observable procedures carried out. As we have seen, it is possible to use translation techniques which are mechanical and encourage word-for-word processing with no space left for discussion or reflection. Likewise, repetition activities may be used which are automatic, inauthentic and virtually meaningless, as choral repetition can be. Memorization activities may involve no more than the learning of long lists of words out of context, or bland texts. Dictation can be conducted exclusively in the traditional way, with slow reading between pauses. Reading aloud may utilize unappealing texts which are to be read in a mechanical exercise around the class without attention to expression. Grammar rules can be presented as an inflexible system which has to be committed to memory without regard for use. And the L1 can be totally banned from the classroom. However, as I have indicated above, things do not have to be done this way. The content of texts and activities alike can be both cognitively and affectively engaging, challenging, playful and have 'depth' (Craik and Lockhart 1972; Fanselow 1978).

148

The why

Teachers need to be clear about the purposes of presenting activities, whether traditional or not. 'Because it's in the coursebook (or syllabus)' is not a sufficient reason. Neither is 'Because it's fun.' Students need to perceive the relevance of what they do, even when they have implicit trust in their teachers. This entails allowing them a voice and encouraging them to develop critical questioning within a framework of choice. This may be at the level of text selection (Which piece shall we translate? Which poem shall we learn by heart?). Or it may be at the level of choice of activity (Shall we use this text to develop an advertisement or to analyse for the verb tenses?). Or it may simply be the right to ask 'Why are we doing this?'

The how

This refers to the manner in which the procedures are carried out. Again, it is clear that activities can be conducted in an authoritarian, top-down manner, with little regard for the personalities, feelings and aspirations of the learners, who are treated like items on a production line needing to be processed for the final exam. Equally clearly, it does not have to be like this (Arnold 1999). Even when working with uncompromising content, teachers can create an effective learning community through their attitude and the atmosphere that it produces (Hadfield 1992; Dörnyei 2001). Teachers need to be authoritative but not get in the way. Students who trust their teachers will engage in the most unlikely activities in the confidence that their teachers know what they are doing (see Candlin and Crichton, this volume). Likewise, teachers need to be able to react moment by moment to the unfolding, emergent pattern of events. They will know when to push and when to wait, when to withhold and when to reveal, when to speak and when to stay silent, when to challenge and when to support (Underhill, 2008, 2009a, 2009b). At their best, such teachers will be creating 'flow' states in which students lose themselves totally in their learning activity (Csikszentmihalyi 1990, 1997). In other words, for effective learning, the way things are done is often more significant than what is done. In the words of the old song, 'It ain't what you do: it's the way that you do it.'

Designer methods and beyond

In this section, I shall be examining some of the so-called 'designer' methods developed in the 1970s, taking each approach on its own, individual merits so as to tease out the underlying principles I am in search of. Given the constraints of space, I shall assume a certain familiarity among my readers with the observable practices of each of them. Detailed descriptions can be found in Richards and Rodgers (2001), and there are perceptive earlier analyses of several of them in Stevick (1976, 1980).

The Silent Way

Students work with minimal inputs provided by the teacher, who remains silent for most of the time while giving non-verbal and non-evaluative feedback. Students are thrown back on their own internal resources. The materials are austere (the coloured rods and the Fidel charts with a pointer) but mesmeric.

What principles underpin this highly unusual and uncompromising approach to language learning?

- The importance of productive silence and time for it to work in
- The value of challenge and stretching the limits of learner capacity
- The high premium placed on independent effort by learners to develop their own 'inner criteria'
- The economy of materials, which produce maximum output from minimal input
- The elegance deriving from the combination of surface simplicity with cognitive depth
- No fixed syllabus: the teacher works with what evolves within a fairly stringent framework
- The importance of the learning community, which pools the resources of individuals for the common good of the group
- The key role of the severe but totally reliable teacher, who is recognized by learners to be working with them in their interests, however uncomfortable this may be at times.

Community Language Learning (CLL)

In one of the key activities in CLL, students sit in an inward-facing circle. They have a small portable tape recorder. The teacher ('Knower') stands outside the circle. When students wish to say something in the foreign language, they call the Knower, who listens, then whispers the translation to the student, who tries to repeat it, addressing another student. A dialogue develops. The utterances are recorded. At the end of a session, time is left for questions and observations. The tape is then played back and transcribed and language items highlighted and discussed.

What principles are at work here?

- The L1 is respected and used as a bridge to the L2.
- The time is given both for production and for subsequent reflection.
- Learners are relaxed and not under too much pressure to perform.

- The formation of a mutually supportive learning community is crucial.
- It is learners who choose the content. They very soon discover what is possible.
- The group is therefore self-regulatory.
- The teacher's role is to be an available resource to provide input, to offer objective feedback, and to lead discussion and reflection.

Suggestopedia

Learners are put at their ease by sitting in comfortable chairs in a room with low lights. They are all given names and life histories in the foreign culture. After an introductory activity, they hear a reading of a long dialogue, which is available to them in English and their own language. In this active concert reading, the teacher reads the dialogue in a dramatic way, coordinated with classical music. There are games and other activities involving the content of the dialogue to activate the material to be learned. Then they will hear what Lozanov termed the 'passive concert', where the text studied is read again but in a normal voice with baroque music in the background.

The main principles here are as follows:

- The importance of relaxing body and mind through the effects of the lights, the comfortable setting and the music
- The use of a foreign language identity to facilitate entry into the new language
- The importance of using the aesthetic aspects in the language teaching/learning process
- Belief in the ability of the unconscious to help to process very large quantities of input
- The use of play to keep the mind away from excessive concentration and 'suffering-to-learn'
- The central role of the teacher in mediating input and in instilling in learners the belief that they 'can'.

Total Physical Response (TPR)

In TPR learners are not required to produce language for quite a long time. Instead, the emphasis is on showing oral comprehension through acting out instructions and other forms of input from the teacher.

The principles here are:

- The importance of linking language learning inputs to physical action

- The need to delay production until learners are ready for it
- The value of a lowered affective filter by removing anxiety at having to produce language prematurely
- The importance of playfulness and enjoyment
- Making language memorable by making it salient through movement
- The importance of forming a close-knit learning community, with memorable shared experiences (the 'storied class'; Wajnryb 2003).

The Natural Approach

In this approach, the emphasis is on comprehensible input offered at an appropriate level of challenge, in a relaxed atmosphere. The activities it draws on come from many sources, so there is no fixed canon of practice: it is highly eclectic.

It involves the following principles:

- Comprehensible and interesting content is key.
- Ample time is left between comprehension and production.
- The focus is on unconscious acquisition rather than on conscious learning.
- Vocabulary is given precedence over other aspects of the language system.
- There is no predetermined syllabus.
- The level of challenge is set at just above learners' current level (i+1).
- There is a conscious effort to lower the affective filter, to develop high learner self-esteem and confidence.
- The teacher has a key role as provider of comprehensible input and to scaffold the ongoing learning.

The present moment

In this section, I shall examine just four of the range of current methodological approaches: Task-Based Learning (TBL), Cooperative Learning, Dogme and Content and Language Integrated Learning (CLIL). Once again, the objective is to winnow out some of the key underlying principles they call upon that could be expected to lead to more successful language learning.

Task-Based Learning (TBL)

The focus in TBL is the engagement with a range of tasks which involve cooperative work from learners, using language to achieve an outcome

(Willis 1996). The primary focus is on meaning, although form-focused activities may follow the successful completion of the task.

Some of the principles underlying TBL would be:

- The primary focus is on successfully accomplishing a task.
- If there is a syllabus at all, it is based on a progression of tasks.
- Language is acquired unconsciously while the mind is engaged with the task via the negotiation of meaning between students.
- Tasks have to be interesting and at the right level of challenge.
- Group cohesion is a key factor.
- The teacher is key to setting up tasks, monitoring and raising awareness of language which occurs.

Cooperative Learning

The key characteristic of Cooperative Learning is that activities are devised to engage learners in groups where cooperation between them is required. Learning is believed to be achieved through the conversations which emerge in the joint completion of the activities by learners.

Here are some key principles:

- Cooperation not competition is the focus to achieve a low affective filter.
- The group, its positive atmosphere and its shared history is paramount.
- Activities centre on mutual help in carrying them out combined with individual accountability.
- Learning takes place through interaction between learners in the carrying out of activities.
- The teacher's role is to direct activities, monitor learner groups, draw out important language for treatment, and ensure that a positive atmosphere is maintained.

Dogme

The Dogme movement aims to free teachers from over-dependence on materials and equipment so that they can focus on the quality of the interaction between the people in the room (Meddings and Thornbury 2009). It aims for a high level of engagement through interactivity and dialogue. The teacher's job is to scaffold the emergent language sparked by using the experience of the learners as input. Essentially, it is conversation-driven, materials light and focused on shaping the emergent language.

Meaningful classroom activity

The principles it is based on include:

- The use of few or no materials in the classroom
- A high level of personal engagement by learners
- Co-construction of content and language through dialogue
- A syllabus that is not predetermined
- A teaching role that involves scaffolding, monitoring and shaping the learning process
- Placing a high value on socialization and the formation of a learning community.

Content and Language Integrated Learning (CLIL)

This is not so much a method as a radically different approach to teaching language. In fact, it is not primarily about teaching language at all. The prime focus is on teaching a subject through the language (not teaching the language through a subject). Although a good deal has been written about CLIL, there have been few clear proposals for using it (Deller and Price 2007; Dale and Tanner 2012).

Major principles of CLIL include the following:

- It is subject-led, not language-led. Language is the means, not the end.
- Content is therefore relevant as it is related to the subject focus.
- Judicious use of the L1 is permitted.
- Depending on the subject area, multiple intelligences come into play – not simply linguistic intelligence.

Some emerging patterns

It is now time to attempt a synthesis of the principles and practices I have been discussing. To what extent do we find common ground between and among approaches which at first sight might seem very different? To what extent are there irreconcilable differences?

I have grouped here principles and factors which are common across many, though not all, of the approaches discussed. I would like to return now to the categories of *what*, *why* and *how*, bringing in patterns I see which might be useful for the teaching/learning process, whatever specific methodology is used.

The what

- The value of productive silence, allowing time for learners (and teachers) to think, reflect and plan

- Related to this, the need to use time creatively and flexibly, and not simply to be in a rush to 'cover' the lesson, the book or the syllabus
- The importance of group cohesion, where the group forms a cooperative, mutually supportive learning community, with a shared history and shared goals
- The importance of economy and simplicity in materials and procedures
- The need to pitch input at a sufficiently high level of challenge, requiring autonomous learner effort
- Related to this, the need to calibrate the quantity of inputs to learner capacity
- The need to make materials and activities salient, through their intrinsic interest, surprise and relevance (Fanselow 1978; Pugliese 2010)
- The need to arrange for materials and activities to have cognitive and affective 'depth'
- The importance of 'talk', in the sense of interaction from which learning can emerge
- The desirability of including playful activities, preferably with a multi-sensory element (Cook 2000)
- The key factor of the teacher as an authoritative (but not authoritarian) source of input, mediation, feedback and support.

The why

Learning purpose is a notoriously slippery concept, and for many learners there is likely to be a complex mix of motivations for learning the language. I have already suggested above that it is nonetheless important that teachers have a clear idea of why they are doing what they do, and that this should be communicated to the learners as clearly as possible. It is important for learners' trust that they have confidence in what their teacher is asking them to do.

Widdowson (1993) makes a useful distinction between *objectives* and *aims*. Objectives are typically short-term (what is expected by the end of the course), limited in scope to pedagogy and relatively easy to measure. Aims, by contrast, are long-term (often lifelong), far more broad-ranging in terms of personality development and quite difficult to measure. Whereas objectives would deal with the language learned, levels of proficiency, etc., aims would cover more broadly educational and psycho-social long-term development. For example, learning how to learn, critical and creative thinking, life-skills, self-awareness, responsibility for self and others, etc. (Maley 2003).

There are many different contexts for the way in which purpose is communicated to learners. They may simply be told that this is what

Meaningful classroom activity

has been prescribed. Or it may be so obvious as not to need articulation, as in CLIL situations. It may on rare occasions be negotiated between learners and teacher. Or it may be simply taken on trust from the teacher. The key thing is that students know why they are doing what they are asked to do, and that they willingly and consciously comply.

The how

The prime role of the teacher is evident in all the approaches discussed. The attitudes and actions which emerge as most important would seem to be the following:

- The teacher shows whole-hearted commitment to the learners and to the act of teaching. It is this manifest conviction which persuades the class of his or her trustworthiness.
- The teacher offers unconditional respect, support and guidance to learners. Feedback is given impartially and objectively.
- The teacher also creates an atmosphere of openness and mutual trust through activities designed to relax learners and reduce anxiety. This makes it possible for the teacher subsequently to engage learners creatively in activities where they can take risks in the certain knowledge that, if they fall, they will not be hurt.
- This atmosphere is made possible partly through giving responsibility to learners to learn independently, by setting up a firm yet flexible structure, by offering choice wherever possible and by not doing for the learners what they can do for themselves.
- The teacher is in a relationship with the class where neither knows what will happen next. The teacher needs to make use of whatever happens to move the activity or the learning forward (Lutzker 2007; Underhill 2008, 2009a, 2009b). This improvisational skill is not easily acquired and forms part of the evolving 'sense of plausibility' mentioned at the beginning of this chapter.
- Needless to say, the teacher also needs the learners, just as they need him or her. A class which becomes a learning community under the influence of the attitudes and actions of the teacher as set out above will necessarily create its own optimal conditions for learning. It will 'take off' and on some occasions will even enjoy a state of 'flow' (Csikszentmihalyi 1990, 1997).

Points of divergence

Clearly, there are also points where approaches are at variance with each other. These are the main ones to emerge from the foregoing discussion:

- Whether the approach treats learning as a conscious, form-focused process or as a largely unconscious, meaning-focused endeavour (Krashen 1985). These are not, of course, irreconcilable positions, and many teachers contrive to include opportunities for both within the overall framework of their teaching.
- Whether the approach strictly limits the quantum of input, as in the Silent Way, or whether it provides large quantities of 'comprehensible input', as in Suggestopedia or the Natural Approach. There seems to be little room for compromise here, since each stance is predicated on a very different set of beliefs about the nature of language learning.
- Whether the approach entails adherence to a set of well-defined procedures or whether it allows for a degree of eclecticism in the procedures it deploys. I would argue that this may be less important in practice, provided that the teacher is acting in the ways described above in 'The how'. What is done may be less important than the way it is done.
- Whether the use of the L1 is proscribed or judiciously deployed. This seems to be a sticking point, where little or no compromise is possible.
- Whether there is a high degree of external control, in the form of a syllabus, coursebook, examination requirement, etc., or whether there is relative freedom to allow the course to unfold organically. In institutional settings, there may be little room for manoeuvre here either.

Conclusion

What seems to emerge from this discussion is the perhaps unremarkable view that people are more central to the learning enterprise than methods or theories or research findings or systems of education. In the words of one teacher quoted in Cook (2010: 48), 'The point is that my concern about my students as individuals, as human beings, at times transcends my concern for the L2 acquisition process.'

How teachers are and the way they carry out their teaching seems to be far more important than any technical skills they may have learned through training. This is doubly important given that students learn their teachers, not simply the subject they teach. And good teachers learn their students too (see Underhill, this volume). It is this enduring memory we carry away from our educational encounters.

What is really important, then, in addition to the basic training which is of course also necessary, is to find ways to develop the teachers' 'sense of plausibility', and to develop those desirable qualities discussed above under 'The how'. In so doing, we would be creating what Dufeu (1994) calls a pedagogy of 'being' rather than a pedagogy of 'having' ('Une pedagogie de l'être, non de l'avoir'). And central to such a way of teaching would be the building of a confident, mutually supporting learning community – the importance of which has emerged time and again in the above discussion. If we can do that successfully, everything else falls into place.

I conclude with a quotation from John Dewey (1963: 48), which underlines the importance of what learners learn over and above what we may imagine we are teaching them.

> Perhaps the greatest of all pedagogical fallacies is the notion that a person learns only what he [or she] is studying at the time. Collateral learning in the way of the formation of enduring attitudes ... may be ... more important than the lesson in geography or history [or language?]. For these attitudes are fundamentally what count for the future.

References

Allwright, R. (1984) 'Why don't learners learn what teachers teach? The inter-action hypothesis,' in Singleton D. M. and Little, D. (eds.) *Language Learning in Formal and Informal Contexts*, Dublin: Irish Association for Applied Linguistics, pp. 3–18.

Arnold, J. (ed.) (1999) *Affect in Language Learning*, Cambridge: Cambridge University Press.

Bilborough, N. (2011) *Memory Activities for Language Learning*, Cambridge: Cambridge University Press.

Butzkamm, W. and Caldwell, J. A. W. (2009) *The Bilingual Reform: A Paradigm Shift in Foreign Language Teaching*, Tübingen: Narr. Studienbucher.

Cook, G. (2000) *Language Play: Language Learning*, Oxford: Oxford University Press.

Cook, G. (2010) *Translation in Language Teaching: An Argument for Reassessment,* Oxford: Oxford University Press.

Cook, V. (2001) 'Using the first language in the classroom', *Canadian Modern Language Review*, 57(3): 399–423.

Craik, F. I. M. and Lockhart, R. S. (1972) 'Levels of processing: a framework for memory research', *Journal for Verbal Learning and Verbal Behaviour*, 2: 617–84.

Csikszentmihalyi, M. (1990) *Flow: The Psychology of Optimal Experience*, New York: Harper and Row.

Csikszentmihalyi, M. (1997) *Finding Flow*, New York: Basic Books.

Dale, E. and Tanner, R. (2012) *CLIL Activities: A Resource for Subject and Language Teachers*, Cambridge: Cambridge University Press.

Davis, P. and Rinvolucri, M. (1988) *Dictation*, Cambridge: Cambridge University Press.

Winnowing the past: towards a principled eclecticism

Deller, S. and Price, C. (2007) *Teaching Other Subjects Through English*, Oxford: Oxford University Press.

Deller, S. and Rinvolucri, M. (2002) *Using the Mother Tongue*, London: Delta Publishing.

Dewey, J. (1963) *Experience and Education: The Kappa Delta Pi Lectures*, London: Collier Books.

Dörnyei, Z. (2001) *Motivational Strategies in the Language Classroom*, Cambridge: Cambridge University Press.

Dufeu, B. (1994) *Teaching Myself*, Oxford: Oxford University Press.

Duff, A. (1989) *Translation*, Oxford: Oxford University Press.

Duff, A. and Maley, A. (2007) *Literature*, Oxford: Oxford University Press.

Fanselow, J. (1978) *Breaking Rules*, New York and London: Longman.

Grellet, F. (1991) *Apprendre a traduire: typologie d'exercices de traduction*, Nancy: Presses Universitaires de Nancy.

Hadfield, J. (1992) *Classroom Dynamics*, Oxford: Oxford University Press.

Helgesen, M. (2006) 'English in 3D: a fresh look at traditional tasks', in Mukundan, J. (ed.) *Focus on ELT Materials II*, Petaling Jaya: Pearson Malaysia, pp. 116–29. Available online at http://tinyurl.com/Helgesen3D.

Howatt, A. P. R. and Widdowson, H. G. (2004) *A History of English Language Teaching*, 2nd edn, Oxford: Oxford University Press.

Kramsch, C. (2009) *The Multi-lingual Subject*, Oxford: Oxford University Press.

Krashen S. D. (1985) *The Input Hypothesis: Issues and Implications*, London: Longman.

Kumaravadivelu, B. (2003) *Beyond Methods: Macrostrategies for Language Teaching*, New Haven and London: Yale University Press.

Lutzker, P. (2007) *The Art of Foreign Language Teaching*, Tübingen and Basel: Francke Verlag.

Maley, A. (1999) 'Choral speaking', *English Teaching Professional*, **12**: 9–11.

Maley, A. (2000) *The Language Teacher's Voice*, Oxford: Heinemann/Macmillan.

Maley, A. (2003) 'Inputs, processes and outcomes in materials development', in Mukundan, J. (ed.) *Readings on ELT Material*, Serdang: Universiti Putra Malaysia Press, pp. 21–31.

Maley, A. (2005) 'The creative spark in ELT: a retrospective, Part 1', *Folio*, **10**(1): 9–13.

Maley, A. (2006) 'The creative spark in ELT: Part 2', *Folio*, **10**(2): 9–13.

Meara, P. (2009) *Connected Words: Word Associations in Second Language Acquisition*, Amsterdam: John Benjamins.

Meddings, L. and Thornbury, S. (2009) *Teaching Unplugged*, London: Delta Publishing.

Nation, P. (2009) *Teaching Vocabulary: Strategies and Techniques*, London: Cengage Learning.

Prabhu, N. S. (1990) 'There is no best method – why?', *TESOL Quarterly*, **24**(2): 161–76.

159

Meaningful classroom activity

Prabhu, N. S. (1998) 'Teaching is at most hoping for the best', *Singapore: Seameo RELC Anthology*, 40: 48–57.
Pugliese, C. (2010) *Being Creative*, London: Delta Publishing.
Richards, J. C. and Rodgers, T. S. (2001) *Approaches and Methods in Language Teaching*, Cambridge: Cambridge University Press.
Schmidt, R. (1990) 'The role of consciousness in second language learning', *Applied Linguistics*, 11(2): 129–58.
Schumann, J. (1999) 'A neurobiological perspective on affect and methodology in second language learning', in Arnold, J. (ed.) *Affect in Language Learning*. Cambridge: Cambridge University Press, pp. 28–42.
Stevick, E. W. (1976) *Memory, Meaning and Method: Some Psychological Perspectives on Language Learning*, Boston: Heinle & Heinle.
Stevick, E. W. (1980) *Teaching Languages: A Way and Ways*, Rowley, MA: Newbury House.
Tannen, D. (1989) *Talking Voices*, Cambridge: Cambridge University Press.
Underhill, A. (2005) *Sound Foundations*, London: Macmillan.
Underhill, A. (2008) 'Work with what comes', *IATEFL Teacher Development Newsletter*, no. 59, pp. 10–12.
Underhill, A. (2009a) 'Make plans ... but if they work out, something may be missing ...', *IATEFL Teacher Development Newsletter*, no. 60, pp. 10–12.
Underhill, A. (2009b) 'Ready to be surprised: improvisation and working with what comes', *IATEFL Teacher Development Newsletter*, no. 61, pp. 6–9.
Wajnryb, R. (2003) *Stories*, Cambridge: Cambridge University Press.
Walter, C. (2011) 'Should we be planning to teach grammar? If so, how?', plenary paper presented at the 45th Annual International IATEFL Conference, Brighton, 15–19 April.
Widdowson, H. G. (1993) *Learning Purposes and Language Use*, Oxford: Oxford University Press.
Willis, J. (1996) *A Framework for Task-based Learning*, London: Longman.

10 Communicative Language Teaching in the twenty-first century: the 'Principled Communicative Approach'

Zoltán Dörnyei

Introduction

Earl Stevick has always been interested in improving language teaching methodology, and he has never been afraid of innovation. His seminal work, *Teaching Languages: A Way and Ways* (Stevick 1980), introduced many of us to Counselling-Learning and Suggestopedia for the first time, and in *Memory, Meaning and Method: A View of Language Teaching.* (Stevick 1996) he discussed a wide range of theoretical and practical considerations to help us better understand the intricate cognitive and interpersonal processes whereby a language is acquired and then used for meaningful communication. The proposal in this chapter to revitalize Communicative Language Teaching (CLT) in the light of contemporary scholarly advances is fully within the spirit of Earl's approach.[1]

By the turn of the new millennium, CLT had become a real buzzword in language teaching methodology, but the extent to which the term covers a well-defined and uniform teaching method is highly questionable. In fact, since the genesis of CLT in the early 1970s, its proponents have developed a very wide range of variants that were only loosely related to each other (for overviews, see Savignon 2005; Spada 2007). In this chapter I first look at the core characteristics of CLT to explore the roots of the diverse interpretations and then argue that in order for CLT to fulfil all the expectations attached to it in the twenty-first century, the method needs to be revised according to the latest findings of psycholinguistic research. I will conclude the chapter by outlining the main principles of a proposed revised approach that I have termed the 'Principled Communicative Approach' (PCA).

[1] This chapter draws on Chapter 7 of my book *The Psychology of Second Language Acquisition* (Dörnyei 2009), where further discussion can be found. The text is an edited version of a plenary talk presented at the 34th National Convention of TESOL-Italy in Rome, 2009, first published in *Perspectives*. I am grateful to the editor of this journal, Lucilla Lopriore, for permission to adapt the text for this volume.

The traditional communicative approach

Communicative Language Teaching was introduced at the beginning of the 1970s by British and American scholars to promote the teaching of usable communicative skills in L2 instruction. Although it was seen by many as a counter-reaction to the Audiolingual method that dominated the 1960s, the main goal of CLT – to develop a functional communicative L2 competence in the learners – was actually similar to the primary audiolingual objective. However, CLT pursued the communicative agenda in a radically different manner. Instead of the audiolingual attempt of trying to build up an implicit L2 knowledge base through drilling and memorization,[2] CLT methodology was centred around the learner's participatory experience in meaningful L2 interaction in (often simulated) communicative situations, which underscored the significance of less structured and more creative language tasks. For this reason, the learning of scripted dialogues was replaced by games, problem-solving tasks and unscripted situational role plays, and pattern drilling was either completely abandoned or replaced by 'communicative drills'.

At the heart of the Audiolingual/CLT difference lay a basic contrast in orientation: audiolingualism was associated with a specific learning theory – behaviourism – and therefore it was the first language teaching method that consciously aspired to build on the principles of the psychology of learning, whereas the communicative reform in the 1970s was centred around the radical renewal of the linguistic course content without any systematic psychological conception to guide the actual process of learning to accompany it. This is well illustrated by the fact that while the linguistic content of communicative syllabuses was informed by a number of cutting-edge theoretical strands, such as Austin (1962) and Searle's (1969) speech act theory, Hymes' (1972) model of communicative competence and its application to L2 proficiency by Canale and Swain (1980) and Canale (1983), as well as Halliday's (1985) systemic functional grammar, the only learning-specific principle that was available for CLT materials developers and practitioners was the broad tenet of 'learning through doing', coupled with the only marginally less ambiguous guideline of developing the learners' communicative competence through their active participation in *seeking situational meaning*. Thus, the conception underlying learning within CLT was confined to the widespread assumption that the

---

[2] Of course, audiolingualism was more complex than that, but a broad characterization is sufficient for the current discussion; for more details, see Castagnaro (2006) and Dörnyei (2009).

learners' communicative competence develops automatically through their active participation in meaningful communicative tasks.

The vagueness of the 'seeking situational meaning' tenet, in turn, resulted in a very wide range of variants of CLT in terms of actual classroom application in both the UK and the USA. Richards and Rodgers (2001: 155) have rightly pointed out in respect of CLT that 'There is no single text or authority on it, nor any single model that is universally accepted as authoritative.' As one extreme, for example, people often associate CLT with a strictly-no-grammar approach, epitomized by Krashen's (1985) *The Input Hypothesis*. In contrast, some of the founders of CLT were quite keen to emphasize a salient structural linguistic component, as illustrated, for example, by the starting sentence of Littlewood's (1981: 1) highly influential teaching methodology text: 'One of the most characteristic features of communicative language teaching is that it pays systematic attention to functional as well as structural aspects of language, combining these into a more fully communicative view.' These contrasting stances – referred to by Thornbury (1999) as 'shallow-end' and 'deep-end' approaches, respectively – correspond to the psychological distinction of *implicit* versus *explicit learning*, and because this distinction will play a central role in conceiving the PCA, let me elaborate on it.

Implicit versus explicit language learning

Explicit learning refers to the learner's conscious and deliberate attempt to master some material or solve a problem. This is the learning type emphasized by most school instruction. In contrast, *implicit learning* involves acquiring skills and knowledge without conscious awareness, that is, automatically and with no conscious attempt to learn them. Amongst language teachers, the emerging view of a typical communicative classroom has been that it should approximate a naturalistic language acquisition environment as closely as possible, thereby providing plenty of authentic input to feed the students' implicit learning processes. This view was partly motivated by the fact that the main language learning model for humans – the mastery of our mother tongue – predominantly involves implicit processes without any explicit teaching: children acquire the complex system of their L1 through engaging in natural and meaningful communication with their parents and other caretakers.

Unfortunately, the problem with implicit language learning is that while it does such a great job in generating native-speaking L1 proficiency in infants, it does not seem to work efficiently when we want to master an L2 at a later stage in our lives. This is regrettable, but the fact is that – alas! – untutored learning through simple exposure to natural language input does not seem to lead to sufficient progress in L2 attainment for most school learners. Strong evidence for this claim has come from two main sources (for a detailed discussion, see Dörnyei 2009): (a) experiences in educational contexts – particularly in immersion programmes – that provide optimal conditions for implicit learning and yet which typically fail to deliver native-like L2 proficiency; and (b) reviews of empirical studies that specifically compared implicit and explicit instruction, which demonstrate a significant advantage of explicit types of L2 instruction over implicit types (for a seminal paper in this regard, see Norris and Ortega 2000).

Thus, the available evidence confirms Lightbown and Spada's (2006: 176) conclusion that 'we do not find support for the hypothesis that language acquisition will take care of itself if second language learners simply focus on meaning in comprehensible input'. In other words, mere exposure to L2 input accompanied by communicative practice is not sufficient, and, therefore, we need explicit learning procedures – such as focus on form or some kind of controlled practice – to push learners beyond communicatively effective language towards target-like second language ability. Ellis (2007: 26) summarizes the overall consensus amongst scholars as follows:

> As with other implicit modules, when automatic capabilities fail, there follows a call for recruiting additional collaborative conscious support: We only think about walking when we stumble, about driving when a child runs into the road, and about language when communication breaks down. In unpredictable conditions, the capacity of consciousness to organize existing knowledge in new ways is indispensable.

It is important to emphasize here that the search for ways of reintegrating explicit learning processes in modern language teaching methodology does not mean that we should regard these processes as replacements of implicit learning. Instead, the real challenge is to maximize the *cooperation* of explicit and implicit learning; accordingly, as will be illustrated below, finding ways of meeting this challenge has been the main driving force of developing the PCA.

The ongoing transformation of CLT

As we saw above, relying on a purely implicit learning approach has turned out to be less than successful in L2 learning in general, and therefore the past decade has seen a gradual transformation of our idealized CLT image. In her summary of this shift, Nina Spada (2007: 271) explains that 'most second language educators agree that CLT is undergoing a transformation – one that includes increased recognition of and attention to language form within exclusively or primarily meaning-oriented CLT approaches to second language instruction'. It was in this vein that in 1997 Marianne Celce-Murcia, Sarah Thurrell and I suggested (Celce-Murcia et al. 1997, 1998) that CLT had reached a new phase that we termed the 'Principled Communicative Approach':

> In sum, we believe that CLT has arrived at a turning point: Explicit, direct elements are gaining significance in teaching communicative abilities and skills. The emerging new approach can be described as a principled communicative approach; by bridging the gap between current research on aspects of communicative competence and actual communicative classroom practice, this approach has the potential to synthesize direct, knowledge-oriented and indirect, skill-oriented teaching approaches. Therefore, rather than being a complete departure from the original, indirect practice of CLT, it extends and further develops CLT methodology.
>
> (Celce-Murcia et al. 1997: 147–8)

As we emphasized, the increasing directness of the emerging principled CLT could not be equated with a back-to-grammar tendency. Rather, it involved an attempt to extend the systematic treatment of language issues traditionally restricted to sentence-bound rules (i.e. grammar) to the explicit development of other knowledge areas and skills necessary for efficient communication. Looking back, I can see that although we did highlight the need to integrate direct, knowledge-oriented (i.e. explicit) and indirect, skill-oriented (i.e. implicit) teaching approaches, we could have gone further in underlining the need to complement the proposed new linguistic content with an awareness of the psychological dimension of learning. It seems to me that this search for integration has been the most fruitful direction of language teaching methodology in the new millennium, with the most forward-pointing developments in research targeting the various modes of the explicit–implicit interface taking place in three central areas: (a) *focus on form* and *form-focused instruction*; (b) *fluency* and *automatization*; and (c) *formulaic language*. All three areas have extensive literatures raising complex issues. Here I will offer a brief sketch of the key topics.

Focus on form (FonF) and form-focused instruction (FFI)

Focus on form (FonF) and form-focused instruction (FFI) indicate a concern with the structural system of language from a communicative perspective. In other words, they represent a halfway position between a concern for communicative meaning and the linguistic features of the language code, calling for a primarily meaning-focused instruction in which some degree of attention is paid to form. Thus, FonF/FFI refer to a new type of grammar instruction that intends to remain fully compatible with communicative principles in that it foregrounds the meaning-focused and personally significant nature of language tasks, and in that sense this approach is a prime example of trying to implement the explicit–implicit interface in actual classroom practice. One of the main proponents of the approach, Rod Ellis (2008), has drawn up the following comprehensive framework of the various form-focused options, distinguishing four macro-options:

- *Input-based options* involve the manipulation of the language input that learners are exposed to or are required to process. The main types of this macro-option are *input flooding* (input that contains an artificially increased number of examples of the target structure), *enhanced input* (input in which the target feature is made salient to the learners in some way, e.g. by highlighting it visually in a text), and *structured input* (input that the learner is forced to process in order to be able to provide a required follow-up response, e.g. ticking an answer option in an opinion survey).
- *Explicit options* involve instruction that can be direct (learners are provided with metalinguistic descriptions of the target feature, e.g. in deductive instruction) or indirect (learners are provided with data illustrating the target feature and are required to 'discover' the rule for themselves, e.g. in inductive instruction).
- *Production options* involve instruction geared at enabling and inducing learners to produce utterances containing the target structure. This type can be further subdivided in terms of whether it involves text-manipulation (e.g. fill-in-the-blank exercises) or text-creation.
- *Corrective feedback options* involve either implicit feedback (e.g. recasts or clarification requests) or explicit correction (e.g. metalinguistic explanation or elicitation), and we can also distinguish between feedback that is input-providing (e.g. recasts or metalinguistic explanation) or output-prompting (e.g. requests for clarification or elicitation).

Fluency and automatization

Everybody who has ever tried to speak in a foreign language knows that the accurate use of linguistic form is not the only, and often not even the most serious, concern with regard to communicative effectiveness. In many respects L2 *fluency* is equally, if not more, important. In the psychological literature, fluency is discussed under the broader concept of 'automaticity/automatization', and the promotion of fluency is usually subsumed under 'skill learning theory'. Thus, from a psychological point of view, the relevant issue to explore is how L2 skills can be automatized.

Skill learning theory proposes the following basic sequence: automatization requires implicit (or *procedural*) knowledge, which in turn requires initial explicit (or *declarative*) input and conscious consecutive practice. Accordingly, a systematically designed fluency-building task will include an initial *declarative input stage* and subsequent *extended practice*, which can be further divided into *controlled practice* and *open-ended practice* (for more details, see Anderson 2000; DeKeyser 2007; Ranta and Lyster 2007):

- The *declarative input stage* is to provide clear and concise rules and sufficient examples that the learner can then interpret and rehearse, thereby raising awareness of and internalizing the skill.
- The *controlled practice stage* should offer opportunities for abundant repetition within a narrow context that still maintains personal significance and communicative meaningfulness (e.g. administering a verbal opinion survey to a group of people in which everybody has to be asked the same questions). Therefore, the key to the effectiveness of this stage is to design interesting drills that are not demotivating (see Dörnyei 2001; Dörnyei and Ushioda 2010) and which are related to some communicative function. The most elaborate operationalization of this stage is offered by the 'creative automatisation' tasks of Gatbonton and Segalowitz (1988, 2005).
- The *open-ended practice stage* involves the continuous improvement in the performance of a skill that is already well established in a wider and wider applicability range. In spite of the unscripted, free nature of this phase, it can still benefit from some added explicit focus, for example by highlighting some L2 functions associated with a list of specific phrases as specific targets for practice.

Interestingly, this *declarative input → controlled practice → open-ended practice* sequence is reminiscent of the well-known methodological progression of *presentation → practice → production* (PPP).

Formulaic language

There is something fundamental about *formulaic language* such as lexical phrases, idioms, conventionalized expressions, collocations, etc. (for overviews, see Schmitt 2004; Wray 2008). Widdowson (1989: 135), for example, argued that 'communicative competence is not a matter of knowing rules ... It is much more a matter of knowing a stock of partially pre-assembled patterns, formulaic frameworks', and indeed many would agree with him that competent speakers of a language are in command of thousands (if not tens of thousands) of language chunks, and use them as basic building blocks in their speech and writing. With his 'idiom principle', Sinclair (1991: 112) also underscores the important role idioms (formulaic sequences) play in discourse. As he concludes, 'The overwhelming nature of this evidence leads us to elevate the principle of idiom from being a rather minor feature, compared with grammar, to being at least as important as grammar in the explanation of how meaning arises in text.'

It is important to note that formulaic language competence is directly linked to automatized, fluent language production. It has been traditionally assumed that formulaic sequences are stored in the memory as single units and therefore their retrieval is cognitively of a relatively undemanding nature. This in turn allows the speaker to attend to other aspects of communication and to plan larger pieces of discourse, which would naturally facilitate fluent language production under real-time conditions.

There has been relatively little research on how to teach formulaic language in classroom contexts; however, things have started to change and some important studies have been published on the classroom practice of promoting chunks and formulaic sequences (e.g. Gatbonton and Segalowitz 2005; Boers et al. 2006; Taguchi 2007; Lindstromberg and Boers 2008). The most principled attempt to develop a coherent approach for the promotion of formulaic sequences has been made by Gatbonton and Segalowitz (1988, 2005); their proposed methodology is called ACCESS, standing for 'Automatization in Communicative Contexts of Essential Speech Segments', and it offers a principled adaptation of CLT that aims to generate fluency by drawing on the theories of automatization and formulaic language.

Conclusion

I have argued in this chapter that the real challenge for language teaching methodology is to specify the nature of the optimal cooperation between explicit and implicit learning processes in a principled manner. Working out the details of a new Principled Communicative Approach is clearly an ongoing process, but we can formulate some key guiding principles based on the available research for the approach. I would like to conclude by offering seven key – and somewhat overlapping – principles that are in accordance with the state of the art of our research knowledge of instructed second language acquisition.

The personal significance principle. PCA should be *meaning-focused* and *personally significant* as a whole. This has been the basic tenet of

168

student-centred CLT, and I believe that this principle is just as valid now as when it was first formulated.

The controlled practice principle. While the overall purpose of language learning is to prepare the learners for meaningful communication, skill learning theory suggests that – similar to the training of musicians or athletes – it should also include *controlled practice activities* to promote the automatization of L2 skills. The purpose of this practice should be clearly explained to the learners and the content/format should be made as motivating as possible within the tasks' inherent constraints.

The declarative input principle. To provide jump starts for subsequent automatization, PCA should contain *explicit initial input* components. This declarative input can be offered in several ways, including the potential utilization of accelerated learning techniques and rote learning.

The focus-on-form principle. While maintaining an overall meaning-oriented approach, PCA should also pay attention to the *formal/structural aspects* of the L2 that determine accuracy and appropriateness at the linguistic, discourse and pragmatic levels. An important hallmark of good teaching is finding the *optimal balance* between implicit and explicit instruction through administering a good mixture of meaning-based and form-focused activities in the dynamic classroom context.

The formulaic language principle. PCA should include the teaching of *formulaic language* as a featured component. There should be sufficient awareness raising of the significance and pervasiveness of formulaic language in real-life communication, and selected phrases should be practised and recycled intensively.

The language exposure principle. PCA should offer learners *extensive exposure to large amounts of L2 input* that can feed the learners' implicit learning mechanisms. In order to make the most of this exposure, learners should be given some explicit preparation in terms of *pre-task activities* (e.g. pre-reading/listening/watching tasks or explanations of some salient aspects of the material) to prime them for maximum intake.

The focused interaction principle. PCA should offer learners ample opportunities to participate in *genuine L2 interaction*. For best effect, such communicative practice should always have a specific formal or functional focus and should always be associated with target phrases to practise.

In sum, the essence of the Principled Communicative Approach (PCA) that I am advocating is the creative integration of meaningful communication with relevant declarative input and the automatization of both linguistic rules and lexical items. In instructed second language acquisition, *the more is not merrier if it is not focused.*

Meaningful classroom activity

References

Anderson, J. R. (2000) *Learning and Memory: An Integrated Approach*, 2nd edn, Hoboken, NJ: John Wiley and Sons.

Austin, J. L. (1962) *How to Do Things with Words*, Oxford: Clarendon Press.

Boers, F., Eyckmans, J., Kappel, J., Stengers, H. and Demecheleer, M. (2006) 'Formulaic sequences and perceived oral proficiency: putting a Lexical Approach to the test', *Language Teaching Research*, 10(3): 245–61.

Canale, M. (1983) 'From communicative competence to communicative language pedagogy', in Richards, J. C. and Schmidt. R. W. (eds.) *Language and Communication*, Harlow: Longman, pp. 2–27.

Canale, M. and Swain, M. (1980) 'Theoretical bases of communicative approaches to second language teaching and testing', *Applied Linguistics*, 1: 1–47.

Castagnaro, J. (2006) 'Audiolingual method and behaviorism: from misunderstanding to myth', *Applied Linguistics*, 27(3): 519–26.

Celce-Murcia, M., Dörnyei, Z. and Thurrell, S. (1997) 'Direct approaches in L2 instruction: a turning point in communicative language teaching?', *TESOL Quarterly*, 31: 141–52.

Celce-Murcia, M., Dörnyei, Z. and Thurrell, S. (1998) 'On directness in communicative language teaching', *TESOL Quarterly*, 32: 116–19.

DeKeyser, R. M. (ed.) (2007) *Practice in Second Language: Perspectives from Applied Linguistics and Cognitive Psychology*, New York: Cambridge University Press.

Dörnyei, Z. (2001) *Motivational Strategies in the Language Classroom*, Cambridge: Cambridge University Press.

Dörnyei, Z. (2009) *The Psychology of Second Language Acquisition*, Oxford: Oxford University Press.

Dörnyei, Z. and Ushioda, E. (2010) *Teaching and Researching Motivation*, 2nd edn, Harlow: Longman.

Ellis, N. C. (2007) 'The weak interface, consciousness, and form-focused instruction: mind the doors', in Fotos, S. S. and Nassaji, H. (eds.) *Form-Focused Instruction and Teacher Education*, Oxford: Oxford University Press, pp. 17–34.

Ellis, R. (2008) *The Study of Second Language Acquisition*, 2nd edn, Oxford: Oxford University Press.

Gatbonton, E. and Segalowitz, N. (1988) 'Creative automatisation: principles for promoting fluency within a communicative framework', *TESOL Quarterly*, 22(3), 473–92.

Gatbonton, E. and Segalowitz, N. (2005) 'Rethinking communicative language teaching: a focus on access to fluency', *Canadian Modern Language Review*, 61(3): 325–53.

Halliday, M. A. K. (1985) *An Introduction to Functional Grammar*, London: Edward Arnold.

Hymes, D. H. (1972) 'On communicative competence', in Pride, J. B. and Holmes, J. (eds.) *Sociolinguistics*, Harmondsworth: Penguin, pp. 269–93.

Krashen, S. D. (1985) *The Input Hypothesis: Issues and Implications*, London: Longman.

Lightbown, M. and Spada, N. (2006) *How Languages Are Learned*, 3rd edn, Oxford: Oxford University Press.

Lindstromberg, S. and Boers, F. (2008) *Teaching Chunks of Language: From Noticing to Remembering*, Innsbruck: Helbling Languages.

Littlewood, W. (1981) *Communicative Language Teaching: An Introduction*, Cambridge: Cambridge University Press.

Norris, J. M. and Ortega, L. (2000) 'Effectiveness of L2 instruction: a research synthesis and quantitative meta-analysis', *Language Learning*, 50(3): 417–528.

Ranta, L. and Lyster, R. (2007) 'A cognitive approach to improving immersion students' oral language abilities: the Awareness-Practice-Feedback sequence', in DeKeyser, R. M. (ed.) *Practice in Second Language: Perspectives from Applied Linguistics and Cognitive Psychology*, New York: Cambridge University Press, pp. 141–60.

Richards, J. C. and Rodgers, T. S. (2001) *Approaches and Methods in Language Teaching*, 2nd edn, Cambridge: Cambridge University Press.

Savignon, S. J. (2005) 'Communicative language teaching: strategies and goals', in Hinkel, E. (ed.) *Handbook of Research in Second Language Teaching and Learning*, Mahwah, NJ: Lawrence Erlbaum, pp. 635–51.

Searle, J. R. (1969) *Speech Acts*, Cambridge: Cambridge University Press.

Schmitt, N. (ed.) (2004) *Formulaic Sequences*, Amsterdam: John Benjamins.

Sinclair, J. (1991) *Corpus, Concordance, Collocation*, Oxford: Oxford University Press.

Spada, N. (2007) 'Communicative language teaching: current status and future prospects', in Cummins, J. and Davison, C. (eds.) *International Handbook of English Language Teaching*, New York: Springer, Vol. I, pp. 271–88.

Stevick, E. W. (1980) *Teaching Languages: A Way and Ways*, Rowley, MA: Newbury House.

Stevick, E. W. (1996) *Memory, Meaning and Method: A View of Language Teaching*, 2nd edn, Boston: Heinle & Heinle.

Taguchi, N. (2007) 'Chunk learning and the development of spoken discourse in a Japanese as a foreign language classroom', *Language Teaching Research*, 11(4): 433–57.

Thornbury, S. (1999) *How to Teach Grammar*, London: Longman.

Widdowson, H. G. (1989) 'Knowledge of language and ability for use', *Applied Linguistics*, 10: 128–37.

Wray, A. (2008) *Formulaic Language: Pushing the Boundaries*, Oxford: Oxford University Press.

171

11 Adapting ways for meaningful action: ZPDs and ZPAs

Tim Murphey

> ... adaptation is inevitable; it ought therefore to receive more attention and more prestige than it usually does. The other theme is that language study is inevitably a total human experience; writers and teachers ought therefore to act as though it is.
>
> (Stevick 1971: vii)

Introduction

This chapter suggests three beneficial shifts concerning change and adaptation in the classroom.[1] The first is to move from seeing learning in terms of the container metaphor, where knowledge is simply transferred by the teacher into a container (the learner's head) as if it were an entity (a thing), to a view of learning as an incremental process over time involving the participants adjusting to each other, the context and their goals. Second, to intensify engagement more with others in order to improve our techniques of observation and interaction. Third, to increase our contact with diversity so as to stimulate innovation and adaptation for a 'total human experience'. I conclude that harmonizing, that is, being in rapport with others and enjoying a learning flow, is not a thing but an activity which demands continual adjusting to the various changes inside and between participants in a complex world.

Learning greatly depends on the ability of the people in learning encounters to adapt to each other in multiple ways to create meaningful actions that engage and motivate. It follows that this is not just a cognitive adjustment, but inevitably a total human experience. Earl Stevick wrote much about adapting and emphasized it often in his work. One

---

[1] This chapter is based in part on the following two conference papers: 'Proactive Adjusting to the Zone of Proximal Development: Learner and Teacher Strategies', in a symposium organized by Gordon Wells entitled 'The ZPD: relationship between education and development', at the 2nd Conference for Socio-Cultural Research Vygotsky-Piaget (celebrating both researchers who were both born in 1896), the Psychological Sciences Research Institute, Geneva, Switzerland, 11–15 September 1996; 'Strategies for Zoning in on the ZPD', in the colloquium on Vygotsky's Zone of Proximal Development, Vancouver, B.C. Canada, American Association of Applied Linguistics (AAAL), 14 March 2000.

of his early books was called *Adapting and Writing Language Lessons* (1971), on which I based my MA thesis, 'Situationally Motivated Teacher Produced Texts', where I proposed that teachers create their own texts adapted to local contexts and student needs. Later, I turned to more 'situationally motivated student produced texts', advocating that students could have a hand in producing many of the materials which would be even more relevant, at their level and intensely student-centred. This necessarily displayed a certain amount of Trust in students as collaborators (see Candlin and Crichton, this volume) and invited more agency. Such adapting to student needs and local conditions is sometimes described as scaffolding (Wood et al. 1976), an attempt to create and interact with students' zones of proximal development (ZPDs), defined as 'the distance between the actual developmental level as determined by independent problem solving and the level of potential development as determined through problem solving under adult guidance, or in collaboration with more capable peers' (Vygotsky 1978: 86).

Stevick also describes teachers adapting the way they use materials, 'the favorable reaction of the users [of the adapted materials] cannot be explained in terms of clever, innovative features of the materials themselves, for there were none. They depended, rather, on the extent to which the staff forced each of the "suggestions for use" to yield both practical and psychological satisfactions' (Stevick 1971: 219). In 1996, at the centennial anniversary conference of Vygotsky and Piaget, I pointed out that teachers and students had variable abilities to adapt or adjust to partners and situations, displaying variable zones of proximal adjusting or ZPAs (Murphey 1996). Obviously, some people can and do adjust in many ways to help themselves and others learn, not only showing knowledge of motivational techniques and needed input and activities, but also giving emotional support and attention to relationship and identity factors. Most of us recognize that we can adjust well in certain situations with certain people and less so in others. Intuitively also, it stands to reason that it is easier for students to adjust to each other than to the teacher or native speakers, who are distant in proficiency, age and possibly in interests.

In Murphey (1990: 168), I playfully explained adjusting in the following manner using Figure 11.1. In the café, you (a) and I (b) are separated somewhat by our different backgrounds and world maps. The distance between our backgrounds (c) will dictate how much we will have to adjust to each other in order to have quality interaction. However, the context (d), the café, is one that is fairly conducive to adjusting. The music is relaxing and there are just a few noises from the kitchen and occasionally the sound of traffic when someone enters (arrows). The different ways we can adjust (linguistically, emotionally, physically, etc.) are represented by

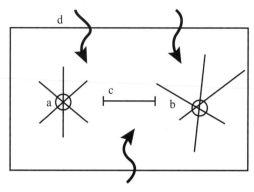

Figure 11.1 Café des Artists

the lines running through each of us. Ideally they match or mirror each other. If they don't match and we are unwilling to adjust to the other, we will have problems communicating (Murphey 1990: 3–4).

Of course a classroom and café are not completely the same environments, but the ways in which we adjust physically, emotionally, linguistically, etc. to interlocutors are quite similar and very important in building good rapport.

Adapting shadowing ways

Vygotsky's experiments had a specific set of questions to act as prompts to measure the ZPD of children, that is to measure what they knew and what they needed for a specific task. However, outside the laboratory, the variable abilities of interlocutors make standard prompts highly unlikely in natural interaction. Aljaafreh and Lantolf (1994: 468) state that the process of adjusting to the ZPD is a 'continuous *assessment* of the novice's needs and abilities and the *tailoring* of help to those conditions'. It is clear that learners are faced with teachers and partners who have varying ability to make those *assessments* and to *tailor* their help, that is, different ZPAs. At the same time, learners vary in that they give different sets of clues as to the input they need for their particular learning at their particular stages. A more silent student is often hard to help because we have little information to go on. Thus, ZPDs and ZPAs are interactive and influence each other considerably, they are not separate but co-constucting and actually everyone has both.

The typical way of thinking about the ZPD is that teachers adjust to learners' ZPDs. However, different teachers have different degrees of

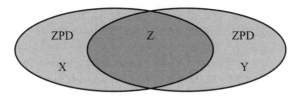

X = area of needs not adjusted to
Y = area of potential to adjust but not appropriate / not needed here
Z = match between ability to adjust and needs

Figure 11.2   The zone of learning flow

flexibility to adjust depending on the learner, topic and process. And learners may have strategies that help others to adjust to them (e.g. shadowing and displaying what they need). Thus, all interactants have both ZPDs and ZPAs, students working together as well as teachers working with students, and while we usually assume that it is the more capable partner who is responsible for adjusting to the less proficient, we all can actually adjust in many ways to each other and everybody has their own ZPD. However, for the sake of simplicity in what follows, we will focus mainly on learners' ZPDs and teachers' ZPAs (but still hopefully teachers are learning at the same time to broaden their ZPD and students are also adjusting to each other in interactive classes). When the ZPDs and ZPAs significantly overlap, as in Figure 11.2 above, there is a good match between students' readiness to learn and a helper's ability to provide what they need.

Shadowing (Murphey 2001a) is one simple strategy that can help interlocutors construct better ZPAs and ZPDs, and, at the micro-interaction level, it seems to hold a lot of promise for giving more actual control of a conversation to the less able partner. Shadowing is simply repeating the words someone says immediately after they say it, on continuums from complete to partial, out loud to silent, and with no interaction to full-blown rejoinders, comments and questions. However, this simple repeating can have a variety of effects psychologically and pragmatically for learning, especially in conversational discourse. Being shadowed usually causes one to chunk ones phrases to the length that a partner can comfortably repeat. In effect, shadowing shows the speaker the moment-to-moment processing that goes on inside the learner's brain so that appropriate adjustments can be made. When working with this in class, I generally ask students to do complete shadowing only at the beginning of conversations and in trouble spots (otherwise Grice's maxim of quantity, saying too much, would be violated). After initially showing what they are capable of through complete shadowing, learners are asked to switch to selective and interactive shadowing with questions and comments, which is actually more like a good, normal conversation with parts of each other's speech being repeated for confirmation and clarification. Research on shadowing (Murphey 2001a) shows that a lot of Long's (1983) strategies and tactics (see Table 11.1) occur automatically when students shadow each other in classroom conversations. Here, ST6, 'Repeat other's utterances', seems to be a simple form of shadowing itself whereas T2, 'Request clarification', is what is implied pragmatically when a repeated utterance is very different, or the shadower stops short or uses rising intonation when repeating. Using these strategies well produces a kind of natural shadowing and helps

Table 11.1 *Devices used by native speakers to modify the interactional structure of NS–NNS conversation (Long 1983)*

Strategies (S) (for avoiding trouble)
Sl Relinquish topic-control
S2 Select salient topics
S3 Treat topics briefly
S4 Make new topics salient
S5 Check NNS's comprehension
Tactics (T) (for repairing trouble)
Tl Accept unintentional topic-switch
T2 Request clarification
T3 Confirm own comprehension
T4 Tolerate ambiguity
Strategies and Tactics (ST) (for avoiding and repairing trouble)
STl Use slow pace
ST2 Stress key words
ST3 Pause before key words
ST4 Decompose topic-comment constructions
ST5 Repeat own utterances
ST6 Repeat other's utterances

develop interlocutors' ZPDs and ZPAs (see Commander and Guerrero 2012; Guerrero and Commander, forthcoming).

Shadowing is also similar to active listening and Rogerian listening, where repeating is done by counsellors and psychotherapists to help speakers hear what they are actually saying better and know also that they are being heard. The positive effect of these ways of interacting becomes evident in the classroom as students pay closer attention to interlocutors and confirm each other's utterances by shadowing.

Stevick (1989) describes shadowing in reference to five students he studied in his book on successful learners. One of them, Ed, describes silent shadowing: 'when my mind works on vocalizing it [what the teacher is saying] inside, I hear the sound. I hear myself saying the sound, in my own voice ... almost as an echo of what the teacher is saying' (p. 83). Later, he provides a good description of conversational shadowing: 'One of the things that I like to do is ... mimic out loud, perhaps in reply to a question. Or not even a question, but in a conversation. I let him say something, and then I just say the same thing back, changing it slightly so that it's suitable as a continuation of the conversation' (p. 97).

We all have variable capacities and techniques to get our interlocutors to adjust to us. To some teachers and helpers with little experience of interacting with learners, the standard adjustment to non-comprehension might simply be (inappropriately) to speak louder. But when learners dare to repeat what their helpers say, however different it may be, they are at least showing *what* they have understood and at the same time what they are capable of to their interlocutors who can then take this information and adjust more qualitatively to what might be needed. Equally, when tutors repeat back what they have understood from learners, they are using shadowing to mediate their ZPA, that is, their situated ability to learn to adjust.

Adjusting, then, is a co-constructing phenomenon that goes on 'inside and between people' (Stevick 1980: 4). Elsewhere, I have described several other mediational tools and activities that allow teachers to adapt more to their students' levels, strategy use, perceptions and values: action logs, newsletters, class publications and students' 'longitudinal self-evaluated videos' (Murphey 2001b, 2007). These tools also allow students to re-view performances and make adjustments that might increase their learning and fluency in subsequent encounters. Timing is also important – individuals and groups of people can be more or less ready for certain changes, certain ideas, and these ideas need to be in relative proximity to what they are already doing and believing for them to consider adopting these new ways of thinking, talking and doing.

It is important to notice that ZPAs, while certainly helping cognitive development, are not merely about adjusting cognitively. Atkinson (2011)

Meaningful classroom activity

described the domineering influence of cognitivism in second language acquisition (SLA) and the need for alternative social approaches. Stevick often emphasized the importance of paying attention to community, emotions, beliefs and attitudes ensure just one character space after full stop and next sentence. Some years ago, Schumann (1997) and Arnold (1999) helped to create interest in affect as a field for SLA inquiry and we are benefiting from a plethora of new studies (Kalaja and Barcelos 2003; Pavlenko 2005; Dewaele 2010). I feel beliefs and attitudes are really the driving force behind opening up ZPAs and ZPDs, and that these zones either shrink or expand depending on the degree of rapport and trust in a group.

Too often adjusting has been seen as unilateral, placing the learner in a passive position at first and the teacher/helper in the active position of doing all the adjusting to the learners' ZPD so the learner learns. However, with our more recent conceptions of negotiation and collaborative construction of understanding, learning is also being co-constructed, although not necessarily the same kind of learning for all parties. Both teachers and students may be learning new ways to adjust, or how to adjust for the particular learner they are with, or learning that some ways are not working well, all of which also adds to their repertoire of adjusting capabilities with future students, thus expanding their zone of proximal adjusting. ZPDs and ZPAs operate dynamically with different partners in different contexts at different moments and their *fit* needs continuous negotiation.

At the metadiscursive level, effective learners often decide to talk more with partners who they know adjust well to them, and thus they shape their environment in order to be with those people with whom they feel they can learn best. Effective learners can and do explicitly ask for reformulation and clarifications, and they interrupt. In other words, they negotiate an understanding of what they are learning. In a general sense they are assertive and more conscious of what they need. In some of my classes I have asked students to check with their conversation partners if they want to be shadowed or not, giving them the choice. This gets them to be more conscious and more in control of how they can actively shape their own learning.

Ways of inviting students to adjust to each other proactively

At the level of classroom organization, simply allowing students to interact with learning material, to teach each other and to co-construct meaning can be immensely beneficial, leading them to model each other not only in the present linguistically, as with shadowing above, but holistically

178

through strategies, beliefs and attitudes. Long and Porter (1985), Varonis and Gass (1985) and Donato (1994) provide evidence that students can help each other co-construct needed input within their ZPDs and scaffold their learning without an *expert*. Oliver (1996) has shown how even small children modify (adjust) their input for NNS children.

As I said above, I believe that it is easier for students to adjust to each other than to teachers or native speakers, who are distant in proficiency and possibly in interests. Learners are often already in proximal relationships. When they interact together, they can become Near Peer Role Models (NPRMs, Murphey and Arao 2001; Singh 2010) for each other, displaying proximal strategies, beliefs and attitudes that other learners feel they can adopt. It is true that some students insist on believing the myth that 'I can only learn from native speakers', but often after experiencing more active learning with their peers the fallacy of this belief is revealed to them. NPRMs can be 'near' in many ways – age, gender, ethnicity, nationality, interests, past or present experiences, aspirations and also in proximity and in frequency of social contact. In the three examples below, I am not so much concerned with cognitive language learning structures as I am with adjusting to and changing emotional/belief systems (which may be a precondition for opening and expanding ZPAs and ZPDs), which seems to happen more easily among NPRMs.

Action logs and newsletters: telephoning in English

Student action logging entails students listing the activities we do in each class and evaluating them, and then writing a general comment about the class or specifically about the homework (as might be directed by the teacher). I read students' action logs weekly and select positive comments from them that I think might be helpful for other students. I place the comments anonymously on a handout, which I call a class newsletter, for all the students to shadow read. In pairs in the next class, one student reads a comment and the other (with their newsletter covered) shadows, summarizes and says something about the comment, perhaps having a short conversation about the topic if they like. They then switch roles with each newsletter comment. In this way students support each others' learning in positive ways. They discover and often adopt new beliefs and strategies that peers are using. (Guerrero and Commander, forthcoming, are experimenting with some very interesting shadowing procedures with reading.)

One typical example often noted in the newsletters at the beginning of a semester is 'telephone homework'. I ask my students to telephone each other in English for homework. At first, about half do not like the activity and, thus, do not get the full benefit of the exercise. However,

Meaningful classroom activity

there are some students who do the activity and enjoy it. I assemble their positive comments about this activity and put them in the newsletter:

> Wow, I called and talked for 20 minutes all in English. It was fun. Of course we talked more than just about the homework. I like this homework.
>
> My mom and dad were surprised! They heard me speak English. And they could not understand! That was fun.

When I pass the newsletters out, I tell students that some people did not like the activity, but some did and that they may be interested in reading about what they liked. Reading their peers' positive comments about the activity helps those that did not like the activity to re-evaluate it. So they usually give it another chance and try it with new enthusiasm. Notice that it is not the teacher who tells learners this is a good and fun way to learn, but rather peers who have similar interests, who are in proximal relationships, and who, as NPRMs, are more believable. Thus, a good activity, but one in which there was little buy-in from the students, has been valorized by some of their peers, which in turn encourages more students to try the activity and benefit from actual language use outside the classroom.

Video interviews of potential NPRMs

In two quasi-experimental studies (Murphey and Arao 2001), learners in a Japanese university English department were shown an 8-minute video of four exemplary, slightly older, Japanese students in the same department who were expressing beliefs and attitudes thought to facilitate SLA. A pre- and post-questionnaire revealed positive changes in viewers' reported-beliefs. In a later study we wished to see the impact of the same video-speakers on non-English majors in obligatory English courses in a different university. The results showed that many of these students' reported-beliefs and behaviours also changed positively after seeing the video and that they seemed to remain more motivated through post observations. Interestingly, the experiment also changed the teacher's beliefs, which made her class more interactive and possibly intensified Near Peer Role Modelling (NPRMing).

While the study above describes the use of short videos of similar students in other classes and how they are powerful NPRMs, the same can and does happen with one's own classmates, especially with a little teacher broadcasting of effective student beliefs and strategies (as with the newsletter above with positive student comments about telephoning). Regular videoing, as with Longitudinal Self-Evaluated Videoing (LSEV, see below), also offers prime opportunities for modelling other learners' attitudes, strategies and beliefs, and can turn a class of individuals into a more cohesive group (Dörnyei and Murphey 2003) as they start noticing the positive attributes of their classmates and emotional contagion spreads (Hatfield et al. 1994).

Longitudinal Self-Evaluated Videoing (LSEV)

I have been videoing my students in classes for over 15 years in a variety of ways and found that it is an ecologically efficient way for them to get feedback on their languaging performances (Swain 2006), which then stimulates adaptive changes on their part.

> In Longitudinal Self-Evaluated Videoing (LSEV), students are periodically video recorded as they perform speaking tasks such as conversations, debates, and presentations in their L2. Students carry out additional tasks as they watch the videos of themselves and sometimes their peers speaking. For example, they transcribe and analyze their conversation, or they note down the main content points of a classmate's presentation, and write a letter to their partner giving feedback both on the content and the delivery of the presentation. These examples show how the procedures of LSEV provide an open platform for a variety of task-based learning activities through collaborative and experiential learning, as well as student-centered pedagogy.
>
> (Murphey and Sakaguchi 2010: 97)

In 2004, Nishimura was a participant observer for a semester in one of my classes where weekly videoing of students' conversations were the main activity. She observed students in general and studied three students in particular. She analysed their end-of-semester videotapes, their learning journals and their final papers, as well as interviewing them through email. While she found evidence of self- and other modelling in students' learning logs, some were more capable modellers than others. Students who seemed to work mostly alone and did not seem to admire others as much, and who may have worked harder than others, still did not seem to progress as much as those who were very open to admiring and imitating others. She concluded that the videoing offered many opportunities to do self- and other modelling, and that the processes were complementary rather than discrete choices (Nishimura 2005). Our original research question had been, 'What are the particular characteristics of other and self-modelling?' This wrongly assumed that they were two separate processes when they actually are one dialectical fusion, or as Aboulafia (1986: 125) says, 'The self sees itself in the other and the other in the self.'

Bakhtin's dialogism helps explain the co-construction of self and other modelling, leading us to understand that the question of 'Who owns or says the words?' is not a helpful question in a co-constructed conversation in which we build on each other's utterances (see Byrnes, this volume). Holquist (2002: 13) says that for Bakhtin, 'utterance is understood as an act of authorship, or ... of *co*-authorship'. Perhaps most relevant to our understanding of self- and other modelling is Bakhtin's explanation of how we position ourselves as others in order to see ourselves:

> in order to see our selves, we must appropriate the vision of others. Restated in its crudest version, the Bakhtinian just-so story of subjectivity is the tale of how I get my self from the other: it is only the other's categories that will let me be an object for my own perception. I see myself as I conceive others might see it. In order to forge a self, I must do so from *outside*. In other words, I *author myself.*
>
> (Holquist 2002: 28)

Watching yourself on video is indeed seeing the self as 'others might see it', and you actually become an 'other'. It can be disconcerting at first and actually many people do not like watching themselves the first few times. But once one gets use to it, the advantages of seeing how you are actually performing are undeniable, as practically any professional athlete, actor or dancer will attest. And language learners can also notice how co-constructed their performances are. Many students actually write about how helpful their partners were in class, and sometimes how unhelpful they were, in their action logs: for example one student wrote in her action log, 'I spoke good today because my partner was funny.' Another wrote, 'What made me upset was my partner was reluctant to join the class.' In Bakhtin's words (1986: 89):

> Our speech, that is, all our utterances (including creative works), is filled with others' words, varying degrees of otherness or varying degrees of 'our own ness,' varying degrees of awareness and detachment. These words of others carry with them their own expression, their own evaluative tone, which we assimilate, rework and accentuate.

Notice that in the above research, students are finding good examples of the proximal changes they deem enriching and finding ways to adjust so that they can do as and believe as their NPRMs. In the first example, students were modelling positive reports of doing the telephoning activity; in the second, when watching slightly older peers express their beliefs, students tended to adopt their beliefs. Lastly, when watching videos of themselves and others conversing, they get to see themselves as others see them and can appreciate both what they and their partners do well and what needs to be improved and take more agentive control over their own adjusting for improvement. Notice also that in many of these examples, participants are choosing to model proactive examples from imagined communities of practice (Norton 2001), that is, communities of others whom they may never meet (e.g. 'Japanese students who speak well' on the video) or who may never even exist in reality (characters in books and movies, see Quinn 2010) but who are nevertheless useful to imagine and can drive one's motivation.

The adjusting harmonizer

Not only do we adjust ourselves to a variety of conversation partners, but we also adjust ourselves to a changing world and the dialectics that we have in mind. Here, too, we have variable ZPDs and ZPAs. Stevick wrote about the dialects of self and community when describing two methods that he had researched in depth. First on the Silent Way:

> The Silent Way … sees the Self of the learner as isolated and independent. It also sees the splendid power that Self can have – that it can develop – when it comes to know itself and so to shape itself. The Self for Gattegno's Science of Education is the 'Invictus' of William Ernest Henley's well-known poem, who thanked 'whatever gods may be / for my unconquerable soul,' and who in defiance cried out to the world that 'I am the master of my fate!' As this finally and fiercely lonely Self develops, it may come to give something of its own to the world in which it finds itself and to some of the other Selves around it, while at the same time learning to learn from those Selves. Among them, a group of such Selves may attain a degree of 'community'.
>
> (Stevick 1998: 168)

And then on Counselling-Learning (p. 168):

> The life-affirmation of Counseling-Learning is in some respects exactly the reverse of the Silent Way's. It too sees the individual as alone. But where the Silent Way affirms the aloneness of the learner and pushes him or her to come face to face with that aloneness and to live through it and beyond it, Counseling-Learning begins by reducing aloneness through the warm, total, womblike support of the counselor-teacher. In addition, the lonely Self of each learner receives support as it finds its place in a developing community of other learning Selves.

Stevick concludes that in both methods, 'the path the learner follows runs between independence and community, but it runs in opposite directions … The Silent Way focuses mainly on the cognitive work – the cognitive adventures – that meet the learning Self. Counseling-Learning gives more explicit attention to interpersonal and intrapersonal forces of all kinds' and despite their differences, he still insisted that each 'is in its own way a fresh and hopeful affirmation of life' (p. 168).

Meaningful classroom activity

Even earlier in his career, Stevick suggested the balancing metaphor of 'harmony' and that learning had more to do with the positioning of one's self in a world of meaningful action: 'My earlier conclusion was that success depends less on materials, techniques, and linguistic analyses, and more on what goes on inside and between the people in the classroom' (Stevick 1980: 4). He emphasized the ever-changing rapport among people as a main inducer of effective learning: 'I have begun to suspect that the most important aspect of "what goes on" is the presence or absence of harmony – it is the parts working with, or against, one another' (p. 5).

In Figure 11.3 I try to schematically translate Stevick's sense of harmony into a diagram, what Galperinz called a SCOBA, a *'schema for the orienting basis of action ... SCOBAs provide learners with resources that are then formulated as a plan of action'* (in Lantolf 2011: 38). Figure 11.3 is merely meant to help us think about how we might adjust ourselves in our various contexts to achieve more meaningful action. I do not equate 'inside and between' with 'intermental and intramental', nor with 'autonomy and community', but they are similar in some obvious ways. A diagram of course is not moving and thus is limited in its capacity to show continual adjusting and the moving of all the parts (please use your imagination). Figure 11.3 attempts to show that there is potential trouble for learners if they go too far towards either extreme (becoming a lone cowboy or a sheep, i.e. being too independent (isolated) or losing the self in the crowd), and there is wisdom in changing and adapting as a person-in-context (Ushioda 2009) and being more or less centred. In the circle below, a person ideally moves about ecologically, adjusting appropriately to needs and enjoying the benefits of all the pairings. At times we might err towards an extreme, but hopefully we are soon brought back into the harmonizing circle which is continually changing – so Figure 11.3 is always in progress.

Figure 11.3   Dynamic Dialectical Adjusting Harmonizer (DDAH)

In a class, an extreme example of the above left-hand point of the diagram might be the somewhat autistic student who has trouble reading and adjusting to others and who stays in his own world. At the other extreme is the student oriented to the right who only wants to do what others are doing and leaves little room for the development of the independent self. A more balanced student takes advantage of what the community offers and feels belonging, but is not totally lost therein. Rather the self becomes stronger as the community develops, and the student still can act with critical thinking and agency of his or her own. Obviously teachers want to have ways of adjusting themselves to these extreme types of students in order to challenge them to become more balanced, benefiting both from community and independence.

In music, harmony exists only in harmonizing patterns of movement, of waves, through the air. No movement, no music, no harmony. We need movement to live, to adapt, to balance, to harmonize. A life in harmony is continually adapting and adjusting to changing circumstances, moving contexts, selves, chaos and complexity, moving to create more harmony.

The ZPD and ZPA of our field

Some people operating in the field of SLA are adjusting so as to look at what they have in common and how they can support each other. The field of SLA most recently has been going through a social turn (Block 2003; Atkinson 2011) and a narrative turn (Swain et al. 2011). Lourdes Ortega (2011) has proposed that we accept, adopt and appreciate 'epistemological diversity'. Her significant contribution is to allow us to see how cognitivists and alternatives overlap and are doing similar things, to discover complementarity where some in both camps could even support each other:

> [W]e have a choice in SLA studies among entrenchment, incommensurability, and epistemological diversity. Entrenchment is likely to be a temperamental reaction that is unsustainable in the long run. Incommensurability is an option that some may find merit in at this juncture in the history of SLA studies. I want to argue that the third option, epistemological diversity, is the best choice.

> (Ortega 2011: 176)

Ortega ends citing Lugones (2003: 177–8) at length and concludes that:

> From traveling to others' 'worlds' emerges the possibility of not only agentive resistance from within accommodation but also empathic understanding of difference, instead of conflictive and hopeless

feelings of entrenchment and incommensurability. If we can experience ourselves as more than one and others as they experience both themselves and us, then perhaps we can also understand how other people understand and judge their own knowledge and theories and how they understand and judge ours. This, in turn, makes it possible to imagine ourselves and others as less epistemologically unitary and impermeable than we may be otherwise inclined to assume.

Conclusions

1. Students learn in different ways, depending at times on partners and contexts, and often because of the variable ZPAs of partners to adjust to their ZPDs.
2. Learners can develop strategies that help others to adjust to them in interaction in the target language, expanding their partners' ZPAs which in turn expand their ZPDs.
3. In negotiated interaction, partners can change and learn new, although perhaps different, things from each other. Everybody has both a ZPD and a ZPA.
4. Highlighting and 'broadcasting' positive examples of practice within a group would seem to be an ecological process of sociocultural change, that is, learning and emotional contagion. They are not only learning more language, but making friends, enjoying themselves and learning about the world, what we might call 'value added language learning'.
5. Being NPRMs for others may facilitate such learning and learning how to 'near' others (get close to people and imagine their worlds, see Ortega above) may create even more learning opportunities, that is, a modelling of diversity.
6 While NPRMing seems to be a natural phenomenon, *diversity modelling* may need the help of educators to eliminate some of the fear of the unknown, opening us up to more *differential harmonies*.
7. Adapting/adjusting to achieve more harmony would seem to be a continual process involving numerous simultaneous and emerging tasks for an individual or a group. This challenge/hope/desire to achieve more harmony apparently pushes and drives much of humanity towards meaningful altruistic action.
8. Time and people and circumstances are continually moving and thus human stories are moving and never ending. And so may our learning be.

From such stances of historical understandings and open epistemological diversity, I believe we can continually develop more *adaptable* frameworks from which to approach our diversity. One that honours and seeks *harmony inside and between* all of us.

References

Aboulafia, M. (1986) *The Mediating Self: Mead, Sartre, and Self-Determination*, New Haven / London: Yale University Press.

Aljaafreh, A. and Lantolf, P. (1994) 'Negative feedback as regulation and second language learning in the zone of proximal development', *The Modern Language Journal*, 78(4): 465–83.

Arnold, J. (ed.) (1999) *Affect in Language Learning*, Cambridge: Cambridge University Press.

Atkinson, D. (2011) *Alternative Approaches to Second Language Acquisition*, London: Routledge.

Bakhtin, M. M. (1986) 'The problem of speech genres', in Emerson, C. and Holquist, M. (eds.) *M. M. Bakhtin: Speech Genres and Other Late Essays*, Austin, TX: University of Texas Press, pp. 60–102.

Block, D. (2003) *The Social Turn in Second Language Acquisition*, Washington, DC: Georgetown University Press.

Commander, M. and de Guerrero, M. C. M. (2012) 'Shadow-reading in the ESL classroom: a brief report', *Peer Spectives*, 9: 7–10. Available online at http://peerspectives.files.wordpress.com/2010/04/shadow-reading1.pdf.

de Guerrero, M. C. M. and Commander, M. (forthcoming) 'Shadow-reading: affordances for imitation in the language classroom', *Language Teaching Research*.

Dewaele, J. (2010) *Emotions in Multiple Languages*, Basingstoke: Palgrave Macmillan.

Donato, R. (1994) 'Collective scaffolding in second language learning', in Lantolf, J. P. and Apple, G. (eds.) *Vygotskian Approaches to Second Language Research*, Norwood, NJ: Ablex Publishing Corporation, pp. 33–56.

Dörnyei, Z. and Murphey, T. (2003) *Group Dynamics in the Language Classroom*, Cambridge: Cambridge University Press.

Hatfield, E., Cacioppo, J. and Rapson, R. (1994) *Emotional Contagion*, Cambridge: Cambridge University Press.

Holquist, M. (2002) *Dialogism: Bakhtin and His World*, London: Routledge.

Kalaja, P. and Barcelos, A. (2003) *Beliefs about SLA: New Research Approaches*, New York: Springer.

Lantolf, J. (2011) 'The sociocultural approach to second language acquisition: sociocultural theory, second language acquisition, and artificial L2 development', in Atkinson, D. (ed.) *Alternative Approaches to Second Language Acquisition*, London: Routledge, pp. 24–47.

Long, M. (1983) 'Native speaker / non-native speaker conversation and the negotiation of comprehensible input', *Applied Linguistics*, 4(2): 126–41.

Long, M. and Porter, P. (1985) 'Group work, interlanguage talk, and second language acquisition', *TESOL Quarterly*, 19: 305–25.

187

Lugones, M. (2003) *Pilgrimages/Peregrinajes: Theorizing Coalition Against Multiple Oppressions.* New York: Rowman & Littlefield.

Murphey, T. (1990) 'You and I, adjusting in interaction to get comprehensible input', *English Teaching Forum USIA*, **28**(4): 2–5.

Murphey T. (1996) 'Proactive adjusting to the zone of proximal development: Learner and teacher strategies', paper presented at the 2nd Conference for Socio-Cultural Research / Vygotsky and Piaget, Psychological Sciences Research Institute, Geneva, Switzerland, 11–15 September.

Murphey, T. (2001a) 'Exploring conversational shadowing', *Language Teacher Research*, **5**(2): 128–55.

Murphey, T. (2001b) 'Tools of recursion, intermental zones of proximal development, and critical collaborative autonomy', *JALT Journal*, **23**(1): 130–50.

Murphey, T. (2007) 'Ventriloquation: the inter/intramental dance in language learning', in Miller, L. (ed.) *Learner Autonomy 9: Autonomy in the Classroom*, Dublin: Authentik, pp. 68–84.

Murphey, T. and Arao, H. (2001) 'Changing reported beliefs through near peer role modeling', *TESL-EJ*, **5**(3): 1–15. Available online at http://tesl-ej.org/ej19/a1.html

Murphey, T. and Sakaguchi, J. (2010) 'Multi-tasked student video recording', in Shehadeh, A. and Coombe, C. (eds.) *Applications of Task-Based Learning in TESOL*, Alexandria, VA: TESOL, pp. 97–110.

Nishimura, C. (2005) 'Exploring self and other modeling: among a group of Japanese university students', unpublished MA thesis, Dokkyo University.

Norton, B. (2001) 'Non-participation, imagined communities, and the language classroom', in Breen, M. P. (ed.) *Learner Contributions to Language Learning*, Harlow: Longman, pp. 159–71.

Oliver, R. (1996) 'Negative feedback in child NS-NNS conversation', *SSLA* 17: 459–81.

Ortega, L. (2011) 'SLA after the social turn: where cognitivism and its alternatives stand', in Atkinson, D. (ed.) *Alternative Approaches to Second Language Acquisition*, London: Routledge, pp. 167–80.

Pavlenko, A. (2005) *Emotion and Multilingualism*, Oxford: Oxford University Press.

Quinn, J. (2010) *Learning Communities and Imagined Social Capital*, London: Continuum.

Schumann, J. H. (1997) *The Neurobiology of Affect in Language*, Malden, MA: Blackwell.

Singh, S. (2010) 'Near-peer role modeling: the fledgling scholars education paradigm', *Anatomical Sciences Education*, 3: 50–1.

Stevick, E. W. (1971) *Adapting and Writing Language Lessons,* Washington, DC: Foreign Service Institute.

Stevick, E. W. (1980) *Teaching Languages: A Way and Ways*, Rowley, MA: Newbury House.

Stevick, E. W. (1989) *Success with Foreign Languages: Seven Who Achieved It and What Worked for Them,* New York: Prentice Hall.

Stevick, E. W. (1998) *Working with Teaching Methods: What's at Stake?*, Boston: Heinle & Heinle.

Swain, M. (2006) 'Languaging, agency and collaboration in advanced second language proficiency', in Byrnes, H. (ed.) *Advanced Language Learning: The Contribution of Halliday and Vygotsky*, London: Continuum, pp. 95–108.

Swain, M., Kinnear, P. and Steinman, L. (2011) *Sociocultural Theory in Second Language Education: An Introduction Through Narratives*, Bristol: Multilingual Matters.

Ushioda, E. (2009) 'A person-in-context relational view of emergent motivation, self and identity', in Dörnyei, Z. and Ushioda, E. (eds.) *Motivation, Language Identity, and The L2 Self*, Bristol: Multilingual Matters, pp. 215–28.

Varonis, E. M. and Gass, S. (1985) 'Non-native/non-native conversations: a model for negotiation of meaning', *Applied Linguistics*, 6(1): 71–90.

Vygotsky, L. S. (1978) *Mind in Society: The Development of Higher Psychological Processes*, ed. Cole, M., John-Steiner, V., Scribner, S. and Souberman, E. Cambridge, MA: Harvard University Press.

Wood, D. J., Bruner, J. S. and Ross, G. (1976) 'The role of tutoring in problem solving', *Journal of Child Psychiatry and Psychology*, 17(2): 89–100.

12 Complex systems and technemes: learning as iterative adaptations

Diane Larsen-Freeman

Introduction

It was in 1959 that Earl Stevick first used the word 'technemic'.[1] 'Technemic' is a portmanteau, a combination of the words *technique* and *emic*. Stevick coined the term to introduce a concept in language teaching, one that I have made significant use of in my own teaching and in my work with teacher interns.

While the meaning of 'technique' is well known, perhaps 'emic' warrants an explanation. In a footnote to his article, Stevick acknowledges his debt to Kenneth Pike for the term 'emic'. Pike was my professor at the University of Michigan, and perhaps that is also why the technemic concept has been so meaningful to me. Pike contrasts an emic approach with an etic approach. The emic approach analyses data in a way which is meaningful to the participants of a community, whereas the etic approach interprets data with reference to an outside perspective or external system. The terms are most often applied in phonology, contrasting sound differences that are phonemic and ones that are phonetic. For example, a phonemic difference exists in English in the contrast between the phonemes /p/ and /b/. The contrast is meaningful to English speakers because the use of /p/ or /b/ results in a meaning difference in, for example, distinguishing *pin* from *bin*. A phonetic difference, on the other hand, does not result in a meaning contrast. For example, in English the first /p/ in *pot* is aspirated, is accompanied by a puff of air, whereas a non-initial /p/ is, as in *spot*, unaspirated. The contrast can be attested to by the outside perspective of linguists, but participants in the community of English speakers do not even notice the contrast because it is not a meaningful one, although the difference between aspirated /p/ and unaspirated /p/ constitutes a meaning difference, in other languages, such as Thai. The phonemic difference between /p/ and /b/ in English and the phonetic difference between unaspirated and

---

[1] At the University of Kentucky Foreign Language Conference. Later published in *Language Learning* (see Stevick 1959).

aspirated /p/ are both real contrasts, but only the former is meaningful to English speakers.

Utilizing the terms and concepts, Stevick suggests that teachers can manipulate an activity in such a way that even the slightest alteration in a technique can potentially make for an emic difference, a meaningful difference, in how the activity is perceived by the students in a classroom community. 'Specifically,' he asks, 'how do the students respond to a change from one of those apparently different techniques to another?' (Stevick 1959: 48). The answer he develops in the article is basically that in order for an emic change to take place, the change must dissipate restlessness among those students for whom things have been moving too slowly and/or not cause trouble for the less advanced students:

> Any pair of techniques which, for a given teaching situation, satisfy either or both of these criteria are then significantly ('emically') distinct in *that situation*: we might call them separate technique-emes, or 'technemes.' In some situations, of course, these usable ('technemic') distinctions will be etically relatively narrow, and in others relatively broad.
>
> (Stevick 1959: 49)

Thus, technemes was Stevick's answer to the question of how to keep students who learn at a faster rate engaged in an activity, while at the same time giving opportunities for further practice to those who need it. It seems to me that there are a few big questions in language teaching, and surely one of them is the challenge of how to attend to the needs of students who learn at different rates. Even language learners who can be characterized as rank beginners in learning another language will, within a short span of time, be clearly differentiated by the pace at which they learn, and thus what they know and can do.

A problem: giving students sufficient practice

The first example: dialogue memorization

Perhaps it would be helpful at this point to consider the first of two examples that Stevick gives. It has to do with etic techniques the teacher can use to promote dialogue memorization (see Figure 12.1). The numbers in parentheses are the number of options of each technique.

Meaningful classroom activity

Listening	Books open
vs.	vs.
Repetition	Books closed
vs.	vs.
Reproduction without direct imitation	Books open but used as little as possible
(3)	(3)
Choral repetition	Repeating each line two or more times
vs.	vs.
Individual repetition	Going straight through the dialogue
(2)	(2)
Calling on students in a fixed order	
vs.	
Calling on them in a random order	
(2)	

Figure 12.1   Stevick (1959): Example 1, dialogue memorization

For instance, when teaching students a dialogue, students can be asked to repeat a dialogue all together in choral repetition while reading the dialogue from their books. Next, they may be asked to repeat the dialogue using their books as little as possible. Finally, the whole class may repeat the dialogue with their books closed. Stevick points out that there are 72 permutations in all among these various options. Every possible etic combination of these 72 represents a potential techneme. Thus, by varying dialogue memorization activities along these dimensions, students who learn at different rates and learn by different means may have opportunities to practise in presumably helpful ways.

Rhythm

It is not only that teachers have a lot of options to exercise in order to address the heterogeneity of the students who make up a given class, but also, note, that the title of Stevick's article contains the words 'the rhythm of class activity'. He writes:

> Even in a homogeneous class, however, the problem of rhythm would remain. No matter what cycle of activity we establish, it will fail if we do not control the rate at which the student encounters difficulties. Too many difficulties per minute will overwhelm him, while too few will leave him restless.

(Stevick 1959: 45)

192

Although Stevick does not say so explicitly, clearly he means that rhythm is important in a class for keeping students engaged. Without that, little learning is likely to take place.

Now, teachers understand this – even if they would not necessarily put it in terms of the etic/emic distinction or in terms of rhythm. They know that when they start to 'lose' students (students' attention starts to wander or wane), either because what students are being asked to do is too easy or too difficult, they must do something different. However, it has been my impression that the usual response to such a situation is that teachers abandon what they are doing and switch to an entirely new activity. That is, rather than exercising a different option (e.g. in terms of dialogue memorization, choosing to have students repeat individually rather than in chorus), teachers abandon one activity for an entirely new one. They go from having students conduct a role play to having them tackle a reading passage, for example.

There are two consequences to this decision. The first is that lesson planning is quite time-consuming because a given lesson must include a number of entirely different activities, rather than emic variations of one or more activities. A more serious problem is that students do not receive the practice that they need on a given day to learn what the teacher intended. Of course, it is always possible, indeed desirable, to return to a given teaching point another time. Still, the same emic/etic approach can provide useful guidance in knowing what to do when one does return.

Let me summarize and make explicit the claim thus far: when students' energy is diverted so that their attention is no longer directed at the learning challenge set before them by the teacher, the teacher will have to make a change to recapture their attention. However, the change need not be a radical one. It may just be that a slight shift is enough to create a techneme and thus sufficient to restore students' attention. In so doing, students receive additional practice, which may be necessary, especially for those who are not as quick to learn as others.

Now, it must be remembered that Stevick was writing at the time that the Audiolingual method was widely practised. It is not surprising, then, that learning a dialogue involved drilling. However, the same principle can be applied creatively to generating technemes for any technique associated with modern-day methods and practices. For example, a typical activity from Communicative Language Teaching is to ask students to work in pairs to compare two different, but similar, pictures. Following students' completion of this activity, a teacher might normally engage students in another activity, such as having them compare one of the scenes in one of the pictures with another scene with which they are familiar, such as one from their home-towns. This activity might be a useful expansion activity, but a technemic approach would invite a lesser change, such as having students close their eyes for a minute and tell each other what they can remember from one of the scenes in the pictures. Then, they could do the same with the other scene. In this way, additional practice with the same vocabulary and syntactic structures can be generated. The point is that the techneme concept is just as applicable to modern methods as it was when Stevick first proposed it during the audiolingual era.

On repetition and iteration

However, one issue that may need revisiting in light of modern-day thinking is the matter of repetition, which figures prominently in Stevick's example of dialogue memorization. Repetition suggests repeated identical performance. It might be the type of learning that actors use to memorize their lines in a drama script or that maths students use to learn a multiplication table. Indeed, the major practice involved in rote learning is learning by repetition. The idea is that one will be able to better recall the material the more one repeats it. It is no wonder, then, that repetition was widely practised in audiolingualism, where verbal behaviour was purported to result from the formation of verbal habits. A major problem with repetition in audiolingualism, however, was that it didn't necessarily require students to use language meaningfully. Repeating the form as precisely as possible was seen to be sufficient.

By way of contrast, there is another term, *iteration*, which I think merits closer attention. Iteration makes explicit the claim that the act of repeating results in a change to a procedure or system. In other words, what results from iteration is 'a mutable state'.

Phoneticians have long known that the same word is pronounced differently by the same person with every use (Milroy and Milroy 1999). Of course it takes sophisticated instrumentation to demonstrate the difference – well beyond what is perceptible to humans. Yet, if this is true of the form of a small linguistic unit, the sound of a word, surely when what is being iterated is something meaningful, the difference between one iteration and the next will be huge. This observation inspires the thought that true repetition does not occur in language production. This last point is perhaps best understood within the context of complex systems.

Complex systems: iteration

When applied to language, an understanding of complex systems suggests that the present level of language development is critically dependent on what preceded it. At the moment at which language is used, humans 'soft assemble' language patterns to create meaning to meet their specific present communicative goals (Thelen and Smith 1994).[2] Through repeated soft assemblies, complex systems iterate. Each iteration reuses the elements generated in the previous procedure(s) of soft assembly, always starting at a different point.[3] By so doing, complex systems are built up. In this way, language is constructed both within the individual and within the speech community. As Caspi (2010) argued persuasively, micro-level changes in word representations in individual minds lead to macro-level changes in the abstract shared entity of language. Gleick captured this bridging dynamic of complex systems when he wrote 'The act of playing the game has a way of changing the rules' (Gleick 1987: 24). Thus, when we entertain a view of language as a complex adaptive system, we recognize that every meaningful use of language changes the language resources of the learner/user, and the changed resources are then potentially available for the user and members of the speech community (Larsen-Freeman and Cameron 2008).

> Perhaps it seems that I am making too much of the distinction between iteration and repetition. Indeed, it would be odd to hear a teacher say 'Iterate after me, now!' And while I would not expect this to occur, nor particularly encourage it, I do think that the distinction has something important to contribute to our understanding of how learning transpires: learning takes place not by repeating forms of a closed, static system, but by *meaningfully* 'playing the game' again and again.
>
> (Larsen-Freeman 2012: 206)

Because technemes have the potential to provide for meaningful iteration, rather than rote repetition, they appear to contribute a solution to one problem in language teaching – how to sustain sufficient learner attention to give learners the practice they need. There is yet a second problem that has plagued language teaching for some time, and one

---

[2] It is called soft assembly because the patterns being assembled and the specific way that they are assembled can change at any moment during a task or from one task to another (Larsen-Freeman 2011: 54). Thus, in contrast to applying immutable rules, soft assembly is a real-time process which takes into account the options that a speaker has available, and their constraints, the intrinsic dynamics of both the speaker and the language, the individual's language-using history, the affordances of the context, and the communicative pressures at the moment.

[3] Complex systems are modelled with differential equations. A differential equation is one where the output of one iteration of an equation (the solution) becomes the input to the next. In other words, each time the equation is solved, a new starting point is defined that initiates the next iteration.

which may also be ameliorated by Stevick's notion of technemes. Here I am referring to the inert knowledge problem (Whitehead 1929). One of the major puzzles both for cognitive psychologists and for learning theorists is to explain why something learned in one context is not available for use in another.

A second problem: getting students to use what they have learned

Of course anyone involved in education wants to engage students in learning experiences that help them go beyond the immediate context, to put the knowledge that they have gained in the classroom to realize their own goals and purposes. One of the impediments to students' doing so, however, is the context-bound nature of what has been learned.

Complex systems: on the contextual basis for knowledge

The claim that knowledge is not independent from context would resonate with complexity theory researchers, researchers who study complex systems. This is because '[C]omplexity theory challenges the nomothetic programme of universally applicable knowledge at its very heart – it asserts that knowledge must be contextual' (Byrne 2005: 97). Van Geert and Fischer (2009) use the example of 'grasping' to illustrate the context-boundedness of human actions. Whether we grasp a kilo of feathers or a kilo of lead, the form of the grasping depends on the thing grasped. In this way, both instances of grasping are not identical, but rather only resemble each other in terms of form–function relationships and results (Van Geert and Fischer 2009: 321). They continue (p. 321):

> There is no intrinsic contradiction in saying that the development of a [mental] concept in a child is in fact the development of a child-context system. The context is not independent of the person because the person seeks certain contexts actively, constructs certain contexts actively, and perceives certain contexts actively. By the same token, the person is not independent of the context since what the person does and can do, feels, perceives and so on depends on the person's current context.

Summarizing, they write: 'development applies not to persons as isolated entities but to intricately interwoven person-context structures' (p. 321).

Applying this insight to language learning, it might be said that the interplay between a person and the context is intricate, and any linguistic representation in the speaker's mind is strongly tied to the experience that a speaker has had with language. The question then presents itself: if what our students learn is bound up with a particular context, how can we teach them in a way that prepares them to transcend contexts, to use their knowledge beyond the classroom? It would be useful at this point to take up Stevick's second example.

The second example: question formation

The second example takes the form of a nine-cell grid to characterize different types of questions (see Figure 12.2). The rows are related to linguistic form. Stevick's specific example entails placing in rows three question types: yes / no questions, alternative questions and Wh- questions. In the columns lie three different types of content to be queried. Stevick based these distinctions on Gurrey (1955). Stage I questions are those where the answers are contained in the wording of a story that students have listened to. Stage II questions are answerable from making an inference about what has been presented in a story, and Stage III questions have to do with some aspect of students' lives that is related to the story. When they are arrayed in tabular form, these two categories of three-way distinctions constitute a nine-cell grid as follows (examples from Stevick):

Here is the information included in the story:

This little boy is holding a broom ... He has cleaned his room ... He has put the toys under the bed ... He is showing his room to his mother ...

The types of questions on this story are as outlined in Figure 12.2:

	Stage I	Stage II	Stage III
Yes / no	Is the boy holding a broom?	Is the boy's mother angry?	Do you clean your own room?
Alternative	Is the boy holding a broom or a toy?	Is the boy's mother pleased or angry?	Do you clean your room, or does your mother?
Wh- questions	What is the boy holding?	How does the boy's mother feel?	Who cleans your room?

Figure 12.2   Stevick (1959): Example 2, question types

Meaningful classroom activity

In the discussion of the grid, Stevick makes two points: first, by posing the questions in each cell in the grid to students following their reading of a story, each cell can comprise a separate technique. Second, there is no reason why there should be only nine cells. For instance, it may be important to distinguish among types of Wh- questions, say subject-based versus object-based, or 'what' questions, which can be answered with a noun phrase, with 'why' questions, which require a clausal response. The point is that techniques are numerous, and that the same pair of techniques which proved to be 'different technemes' in one situation might in some other situation fail to satisfy either of Stevick's two criteria of dispelling restlessness in faster students without causing undue difficulty for the slower students. Importantly, this rich array of options and a teacher's skilful use of technemes can also teach students to adapt what they know to different contexts so that their language use can transcend contexts.

Complex systems: adaptation

A subset of complex systems is referred to as complex adaptive systems. What this means is that such systems are capable of 'adapting', improving their condition in relationship to their environment. As applied to language, Larsen-Freeman and Cameron have put it this way:

> Embodied learners soft assemble their language resources interacting
> with a changing environment. As they do so, their language resources
> change. Learning is not the taking in of linguistic forms by learners,
> but the constant adaptation and enactment of language-using patterns
> in the service of meaning-making in response to the affordances that
> emerge in a dynamic communicative situation.

(Larsen-Freeman and Cameron 2008: 158)

In other words, what is learned is not simply meaningful patterns, but the process of moulding them to fit the present context appropriately. As van Lier (2000: 246) states, 'learning is construed as the development of increasing effective ways of dealing with the world and its meanings'.

Thus, a partial solution to the inert knowledge problem, within a unified view of context and learner, lies in the recognition that giving learners an opportunity to do something a little bit different each time they engage in a particular activity is good training for being able to make the adaptations they need when faced with a different context or task. This is what I think Stevick's technemes provide.

Iteration, then, is important – but so is adaptation. As a matter of fact, I have come to believe that what we should be teaching is not only language, but also the process of adaptation: teaching students to take what they know and mould it to a new context for a present purpose. One way to accomplish this is to present students with slightly varied activities in which they must enact and adjust their language-using resources – and this is what the variations on a theme that technemes affords gives them.[4]

Segalowitz and Trofimovich (2012) underscore this point by noting that instructional activities should include variational elements, by which they mean variation in the cognitive demands that they place on learners. They suggest that a variational continuum exists between closed- and open-skill environments. In closed-skill environments, there is minimal variation in the conditions under which performance takes place so that performers can learn by repeating an action as precisely as possible. In contrast, open-skill environments, where natural communication takes place, are much more demanding. In such contexts, performers have to deal with unpredictability, interruptions and distractions in the environment. In such cases, performers have to notice changes in the environment and respond to them rapidly. Thus, performers have to learn to deal with changes as they occur in real time (e.g. adapting to an interlocutor or to different task demands).

I submit that one of those cognitive processes is accommodating to shifting task demands, and giving students practice in adapting to the shifts is another pedagogical contribution of technemes.

Conclusion

One of the first lessons I received from Earl Stevick had to do with the value of technemes. I have used the concept many times in working with language teacher interns. I have helped the interns see that they can establish a rhythm to class activity that is more conducive to learning than one which lunges from one activity to another. However, working with complexity theory in recent years has helped me to understand most clearly why technemes are an important contribution to language teaching. I have used the opportunity afforded me in writing this chapter to both celebrate Earl Stevick's gifts to language teaching and to theorize why they are important.

What this exploration has revealed to me is that technemes are useful for giving students practice that is iterative, not repetitive. Such practice starts at a different point (what complexity theorists call 'the initial condition') with each iteration, always revisiting the same, though

[4] See Murphey (this volume) for further discussion of adaptation.

Meaningful classroom activity

not identical, territory. I have also proposed that the use of technemes helps students to move beyond the classroom context to adjust their language resources to changing task demands. Practice in which learners engage meaningfully in the classroom is not rehearsal; if skilfully planned and executed, it is about adapting one's language resources to new purposes.

I note that although technemes were first discussed in Stevick's 1959 article, his line of thinking can be traced through his other contributions. For instance a major contribution of Stevick's *Images and Options in the Language Classroom*, published almost 30 years later, is the way that Stevick illustrates the choices teachers have in generating teaching techniques based on textbook material.

In conclusion, Stevick's concept of technemes remains vital today. To my mind, technemes are valuable not only in guiding teachers to renew students' attention, as technemes were originally intended. They are also valuable because they can encourage meaningful iteration, and they can teach adaptation. Iteration and adaptation are critical components not only of learning in the classroom, but also of mobilizing learning beyond the classroom (Larsen-Freeman forthcoming). After all, second language acquisition is not a matter of conformity to uniformity (Larsen-Freeman 2003), and language is not fixed but is, rather, a dynamic system (Larsen-Freeman 1997).

References

Byrne, D. (2005) 'Complexity, configuration and cases', *Theory, Culture & Society*, **22**: 95–111.
Caspi, T. (2010) 'A dynamic perspective on second language acquisition', PhD dissertation, University of Groningen, the Netherlands.
Gleick, J. (1987) *Chaos: Making a New Science*, New York: Penguin Books.
Gurrey, P. (1955) *Teaching English as a Foreign Language*, London: Longman.
Larsen-Freeman, D. (1997) 'Chaos / complex science and second language acquisition', *Applied Linguistics*, **18**: 141–65.
Larsen-Freeman, D. (2003) *Teaching Language: From Grammar to Grammaring*, Boston: Heinle/Cengage.
Larsen-Freeman, D. (2011) 'A complexity theory approach to second language acquisition/development', in Atkinson, D. (ed.) *Alternative Approaches to Second Language Acquisition*, Oxford: Oxford University Press, pp. 48–72.
Larsen-Freeman, D. (2012) 'On the roles of repetition in language teaching and learning', *Applied Linguistics Review*, **3**: 195–210.
Larsen-Freeman, D. (forthcoming) 'Transfer transformed', *Language Learning*, special issue.

Larsen-Freeman, D. and Cameron, L. (2008) *Complex Systems and Applied Linguistics*, Oxford: Oxford University Press.

Milroy, J. and Milroy, L. (1999) *Authority in Language*, 3rd edn, New York: Routledge.

Segalowitz, N. and Trofimovich, P. (2012) 'Second language processing', in Gass, S. and Mackey, A. (eds.) *Handbook of Second Language Acquisition*, London: Routledge, pp. 179–92.

Stevick, E. W. (1959) 'Technemes and the rhythm of class activity', *Language Learning*, 9: 45–51.

Stevick, E. W. (1986) *Images and Options in the Language Classroom*, Cambridge: Cambridge University Press.

Thelen, E. and Smith, L. (1994) *A Dynamic Systems Approach to Development of Cognition and Action*, Cambridge, MA: MIT Press.

Van Geert, P. and Fischer, K. (2009) 'Dynamic systems and the quest for individual-based models of change and development', in Spencer, J. P., Thomas, M. S. C. and McClelland, J. (eds.) *Toward a New Grand Theory of Development? Connectionism and Dynamic Systems Theory Reconsidered*, Oxford: Oxford University Press, pp. 313–36.

van Lier, L. (2000) 'From input to affordances', in Lantolf, J. (ed.) *Sociocultural Theory and Second Language Learning*, Oxford: Oxford University Press, pp. 245–59.

Whitehead, A. N. (1929) *The Aims of Education*, New York: Macmillan.

13 The Inner Workbench: learning itself as a meaningful activity

Adrian Underhill

Introduction

The 1970s and 1980s were, for me in the UK, a time of professional excitement in the ELT world. I found myself teaching in a milieu in which my colleagues and I explored, discussed and adapted the educational and psychological theories and practices of learning and teaching around at the time, exchanging experiences and pushing our own boundaries. This formative time was rich in influences that shaped my experience and the development of my values and assumptions, which affect what I notice, how I respond, what I write about and how I write. I will start by identifying some of the assumptions or biases that I hold, that may colour what I say in this chapter:

- Learning *itself* is engaging and personally meaningful. In fact humans are designed for learning, we are learning beings. I value activities that uphold this.
- The meaning experienced in the *activity of learning* is different from, though not unconnected to, the significance that the *content of the learning* may have for the learner.
- Part of the meaning I experience in the activity of learning is that it seems to allow me the feeling of being more myself, almost as if I am coming home to something. I can imagine that this relates to the innate biological urge to learn, and I can imagine that it relates to a purposeful sense of using myself, or even 'making myself', but this is imagination and I do not wish to take it further here, except to say that I think I recognize this in others when they are learning, especially my students, and furthermore my own experience of learning can be enhanced when in the company of others who are similarly engaged, as in my classroom.
- There is something about engaged learning that is contagious (Gattegno, personal communication). Thus if you want learning, show learning. I feel that my students' learning is in some way dependent on my own learning at the same time in the same room, so that a core part of my job as teacher/facilitator is to serve the learning of the learner by creating the conditions for their engagement to emerge, for

their curiosity to fire up, which necessitates my own learning in the same moment. I see myself as a *learning companion*, helping them by learning alongside them.

- Teachers can develop these skills and sensitivities if they want to, but there are obstacles, such as the accumulated experiences of imposed or forced learning, inflicted with good intent but out of kilter with the robust self-learning which we experienced as babies and, I believe, yearn for later.
- It is one thing to see and articulate one's values as they develop and move in and out of view, and another to connect them with one's practice in life. Whitehead (2005) writes of the moments when we find that our practice contradicts our values, and of the consequent experiencing of ourselves as a 'living contradiction', a potentially creative state and an impetus for inquiry. Lewin (2001) suggests that when people are aligned to their purpose, when the gap between values and behaviours closes, what people experience is a 'stream of ease'. With regard to the activity of learning, I experience both 'stream of ease' moments, powered by a sense of synergy with my purpose, and 'living contradiction' moments when a value I hold is contradicted by my own actions. Therefore, I also value the practice of reflection on my learning, learning about my learning.

The riddle

I read *Memory, Meaning and Method* (Stevick 1976) soon after it was published and was excited by its resonance with the questions I and my colleagues were asking. Stevick put forth a riddle, which I can summarize as follows: you can have two quite different methods, Method A and Method B, based on different assumptions about how people learn, yet one teacher gets excellent results with A and another gets comparable results with B. How is this possible? (For other responses to this riddle, see also chapters by Maley and by Clarke, this volume). In addition he asked why it is that Method A (or B) sometimes works so beautifully and at other times so poorly. He suggests that if we just discuss the visible differences between A and B, if we remain on the plane on which methodological matters are usually discussed and defined by linguistic analysis and overt classroom behaviour, we may miss something else that is going on when each of these methods is used well: that is, that each method regardless of its surface methodology can fulfil a set of other requirements that goes 'beneath and beyond any of them', that is outside the description of the method. So what is going on that makes the real difference? What are these other requirements? Stevick (1976: 109–10) proposes that the '"the deeper" the source of a sentence within the student's personality, the more lasting value it has for learning the language', adding that while such a statement may not be too controversial, what might be more so is the further assertion that 'this same "depth" factor … is in fact more to be reckoned with than technique, or format, or underlying linguistic analysis' Stevick (1976: 110). The idea that there is a less visible process going on, which does not belong to the surface method employed, and that it might make more difference to the quality of learning than the method itself, was what I and my colleagues were thinking, and we were encouraged to find this argued succinctly and with such elegant authority.

Stevick goes on to describe a range of classroom activities, moving away from mechanical ones, where action rather than personal meaning is the aim, towards those that invite learners to find personal meaning and engagement. This depth or meaning factor provides Stevick with the beginnings of his tentative answer to the riddle and provided me with encouragement for my own search. Trying to make experiential sense of the riddle led me to propose the idea of three zones of expertise of a fully functioning teacher: knowledge of the topic, skill with classroom methods and competence with inter- and intrapersonal relationships and the psychological learning atmosphere of the group. The first two I felt were more or less adequately covered by ELT teacher education. It was the third zone that I felt was additional and that held the key to the riddle.

The atmosphere of the teacher

Like many teachers and students, I am struck by the different learning atmospheres prevailing in the classes of different teachers and often wonder to what extent this is a significant variable. This gives rise to another riddle: 'The same lesson taught by *different teachers* can have very different outcomes. Why?' To approach an understanding, let's try a thought experiment about personal atmosphere: identify at random one of your work colleagues, and in your mind's eye imagine the two of you are sitting together at a table, perhaps drinking coffee. Picture your colleague's face and hear his or her voice tone, and be aware of the personal atmosphere that may seem to extend from him or her. In that setting, what are the things you are likely to talk about or to avoid? What might you laugh about or not? What is possible or not possible and how does it feel just to be with that person? As a check, let go of the image of that person and do the same with another colleague.

Most people say they notice a difference between the recalled psychological atmospheres of the two colleagues, and that it affects how they think, feel and speak. What is missing from the picture is our own personal atmosphere, emanating from ourselves and felt just as acutely by the other person. And this is the problem: we seem to have a blind spot for our own personal psychological atmosphere, though not for the other's, albeit seen through our own filters. Try a second thought experiment: choose any teacher, past or present, whom you have had as a learner ... imagine yourself again in his or her learning space, and recall the teacher's appearance, voice tone and so on. Now, consider the atmosphere that this teacher creates for you. How does it affect the kind of learning you can do? Which of your talents are drawn out? As a check, do the same for a different teacher. What do you conclude from this? My conclusion is that we teachers create a personal atmosphere in our classes, that it is perceivable to everyone except ourselves, that it makes a difference to the learning that takes place there, and that it is difficult to get a strong impression of what our own atmosphere 'tastes' like to others.

Mainstream methodologies in ELT have appeared not to address the personal atmosphere and relationship issue, perhaps taking the line that this involves factors that are not identifiable, or not significant, or not susceptible to development or change. Conventional methods appear to me to steer away from the human qualities of learners and teachers rather than to inquire into other ways of knowing these elusive qualities. However, Suggestopedia and Community Language Learning, to mention only two of the non-mainstream approaches, emphasize the importance of the interpersonal skills and sensitivities of the teacher. Carl Rogers (Rogers and Frieberg 1994) asserted that the presence of three core qualities of the facilitator were necessary and sufficient to enable significant learning to take place: empathy, genuineness and non-judgemental regard. In clinical psychology the therapeutic alliance (i.e. the relationship between therapist and client) is known to be a strong predictor of outcome in individual psychotherapy across diverse treatment orientations and modalities (Martin et al. 2000). Postman and Weingartner (1987) propose that in the end we simply teach what is going on in ourselves. The point is that practitioners across disciplines believe that a major variable in successful learning lies in a zone beyond both the topic being learned and the teaching method employed, and that it has to do with relationship with oneself and with others.

The three zones of expertise of a fully functioning teacher

I identify these three domains (or zones of expertise) with the terms
Lecturer, Teacher and Facilitator (Underhill 1989, 1999), which I use
with specific restricted meanings (distinguished by the initial capital
letter) to refer to three different kinds of teacher (see Figure 13.1):

- Lecturer: a teacher who has a knowledge of the topic he or she teaches
  but has not attended to developing special skills in the techniques and
  methodology of teaching it.
- Teacher: a teacher who has knowledge of the topic and is also familiar with a range of principled methods and procedures for presenting,
  practising and testing the subject matter.
- Facilitator: a teacher who understands the topic, is skilled in the use
  of teaching methods and techniques, and who actively studies and
  pays attention to the psychological learning atmosphere and to the
  impacts of his or her intentions and interventions.

Simply training and working in the current culture of ELT is likely
to expose a teacher to expertise in the first two domains, but not to
expertise in the third, that of the Facilitator. One has to go outside the
world of ELT and look at the work of, for example, Carl Rogers or
John Heron to see what effective, purposeful training on such facilitative skills is like. This facilitative domain includes not only the question
of teacher atmosphere, discussed above, but sheds light on the idea in
Stevick's riddle that, regardless of surface methodology, there are other

Teacher as 'Lecturer'	Topic knowledge of subject matter		
Teacher as 'Teacher'	Topic knowledge of subject matter	Methodology practical skills and methods	
Teacher as 'Facilitator'	Topic knowledge of subject matter	Methodology practical skills and methods	Relationship beneath and beyond methodology

Figure 13.1   Three zones of competence of a fully functioning teacher

dimensions of teaching and learning that go 'beneath and beyond' and exert a profound effect. Paying attention to competence in all three domains is, I suggest, a more complete way of describing a fully functioning teacher.

An 'aha' teaching moment

For the first years of my teaching career I worked with groups of about 18 learners at all levels. Then I began to spend my time teaching scientists, doctors and business people in small groups or one to one, perhaps spending hours across a table from a single learner. In the absence of the clamour of a group, I could focus my attention on what my student was thinking, and I learned to watch and wait, to track the student's processing and include this in our learning conversation. I was not especially aware of doing this until two years later when I returned to teaching larger groups and found I could maintain this individual focus even within a larger group. I had a new and startling impression of a closer relationship with each learner in spite of the group size. My one-to-one experience had enhanced my confidence and ability to follow an individual learner's subtle inner moves of learning, sense-making and insight, or at least to recognize them and to endeavour to make them more visible using a variety of interventions. I think of this relationship as *close-up teaching* simply because I feel closer to the learning moves the student is making, as if putting on spectacles that *see learning*. In the next section I will describe one aspect of this kind of facilitation using what I call the Inner Workbench, which I see as a powerful and easily accessible resource in the Facilitator domain.

The Inner Workbench

Although it is possible for learning to be experienced as an inner activity, much of what happens in classrooms focuses on external, observable and measurable activities. Classroom activities generally involve practice, demonstration, performance, feedback, correction and evaluation, writing, communication and exchange of information and so on. Most of the discourse focuses on the subject under study, and the inner learning movements of the mind tend to remain untalked about, unremarked on, unseen by the teacher, unrelated to the activities and hidden from the rest of the class. As a result such movements take a low priority in the attention of the student too, simply because no-one takes an active interest in what happens 'inside'. This may give the impression that the internal movements of learning are too subtle to be seen, cannot be worked with directly by the teacher and cannot play an active part in the overt learning processes of the class. But is this really the case? De Guerrero (2005: 77) quotes Vygotsky's comment that inner speech 'serves as preparation for external speech'. Is it not then possible that inner speaking could be deliberately and systematically exploited in language learning? And as de Guerrero further points out (p. 208) 'awareness of inner speech is not something that comes automatically ... Neither are people very conscious of the possible benefits of engaging deliberately in inner speech.' And for this reason it is of particular importance that the teacher takes the initiative to introduce the Inner Workbench into language learning.

An individual's inner moves cannot be directly registered by others. In the case of language learning, they have to be amplified (through the muscles) into visible behaviour, such as speech or writing or some other response. Illustrations of this amplification of a non-physical inner movement through to a physical outer movement can be found in other disciplines. An example is the way musicians and athletes can rehearse and prepare without moving a muscle. The violinist may without moving a muscle play through the whole piece, perhaps seeing the notes with the mind's eye and hearing them with the mind's ear and even activating the neural pathways that move the fingers, though stopping short of activating the muscles themselves, so that only the 'mind's fingers' and not the 'physical fingers' are moving. Athletes may also spend time working with the movements of their sport without activating the muscles themselves. I have found it useful to conceive of this kind of activity as being more than just visualization, it is actually doing it, but with the muscles 'switched off'. This enables me to think of activities taking place 'before' muscles (a vivid neural activity without muscle movement) and 'after' muscles (the actual physical playing of the tune or speaking of the sentence or sprinting down the track). I want to show that making these inner moves visible means that they can be exploited for learning a language. The world of the Inner Workbench is not new, but what would be new is to make it perceptible, discussible and integral to learning a language.

I'd like now to describe a number of activities that can make some of these inner moves of learning visible to teacher, learner and the rest of the class.

Activating the Inner Workbench in a class

Imagine a group of 10 or 20 students seated around an empty table or floor space. I give the following instructions, though maybe not all at once:

> You may have played this game before, but these rules are a bit different. In a minute I will ask each of you to find an object from your bag or the room or just outside and put it in the middle. Then we will sit silently for a minute while you use any mental strategy you like to commit the objects to memory without writing or talking. After that I will ask you each to remove the object you put there and place it out of view. Then, still silent, I'd like you to write down all the objects you can recall. And the sign of success will be not *how many* items you recall, but *noticing how you go about it*, observing the strategies you use to commit the items to memory and to write them down.

We do the activity. The objects may be things like handbag, pencil case, bicycle pump, sun glasses, pen, purse, mints, etc. The students have a minute to look at them in silence, the objects are removed one by one by the owner, and then I ask them to write down the objects. When the writing slows up I say, 'Now take a minute to describe to someone else the strategies you used to help you to memorize and retrieve these items' (and this could be done in the mother tongue). This gives them the experience of recalling and hearing themselves articulate the processes they noticed in themselves. Then I invite a few individuals to give a brief account to the whole group of how they went about the memory and recall, which will have been made easier by having spoken to the partner. A noteworthy aspect of this activity is how eager people are to talk about their strategies, as if doing so gives meaning to their own unique process. Some of the strategies described may be:

I made a story linking them together …

I took a mental photo of the items, like a picture

I divided the items into different groups …

I kept saying them to myself, in English and in my language …

I felt each one in my hand …

I associated the articles with the person that put them there …

and so on.

Meaningful classroom activity

As people tell their stories I help them thicken their description with prompts such as:

And while you were doing this, did you speak to yourself inside?

Did you hear the objects spoken in your inner ear?

Was that in your voice or some other voice?

Did you see the objects in your mind's eye when you recalled them? Did you see them in colour? Did you get stuck at all? How? How did this affect you?

Did anyone try more than one strategy?

Some of the outcomes I want from this activity are: seeing and articulating one's own inner moves; hearing similarities and differences and noting other strategies worth trying; finding that inner moves can be talked about and enjoyed; seeing (gradually perhaps) that this is helpful in learning language and that strategies don't only 'happen' but can be deliberately chosen; making meaning from experience. This game is good for connecting people with their Inner Workbench, arousing curiosity and generating discussion. De Guerrero (2005) describes the 'working memory' model (of Gathercole and Baddeley 1993) as involving a kind of 'phonological loop' that holds information in phonological form and keeps it fresh through a process of articulatory rehearsal involving inner speech that uses both inner ear and inner voice. I want students to start observing this in themselves, and the next activities demonstrate ways of putting this phonological loop to work in an English language lesson with almost any group of learners, no matter what their language level.

Activating the inner ear and the inner voice

The aim here is to enable learners to listen internally to something they have just heard externally. This is good for sounds, words and short bits of connected speech (for example /ɪə / or 'wonderful!' or 'it's warm today!' or any language item needed at that moment in that class). So let's take single sounds as the first example. I say to the class 'I'm going to say an English sound, just once. But don't repeat it, just listen to it inside several times over, even though I only say it once.' I leave a second of focused silence and say a sound, perhaps: /aʊ/. Then I am silent for two or three seconds, but I keep their attention, imagining them hearing it several times in their mind's ear. I may say in a quieter voice, 'Can you still hear it?', and mostly they nod. Then I might say,

'In my voice?' and after a moment I ask, 'Would you like to hear the sound again?' If they indicate yes, then I give it. In this second hearing they listen more discerningly, because they have already invested in the sound internally, and perhaps located the 'tricky bit'. Then we may do this with one or two other sounds to get the hang of it. The same procedure can be used for learning a word or a phrase or sentence, which I will invest with some expression or feeling.

In this introductory activity, which takes only a moment, students are observing the phenomenon of their inner ear. They find they can hold something in their inner ear and listen to it several times. This may be contrary to their habit of panicking when the teacher gives a new language item, and of immediately asking for it again because they could not listen well the first time. And they are now looking inside at the inner movements that take place when doing an activity.

Then we add the inner voice. This activity begins as above by giving the single model, but then I may say, 'Can you still hear it? Whose voice can you hear it in? Mine ...?' (Usually their internal repetition is in my voice.) 'Now change it to *your* voice. Listen to your own voice inside, and notice any differences. And now get ready to say it aloud, but don't ...' At first they may not distinguish inner hearing from inner speaking, but after a while may find that the inner voice seems closer to the muscles of speech as if they are just beginning to twitch, or receiving some neurological message to activate.

Adding the outer voice

I do as above, and then I say 'OK, now say it aloud', and I ask them to say it to themselves, or their neighbour, or I select a few to say it to the whole class so that we can all hear. This step completes a small journey starting with listening in the inner ear, adding the inner voice and then adding the outer voice. And what we have here is an elegant alternative to the traditional repeat-after-me modelling technique in which typically the teacher says the prompt (sound, word or phrase) three times and the students repeat together in chorus several times. Instead they hear the model once, there is silence while they listen to it several times internally, they then rehearse it internally and then say it aloud. I find this alternative more powerful because (1) the students learn to listen with better attention, (2) they start to make use of the natural faculty of listening again in the inner ear and (3) they find that they can also say it and rehearse it internally while maintaining a critical inner ear (Underhill 2004)

Then I ask them to notice any difference between what they heard in their inner voice and the outer voice with which they just spoke. 'Are they the same? What difference can you hear?' (for example in tone or pronunciation). And they find that they *can* hear a difference between the two, thus opening up a new channel for critical discernment.

Between the inner ear and the outer voice is the inner voice. I know when I am activating the inner voice because I may sense my articulatory muscles inclining to engage and to shape themselves according to the sounds in the inner ear. I also have the impression of my attention moving from my ears to my mouth and throat. Though this may be partly imaginary, my students also report the same thing. It's as if the accent of the inner ear is more accurate than the accent of the inner voice, which in turn may be more accurate than the accent of the outer voice. This is something you can verify for yourself (see the 'cake shop' experience on p. 215). Here are some further uses of this resource for language learning activities.

Counting sounds, syllables, stresses or words on the Inner Workbench

This is a powerful way to get students to examine a piece of language close up, using the simple activity of counting. For example, I say a word once, with the usual invitation to them to listen to it several times internally as described above. Suppose we are encountering the new word *adventurous*.

I say it once, the students listen to it internally, and I ask 'How many sounds does it have?' They count internally and call out a number, perhaps 10, 13, 12, etc., usually both correct and incorrect numbers are called. Once they have counted, I get them to say the sounds one by one out loud, while I count them on my fingers. In fact the number of sounds is immaterial as the power of this activity lies in what the learner has to do in order to count the sounds, that is to hold the word in the inner ear, slow it down enough to separate and distinguish the sounds, listen internally to the representation of each sound in turn while also counting them. The aim is to get learners used to holding, identifying and separating sounds rather than to elicit the right number, though the number they offer also indicates something about how they are hearing the word. Note that whenever my students say a word 'correctly', sound by sound, I always then say to them, 'Now in English!', which they know means they should join the words up into a connected flow of English sound, adopting appropriate simplifications and stresses. The same applies to sentences.

This is a way to keep pronunciation in circulation while learning new vocabulary, and to focus attention on the sounds, the muscular movements of the sounds and the memory for that word afforded by an insightful pronunciation. But it is more than integrated pronunciation; it is a physical portal to language itself. Variations include asking how many syllables the word has, and if working on a phrase or short sentence, then how many words there are.

Preparing given language to speak after listening to it

This is for use when students need to listen to a sentence or phrase and then repeat it in an exact or similar way. I say something like 'I am going to say/play this sentence just once. Don't repeat it, but keep hearing it in your inner ear, and then I'll add another instruction.' So let's take this sentence:

The cat crossed the courtyard and jumped onto the wall.

I say/play it, then after a couple of seconds I might lead them to reflect on the phrase, using the following prompts:

Can you still hear it? ... whose voice is it in?

How many words ...?

Notice the stressed syllables. Which syllable is the highest pitch? Which is the lowest?

All of this is done in the Inner Workbench, requiring students to go back inside and listen again to the internal registration of the sentence without a second rendition of the model, though if they need it I give it.

Now listen to it in *your* voice, and notice any changes you make ...

Get ready to say it yourself, your way

Where do you want to put the stress? How do you want your intonation? What is the meaning you want?

Hear yourself saying it internally

During this phase of a few seconds, they all prepare and internally rehearse the sentence, and I might prompt them with:

Now say it aloud.

Was that the same as you heard in your inner ear?

What was different?

Try it again ...

And perhaps they go back inside and re-rehearse.

This gives students a liberating strategy of self-reliance by activating the faculty to rehearse a sentence in the inner voice before amplifying it externally.

Preparing given language to speak after reading it

This is for use with students in a similar way to that described in the previous section, but this time the student *reads* the printed sentence without hearing it, and prepares it for speaking on the Inner Workbench. (The sentence may be in a coursebook, or written on the board by the teacher or a student.)

The teacher might give the following sequence of instructions interspersed with occasional student activity:

Read this sentence. In a moment you will say it aloud, but how would you like to say it?

What meaning do you want to give it?

Say it in your inner voice. Where do you put the stress?

Choose your intonation and feeling. Which syllables are unstressed? Which words are joined together?

They prepare it for a few seconds.

Hear yourself saying it like this internally.

They rehearse it for a few seconds.

Now say it aloud.

A useful application of this is when using a coursebook dialogue. Before listening to the recorded version, ask students to read the dialogue and then rehearse it internally based on their own interpretation of the meaning. Then when they listen to the recorded version, they will hear it freshly and with more discrimination, noticing nuances and differences between the recorded dialogue and their internal rendering.

Preparing new language to speak aloud

In this case the students are preparing whole sentences, perhaps in the course of doing a standard activity, for example to show they have understood and can manipulate verb tenses. I indicate a question to be answered and ask the whole class to formulate the answer in their inner voice, before saying it out loud. By doing this, students may deal with careless slips before speaking aloud, so this functions as a kind of 'anti-blurt device'. When doing exercises such as the archetypal put-the-verb-in-brackets-in-the-correct-tense, I do not simply accept the right words in the right order as being correct. Instead, I demand that any utterance is also spoken with the maximum fluency and connectedness possible for that student. Thus, I make a physical demand on top of the cognitive demand, and the student almost certainly will need to say it twice, first to get the right words in the right order, and then to create a connected up-flow of energized English.

One can apply the resources of the Inner Workbench to many activities, thereby requiring the student to pay close up attention to their inner process. Such 'close-up teaching' brings teacher and student closer to the student's inner process, requiring the teacher to be constantly learning the student, second by second. For further perspectives on the use of the inner voice in language learning, see Tomlinson (2001) and (2003).

The 'cake shop' experience

This is probably familiar to you, and it illustrates the Inner Workbench in natural use. Imagine you are in a country where you speak only a little of the language. You are outside a cake shop and see in the window a cake that you want to buy. You stand by the window for a moment and rehearse, in your mind's ear, the words in this foreign language that you will need to ask for and buy the cake. You assemble the words and the stress and intonation you will use, and internally massage the utterance into shape and rehearse with your inner voice. It sounds good. You push open the door and enter the shop, and then open your mouth and speak. But what comes out is not the same as you just heard in your inner rehearsal. Ideally, you should then go back and listen again to the mind's ear, re-rehearse it internally, and try for the cake again. But the pressures of the cake shop do not usually allow for this, and other strategies must be employed.

This shows how a sentence can be composed and polished to a high quality using the inner ear and the inner voice, yet when amplified through the muscles of speech, it may lose that quality. Here lies a rich resource, the ability to create and compare two versions of the same utterances, the inner one, and the outer one that gets distorted by the muscular grip of the mother tongue habit. This comparison opens up to the learner a way into self-reflection, a position from which to view personal learning processes, to glimpse some of the internal movements of learning and to compare, critique and choose learning strategies.

215

I have tended to dwell on the phonological aspects of the Inner Workbench. This is partly because pronunciation involves the musculature which has a clear-cut physical aspect and thus offers an accessible starting point to become more sensitive to 'seeing' the inner moves of learning. I use this as a natural first step in developing both the *teacher's* sensitivity to the strategies, thoughts, feelings and insights of the students as they work with the material at hand, and vitally to develop the *student's* own 'in-sight' into the moves taking place within them, in which they can participate and intervene more fully and at will only as they begin to see them. Beyond pronunciation and its physicality, the Inner Workbench principles also apply to the exploration of semantic and syntactic structures of a language.

Not only does awareness of their inner learning moves offer a richer learning experience for the student, it offers teachers a richer experience too, enabling them to see their own impact on the student processes, to act to avoid any imbalance their interventions might bring, and to be guided by the student in a way that might be called not just learner centred, but *learning* centred.

Conclusion

In this chapter I have described the Inner Workbench as consisting, amongst other things, of the inner ear and the inner voice and the capacity to observe and use both of them intentionally. These features come ready installed, so to speak, in each learner, enabling inner processes that support external activities of speaking, listening and language learning generally, such as listening multiple times internally to samples heard externally, constructing, shaping, composing, correcting and rehearsing new utterances, noting both phonological and connected-up features of speech, and spotting and correcting errors. Unexpected features include the ability to hear a sentence in the inner ear and then to discern how different it may sound when first spoken aloud, allowing for critical discrimination and informed second attempts. I see intentional and conscious activation of the Inner Workbench in language teaching as an important subdivision of the domain of facilitation, requiring the teacher to attend to, relate to and learn the student processes. Such teacher learning completes a virtuous circle as the student's learning and the teacher's learning evoke each other. Thus, teachers can use their sense of learning as one measure of how they are creating conditions for student learning.

The Inner Workbench: learning itself as a meaningful activity

Finally, I am suggesting that learning can be experienced as meaningful and worthwhile in itself. Meaning is to be found not only in the personal relevance of the *content* of the learning but in the experience of finding oneself to be a *learning being*. Perhaps such meaning is taken for granted and so becomes invisible in our current methodologies, just as the Inner Workbench is assumed and thus invisible in the workings of language activities in the classroom. However, by surfacing and unpacking these processes we can develop finer tools for finer interventions, bringing us closer to learning as it happens. Imagine a dentist attempting a delicate dental task with the tools of a carpenter, tools of quality yet the wrong size for the job. Perhaps we need to develop tools that are the right size for the delicate learning work we are attempting. We have conversations about listening texts and how to choose them, about their authenticity and whether to grade the text or task, and about whether to ask questions before or after. What would it be like to have equally exploratory conversations about what it takes to make the inner moves of learning more visible, and how we might explore this in any lesson and how we could recognize whether we are doing so? Such conversations could take us to territories of teaching and learning that lie beneath and beyond the surface methodologies, and closer to where the apparent contradictions of Stevick's riddle may resolve themselves.

References

de Guerrero, M. C. M. (2005) *Inner Speech-L2: Thinking Words in a Second Language*, New York: Springer.
Gathercole, S. E. and Baddeley, A. D. (1993) *Working Memory and Language*. Mahwah, NJ: Lawrence Erlbaum.
Lewin, R. (2001) *Weaving Complexity and Business: Engaging the Soul at Work*, New York: Texere.
Martin, D. J., Garske, J. P. and Davis, K. M. (2000) 'Relation of the therapeutic alliance with outcome and other variables: a meta-analytic review', *Journal of Consulting and Clinical Psychology*, **68**: 438–50.
McNiff, J. and Whitehead, J. (2005) *Action Research for Teachers*, London: David Fulton.
Postman, N. and Weingartner, C. (1987) *Teaching as Subversive Activity*, New York: Laurel Press.
Rogers, C. and Frieberg, H. (1994) *Freedom to Learn*, 3rd edn, New York: Merrill.

Meaningful classroom activity

Stevick. E. W. (1976) *Memory, Meaning and Method: Some Psychological Perspectives on Language Learning*, Boston: Heinle & Heinle.

Tomlinson, B. (2001) 'The inner voice: a critical factor in L2 learning', *The Journal of the Imagination in Language Learning and Teaching*, 6. Available online at http://www.njcu.edu/cill/vol6/tomlinson.html (accessed 22 July 2011).

Tomlinson, B. (2003) 'Helping learners to develop an effective L2 inner voice', *RELC Journal*, 34(2): 178–94.

Underhill, A. (1989) 'Process in humanistic education', *ELT Journal*, 43(4): 250–60.

Underhill, A. (1999) 'Facilitation in language teaching', in Arnold, J. (ed.) *Affect in Language Learning*, Cambridge: Cambridge University Press, pp. 125–41.

Underhill, A. (2004) *Sound Foundations*, Oxford: Macmillan ELT.

Part C

Frameworks for meaningful language learning

Stevick has eloquently stressed the importance of meaning-making for language use and language learning and teaching. This also extends to issues of planning and establishing the structures and conditions which in one way or another support the language learning process by affording possibilities for engagement, belonging, challenge, agency, motivation and other facilitating factors. Hanks (1991) said that 'structure is more the variable outcome of action than its invariant precondition'. This way of understanding structures as emerging from action correlates with much of what we know about effective ways to promote second language acquisition. For example, we take action to know our students and do activities with them that we expect may relate to their needs, and thus classroom structures emerge from our interactions to serve these needs.

Language learning and teaching entail a host of interrelated systems that as Larsen Freeman and Cameron (2008) have shown are dynamic, complex and emerging. In this part the authors look at individuals and classrooms but also bring in larger systems and networks of support for language education, as well as new ways to conceptualize language and language learning.

In Chapter 14 Heidi Byrnes argues for a reorientation in our understanding of the nature of language if our language classrooms are to prepare students for the complex demands of meaning-making that they face in an increasingly multicultural and multilingual world. Expanding Stevick's notion of 'personal competence', she presents language and learning as quintessentially social and meaning-oriented. That means that we are always engaged with an Other, that we are borrowing words that have been used by others who gave them particular meanings, and that learning to be a competent user is learning to respect those earlier, socioculturally embedded meanings while also giving them one's own particular meanings.

In support of an ecological view of ways to structure classroom interaction, Leo van Lier stresses in Chapter 15 the importance of the classroom atmosphere and develops Stevick's idea of control and initiative on the part of both the teacher and the students, opening up possibilities for meaningful action. Van Lier looks at other related terms (constraints and resources; structure and process) that can have implications of an institutional nature and that affect the conditions for developing learner agency and the classroom community. In his opinion (van Lier 2000: 246), 'the learner is immersed in an environment full of potential meanings' and learning is not just getting things inside the learner's head but more 'the development of increasingly effective ways of dealing with the world and its meanings'.

Madeline Ehrman in Chapter 16 provides a personal narrative which reviews her varied language learning experiences and her explorations of ways to help others learn more effectively, especially taking into account learners' individual differences and the application of principles from the field of psychology. These experiences have led to the development of the Learner Consultation Service, which was created to deal with orientation and problem-solving in the process of language learning at the Foreign Service Institute of the US State Department. She provides a useful example of consultation and shows us how to work with it reflectively as an option for the structuring of more effective language instruction.

In Chapter 17 Donald Freeman examines the relationship among three different but strongly interrelated areas: the preparation teachers receive, what they then do in the classroom and what students learn. He points out that one does not automatically determine the other and gives suggestions to illuminate the connections that can be predicted between learning and teaching. He then analyses five pairs of concepts which help to structure thinking about what teachers can be expected to take from teacher education and use in the classroom and then what students in the end 'learn'.

The approach to language learning taken by Mark Clarke in Chapter 18 is informed by systems theory, sociocultural and historical perspectives of education, as well as constructive-developmental psychology, and is based on the belief that we need to understand how organizational and individual identities construct each other if we are to make significant changes in the ways we teach or in the impact our teaching has on student learning. Clarke deals with the central problem of resistance to change and describes an action research project designed to reveal the organizational, interactional and psychological factors that contribute to this phenomenon of resistance to change while also pointing out possible roads towards greater acceptance of innovation and transformative learning at the individual and institutional levels.

References

Hanks, W. (1991) 'Forward', in Lave, J. and Wenger, E. (eds.) *Situated Learning: Legitimate Peripheral Participation*, Cambridge: Cambridge University Press, pp. 13–24.

Larsen-Freeman, D. and Cameron, L. (2008) *Complex Systems and Applied Linguistics*, Oxford: Oxford University Press.

van Lier, L. (2000) 'From input to affordance: social interactive learning from an ecological perspective', in Lantolf, J. (ed.) *Sociocultural Theory and Second Language Learning*, Oxford: Oxford University Press, pp. 245–59.

14 Renting language in the ownership society: reflections on language and language learning in a multilingual world

Heidi Byrnes

Introduction

Re-reading some of Earl W. Stevick's publications in anticipation of contributing to this volume, I was struck again by the central role he accorded to what he refers to as 'humanistic' language teaching and learning. That focus is unmistakably stated in the title of one of his late works, *Humanism in Language Teaching* (1991). But an interest in 'humanistic' approaches had long permeated his scholarly output. Thus, the preface to *Memory, Meaning and Method: Some Psychological Perspectives on Language Learning* (1976) reiterated a belief that he had already stated earlier on, namely that language study was to be regarded as a 'total human experience', as being oriented towards the whole person who is acting and interacting in the classroom. Accordingly, while the opening sections of that book dealt with the biological bases of memory and diverse experiments on verbal memory and verbal learning, Stevick left little doubt in the treatment of 'meaning' and 'method' in the remainder of the volume that his real concern was, to use his plain-spoken, memorable phrasing, with 'what goes on inside and between folks' (1976: 119).

That turn of phrase provides a useful first-hand characterization of the intended focus. Even so, reference to this interest as being 'humanist' or indicating 'humanism' might, in light of current use, appear to be somewhat oddly placed, perhaps even overstated. However, Stevick's publications, especially *Teaching Languages: A Way and Ways* (1980) and his responses to diverse interpretations, over-interpretations and misinterpretations of that work by contemporary scholarship (see Stevick 1983 and other contributions in Clarke and Handscombe 1983), are unequivocal in the matter. To him, *Teaching Languages* presented an expansive personal reflection on three contemporary teaching methods that, despite their differences, were unified by what he called their 'humanistic' approach: Gattegno's the Silent Way, Curran's Counselling-Learning / Community Language Learning and Lozanov's Suggestopedia (see Maley, this volume).

What makes them 'humane' or 'humanist' is the central role they accord in the processes of teaching and learning to learners' feeling, both emotional and aesthetic; to social relations, including friendship and cooperation; to responsibility; to critical reasoning abilities; and to self-actualization that pursues a path towards individuality. To advance the point even more forcefully, a subsequent interpretation by Stevick himself of his own writing includes this pointed question: 'to what extent should our goals be confined – *can* our goals be confined – to the linguistic competence and the communicative competence of our students? On the other side of this issue, to what extent can we, or should we, pay attention to how our teaching affects what in teaching and learning languages I am calling the "personal competence" of the student?' (1983: 68). This 'personal competence' encompasses a great deal:

> [It] includes knowledge of learning techniques, but it also includes awareness of how one's own mind works through various techniques, and awareness of how one adopts or adapts techniques, and of how one deals with the emotional side effect of the study experience. It even carries over into the student's changing attitude toward the foreign culture, and toward his/her own fitness to deal with foreigners and their languages. (p. 68)

Closing the loop between his humanist impetus, his personal reflections on three methodological options that realize diverse aspects of that impetus and his focus on the personhood of the learner, he is wary of what he bluntly terms 'whole-hog humanism' with its 'nice moral sheen' (p. 69). At the same time, he describes *Teaching Languages* as a set of explorations 'in the identification and development of personal competence in students of foreign languages' (p. 69).

From personal competence in the classroom to dialogical competence in a multilingual world

It is this notion of 'personal competence' that is the focus of my chapter. Like other contributors to this volume, I am much attracted to particular lines of Stevick's thinking, even as the contexts and scholarly dynamics that led him to foreground specific issues, including his understanding of the notion of personal competence and how it might be developed in the interactions of the classroom, have surely changed over the last three decades or so. For example, Stevick's lifelong probing into the culture of language classrooms and the methods being used was animated by the phenomenon that learning outcomes can vary considerably, within classes and across them. Today, in a post-methods era, we are less inclined to seek answers in terms of teaching methods, even humanist teaching methods. Rather, we would be more prone to seek information about cognitive, educational, social and environmental factors that might influence the affordances and obstacles for learning that characterize a particular learner's forms and levels of engagement and, by extension, his or her facility with the language. In other words, we have come to consider a number of important aspects subsumed under Stevick's notion of personal competence.

To some extent this shift reveals the impact of a more pronounced sociocultural orientation regarding teaching and learning (e.g. Lantolf 2005) than prevailed in the late 1970s. Also, our heightened awareness of the dynamic non-linearity of language development, as that has been persuasively laid out in dynamic systems theory (de Bot et al. 2007), now predisposes us to expect learner and learning differences rather than not to do so. At the same time, we might not designate the kind of teaching Stevick described and advocated as 'humanist', even though most of us have endorsed interactionist notions of teaching and learning. However, exactly that link is made by Richards and Rodgers (1982) in their seminal article on approaches, designs and procedures in teaching methods when they associate giving prominence to interaction with humanistic approaches. Finally, in the multilingual and multicultural classrooms in which many of us teach, the effects of multiple cultural and linguistic beliefs, values and identities are constantly being brought home to us. For that reason Stevick's focus on the importance of learners' self-esteem and identity as ways of seeing themselves now and projecting themselves into the future are likely to resonate strongly with many language educators (see the contributions by Kristjánsson, and Arnold, this volume).

Those developments in the direction of emphasizing 'personal competence' notwithstanding, I believe additional, deeper probing is necessary to appreciate more fully its relevance and implications. Specifically, I identify two interrelated phenomena within that construct that to me are crucial in our age, an age that we customarily refer to in terms of globalization, that we summarize as multilingual, multicultural, multiethnic and multi-religious, and that we experience within multimodal, ever more expanding, complexly mediated, functionally differentiated and hybridized forms of communication.

The first refers to teaching and learning, Stevick's own passionate preoccupation. The question to be posed nowadays is this: how can we enable learners, even those that primarily learn a second language in the environment of the language classroom, to become and to be makers of meaning as they interact with others in and through several languages in various and variously configured cultural contexts? That focus on the phenomena of meaning-making is a marked repositioning of what might have been a peripheral concern with the foreign, the foreigner and the foreign culture of language classrooms even in the not so distant past. Not only is sidelining meaning no longer viable, the very distinction of the native and the foreign has lost its erstwhile taxonomic purity. For example, a much-discussed report by the Modern Language Association of America (MLA 2007) proposed as the desired goals of language education in the twenty-first century that students should become translingually and transculturally competent. Similarly, and focusing on the whole, embodied person, Kramsch (2009) highlights that language users are sign users, that using signs is all about meaning-making and that language learners as multilingual language users are participants in and shapers of an expanding and complex symbolic power, all of which affects their subjective experiences of conducting their lives as multilingual subjects in continually changing symbolic realities.

The second phenomenon that challenges us in conjunction with the construct of personal competence is therefore language itself: how might we go about redirecting our understanding of language in a way that sees language as a semiotic system, that is, as a meaning-making system that constitutes a resource, not a rule-governed 'object' to be 'acquired' in language acquisition? Language exists as a semiotic *potential* that is realized only as it is being used in particular contexts of situation within larger contexts of culture by particular language users. For the emergent multilingual user whom we call the foreign/second language learner, that potential for meaning-making through the semiotic systems of now several languages becomes exponentially more expansive – and with it the challenge to come to use it for one's personal good as well as for the good of others and society. Seen in this way, language learning might aptly be described as an evolving awareness of and ability to engage with those expanded resources, what we have come to call 'multicompetence' (e.g. Cook 1992).

Importantly, like all semiotic systems language is a shared resource because meaning itself is a shared resource. Even though Stevick seemingly highlights a path to *individuality,* I suggest that his concern with the individual is not the culturally solipsistic notion of American individualism that Scovel in his discussion of Stevick's work roundly critiques (1983: 90). Stevick's simultaneous emphasis on affect, emotion and identity, not to mention responsibility, inherently points to social acts, that is, to forms of exchange between two or more parties. In other words, meaning-making, and most especially meaning-making with language, is inherently social and involves another. Indeed, the very system of language is not individually owned but resides at the dynamic intersection of individual choice and the conventions and typicalities of language use as the user community has gradually developed them into oral and written genres and their registers. For that reason, we rightly speak of *dialogue* as perhaps the most central manifestation of our human capacity to be a languaging species.

To sum up, I propose a focus on the fundamental *dialogicality* of all meaning-making and the consequent situated and contingent nature of meaning-making as a way of establishing a rich theoretical grounding for the notion of personal competence that we hope to enable through our pedagogies. I am aware that our field has only recently shown some measure of support for such a notion. For that reason, rather than simply assuming agreement on the central role of dialogicality for how we understand language itself (as contrasted with pedagogical activities), I begin by taking a more indirect path, namely via the related notion of ownership and its correlative term of rental, using that nexus as a *leitmotif* for a meaning-oriented understanding of language. Ultimately, of course, any such theorizing is interesting to the extent that it is 'appliable', to use Halliday's wording (2010), to the complex environments of communication that a 'personally linguistically competent' language learner will need to be able to negotiate in the age of global communication. Closer to the concerns of this volume, it is interesting to the extent that it can help us understand and guide the complex performances by all actors in the language classroom.

Reconsidering the metaphor of ownership

I have chosen four perspectives for moving us, step by step, from notions about individuals 'acquiring', 'owning' and 'controlling' language by means of adhering to rules towards more interconnected notions of how we go about making meaning through language and, by extension, how we go about learning to use language in the complex give and take of different social spaces, including virtual spaces of communication.

Who owns language and languages?

In a 1996 article that appeared in *Die Unterrichtspraxis*, a journal by the American Association of Teachers of German (AATG) devoted to pedagogical issues of German as a foreign language, Kramsch posed the provocative question 'Wem gehört die deutsche Sprache?' (To whom does the German language belong?) In a first take she answered it unequivocally as 'Why, to the Germans, of course – also to the Austrians, the

Swiss, to all those for whom German is the native language' (1996: 1). However, further elaborating on her answer, she used the notion of ownership to expose the problematic consequences of the long tradition in second language acquisition (SLA) theorizing and practice of assigning normative prominence to native speakers to the detriment of non-native speaker-learners and their use of the foreign language.

Since then, Kramsch's critique has gained strength through numerous publications and presentations (e.g. Cook 1992; Kramsch 1997; Ortega 2010; Pavlenko 2011). In what has been called the 'bilingual turn' in language studies, authors find fault with (1) the undue weight being given to an accident of birth and a concomitant denial of the effects of history, culture and societal use; (2) the undisputed authority and legitimacy in representing and arbitrating standards of form and use enjoyed by native speakers; and (3) the troubling disregard of current social, political and cultural realities of multilingualism and ever-changing forms of hybridity between multiple languages as learners adopt and adapt various identities in diverse circumstances of life.

In short, the contested space is the L2 learners' fully legitimized participation in shaping and using language in a multilingual environment, including the foreign language classroom. Most language teachers are, of course, well attuned to the kinds of dynamics that I have just identified. Even so, professional discourse practice continues to express language development in terms of complexity, accuracy and fluency (typically abbreviated as CAF), despite the fact that such indicators privilege an exclusionary stance toward L2 learners and do not entirely account for what actually takes place and what matters in L2 learning once we 'sanction' it in terms of meaning-making. One need not draw the same conclusion as Widdowson does when he suggests that 'the extent to which it [i.e. the learner's capacity for making meaning] produces native speaker competence is of secondary and contingent concern' (1983: 106) and yet be able to appreciate the fact that 'accuracy', typically associated with native-like behaviour and, not coincidentally, the privileged performance characteristic targeted in testing, is secondarily related to learners' primary task of exploring languages as semiotic resources. That statement in no way invalidates affirming the critical importance of precise (and accurate) ways of conveying one's intended meanings. But it reprioritizes how we as language teachers see language and engage our learners and how they themselves engage creatively as they learn a second language in order to be able to engage in acts of meaning (for a theoretical treatments of these matters, see Larsen-Freeman 2006; Norris and Ortega 2009; for a discussion of the consequences for individual learners, see Kramsch 2009).

227

Frameworks for meaningful language learning

The conduit metaphor of language

The second perspective takes us even closer to practices in research and instruction that can prevent us from seeing language as a functional, meaning-making resource which, at its core is contingent and negotiated dialogical give and take. At the same time, these practices uncover broad societal stances towards language that confine it in a narrow framework of ownership – in Western societies naturalized as *individual ownership.*

With respect to the difficulties practitioners have with understanding the results of language learning research, Stevick speculated that common terms like 'strategies' or 'filter' or 'networks' are subject to a 'kind of insidious reification, that is to say, a tendency to think of an abstraction as if it were a thing' (1990: 146). In a seminal article, Reddy (1979) uncovered one of the most consequential instances of such reification, referring to it as the conduit metaphor. He began investigating how we imagine, metaphorically, the nature of communicating with language by focusing on unsuccessful communicative events. There he cited expressions such as:

Try to *get* your *thoughts across* better.

None of Mary's *feelings came through to* me with any clarity.

You still haven't *given me* any *idea* of what you mean.

In a similar vein, academics critiquing student writing might make comments like these:

You have to *put* each *concept into words* very carefully.

You have to *pack* more *thoughts* into fewer *words.*

Insert those *ideas* elsewhere *in* the *paragraph.*

Further extensive study of numerous areas of language use led Reddy to conclude that speakers of English routinely refer to ways of communicating with each other in terms of a conduit through which we send words, like packages, from one person to the other. Such imagery is by no means innocent inasmuch as it suggests that it is the words themselves that contain thoughts and feelings, and that the meanings contained in those words somehow travel 'unfettered and completely disembodied, into a kind of ambient space between human heads … independent of any need for living human beings to think or feel them' (Reddy 1979: 170). For Reddy, such notions risk leading us down a blind alley of 'mass communication systems coupled with mass neglect of the internal, human systems responsible for nine-tenths of the work in communicating' (p. 188).

How Reddy's insight manifests itself in language teaching and learning is well worth considering: by suggesting that we are 'capturing ideas in words' (Reddy 1979: 188), the conduit metaphor plays right into an interrelated set of illusions in L2 instruction: (1) it suggests that meanings exist independently of language, therefore what another language expresses in its words is essentially the same thing being expressed in the native language, except in 'strange' ways; (2) it absolves the language learner of responsible engagement with the nature of meaning-making that characterizes a particular language as it resides within a particular sociocultural environment; (3) it occludes an understanding of language learning as being about learning how to mean in a new language, where the lexicogrammatical resources made available in that language potentially create semantic spaces that differ considerably from those provided in the native language; and (4), correlatively, it easily overemphasizes the role of individual lexical words rather than focusing on the entire lexicogrammatical system of a language as a resource and a *potential* for meaning-making, one that language learners themselves need to *realize* in particular instances of oral and written communication – in the multiple meanings of that word – in their own evolving L2 language use.

Virtual spaces and the refiguration of language-based social practices

A growing experimentation with different forms of realization and participation – that is, with different ways of being through languaging – is particularly noticeable among young people. It seems that the exuberantly hybrid environment that technology creates for communication also leads to the development of different forms of identity, linguistic innovation, language play and voicing in their native languages as well as in a second language (Belz 2002; Belz and Thorne 2006; Lam 2006). For L1 language use in cyberspace, young people's language use includes

- affinity groups that develop 'through networking, collaborating, and affiliating, sometimes across distance, around common interests, joint endeavors, and shared causes' (Lam 2006: 219);
- the creation of what have been called 'glocalized' identities, whereby locally valued forms of identity and communication are referenced to and aligned with globally available forms of ethnic belonging and participation;
- the recognition that rather than building on fixed forms of ownership, identity construction and learning proceed through 'the production of intercultural capital, cosmopolitan identities, and sites of digital transcultures' (Lam 2006: 228).

Frameworks for meaningful language learning

For L2 language learning researchers have identified similar tendencies, leading to

- the potential of language play across languages as enabling the acquisition of L2 language forms;
- such engagement serving as 'a textual icon for learners' growing multicompetence (i.e., the distinct state of mind with 2 or more grammars ...) [and] learners' sense of self and their ways of interacting with the world' (Belz 2002: 13); and
- such hybrid practices strengthening 'the ecological relations between language practices and identity dispositions developed within both instructional L2 settings and the plurilingual world outside of school' (Thorne 2009: 91).

The reality of multilingual, multicultural societies

As the previous examples indicate, the foundational equation for much of our understanding of language, namely nation = language = culture, no longer holds. What was once the ideal and idealized single normed language now resides within a multiplicity of horizontally stratified and functionally differentiated versions with different roles, forms of access and participation for individuals, groups of people and across states.

Mobility and migration produce additional shifts across individual lifespans and for entire social groups. Specifically, migration by individuals and groups is frequently accompanied by demands for different levels and different kinds of literacies within the same language. These demands extend all the way to the need for groups of people to conduct their entire lives in functionally highly differentiated multiple languages. As a result, what is a native and what is a foreign language becomes blurred by contexts of use. Not surprisingly, education plays a critical role in the maintenance, acquisition and disappearance of available varieties – all processes that are linked to access and social power and that affect and are affected by notions of ownership. In other words, repeated refigurations of multilingualism become the norm rather than the exception, much less a deviation from 'properly' functioning societies.

Furthermore, the pursuit of tertiary education, and that includes instruction in professional forms of language use, is no longer a privilege for the few but a necessity for the many. Language education must therefore attend to this increase in functional uses to which learners might, in the future, put their several languages. That translates into an expanded set of educational goals, potentially including language use in the professions, such as healthcare, engineering and the business world, to name but the most obvious areas. At the same time, the observed expansion signals that who 'owns' a language and what constitutes its competent performance has to be thoroughly rethought, a requirement that is well illustrated by the fact that healthcare in many countries around the world is increasingly being delivered by non-native users of the local language. As a result there is an urgent need for heightened attention to the nature of language use by all parties, especially on the part of healthcare professionals (Slade et al. 2008).

Finally, in a kind of ironic twist, the prominence of the global lingua franca English by now undermines the very notions of ownership and its association with an elevated position for the native speaker that had originally propelled the spread of English (Graddol 2006).

How do these four perspectives illuminate the topic at hand? The reality of multilingualism and hybridity foregrounds the crucial function of the context of an utterance. Agar (1994) has coined the apt term of 'languaculture' to highlight the intricate and dynamically changing relationship between the environment of use and the various languages users deploy in a particular context. Language means in a context of culture and in a context of situation. If, then, we are to 'own' its meanings in a new way, we will have to become exquisitely aware of the contexts that brought them on in the first place. Recognizing the need for such forms of appropriation is another way of signalling that 'singular ownership' is increasingly insufficient for successful communication.

For L2 learning in a global environment, the challenge might then be stated like this. At a first level, language instruction must find ways in which *language and context* can be incorporated into language teaching and learning, right from the beginning of instruction, even in a foreign language teaching setting that might be far removed from the L2 culture. Recent years have provided convincing evidence for the proposal that a genre- and text-based approach is likely to be the most advantageous way for creating that kind of heightened awareness and self-reflexivity about the nature of meaning-making. This is so because genre-based teaching can enable learners to develop an increasingly differentiated meta-awareness about the intricate link between the lexico-grammatical patterns that are characteristic for a particular genre and social activity. As Martin states so aptly: 'Genres are how things get done, when language is used to accomplish them' (1985: 250). In other words, through genre we are not only able to foreground that we make meaning through oral and written texts – from very short to very extended; we concurrently model the link between textual form and social context and social context and textual form (for an overview, see

Rose 2011; for L2 instructional application, see Byrnes et al. 2010). At a second level, instruction will then be able to highlight that 'words matter' but do so in relation to the context of their use and the particular instance of use. In contemporary language learning, recognizing that fact will be just as much a task as learning the wordings themselves, a way of instilling in learners a responsibility towards present audiences and, through technology, increasingly also towards non-present, imagined audiences – in short, a way of being 'personally competent' in the way I believe Stevick intended.

To sum up, communication and its success are potentially ever more fragile because ownership is not simply given and cannot simply be claimed. Recognizing the fragility but also the surfeit of meaning-making potential that inheres in the situation, communicative partners must develop a sophisticated, multilayered awareness of the innumerable transculturally and translinguistically derived meaning potentials that a particular context affords in order to position themselves and others responsibly and constructively within them. That is a tall order when communication takes place among members of the same social and linguistic group. It is a particularly tall order for the foreign language classroom to prepare students to operate in such contexts. But unless we understand it as such, we have little chance of making our classrooms environments that even begin to address this challenge.

Bakhtin and Halliday: from owning to renting language

Thus far I have emphasized ownership and its limitations as a way of illustrating the importance of the interpretive frameworks we choose for how we shape the field of language teaching and learning. To make the case more strongly, I now turn to the correlative term of rental, the second guiding metaphor for this chapter.

Bakhtin's reflections on language, many of which hail from the politically, socially and intellectually turbulent times of Russia in the twenties and thirties, attenuate fixed notions of ownership inasmuch as he points out intertextual, dialogic and contextual aspects of meaning-making, most especially through the notion of socially agreed upon genres. Complementing Bakhtin's textual orientation is Halliday's systemic functional theory of language with its affirmation of the embeddedness of language in social activity, another way of reassessing language 'ownership'. Not only is language use functional but the system of language itself in its lexicogrammatical resources is functional with regard to cultural, historical and therefore contingent and changing perspectives, interests and purposes. For that reason, a theory of language that would be usable and useful in L2 teaching and learning must centrally focus on explicating the consequences of opting for this wording vs another wording that might also have been used in order to convey the generally intended particular *meaning*. Linguistic theory refers to this as the vertical axis of choices within a paradigm, the paradigmatic axis. This perspective contrasts with the horizontal, syntagmatic axis of syntax, where the emphasis is on structure, that is, what word, phrase, clause follows the previous one according to *structural rules*, generally stated with little regard for meaning. As we know too well, it is the latter which has constituted the prevailing emphasis in much language instruction.

As for the notion of 'rental' itself, its original motivation comes from Bakhtin's extensive analysis in 'Discourse in the Novel' (1981: 293–4), where he makes the following observation:

> The word in language is half someone else's. It becomes 'one's own' only when the speaker populates it with his own intention, his own accent, when he appropriates the word, adapting it to his own semantic and expressive intention. Prior to this moment of appropriation, the word does not exist in a neutral and impersonal language (it is not, after all, out of a dictionary that the speaker gets his words!), but rather it exists in people's mouths, in other people's contexts, serving other people's intentions: it is from there that one must take the word, and make it one's own.

But Bakhtin hastens to caution that

> not all words for just anyone submit equally easily to this appropriation, to this seizure and transformation into private property: many words stubbornly resist, others remain alien, sound foreign in the mouth of the one who appropriated them and who now speaks them; they cannot be assimilated into his context and fall out of it; it is as if they put themselves in quotation marks against the will of the speaker. Language is not a neutral medium that passes freely and easily into the private property of the speaker's intentions; it is populated – overpopulated – with the intentions of others. Expropriating it, forcing it to submit to one's own intentions and accents, is a difficult and complicated process.

My choice of 'rental' over 'ownership' as a more desirable metaphor refers to some of these aspects, most especially its strong relational quality. If a word is 'half someone else's', that is, if we half own the word, the nature of such 'appropriation' or 'ownership' is likely to be determined by the specifics of a particular case. Whatever the configuration, we can no longer speak of non-contingent individual 'ownership' (as a narrow interpretation of copyright law or the prominence of dictionary definitions does) but must acknowledge the socially shared nature of meanings and meaning-making, synchronically and diachronically, across texts. The choice of 'rental' signals as well that, though some rights accrue to the renter, these, too, will have to be rethought in line with responsibilities and obligations. Linguistic renters gain a framework for expression that facilitates their expressive capacities, and they gain the capacity to participate in communication, the freedom to mean. But they gain both because others can and, ideally, will acknowledge that freedom in the first place.

In the process, both parties will foster and expand their ways of thinking for speaking, thinking for reading, thinking for listening and thinking for writing, as Slobin (1996) aptly calls this intimate link between culturally steeped shared thought that nevertheless evolves individually through languaging. In this fashion also, we create the new sources of multiple identities, the new sources of the self that seem to be at the heart of multicultural societies.

On that background, we can now look more closely at specific positions taken by Bakhtin and Halliday.

Exploring Bakhtin's dialogic self

The master trope at the heart of all of Bakhtin's reflections on language is the notion of heteroglossia or polyphony (Holquist 2002: 15). It is a concern for dialogism that Bakhtin expresses like this (1981: 272): 'every utterance participates in the "unitary language" (in its centripetal forces and tendencies) and at the same time partakes of social and historical heteroglossia (the centrifugal, stratifying forces)'. Language as a system of meaning exists and changes within these two forces – unifying (centrifugal) forces that assure successful communication and expanding (centripetal) forces that constitute creative adjustment to new communicative situations and needs.

Given the prevalence of notions of fixed ownership in how we imagine language, it is fair to ask: what is gained by beginning our reflections on the nature of language with polyphony, with multiplicity, with multivoicedness? First, it is the potential for an exquisite awareness of the social foundation of language, of the process of meaning-making and the extraordinary fragility of human cultural work, both on the individual and on the social plane among different societal groups. By extension, such a stance foregrounds the inherent historicity of languaging and of ways of meaning and being through language, whether that 'being' is focused on the individual or an entire social group. Second, it is a way

234

of acknowledging that the primal use of language is in dialogic settings, where we direct our speech to a particular addressee and expect that addressee to participate in the work of understanding. In other words, for communication through language to 'work' exquisite awareness of the Other is a *necessity*, not the ancillary accident that can be added *after* particular wordings have been chosen.

Dialogicality so understood is far from an endless and ultimately irresponsible relativity, not a vapid 'liberating licentiousness' nor 'no more than multiple point of view' [*sic*] (Holquist 2002: 108). Instead, it has two powerful anchors. The first is provided by the centring forces of the language system itself. Recognizing its inherent dialogicality, Wertsch (2006) calls it 'a generalized collective dialogue'. The second is flexible, creative and multivocal, and heteroglossic language use in the here and now. Both take place in a simultaneity of time and space, inasmuch as a language incorporates in itself the present as well as the history of an entire linguistic group. Here Bakhtin incorporates into his understanding of language insights that he gained from quantum physics. I suggest that such considerations are remarkably close to those expressed by Stevick: it is within this dialogicality of the system and the unique instance of meaning-making, both for the native language user and the L2 language learner, that the present and the past, that synchrony and diachrony, language use and language change, meet up. Individual language learning and the continuity of the system across generations of a speech community are sustained even as imperceptible innovations are accumulated over time.

Halliday: choices in contexts of culture and contexts of situation

We have thus arrived at foundations for a theory of language that explicitly point to the external cultural context in its multiplicity while also expressing its necessary dynamic stability. It links the multiplicity of individual ways of going about meaning-making to an encompassing frame of reference for meaning-making, the language being used and the languages being learned, perhaps over a lifetime.

To be useful for educational contexts, such a theory must possess a level of transparency that enables researchers, teachers and the general public to understand how we go about making nuanced choices, nuanced expressive choices and nuanced interpretive choices. In his *Introduction to Functional Grammar* (1994), Halliday takes a crucial initial step towards that goal by identifying the functionality of language from three perspectives. First, language is functional in terms of how it is used in society because everything said or written occurs in some context of use. Second, it is functional in terms of its macro-components, which he identifies as the ideational component (how we understand our environment) and the interpersonal component (how we act on and interact with others). Realizing both is the textual component, which is the way the ideational and the interpersonal metafunctions are instantiated in a particular spoken or written text. Finally, it is functional because each element of the language is functional with respect to the whole language system, words and grammatical markers within clauses, clauses within sentences, sentences within textual episodes and so forth.

As a semiotic (i.e. a meaning-oriented) system, language use is about choices in wording that reveal the perspectives users take within the overall context of culture and in response to particular contexts of communication as they see them. Martin takes the trajectory of context of culture – context of situation – preferred register of language one step further through the construct of genre: they are 'linguistically realized activity types which comprise so much of our culture' (1985: 250) and 'verbal strategies used to accomplish social purposes of many kinds' (p. 251). The key distinction between genre and register is that genre can be analysed in terms of schematic textual structures, thereby allowing genre to become sites for investigating the typicalities as well as the choices that are available for linking formal structure and meaning at the textual level, and thus becoming sites of learning to mean in a personal way.

Specifically, through extensive textual modelling and scaffolding it is possible to work towards the educational goal of rendering meaning-making transparent for both teaching and learning. From the side of the teacher, Cope and Kalantzis (1993: 1) note that 'a genre approach to literacy teaching involves being explicit about the way language works to make meaning'. From the perspective of both teacher and learner, genre teaching, according to Christie (1999: 762), 'offers the capacity for initiating students into ways of making meaning that are valued', and also for 'reflecting on and critiquing the ways in which knowledge and information are organized and constructed' in a particular language. For foreign language teaching and learning, Byrnes et al. (2010) have foregrounded the need to socialize learners into beliefs, attitudes, values and ways of thinking: it is here that working with multiple textual genres affords learners multiple experiences with the moral, intellectual and aesthetic dimensions of variously configured texts, thereby preparing them to participate in the multiplicity of meaning-making of contemporary societies.

Conclusion

In conclusion, let me return to the central notions of ownership of language and of the suggestion that a dialogically constructed notion of languaging, here expressed in terms of 'renting', might be an appropriate way of constructing responsibility and freedom in the contemporary multilingual and multicultural world – of enabling an enlarged vision of Stevick's 'personal competence'. In such a world our intellectual and educational interest is to enable students to work with a multiplicity of expressive forms, in the context of different social languages, public life, the professions and institutions, many of which will reflect different ideologies. If such an educational goal is to become a reality, a meaning-oriented theory of language is likely to be indispensable. In addition, a genre-based literacy has much to recommend itself inasmuch as it focuses on how human beings, over time, proceeded to make sense of the phenomena around them by communicating about them in a certain fashion (see Hasan 1996: 21), whether that communication pertains to our private or our public lives or whether it is in the humanities, the social sciences or the natural sciences.

Not too long ago we could still conceive of all of this happening within one language and one cultural group. Now, however, we must conceive of it as happening in the hybrid spaces of translingual and transcultural communication. If that is so, our attention needs to be directed towards assuring a sophisticated awareness of the complexity of intersecting and overlapping discursive spaces – Discourses with a capital D as Gee calls them (2004) – a project that will continually require further negotiation so as to enable further creativity and freedom.

In a thoughtful discussion of the consequences of such a stance for curriculum building, Scarino (2010: 168–9) makes this point about intercultural learning: 'Learning to communicate inter-culturally also entails learning to reflect on one's own enculturation. It is this enculturation that constructs a person's linguistic, social, cultural, and social identity; that is, the *intra*-cultural dimension of one's own learning and communication' (italics in original). In that case, a metalinguistically reflective engagement with and appropriation of a rich array of social languages within ideologically marked Discourses might bring us closer to the foremost educational task facing multilingual societies. Stevick called the required sensitivity and responsibility 'personal competence'. Gee referred to the task as enabling contemporary learners to become moral agents as they appropriate the 'political geography of Discourses' (2004: 31). I have referred to it as responsible forms of renting language in the ownership society within a multilingual world.

Frameworks for meaningful language learning

References

Agar, M. (1994) *Language Shock: Understanding the Culture of Conversation*, New York: William Morrow.

Bakhtin, M. M. (1981) 'Discourse in the Novel', in Holquist, M. (ed.) *The Dialogic Imagination: Four Essays by Mikhail Bakhtin*, Austin, TX: The University of Texas Press, pp. 259–422.

Belz, J. A. (2002). 'Second language play as a representation of the multicompetent self in foreign language study', *Journal for Language, Identity, and Education*, 1: 13–39.

Belz, J. A. and Thorne, S. L. (eds.) (2006) *Internet-mediated Intercultural Foreign Language Education*, Boston: Thomson-Heinle.

Byrnes, H., Maxim, H. H. and Norris, J. M. (2010) 'Realizing advanced foreign language writing development in collegiate education: Curricular design, pedagogy, assessment', *The Modern Language Journal*, 94: Supplement s-1.

Christie, F. (1999) 'Genre theory and ESL teaching: a systemic functional perspective', *TESOL Quarterly*, 33: 759–63.

Clarke, M. A. and Handscombe, J. (eds.) (1983) *On TESOL '82: Pacific Perspectives on Language Learning and Teaching*, Washington, DC: TESOL.

Cook, V. (1992) 'Evidence for multicompetence', *Language Learning*, 42: 557–91.

Cope, B. and Kalantzis, M. (1993) 'Introduction: how a genre approach to literacy can transform the way writing is taught', in Cope, B. and Kalantzis, M. (eds.) *The Powers of Literacy: A Genre Approach to Teaching Writing*, Pittsburgh, PA: University of Pittsburgh Press, pp. 1–21.

de Bot, K., Lowie, W. and Verspoor, M. (2007) 'A dynamic systems theory approach to second language acquisition', *Bilingualism: Language and Cognition*, 10: 7–21.

Gee, J. P. (2004) 'Learning language as a matter of learning social languages within Discourses', in Hawkins, M. R. (ed.) *Language Learning and Teacher Education: A Sociocultural Approach*, Clevedon: Multilingual Matters, pp. 13–31.

Graddol, D. (2006) *English Next: Why Global English May Mean the End of English as a Foreign Language*, London: British Council.

Halliday, M. A. K. (1994) *An Introduction to Functional Grammar*, 2nd edn, London: Edward Arnold.

Halliday, M. A. K. (2010) 'Putting linguistic theory to work', keynote address delivered at the annual meeting of the American Association for Applied Linguistics, Atlanta, GA, 6–9 March.

Hasan, R. (1996) 'What kind of resource is language?', in Cloran, C., Butt, D. and Williams, G. (eds.) *Ways of Saying, Ways of Meaning: Selected Papers of Ruqaiya Hasan*, London: Cassell, pp. 13–36.

Holquist, M. (2002) *Dialogism: Bakhtin and His World*, London: Routledge.

Kramsch, C. (1996) 'Wem gehört die deutsche Sprache?', *Die Unterrichtspraxis*, 29: 1–11.

Kramsch, C. (1997) 'The privilege of the nonnative speaker', *PMLA*, 112: 359–69.

Kramsch, C. (2009) *The Multilingual Subject: What Foreign Language Learners Say about Their Experience and Why It Matters*, Oxford: Oxford University Press.

Lam, W. S. E. (2006) 'Culture and learning in the context of globalization: research directions', *Review of Research in Education*, 30: 213–37.

Lantolf, J. P. (2005) 'Sociocultural and second language learning research: an exegesis', in Hinkel, E. (ed.) *The Handbook of Research in Second Language Teaching and Learning*, Mahwah, NJ: Lawrence Erlbaum, pp. 335–53.

Larsen-Freeman, D. (2006) 'On the need for a new understanding of language and its development', *Journal of Applied Linguistics*, 3: 281–304.

Martin, J. R. (1985) 'Process and text: Two aspects of human semiosis', in Benson, J. D. and Greaves, W. S. (eds.) *Systemic Perspectives on Discourse*, Norwood, NJ: Ablex, pp. 243–74.

MLA Ad Hoc Committee on Foreign Languages (2007) 'Foreign languages and higher education: new structures for a changed world', *Profession 2007*: 234–45.

Norris, J. M. and Ortega, L. (2009) 'Towards an organic approach to investigating CAF in instructed SLA: the case of complexity', *Applied Linguistics*, 30: 555–78.

Ortega, L. (2010) 'The bilingual turn in SLA', keynote address delivered at the annual meeting of the American Association for Applied Linguistics, Atlanta, GA, 6 March. Available online at http://www2.hawaii.edu/~lortega/

Pavlenko, A. (ed.) (2011) *Thinking and Speaking in Two Languages*, Bristol: Multilingual Matters.

Reddy, M. J. (1979/1993) 'The conduit metaphor: a case of frame conflict in our language about language', in Ortony, A. (ed.) *Metaphor and Thought*, 2nd edn, Cambridge: Cambridge University Press, pp. 164–201.

Richards, J. C., and Rodgers, T. (1982) 'Method: approach, design, and procedure', *TESOL Quarterly*, 16: 153–68.

Rose, D. (2011) 'Genre in the Sydney School', in Gee, J. P. and Handford, M. (eds.) *The Routledge Handbook of Discourse Analysis*, London / New York: Routledge, pp. 209–25.

Scarino, A. (2010) 'Language and languages and the curriculum', in Liddicoat, A. J. and Scarino, A. (eds.) *Languages in Australian Education: Problems, Prospects and Future Directions*, Newcastle upon Tyne: Cambridge Scholars Publishing, pp. 157–77.

Scovel, T. (1983) 'Emphasizing language: a reply to humanism, neo-audiolingualism, and notional-functionalism', in Clarke, M. A. and Handscombe, J. (eds.) *On TESOL '82: Pacific Perspectives on Language Learning and Teaching*, Washington, DC: TESOL, pp. 85–96.

Slade, D., Scheeres, H., Manidis, M., Iedema, R., Stein-Parbury, J., Matthiessen, C., Herke, M. and McGregor, J. (2008) 'Emergency communication: the discursive challenges facing emergency clinicians and patients in hospital emergency departments', *Discourse and Communication*, 2: 271–98.

Slobin, D. I. (1996) 'From "thought and language" to "thinking for speaking"', in Gumperz, J. J. and Levinson, S. C. (eds.) *Rethinking Linguistic Relativity*, Cambridge: Cambridge University Press, pp. 70–96.

Stevick, E. W. (1976) *Memory, Meaning and Method: Some Psychological Perspectives on Language Learning*, Boston: Heinle & Heinle.

Stevick, E. W. (1980) *Teaching Languages: A Way and Ways*, Rowley, MA: Newbury House.

Stevick, E. W. (1983) 'My view of *Teaching Languages: A Way and Ways*', in Clarke, M. A. and Handscombe, J. (eds.) *On TESOL '82: Pacific Perspectives on Language Learning and Teaching*, Washington, DC: TESOL, pp. 63–75.

Stevick, E. W. (1990) 'Research on what? Some terminology', *The Modern Language Journal*, 74: 143–53.

Stevick, E. W. (1991) *Humanism in Language Teaching: A Critical Perspective*, Oxford: Oxford University Press.

Thorne, S. L. (2009) 'Community, semiotic flows, and mediated contribution to activity', *Language Teaching*, **42**: 81–94.

Wertsch, J. V. (2006) 'Generalized collective dialogue and advanced foreign language capacities', in Byrnes, H. (ed.) *Advanced Language Learning: The Contribution of Halliday and Vygotsky*, London: Continuum, pp. 58–71.

Widdowson, H. G. (1983) 'Competence and capacity in language learning', in Clarke, M. A. and Handscombe, J. (eds.) *On TESOL '82: Pacific Perspectives on Language Learning and Teaching*, Washington, DC: TESOL, pp. 97–106.

15   Control and initiative: the dynamics of agency in the language classroom

Leo van Lier

Introduction

For most language learners, the world over, the success or failure of their language studies depends in large measure on the classrooms that they are in or have been in. A lifelong champion of classroom quality, Dick Allwright, says the following:

> The quality of classroom life is itself the most important matter ...
> for the sake of encouraging people to become lifelong learners, rather
> than people resentful of having to spend years of their lives as 'captive'
> learners, and therefore put off further learning for life.

> (2006: 14–15)

There are of course other factors, such as the learners' goals and aspirations, interests and engagements, the teacher's enthusiasm and support and so on, but these things in themselves also depend a great deal on the atmosphere that is created in the classroom.

Over the years, Earl Stevick has tirelessly advocated for a classroom that promotes a 'feeling of community' and thereby creates a 'world of meaningful action' (1980: 26). Other researchers and practitioners likewise have argued for the importance of classroom quality (Gieve and Miller 2006), investigated the properties of 'the good language class' (Senior 1999) and documented interaction, collaboration, autonomy and so on (Allwright 1988; Benson 2001; Breen 2001). There is no shortage of opinions or desired features regarding what it takes to create a high-quality classroom or lesson.

In this chapter I will focus on the crucial distinction that Stevick (1980) has drawn between 'control' and 'initiative' and the dynamic relationship between them. I will do this by drawing on my own work on classroom interaction, and expand the discussion by looking at related distinctions such as 'constraints and resources' (van Lier 1998) and 'structure and process' (inspired by the insights of the great physicist and thinker David Bohm 1998).

My focus will be to take an ecological perspective that looks at three spatio-temporal scales: the institutional scale, the interpersonal scale and the (intra-)personal scale. These scales are equivalent to the three 'lenses' or 'planes' that Rogoff has postulated (1995: 158) and are given

241

an ecological flavour by emphasizing different spatial and temporal dimensions. On the institutional scale, there are standards, frameworks, assessment demands, budget issues, mandated textbooks and other macro-level concerns that have an impact 'from above' on what happens in the classroom. On the interpersonal scale there are the ways in which teachers and learners interact in the classroom: lecturing, question and answer routines, scaffolding and so on. On the intrapersonal scale we find the cognitive and affective processes of understanding, as well as the physical engagement with materials, the social engagement with other learners, the enactment of identity and everything else that 'moves' the learner (in a word, the learner's agency).

Control and initiative

For Stevick, control consists of two essential elements: the structuring of classroom activity and the provision of feedback. In this sense, control is very much a teacher function, although some control can gradually be shared with the students. In his view, the centrality of the teacher is important: the teacher rightfully demands and accepts the centre of the stage. However, this centrality of the teacher does not have to conflict with the centrality of the learner, which is expressed through initiative. The teacher can have 'nearly 100% of the control', and the students can have 'nearly 100%' of the initiative (1980: 17). Initiative, in Stevick's terms, refers to 'decisions about who says what, to whom, and when'. For the students to be able to make those decisions, and to play an 'active, central, self-validating role', the teacher must have provided a 'world of meaningful action', and this is the main purpose of the teacher's control (1980: 17–19). In other words, control in this view is enabling and supportive, and thereby it facilitates initiative.

A question arises immediately: how does the teacher go about controlling the environment in such a way (or such ways) that the student is enabled to enact his or her initiative? This is one of those questions that can be examined along the three scales mentioned above. First, on the institutional or community scale, educational contexts have certain rules and demands that – over time and within specified parameters – create certain ideas and expectations that particular instantiations of educational activity (such as language lessons) are held to. As an example, one such long-standing notion, deeply engrained in the folk wisdom, is that the target language is a distinct and autonomous code that must be pursued in a spirit of purity and perfection. This is sometimes called a monolingual or monoglossic ideology (García 2009; Ortega 2010), and it reverberates down to the interpersonal scale, disallowing translanguaging, an approach to bilingual pedagogy (and language use in general), in which different languages are used as part of meaning-making processes (Creese and Blackledge 2010), and to the intrapersonal scale, fostering a sociocognitive mindset that encourages students to keep their languages separate 'in their brain' so as to avoid contamination, pidginization or worse.

When Stevick's teacher crafts the controls to facilitate initiative, his or her adherence to (or rejection of) this monoglossic ideology will colour heavily the sorts of initiative that are legitimized in the classroom. The students themselves may not see their own emergent 'multicompetence' (Cook 1995) as a resource that they can legitimately use to mediate their cognitive and interactional exploits and experiments, inside or outside the classroom.

The student and the teacher therefore may operate inside a controlling carapace of linguistic and pedagogical expectations and rules. This may or may not be overtly visible or audible in classroom discourse, it may or may not be explicitly referenced as a guiding rule set (except when the rules are broken and explicitly invoked), but it may nevertheless be there, thus causing problems for a researcher conducting a conversation-analytical or ethnographic analysis of documented interaction. In a sense, absent voices, inaudible and unaddressed, may speak powerfully as silent yet controlling participants in discourse.

Setting aside these problems for the moment, teachers' controlling actions and students' initiating actions are fruitful topics of research. In my own early classroom interaction research (1988), I took stretches of teacher–student interaction, and stretches of student–student interaction, to get hold of the notion of initiative, that is, the idea of when and what is said, and by whom. Basically, by focusing on such agentive expressions as turn-taking, topic change, agreement, disagreement, turn allocation and sequencing work, it was possible to create an evaluative scale of initiative (from more to less) that showed relative initiative-taking of individuals within dyads and groups. Needless to say, the teacher always appeared as main initiative taker when he or she was in the interaction, but when looking at group work, interesting patterns of agency emerged. The explanatory value of this work is of course limited, but it is nevertheless revealing in terms of what students do or do not know, given certain activity types in the classroom (van Lier 1988; Kinginger 1994).

Constraints and resources

Constraints and resources are terms that cast the conceptual net into waters that are both wider and deeper than the earlier set of control and initiative. The philosopher Immanuel Kant said, in a famous aphorism, 'the light dove cleaving in free flight the thin air, whose resistance it feels, might imagine that her movements would be far more free and rapid in airless space' (1934: 29). The dove feels the air that pushes against its wings as a constraint, yet it is at the same time the resource that enables its flight. There are things we cannot do in classrooms, as teachers or as students, but to what extent are these things hindrances, and to what extent are they enablements? Let's give an example, first from a game of chess, then from a classroom. In chess, you can move the knight only in this way or that, the bishop in another way and so on. You might like to be able to move any piece in any way you want to, but then the game would deteriorate into chaos very quickly. The same is true in the classroom.

Constraints are not only brought into the learning arena by teachers or curricula (or a variety of institutional/societal strictures), but may derive from a multitude of interrelated forces that include the instructional ones mentioned, but also many other possibilities. At the cognitive (intrapersonal) level, for example, Piagetian developmental stages function as constraints: you cannot conceive of abstract functions, before relevant practical experiences. At the linguistic level, cognitive complexity of structures functions as a source of constraints, and at the pragmatic level, complexities of discourse, genre and so on provide constraints. You cannot express embedded questions unless you have learned to ask simple ones. At a pedagogical and instructional level, resources may be made available for students to overcome constraints of an institutional, linguistic, cognitive and sociocultural nature, and indeed, the constraints themselves may be turned into enabling resources through carefully designed collaborative work of an abductive nature, which involves active experimentation and the search for possible meanings, including the formation of hypotheses. Good examples of such work, which focuses on creative exploration, investigation and reflection, can be found in the work on exploratory practice of Dick Allwright and associates (Allwright and Hanks 2009; Gieve and Miller 2006; Yoshida et al. 2009). As an example, Allwright and Hanks report that in an EFL class, students felt significant constraints against using the L2 with their fellow students (they thought it was artificial, and they simply did not like it). At the same time, the curriculum strongly constrained and disapproved of the use of the L1. It seemed that neither L1 nor L2 use was enabled. The students resisted L2 use, and the curriculum minimized L1 use. After discussing, analysing and reflecting on their feelings about these issues, the teacher noted a much more proactive approach to using the L2 (p. 157).

In general, constraints of various kinds may create boundaries that can be difficult to cross for a learner or a teacher. We might take as an example the Piagetian experiments on scientific understandings, such as conservation of liquids and so on. According to Piaget, the boundary between non-understanding and understanding could be crossed only through a natural conceptual maturation, not through explicit instruction. Interestingly, Piaget maintained that it was easier for students at the same level to jointly cross such a boundary through dialogue, than through explicit instruction from a teacher (this, incidentally, was a major point of difference between Vygotsky and Piaget, since according to Vygotsky the only good learning is that which is ahead of development; see Vygotsky 1978).

Let me give a practical example from my own experience. I once observed a high school chemistry lesson somewhere in the USA. The students were working in groups using various liquids and powders to create a variety of compounds. I am not well versed in chemistry or physics, so I basically walked around the room taking notes on the interactions among the students (the teacher was at the desk in front, working with individual students on their previous homework). While I walked around the room, one group appeared to be discussing some sort of problem. As I observed them (not knowing what was going on), one student asked me, 'Excuse me, can you explain the difference between *melt* and *dissolve?*' I tried to explain it, but got confused, and decided to ask the teacher if he had a good definition and a couple of clear examples. The teacher's answer was, 'Oh no, I don't explain these concepts, the students will understand them when they are ready, through their collaborative work and discussions.' In other words, the message seemed to be, just keep working on it until the problem is resolved. I think many language teachers might be sceptical about how that would work in acquiring complex grammatical structures, but others might agree that it is the only way to come to grips with such perennial problem areas as the English article system, the Spanish subjunctive or the choice between *wa* or *ga* in Japanese.

Constraints – such as a gap in understanding – are conceived as opportunities for learning in the above pedagogical example. Trying to remove a constraint through explanation, in that view, means the loss of a learning opportunity. Applied to language teaching, this would mean that common practices such as explaining grammar rules and difficult words (a deductive approach) would be rejected in favour of an inductive one. Not all pedagogical theories adhere to this particular view of the relationship between constraints and resources. For example, systemic-theoretical instruction posits that 'mental activity is controlled by three processes: orientation, execution and control' (Lantolf and Thorne 2006: 304). This approach proposes that a high level of explicit knowledge is required at the outset of studying a particular linguistic feature (such

245

as aspect in Spanish; see Negueruela 2003). In this view, sometimes known as Systemic-Theoretical Intruction or STI (Lantolf and Thorne 2006), a high level of conceptual knowledge is a resource needed for successful learning, whereas in the example above, the focused activity itself is the resource that leads to conceptual knowledge. It is possible that both approaches may be effective, perhaps for different kinds of work and knowledge, or in some dynamic combination.

In the above, I have given examples of constraints of a cognitive or linguistic kind. The constraint of not allowing the use of the learners' L1 is another type of constraint, also introduced above, and we have to ask what it might enable in terms of learning opportunities in the L2. A further constraint is of course the institutional/political requirement of passing high-stakes tests at certain intervals. Teachers and policy-makers should ask themselves what these – and many other – constraints afford in terms of learning opportunities and progress.

The curriculum as structure and process

On the surface it would seem that the two terms *structure* and *process* are opposites, just like the earlier sets. However, on closer inspection it turns out that they, too, can actually be mutually constitutive, as the originator of the concept of 'structure/process' unity in nature, the physicist David Bohm, has argued. An example from a classroom may illustrate how structure and process might work together.

The following extract is taken from research on students working on a content-based unit on the brain in a class of English language learners in a high school in the USA (Crescenzi and Walqui 2010). In the lesson in question, learners in groups of four have read different case studies on brain injuries and their effects. In each group the learners have to compare notes and complete a matrix that answers four questions. Their answers have to be identical, since every member has to take this matrix to a new 'expert group' in which the case study in question is compared to three other case studies (the four cases are Phineas Gage; Stephen Hawking; Ellen G. White; and Charles Whitman). This particular group is studying Phineas Gage, a railway worker who got a tamping rod through his skull. A rule for completing the matrix is that students cannot copy from one another, but have to read and spell difficult words for each other. In the following scene, a student is preparing to copy a word from another student's worksheet, but the teacher intervenes:

S2:   Why can't I just copy it?

T: It doesn't help you practise the language. Doesn't help
          <u>HIM</u> practice the language. I want you to be able to
          use these academic terms.

S2:   But I <u>KNOW</u> English.
T: Yes, but psychoLOgical English.

This small example can be analysed from each of the three perspectives: control and initiative, constraints and resources, and structure and process, and in each case interesting information will come to light. For example, the teacher controls what the students can and cannot do in the activity. At the same time, the content of the matrix is based on the students' initiative on how to conceptualize and write down the content. At the constraints/resources level, we can see how conversational resources can enable academic language development.

Seen from the structure/process perspective, we can note an activity structure that has been specifically set up to enable the process of developing academic language by using academic language, one of the explicit requirements for academic success. At this early point in the structure/process activity, the structure is still seen as an imposition (a control) that impedes the smooth and rapid flow of work. Indeed, these students 'know English', since they are second-generation immigrants, and they have grown up using English conversationally. However, it is also a fact that such students face massive challenges in 'languaging' complex concepts in academic genres, and often resist expanding their identities to incorporate such genres. As one student complained, 'Why do we have to use these difficult words?'

Thus, the (initially imposed) structure is aimed at bringing about new processes of languaging, that is, the use of linguistic and other semiotic resources as part of sense-making (Garcia and Kleifgen 2010). This languaging allows the students to discuss academically complex concepts and events, and reorganize (restructure) their discursive and agentive space. Eventually, newly created discursive structures permit the students to expand their expressive repertoires without having to be externally imposed. The initially imposed structures therefore serve to prime the pump, as it were, of academic development without compromising the students' identity as competent users of English. They thus become multicompetent users (Cook 1995), capable of translanguaging between conversational and academic language, as in the following example, taken from a reflective interview after finishing the unit (S2 is the same student as in the extract above):

S2:   It was really cool. This guy Phineas Gage, a long time ago, working on a construction, had an accident, a rod penetrated Phineas' head. He did not die, he had frontal lobe damage, and he became angry, impatient. Before the accident he had been a nice man.
Interviewer: Why is he famous?

S2:   Because that was the first time that doctors studied
                       why people change their personality. Sometimes it is
                       brain damage.

Conclusion

In this chapter I have taken Stevick's original distinction between control and initiative, and added two related distinctions: constraints and resources, and structure and process.

The discussion has shown that Stevick's insightful remark that 100% control is compatible with 100% initiative is quite apt. There can be a productive tension between all three of the sets of terms, at different levels and layers of school work:

• Teacher expertise and learner autonomy
• Material resources (e.g. textbooks) and lesson/task design
• Curriculum design (planning) and interactional dynamics (improvisation).

Ideally, these dynamic forces or ingredients work together in mutually enhancing ways. However, the productivity, the positive energy, does not happen automatically. It is frequently the case that control/constraints/ structure kill off creativity and initiative, prevent the location and exploitation of resources or affordances and stifle emergent processes (van Lier 2000). It is therefore essential that the 'left-hand' terms of the three sets are designed to enable, free up and stimulate the 'right-hand' terms, and this is the crucial task of a curriculum. The balance required will be different in every context, but unless this is seen as a central goal, the curriculum will either rigidify or descend into chaos, and in both cases the pedagogical support for development may grind to a halt.

I will close with one more small extract, this time from a class in linguistics in a New York City high school. The students are studying aspects of language and are tasked with writing five letters on different aspects of language to a person of their choice (family member, friend, teacher, etc.). Here, Lavinia is reading the first paragraph of her first letter to the class. A short excerpt of the event follows (see also van Lier 2008):

[*L reading from her draft that is taped to the blackboard*]
L: I fou-uhhh ... I found from my research that
                       animal communication is not a language. Animal
                       communication is different from the human
                       communication because in case of dolphins they
                       communicate through ultrasonic pulses that cannot

	be heard by the human ear. I don't think that there are languages better than other. This is about it, because I do not have enough time. But I appreciate that you teach me these things and I consider you the best teacher that I ever had in my life.
T:	Amen, very nice job
(All):	[*Clap, laugh*]
J (to L):	Animal communication is not a language ... it IS a language, that's what I think. Because they are communicating with each other.
L:	But they do not speak
	[*Lots of talking*]
J:	(You can have) everything in a language; you can have words, sounds and everything ...
L:	But they don't have words. They don't say 'Mama'.
J:	It is a characteristic, and in animal language some of the characteristics that YOU [pointing to T] said ... it IS a language.

We see here that a new discursive organization is emerging after J addresses L and initiates a debate on whether animal communication is or is not a language. At this point, the structure (i.e. the activity of reading from an example on the board) gives way to a process (a multivoiced classroom debate) that was not planned or anticipated. Interestingly, the teacher steps back and lets the students voice their opinions. However, later in the class (not included above, but see van Lier 2008 for a longer transcript), he retakes control and restructures the discussion (which is loud and somewhat chaotic) by summarizing the controversy and allowing several students a turn to give their opinion. He then releases the organization once more and a new process of multivoiced debate ensues. The larger event shows a rhythmic alternation between constraining and releasing (structure and process), almost a discursive dance in which pulling back and letting go alternate (see Valsiner 2006 for further discussion).

In sum, the pedagogical classroom game is not one in which either a well-managed carefully planned, and above all orderly sequence of events unfolds, or one in which order has broken down and chaos reigns, but rather, it is a moving ritual that is at times tightly orchestrated, and at times free-flowing (or 'carnivalesque'; Bakhtin 1981; DaSilva Iddings and McCafferty 2007). Without structure, there is no process. Without process, structure is futile.

Finally, I return to the question I posed earlier: how does the teacher go about controlling the environment in such a way (or such ways) that the student is enabled to enact his or her initiative? To answer this, I would like to refer to Deci and Flaste (1995), who say that teachers' actions in the classroom can be either controlling or autonomy supporting. The former are detrimental to establishing a favourable pedagogical environment; the latter promote such an environment. I have no doubt that we can and should read Stevick's conceptualization of control as one that is entirely autonomy supporting – thus enabling him to claim, as mentioned earlier, that the teacher can have 100% control and the students 100% initiative.

References

Allwright, D. (1988) *Observation in the Language Classroom*, New York: Longman.

Allwright, D. (2006) 'Six promising directions in applied linguistics', in Gieve, S. N. and Miller, I. K. (eds.) *Understanding the Language Classroom*, Basingstoke: Palgrave Macmillan, pp. 11–17.

Allwright, D. and Hanks, J. (2009) *The Developing Language Learner: An Introduction to Exploratory Practice*, Houndsmills, Basingstoke: Palgrave Macmillan.

Bakhtin, M. M. (1981) *The Dialogical Imagination*, Austin, TX: The University of Texas Press.

Benson, P. (2001) *Teaching and Researching Autonomy in Language Learning*, London: Longman.

Bohm, D. (1998) *On Creativity*, London: Routledge.

Breen, M. (ed.) (2001) *Learner Contributions to Language Learning*, London: Longman.

Cook, V. J. (1995) 'Multi-competence and the learning of many languages', *Language, Culture and Curriculum*, 8(2): 93–8.

Creese, A. and Blackledge, A. (2010) 'Translanguaging in the bilingual classroom: a pedagogy for learning and teaching?', *The Modern Language Journal*, 94(1): 103–15.

Crescenzi, S. and Walqui, A. (2010) 'Brain injury jigsaw project (DVD)', San Francisco: WestEd.

Deci, E. and Flaste, R. (1995) *Why We Do What We Do: The Dynamics of Personal Autonomy*, New York: Putnam's Sons.

DaSilva Iddings, A. C. and McCafferty, S. G. (2007) 'Carnival in a mainstream kindergarten classroom: a Bakhtinian analysis of second language learners' off-task behaviors', *The Modern Language Journal*, 91(1): 31–44.

García, O. (2009) *Bilingual Education in the 21st Century: A Global Perspective*, Oxford: Wiley-Blackwell.

García, O. and Kleifgen, J. A. (2010) *Educating Emergent Bilinguals: Policies, Programs, and Practices for English Language Learners*, New York: Teachers College.

Gieve, S. N. and Miller I. K. (eds.) (2006) *Understanding the Language Classroom*, Basingstoke: Palgrave Macmillan.

Kant, E. (1934) *The Critique of Pure Reason*, London: Dent.

Kinginger, C. (1994) 'Learner initiative in conversation management: An application of van Lier's pilot coding scheme', *The Modern Language Journal*, 78: 29–40.

Lantolf, J. P. and Thorne, S. L. (2006) *Sociocultural Theory and the Genesis of Second Language Development*, Oxford: Oxford University Press.

Negueruela, E. (2003) 'A sociocultural approach to the teaching and learning of second languages: systemic-theoretical instruction and L2 development', PhD dissertation, Pennsylvania State University, University Park, PA.

Ortega, L. (2010) 'The bilingual turn in SLA', plenary address at the annual meeting of the American Association for Applied Linguistics, Atlanta, GA, 6–9 March.

Rogoff, B. (1995) 'Observing sociocultural activity on three planes: Participatory appropriation, guided participation, and apprenticeship', in Wertsch, J. V., Del Rio, P. and Alvarez, A. (eds.) *Sociocultural Studies of Mind*, Cambridge: Cambridge University Press, pp. 139–64.

Senior, R. (1999) 'The good language class: teacher perceptions', unpublished PhD dissertation, Edith Cowan University, Perth.

Stevick, E. W. (1980) *Teaching Language: A Way and Ways*, Boston: Heinle & Heinle.

Valsiner, J. (2006) 'Beyond the first language: acquisition without learning', invited presentation at the 13th Annual Sociocultural Theory and Second Language Research Working Group, Amherst, MA.

van Lier, L. (1988) *The Classroom and the Language Learner*, London: Longman.

van Lier, L. (1998) 'Constraints and resources in classroom talk: issues of equality and symmetry', in Byrnes, H. (ed.) *Learning Foreign and Second Languages: Perspectives in Research and Scholarship*, New York: The Modern Language Association, pp. 157–82.

van Lier, L. (2000) 'From input to affordance: Social-interactive learning from an interactional perspective', in Lantolf, J. (ed.) *Sociocultural Theory and Second Language Learning*, Oxford: Oxford University Press, pp. 245–59.

van Lier, L. (2008) 'Agency in the classroom', in Lantolf, J. P. and Poehner, M. E. (eds.) *Sociocultural Theory and the Teaching of Second Languages*, London: Equinox, pp. 163–86.

Vygotsky, L. S. (1978) *Mind in Society: The Development of Higher Psychological Processes*, ed. Cole, M., John-Steiner, V., Scribner, S. and Souberman, E.,Cambridge, MA: Harvard University Press.

Yoshida, T., Imai, H., Nakata, Y., Tajino, A., Takeuchi, O. and Tamai, K. (eds.) (2009) *Researching Language Teaching and Learning: An Integration of Practice and Theory*, Bern: Peter Lang.

16   From language learner to learning advisor

Madeline Ehrman

Introduction

This is the story of a journey, less of geography than mind. It begins before I learned my first foreign language – Latin – and continues through my insights about learning to helping others succeed at the demanding task of reaching high levels of proficiency in the foreign languages taught to members of the US foreign affairs community.

The culmination of the journey is the establishment of the Foreign Service Institute's (FSI) Learning Consultation Service, an advisory learning programme to assist the educated, adult (average age around 40) and often highly driven students of the FSI intensive language programmes. The narrative is a chronological description of insights and experiences that led me to found this now well-established pro-gramme. It is followed by a description of the Consultation Service and of important lessons I have learned over the course of my career, many of which were influenced by my association with Earl Stevick while he was at the FSI.

Personal narrative

There is considerable work to show how a single case history can serve as the source of useful insights and raise questions for future research. Narratives help us generalize. Researchers have pointed out that 'showing concrete details of a specific life can convey a general way of life' (Ellis 1998: 1) and that 'it is valid and effective to draw on personal experiences ... to explore a topic, as well as a prime source of data' (Gaitan 2000: 9). Narratives can help make the abstract more concrete and thus more comprehensible. For example, Bruner (1996: 90) points out, 'telling stories in order to understand is not mere enrichment of the mind; without them we are, to use [Kierkegaard's] words, reduced to fear and trembling'. Another, less poetic, way to say it is that without stories and examples, we often have difficulty grasping abstractions, as useful as said abstractions may be. (See also Chapter 1 of this volume.)

In addition, narratives are rich in ways that experimental research reports cannot be. Pavlenko and Lantolf (2000: 161) state, 'Most importantly, narrative-based theory and research also has ecological validity as that which "has something to say about what people do in real, culturally significant situations"' (Neisser 1976: 2). Thus, in the context of teaching, 'it explores the messiness of what it means to become a teacher. It situates the researcher as text' (Renner 2001).

The earliest steps

My own journey as a language learner actually began in childhood when my parents used the little French they knew when they didn't want me or my brother to understand what they were saying. At the same time, however, they also arranged for me and some neighbourhood friends to be given French lessons. These consisted of the teacher pointing to pictures in one of her many large scrapbooks and giving us the French word. But what good did it do to know that the picture of something with beak, wings and feathers was a *oiseau*? Needless to say, motivation lapsed altogether among her young pupils, and the French lessons ended not long after they began.

In the classroom

In spite of this less than encouraging beginning, I wanted very much to learn a foreign language. Finally in high school, I had the opportunity to study one in a classroom – Latin – which I enjoyed so much that my father lent me a copy of Leonard Bloomfield's *Language* (1933), and I learned of an obscure field called linguistics. From there my academic future was set.

I also studied Spanish and French. My learning became more systematic, guided by the texts and curricula of my several language courses. But something was missing ... We had no opportunities to use these two romance languages for communication.

Beyond romance

My language learning career blossomed when I entered the university. I began with another semester of French and a year of German. Then I undertook two years of Chinese and then Russian, which culminated in a summer language tour to what was then the Soviet Union. With plenty of opportunity to use the language with native speakers in conversation, my Russian reached a level of fluency beyond that of any previous language I had studied.

Language in context

In graduate school, I pursued ancient Germanic languages such as Gothic but also had a course in linguistic field methods. Our native-speaker 'informant' was a Filipino whose mother tongue was Pangasinan, spoken north of Manila. It was up to us to elicit his language from him. Both the elicitation process and the language itself proved gratifying, with the result that I arranged to do linguistic fieldwork in the Philippines for my dissertation. In preparation, I studied Tagalog for use in general, and my language of study, Bolinao, with a native speaker.

Over the course of my on-site research during my six weeks in the Philippines, I learned to speak Bolinao to a decent level of proficiency, and that was one of the most exciting aspects of the experience. It was also motivating to see how the abstractions in my notes that I had taken at the university came to life in context among real people for whom the language was native. The language seemed as alive as its speakers.

So my journey had taken me from interest in foreign languages through experiences with learning parts (words, transliteration and some basics), through conventional classroom experiences and finally to full-fledged oral communication. Each step increased my motivation, though as yet I was not introspective about how I was learning.

Widening experience

Working then at the US State Department's Foreign Service Institute, as part of the supervisory staff of its School of Language Studies, I spent some years taking advantage of the opportunity to learn multiple languages as I became the supervisor of the teachers of these languages: Vietnamese, Cambodian, Indonesian, Malay, Tagalog, Thai, Burmese, Korean, Japanese and Turkish. My initial assignment was to the Vietnam Training Center where we were preparing Foreign Service officers for civilian service, so naturally I bent every effort into learning Vietnamese, and I became increasingly aware of language learning as a vehicle for building relationships.

A year later, I was sent on a fact-finding trip to Cambodia and Indonesia to look into the US embassy language programmes as well as actual language use by mission staff. In Cambodia, the embassy arranged for me to stay with a Cambodian family, which began a relationship that lasted for many years afterwards. This meant that in addition to my work at the embassy, I could also spend time on learning Cambodian, which greatly helped me to develop proficiency.

A lasting observation from that trip was the importance of encouragement by one's supervisors (parent-figures) for learning and continuing to work on a difficult and obscure language. Many of the embassy employees were convinced that French was sufficient for their work, and in a way, they were correct. But I saw how much more insight I had into the culture and the more trusting relationship I had with Cambodians by virtue of my interest, efforts and increasing proficiency in their language and culture.

This episode highlights motivation. Those few of us who worked on and gained proficiency in Cambodian at that time were not motivated solely by job rewards, important as they might be. We delved into this language that could be used in only one country because, to put it simply, it was fun, exciting and personally relevant for us. This kind of motivation is referred to as intrinsic, because it comes from inside the learner, whereas extrinsic motivation normally comes from outside in the form of payments, advancement and the expectations of others. Both kinds of motivation can be effective, but when the external rewards go, all that's left is intrinsic motivation. Similarly, though perhaps less effectively, when intrinsic rewards are missing, extrinsic factors can motivate effort. Unfortunately, it has been my experience with the learners at the Foreign Service Institute that such extrinsic motivators as the end-of-training test and financial incentives for high scores tend to arouse debilitating anxiety that can cancel out their motivational effects.

Next, I was sent on a two-year tour of duty as regional language officer for Southeast Asia, based in Bangkok. Along with my work helping teachers and students in the language programmes at the various American missions, I also continued work on a massive Cambodian language textbook series begun before my departure. Whenever I could, I went to Phnom Penh to stay with my host family there. I took every opportunity to speak the language of whichever country I was visiting, though my fluency varied greatly from one language to another.

During this time I learned more about my language learning. I discovered how helpful reading can be by virtue of making my way through a fascinating historical novel in Thai, whose title is translated as *Four Worlds*. Because I was reading for pleasure at least as much as for learning Thai, I came on my own to such often-taught strategies as skimming, scanning, massive guessing from context, knowing which lexical items to skip over because they did not make a direct and central contribution to meaning. Reading in Cambodian was also enhanced through the ongoing materials project that I had taken to Thailand with me. Throughout this process, I was always on the watch for something new, interesting or that contrasted with what I already knew. I was constantly *noticing*, whether I took immediate action or not. (Noticing is now considered an important element of high-level language learning success (Tomlin and Villa 1994)).

A change in direction

It is at this point that my main focus changed from personal language learning to how to help others learn.

While in Southeast Asia, I became aware of the dependency of most of our training graduates on continued structured language teaching. I wondered why they couldn't do what I do: just go out and try to talk, take risks, learn how to say what they want to say without a teacher. I finally came to the conclusion that we were short-changing our students by not helping them develop ways to learn independently once they left our classrooms. On my return from Southeast Asia, I discussed this matter with my colleague Earl Stevick, who introduced me to then new methods for language teaching: the Silent Way and Community Language Learning. Both emphasize developing student autonomy, each in a different way. These approaches seemed like the answer to my concerns. However, when we tried to introduce them to our FSI classrooms, they were much less successful.

What went wrong? Some of the problem was with insufficiently trained (and committed?) teachers. But much of it had to do with the way many of our students preferred to learn. They were comfortable with the highly structured Audiolingual method with its dialogues to memorize and 'burn it into the brain' drilling. Only a relatively few shared the liberation I had felt when I discovered the much more open-ended methodologies. This was my first insight into language learning styles. Nowadays I would refer to the two styles as *sequential* and *random*. Realizing that simply teaching people language in a classroom would not provide the skills needed to continue learning outside of it, I thought learning styles might provide a productive direction for helping learners gain autonomy, a goal Earl Stevick seemed to feel at least as strongly about as I did.

The Foreign Service Institute is a splendid laboratory for language learning and training experiments, and I was involved in a number of curriculum innovations over the next 10 years. The successes and failures of these initiatives brought me closer to an interest in learning styles, as did my increasingly wide scope of responsibility within the School of Language Studies. The opportunity to work closely with Earl Stevick during this time had a major impact on my thinking, as his thoughts about structure and freedom, most clearly described in *A Way and Ways* (1980), not only converged with many of my own, but enhanced and deepened them. It was my extraordinary privilege to read each chapter of that work as he wrote it, critique it and discuss it with him in depth. This process taught me at least as much as it may have helped him.

When I became the chairperson of the Department of Asian and African languages, I was able to bring in a consultant to administer and interpret the Myers–Briggs Type Indicator or MBTI (Myers et al. 1998), a psychological questionnaire based on Karl Jung's theory of psychological types (Jung 1971) (see Appendix A of this chapter), the intended use of which is to enable individuals to appreciate each other's differences. In addition to team-building in the department, one of my aims was to investigate the MBTI model as a vehicle for understanding language learning differences.

For my research efforts, I needed something with which to correlate my styles model – the MBTI – in order to see the effects its constructs might have on our language learning and teaching. Actual learning techniques, widely called learning strategies, seemed a likely candidate, and so I began very productive joint research with Rebecca Oxford, whose Strategy Indicator for Language Learning or SILL (1990) was very useful as a beginning to my research on learning styles and individual differences.

A parallel path

My initial work with the MBTI and the SILL provoked a long-dormant interest in psychology. Discussions with colleagues at FSI brought to my attention a non-traditional, though regionally accredited institution that featured a great deal of self-direction and a flexible path, called at that time the Union for Experimenting Colleges and Universities. (The name has since been changed to the Union Institute and University.) The Union is the outcome of a consortium of universities led by Antioch College to pursue greater independence in learning and more self-direction. It serves as a working model for the principles espoused by Carl Rogers in *Freedom to Learn* (1969). It was a perfect match for my work situation and for my very independent and experimental learning style. I was accepted into their doctoral programme and, with a great deal of cooperation from my supervisors at FSI, embarked on an exceptional educational experience.

My topic was clinical psychology, but as there was an interdisciplinary requirement for the degree, applied linguistics was a natural fit and was included in the programme both through study and through my research. After I received my degree, I made an increasing commitment to psychoanalytic psychology, including five years of continuing education in theory and practice which offered me supervised experience as a psychotherapist. This training was to serve me well later on as I explored the impact of emotional as well as cognitive processes on FSI language learners and teachers.

The paths meet

It became clear early that while the MBTI model clarified a great deal, it did not account for a great many of the differences I was finding among learners, especially after my doctoral studies had revealed to me many more aspects of human psychology.

In the early 1990s, I received permission to begin an official pilot research programme to investigate learner differences among the students in FSI's School of Language Studies. Thanks to support by colleagues and managers, on this project we had the time to experiment with various measures until we came up with the ones we thought gave us the best information to use with our adult, educated, and career-driven students and their teachers. My initial work was with the MBTI and Oxford's SILL, as well as other models and instruments. None of the usual learning style instruments supplemented the MBTI in the ways I was looking for, that is, adding more granularity to the relatively general styles that the MBTI yields. Ultimately we found two of use for the purpose, one that addresses tolerance of ambiguity, the Hartmann Boundary Questionnaire (Hartmann 1991), and one that Betty Lou Leaver and I developed to add the desired detail and specificity to cognitive styles, the Ehrman and Leaver Learning Styles model (Ehrman and Leaver 2003).

Origins of the consultation service

While this research was taking place, an occasional teacher or supervisor would ask us to administer the instruments to struggling students and attempt to use the results to provide advice. These occasional, ad hoc interviews were the germ of what eventually became our Learning Consultation Service, now an established and popular programme in the School of Language Studies. In these interviews I began to apply such basic clinical skills as listening for both thought and feelings, my own intuitive responses to what I was hearing and seeing from the students and gentle but relatively deep inquiry to test my hypotheses.

I emphasize that I was not practising psychotherapy at FSI, nor have I ever done so. I have, however, benefited enormously from the clinical training and simultaneous and consequent personal growth in empathy and trust in my intuition that I gained from my background in psychology. I believe I am a far more effective diagnostician and interviewer because of the skills and sensitivities developed in my clinical training. For example, I am sensitized now to the complexities of anxiety, defensive behaviour and interpersonal issues that are not normally part of student counselling and can address them far more compassionately than I could before my studies.

Recognizing that learning styles are preferences, not activities in themselves, I experimented with the delivery of learning strategy workshops, offered at the beginning of training and at intervals during the training period. These were not very successful, and examination suggested that the root was the heterogeneity of the participants. I found no way to reach everyone in a group that might go from first-time language learners to the four- or five-language virtuoso and everything in between, to say nothing of the multiple personality types likely to be present. Furthermore, I realized that in a workshop, strategies are an abstraction. The place to work on learning strategies is when you need them, not so long before you need them that you forget them by the time they are called for. What we needed was just-in-time learning strategy training.

At this time, the individual differences project was incorporated into a school-wide initiative called The New Orientation as one of its three main parts. The other two were enhanced linguistic preparation for post-classroom professional responsibilities and the use of educational technology, in its infancy at the time. The New Orientation Pilot Program enabled me to train the first group of 'Learning Consultants', language teachers who were to be empowered to assist students with learning strategies when they need the help – the just-in-time assistance I was looking for. The Learning Consultant role has expanded considerably since this time, but one of their main responsibilities continues to be to help students improve their learning strategies.

During the mid-1990s, Betty Lou Leaver and I developed a new learning styles scale in response to dissatisfaction with aspects of the models then currently used by applied linguists, to avoid conflating separate dimensions and to provide more granular differentiation that could be provided by, for example, the then popular 'global-analytic' model. For lack of a better name, we call it the Ehrman and Leaver (E & L) Learning Styles model. We also developed a simple instrument to test and apply it.

The E&L model comprises ten bipolar scales, most of which are adaptations from earlier work on learning differences and a few of which are original. Among the most frequently used scales are the previously mentioned random-sequential dimension, together with inductive vs. deductive learning, synthetic-analytic, levelling-sharpening. Those listed first in each pair are classified as 'synoptic', suggesting understanding or insight arrives in consciousness without awareness of the process that took place to achieve the insight, whereas those listed second are called 'ectenic' to suggest a more drawn-out process of taking conscious control of the learning process. These terms are neologisms used deliberately to indicate that the model is different from similar but less complete distinctions between, for example, holistic and atomistic. All ten of the scales are listed with brief descriptions in Appendix B of this chapter. The E&L model has proved very useful in student counselling and teacher-training activities, as it provides both logical consistency and a degree of detail, specificity and differentiation among students not found elsewhere.

Our work with individual referrals and with teachers seeking advice increased with our success. The ranks of the Learning Consultants were growing and the Learning Consultation Service was made official in 1995. At the time of writing, there are four full-time counsellors who administer and interpret the diagnostic instruments, train Learning Consultants and provide general staff development workshops. Their work is leveraged by trained Learning Consultants throughout the over 60 languages taught at FSI. (More description of the Consultation Service can be found in Ehrman 2001.)

What follows is a look at how the Learning Consultation Service works. I include it not only to show the work of a Learning Consultant, but also to suggest how it can be useful for classroom teachers and their supervisors

A typical student in trouble

This student is fairly typical of learners who are struggling. The description by his teachers is what a supervisor or advisor is likely to hear. What does it tell us? As you read, stop for a moment and think about your reactions to this short vignette as if you were a Learning Consultant: what are your initial conclusions? Even more important, what else would you like to know?

> *PART 1:* Jim has been referred to you by a supervisor in your language section. He is an early-career student, 28 years of age who is studying a language in the category of those most difficult for English speakers (includes Arabic, Chinese, Japanese and Korean). Before he will be authorized to depart for his assignment, he must demonstrate that he

has achieved the goals set for the position he will occupy overseas in a rigorous end-of-training test. This high-stakes test includes an oral interview and an interactive reading portion; it usually takes 2–3 hours.

The programme supervisor has informed you that Jim has 'frozen up' on his attempt at the end-of-training test and fell well below the required score. The supervisor indicates that the student is suffering from test anxiety but also worries that he does not yet have the language skills needed to achieve the required score. The supervisor also says that Jim's teachers believe that he does not study enough.

Take some time to think about this information before reading further. These questions are part of the routine of every Learning Consultant.

- What are your initial reactions to it and to Jim?
- What do you know about Jim?
- What are your initial guesses about what is going on with him? What do you base them on?
- What more do you need or want to know?

Here is some more information about Jim. It may answer some of your questions, and it may help confirm or disconfirm your initial guesses about what is going on. It may also raise more questions.

PART 2: You meet with Jim, who tells you that he cannot speak in the language he is studying because he is so 'tied up in knots'. He freezes up and has trouble breathing whenever he attempts to say something. All he can think about is whether he is going to make a mistake. He says he is forgetting words he knows well and is making many more errors than he did in previous months. He reports that nothing is sinking in, especially grammar, though he believes he is working very hard and constantly studying. He feels as if he is grasping at straws and that learning is merely hit and miss for him.

What are your reactions now? Again, try to think as if you were a Learning Consultant.

- What more do you know about Jim?
- What are your current guesses about what is going on? What do you base them on?
- What more do you want to know? What would you like to ask Jim?

Here is some final information about Jim. Do your conclusions and questions change?

PART 3: Additionally, Jim is worried about what colleagues at post will think about his needing an extension of his language training in order to achieve the position goals. He says that he just wants to get to post and that he believes he would be able to achieve his goal easily after time interacting with native speakers in the immersion environment. He reports that he cannot sleep, is no longer motivated and dreads coming to class in the morning.

What would you say about this case now?

- What more do you know about Jim?
- What are your thoughts about what is going on with him? What do you base them on?
- How would you start working with him?
- What more would you like to know?
- What is your opinion of the teachers' assessment of Jim as reported by the supervisor in Part 1 of the case?

Training Learning Consultants

This kind of case is used frequently in training Learning Consultants. A key feature lies in the questions asked at the end of each segment here: in the training we emphasize keeping an open mind and gathering information, holding multiple hypotheses in mind while seeking and evaluating evidence. This process includes trying out interventions based on the working hypothesis or hypotheses to see if they help. If they help, continue, but if they do not, look elsewhere.

We also emphasize communication skills, especially active listening, where the listener only reflects and does not impose any of his or her own thoughts on the interaction. This is probably the single most effective tool we have for information gathering, including development of hypotheses that may not have come up before. For example, in Part 3, Jim mentions that he thinks he could learn well in direct interaction with native speakers in natural context. This introduces something new in to our picture of Jim. How might you pursue that remark to find out more? And what would you want to know?

The theory component of the training additionally includes learning styles and strategies, basics of brain and memory, affective factors and working with colleagues. We conduct the training sessions in the style of a graduate seminar. The sessions include not only theory but also cases, role plays and skill practice.

The case in my journey

The apprentice. During the time before my tour of duty in Thailand, I probably would have taken most of my information from Part 1 and never reached Parts 2 and 3. My initial reaction to Jim might have been that he's something of a mess, and possibly not a very good language learner. I might well have taken the teachers' comments as reported by the supervisor at face value. When Jim said he was spending a lot of time studying, I might have been curious about how he was spending it, but I would have had relatively few tools for helping him use his time better. My own learning strategies were developed intuitively, so I had little understanding of how others might need to learn them. Jim's anxiety would have seemed a nuisance and impediment to the 'real' issues; I probably would have attempted to reassure him and perhaps ensure that he got a fair chance in the next round of end-of-training testing. I fear I would not have been much use to him.

The journeyman. Insights achieved during and after my overseas tour of duty would have led me to focus primarily on Jim's study habits and his motivation. I would question his study habits more closely than I would have done before and look at ways to change them. I probably would have attempted to enhance his motivation by finding out what his interests are and suggesting that his teachers use them as a focus for conversation and reading. I would recognize his test anxiety as an important factor and attempt to address it both by providing information such as the goals of the testing team, for example achieving a rateable sample, and by offering practice tests. I might have suggested changes in the actual test routine that might help alleviate Jim's anxiety, such as using a classroom rather than a testing cubicle. The intensity of Jim's feelings would still raise anxiety in me, so I would probably not address them beyond reassurance.

Seeking mastery. Today, I would recognize Jim's anxiety as central, and I would work with it directly. I would look for sources, especially sources beyond the ones he describes, particularly having to do with his self-image. I would want to find out more about his relationships with his classmates and colleagues, as he seems to indicate fear of their reactions. Second, I would also review his learning strategies, as he appears to be working hard but not 'smart' (i.e. not efficiently). Improved learning strategies might lead to increased self-confidence as a learner, which in turn would have an effect on his profoundly debilitating anxiety. Third, I would be concerned with issues of his learning style and its fit with the classroom along with his use of metacognitive strategies to use his time more effectively. In line with investigation of his learning style, I would investigate the remark about in-country learning: has he done it successfully before? Is there is a conflict between the teaching methods used in his classes and his learning style, how can it be managed to enhance his success?

Throughout, I would anticipate doing a great deal of active listening, in the hope that through indirectly hearing himself he might gain insights and attempt change.

Conclusion

Of all the many lessons I have learned to this point, the most important have to do with nuanced thinking and the importance of feelings: the student's, those of the teaching staff and my own.

One of the benefits of doing research with real people is that there are always outliers and contradictory data. Many of my best insights came from the need to reconcile contradictions in learning styles data and in student interviews. For example, why do Jim's teachers say he's not studying, when in fact he tells us that he's putting in a great deal of time and effort. Usually I found that an attempt to make sense of the contradictions at a higher level of abstraction brought resolution and a new piece of 'theory'. For example, Jim's teachers see only the weak results of his work, whereas Jim is focused on his learning process and is aware that it is not adequate. Another example: when I found that some students with high scores on the Modern Language Aptitude Test did not learn well, I was led to look at other factors, one of the most important of which turned out to be tolerance of ambiguity. This helped me understand language learning aptitude as a combination of both cognitive and affective factors, especially motivation but also including open-mindedness and tolerance of ambiguity.

Staying open comes into play in the use of skilled listening. Active listening is one of my most effective tools for both information gathering and assisting students to insight (as they overhear themselves through my reflections). This skill is not easy for most of us to learn: it is not how we normally conduct a social conversation with people we like and want to like us. Our Learning Consultant trainees have to overcome a desire to reassure, share their own stories and solve problems. It is not easy, but those who stick to it and gain some proficiency become enthusiastic about the effectiveness of the skill.

Learning styles are preferences. That means that students may well indicate that they prefer one way of doing things but then spend a lot of time doing the other. The ability to 'style-flex' is desirable and even necessary in life as well as school, but working outside of one's preference much of the time raises questions about what may be going on

264

with the student (e.g. trained not to use their preference, responding to perceived norms, etc.).

Learning styles are somewhat controversial, as some studies (e.g. Landrum and McDuffie 2010) have concluded that there is no such thing. Observation tells me otherwise, and I have found the concepts highly useful as a shortcut to understanding and addressing difficulties. For example, I have increasingly come to see these preferences as ways to manage cognitive load: some students prefer to 'fly now and pay later'; these, for example, might be deductive learners who would like to focus on the learning product rather than 'waste time' on a puzzle-solving process. Others prefer to make their investment early with the expectation of later payoffs; among these are likely to be inductive processors who prefer to figure out language puzzles for themselves. The deductive learner delays the cognitive load entailed by full mastery; the inductive one takes on many more cognitive demands in the interest of fuller and wider mastery sooner.

Difficulties do not belong only to slow students. Fast and accurate learners can run into trouble if they find a profound classroom mismatch with their learning approach, for example a successful random learner in a traditional sequential classroom. They may also experience interpersonal difficulties with classmates. And in some cases their ability may lead to overconfidence.

A key to much of what we do is metacognition. Students who flounder and work hard but not smart usually lack metacognitive strategies to plan, monitor, evaluate and change the way they work. Furthermore, learner autonomy depends heavily on the ability to make effective decisions and follow up on them. Much of what we do in the Learning Consultation Service becomes development of the metacognitive skills of those with whom we work (including teachers!).

In nearly every student and/or teacher consultation, go for the feelings early. Usually, even if they are not at the root, as they were for Jim, they can become a very debilitating consequence of such difficulties as poor learning techniques. Most students appreciate acknowledgement of their feelings, both positive and negative, especially in an active listening context. This may have been my latest and most important lesson: feelings are profoundly important in every endeavour, not just learning.

It has been a long journey, a worthwhile one, and one I hope has not yet ended. May more discoveries lie ahead!

Appendix A: Myers–Briggs psychological type

Jung's theory posits two attitudes towards life, **extraversion** and **introversion**, and two sets of cognitive functions, **sensing-intuition** and **thinking-feeling**. In an effort to determine which of the functions was the most central for each individual, Myers and Briggs added another attitude set, **judging** and **perceiving**.

Extraversion represents a preference for receiving stimulation and energy from outside the self, whereas introversion indicates a preference for generating energy and stimulation internally. Needless to say, extraverts also receive internal stimulation, and introverts take in much from outside, but those are not their preferred patterns.

The perceiving functions, sensing and intuition, are ways of taking in information – of learning: the former focuses on the concrete world of the traditional five senses and what the facts are now, whereas the latter also finds the 'sixth sense' of insight of special interest and seeks meaning in the facts.

Thinking and feeling are called the 'judging functions', to suggest that they are used for decision-making. Thinking seeks to use logic and to remove personal feeling and opinion as much as possible; feeling bases decisions on personal values even if they conflict with normal logic.

Finally, judging and perceiving reflect the individual's approach to managing tasks and time. The judging type (note, not judgmental) attempts to create an ordered, largely predictable life, with schedules and systematic management of objects. In contrast, the perceiving type wants above all to maintain flexibility in life and to keep options open as much as possible.

There is far more to MBTI theory, including the 16 possible combinations of these four scales, which are more than a simple sum of their parts. The Manual (Myers et al. 1998) provides much of this information.

Appendix B: The Ehrman and Leaver Learning Styles model (adapted from Ehrman and Leaver 2003: 404)

SYNOPTIC	ECTENIC
FIELD-SENSITIVE	FIELD-INSENSITIVE
in-context material	lack of field sensitivity
sensitive to socio-emotional content	does not pay attention to whole context

may need discrimination exercises	may miss socio-emotional clues
'floodlight'	
incidental learning	
FIELD-INDEPENDENT	**FIELD-DEPENDENT**
out-of-context material	lack of field independence
focuses on grammar rules	needs context
likes discrimination exercises	does not discriminate easily
'spotlight'	needs assistance pinpointing important/priority items
awareness and focus on most important things	
RANDOM	**SEQUENTIAL**
start where it seems best, even the middle	start at the beginning
unpredictable paths through material	one step at a time
neatness may be a low priority	orderly
follows internally generated order	follows externally provided order
GLOBAL	**PARTICULAR**
searching for the main idea before details	awareness of details before main idea
conversing without knowing all the words	control of most structural forms
top down	bottom up
'forest'	'trees'

INDUCTIVE	DEDUCTIVE
specific to general	general to specific
uses examples to make rule	applies and tests rule
starts with examples	starts with rules
SYNTHETIC	ANALYTIC
learns by putting words, sentences together	dissects words and sentences
seeks to create something new	contrastive analysis
assembly	disassembly
ANALOG	DIGITAL
metaphorical	direct, literal
symbolic	realistic
'deep' strategies	'surface' strategies
CONCRETE	ABSTRACT
experience	theory
using language	knowing about language
application of knowledge	formal rendition of knowledge
LEVELLING	SHARPENING
looks for similarities	notices differences
seeks to reduce disparities	explores and tries to account for disparities
may tune out relations among parts	often aware of relations among parts

IMPULSIVE	REFLECTIVE
moves and thinks fast	hates acting too quickly
excitable	likes to think before speaking
easily bored	thoughtful and careful
needs variety	often works slowly

More information can be found in Ehrman and Leaver (2003) and Leaver et al. (2005). A thorough discussion of the Field Independence–Field Sensitivity model used here is contained in Chapter 5 of Ehrman (1996) and somewhat refined in Ehrman (1997).

References

Bloomfield, L. (1933) *Language*, London: George Allen and Unwin.
Bruner, J. S. (1996) *The Culture of Education*, Cambridge, MA: Harvard University Press.
Ehrman, M. E. (1996) *Understanding Second Language Learning Difficulties*, Thousand Oaks, CA: Sage Publications.
Ehrman, M. E. (1997) 'Field independence, field dependence, and field sensitivity', in Reid, J. (ed.) *Understanding Learning Styles in the Second Language Classroom*, Englewood Cliffs, NJ: Regents Prentice Hall, pp. 62–70.
Ehrman, M. E. (2001) 'Bringing learning strategies to the learner: the FSI language learning consultation service', in Alatis, J. E. and Tan, A. (eds.) *Language in Our Time: Bilingual Education and Official English, Ebonics and Standard English, Immigration and the Unz Initiative*, Washington, DC: Georgetown University, pp. 41–58.
Ehrman, M. E. and Leaver, B. L. (2003) 'Cognitive styles in the service of language learning', *System*, 31: 393–415.
Ellis, C. (1998) 'What counts as scholarship in communication? An autoethnographic response', paper delivered at a National Communication Association Research Board Session. Available online at http://acjournal.org/holdings/vol1"\t"_blank"acjournal.org/holdings/vol1/Iss2/special/ellis.htm (accessed 24 July 2001).
Gaitan, A. (2000) 'Exploring alternative forms of writing ethnography: review essay', *Forum: Qualitative Social Research*, 1(3). Available online at http://www.qualitative-research.net/index.php/fqs/article/view/1062/2302 (accessed 23 January 2012).
Hartmann, E. (1991) *Boundaries in the Mind: A New Psychology of Personality*, New York: Basic Books.

Jung, C. G. (1971) *Psychological Types*, in Read, H., Fordham, M., Adler, G. and McGuire, W. (eds.) *Collected Works of C. G. Jung*, Vol. VI, Bollingen Series 20, Princeton, NJ: Princeton University. (Original work published 1921.)

Landrum, T. J. and McDuffie, K. A. (2010) 'Learning styles in the age of differentiated instruction', *Exceptionality*, 18(1): 6–17.

Leaver, B. L., Ehrman, M. E. and Shekhtman, B. (2005) *Achieving Success in Second Language Acquisition*, Cambridge: Cambridge University.

Myers, I. B., McCaulley, M. H., Quenk, N. L. and Hammer, A. L. (1998) *MBTI Manual: A Guide to the Development and Use of the Myers-Briggs Type Indicator*, Palo Alto, CA: Consulting Psychologists.

Neisser, U. (1976) *Cognition and Reality*, San Francisco, CA: Freeman.

Oxford, R. L. (1990) *Language Learning Strategies: What Every Teacher Should Know*, New York: Newbury House.

Pavlenko, A. and Lantolf, J. P. (2000) 'Second language learning as participation and the (re)construction of selves', in Lantolf, J. P. (ed.) *Sociocultural Theory and Second Language Learning*, Oxford: Oxford University Press, pp. 157–80.

Renner, P. (2001) 'Evocative narrative as educational research'. Available online at http://www.adulterc.org/Proceedings/2001/2001renner.htm (accessed on 23 January 2012).

Rogers, C. (1969) *Freedom to Learn: A View of What Education Might Become*, Columbus, OH: Charles Merrill.

Stevick, E. W. (1980) *Teaching Languages: A Way and Ways*, Rowley, MA: Newbury House.

Tomlin, R. S. and Villa, V. (1994) 'Attention in cognitive science and second language acquisition', *Studies in Second Language Acquisition*, 16(2): 183–204.

17 A dilemma of prediction: how teacher education is 'piped' to classroom teaching and student learning

Donald Freeman

Introduction

Drawing connections among complex human activities is a commonplace but imprecise undertaking. From economics to lifestyle choices to education, a great deal of time and energy is spent in trying to understand how one domain of activity may influence another. In this chapter, I explore one particular trajectory of these connections: those that try to link what teachers learn through professional education to what they do day to day in their classroom teaching; in essence, how teachers' knowledge becomes available to their students. These connections are generally assumed but not often closely examined, the problem being that these three domains of activity – teacher education, classroom teaching and student learning – are distinct and yet interrelated. However, what happens in one domain cannot *cause* things to happen in the others. Therefore, characterizing the connections across them amounts to a matter of guesswork, which leads to the dilemma of prediction.

'Piping' as a metaphor for the problem of connection

In the second chapter of *Teaching Languages: A Way and Ways*, Earl Stevick begins his discussion of teaching with a story about religion, faith and access that offers a useful metaphor for this connection problem. The story is about a preacher at a revival meeting, which Stevick relates as follows: 'When the time came to pass the collection plate, a man in the congregation stood up and shouted, "Hey Brother, I thought you said salvation is as free as the rain that falls from the heavens! Then why are you asking us for money?" To which the preacher replies, "Yes, Brother, salvation is ... free ... But you have to pay to have it piped to you!"' (1980: 16). What is great about this story is how it distills the problem of instructed language learning and teaching. There is a contradiction in saying that to acquire things you can 'get for free', like religious beliefs or languages, you need to participate in organized settings, like churches or classrooms. But it is often the case.

The dilemma lies in how language teaching connects to language learning, since much of both contents (of teaching and of learning) can be 'got for free' in the world outside the classroom. In teacher education, it is the dilemma of how individuals (as learners of teaching) learn to teach students in classrooms, since many aspects of the knowledge used in language teaching are portrayed as 'free': learned through experience or by birthright (as in the case of teaching one's 'native' language). In the classroom, the dilemma is how students learn the new language, having learned their first language 'for free' in the world. And these two dilemmas are interconnected since what teachers learn to do somehow links to what students know. It is this problem of connection that is the focus of this chapter.

As I will argue later, these connections between teaching and learning have generally been thought of as fairly straightforward in a classroom context. However, there are obvious fallacies in this assumption since students can – and often do – learn languages as well or better out of school. As Stevick points out:

> Quite possibly our students, even our adult students, could learn languages without us if they were placed under the right conditions in the right cultural and linguistic environment. But *with the world the way it is*, these conditions and this environment are extremely rare.

(1980: 16, italics added)

This phrase, 'with the world the way it is', both in the classroom and the wider world, goes to the heart of the problem. In the world of schools, we expect a basic syllogism to be true: teachers teach *so that* students learn; therefore, *if* students do not learn, the teacher must not have taught them well (Freeman 2006).

This societal expectation certainly makes intuitive sense – that what teachers know and do in their classroom teaching should in some way impact on what their students learn. However, the connection is quite complicated, as Stevick (1980: 16) explains, 'There can, after all, be "learning" without "teaching", but one cannot claim to have "taught" unless someone else has learned.' This stark syllogism lays out a pedagogical necessity: to link what teachers know to what they do in classroom teaching, and that to what students come to know through classroom activity. Aligning these three domains – of professional learning, classroom teaching and student learning – is the central problem of connection; it lies at the heart of the 'piping' problem.

The connection problem can be unpacked along two dimensions, which are represented in Figure 17.1. One is what we could call the *knowledge dimension*. Teachers acquire professional knowledge in formal and non-formal teacher education; this is '*what* teachers know'. This 'what' translates or morphs into classroom activity and becomes

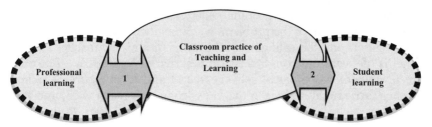

Figure 17.1   Knowledge and delivery as two dimensions of the connection problem

Formulated as:		
what teachers know	>>	Professional learning
what they do with what they know in the classroom	>>	Classroom practice
what students come to know	>>	Student learning

'*what* they do in classroom teaching'. However, in the process of moving from the first to the second domain, the 'what' changes in subtle and substantial ways (Freeman and Johnson 2004). When students interact with this second 'what' as the content in the classroom, it morphs again. And again things can leak since 'what' each student comes to know from the lesson as it is taught varies. Some of what students take away will be common across the class; these are captured in the broad outcomes of the lesson. Other 'take-aways' may be idiosyncratic, based on, for example, who the student was seated next to, or worked with or talked to during the lesson.

Simply put, in connecting what teachers know to what they do, to what their students learn, the 'what's' are not the same. Using the metaphor from Stevick's story, the knowledge actually changes or is (re)shaped as it is 'piped' from the teacher through classroom activity to students, and beyond that to how students subsequently use what they have learned. It is interesting to note that when we talk about 'piping' teaching to learning in classrooms and schools, we conventionally apply the term only at the end of the process, to 'what students have learned': the uses that learners make of what they have been taught. This is the social metric of teaching. Measures of accountability, like tests and national exams, focus exclusively on this learning as output from the teaching process, a point that I will return to.

The transformation of knowledge is one dimension of the challenge of connecting teaching to learning in classrooms; delivery, or *how* that knowledge is 'piped' across domains, is another. When we focus on the *delivery dimension* of the problem, we typically focus on what happens in the classroom. We talk about it in terms of how the teacher's knowledge is 'delivered' through classroom activities to students. But there are actually two versions of delivery (see #1 and #2 in Figure 17.1): how teachers are taught and learn the knowledge they teach with, and then how they make use of that knowledge in teaching their students. So the delivery dimension is both a problem of professional learning for teachers (and therefore of teacher education (see #1)) and a problem of classroom learning for students (and therefore of classroom practice (see #2)). These two types of delivery are connected if we agree that teacher education does somehow shape what teachers do and what their students learn. All of which complicates the piping problem.

Many public discussions of teaching – teacher quality and accountability are prime examples – greatly simplify this complexity. They do so by making student learning the outcome variable, while teaching (and by extension teacher education) are the inputs. This calculus casts the connections as a straightforward matter of cause and effect: teaching inputs 'lead to' learning outcomes in both teacher education and classroom teaching. Were it that simple, however, improving inputs would change outputs; educational systems would function effectively, and there would be little need for educational reform. Rather, connecting teaching to learning is a messy business precisely because there is no clear cause–effect relationship. It is a challenge of predicting one based on the other. These predictions involve forecasting connections between what teachers learn through teacher education, how they use this knowledge in classroom teaching, and what their students take (or 'learn') from that teaching.

To elaborate this problem of predicting connections, I want to examine five pairs of concepts: about learning outcomes versus opportunities to learn; about causing versus influencing learning; about teacher education versus professional learning; about scalability; and about sustainability. The ideas in each pair are intra-related, and the pairs themselves are interrelated. Together these pairs of concepts can help to elucidate the messiness and complexity in the problem of 'piping' teaching to learning.

Concept pair #1: *learning outcomes vs. opportunities to learn*

The first pair of concepts addresses how teaching leads to learning. The problem is that teaching combines broad social expectations and specialized professional knowledge. On the societal level, teaching is something that many people think they know how to do based on their experience as students (Lortie 1975). These ideas about teaching are part of a social fabric that stretches in time from childhood through schooling to parenthood; through relationships, from families to communities to classrooms, and across space from home to school to the workplace (Christie and Martin 2000). Tracy Kidder (1989: 49), in his ethnographic account of a year in the work of urban elementary schoolteacher Christine Kajak, comments on this societal grounding of teaching:

> [It] is an anomalous profession. Unlike doctors or lawyers, teachers do not share rules and obligations that they set for themselves. They are hirelings of communities, which have frequently conceived of them as servants and have not always treated them well.

This persuasive sense of understanding – that we know what teaching is – leads to many assumptions, among them that teaching is common knowledge, that it is easy work to do, and that when things don't work out and teaching doesn't lead to learning, the fault lies with the teacher. The problem with this view, as Cohen et al. (2003: 120) point out, is that:

> What we casually call 'teaching' is not what teachers do, say, or think, though that is what many researchers have studied and many innovators have tried to change. Teaching is what teachers do, say, and think with learners, concerning content, in particular organizations and other environments, in time.

Teaching is embedded in interactions; it is relational work in a particular setting that connects the teacher, the students and the content. This notion is distilled in Stevick's well-known aphorism that language teaching is 'what goes on inside and between people' (1980: 4).

When understood in this way, the focus shifts from what teaching *produces* – often referred to as 'learning outcomes' – to what teaching *does* – to the 'learning opportunities' that it creates. As we have come to understand, participating in learning opportunities involves developing new identities. As students learn language, the process is not so much one of accumulating new knowledge as one of becoming new language users.[1] Writing about this interaction of new knowledge and new identity, James Gee (2008: 82) observes:

> Any actual domain of knowledge is first and foremost a set of activities (special ways of acting and interacting so as to produce and use

[1] Interestingly, Stevick's observation in *Memory, Meaning and Method* (1976) that adult students may avoid acquiring 'native-like' pronunciation in order to maintain their L1 identity presaged by two decades what became broad and complex discussion of second language learning and learner identity (e.g. Peirce 1995).

knowledge) and experience (special ways of seeing, valuing, and being in the world). Physicists do physics. They talk physics. And when they are being physicists, they see and value the world in a different way than do non-physicists.

The same is true of new teachers. They are not simply learning new professional knowledge that they will later apply; rather, as they participate in their professional education in pre-service training or later in in-service development, they are developing new social identities. This emerging teacher identity brings together socialization as students in schools, what sociologist Daniel Lortie (1975) referred to as the 'apprenticeship of observation' – the time spent as a student 'observing teachers and participating in their work' – and experiences they participate in as they are becoming teachers (Freeman 1996).

This focus on experience and socialization, in contrast to teaching inputs and learning outcomes, raises the question of what teaching activities are, in language classes or teacher education programmes, and how they develop these new identities. In referring to this messy process as creating *learning opportunities*, we take a conventional concept and place it in the relational context of 'what goes on inside and between people'. For the last two decades of US educational policy, the notion of 'opportunity to learn' has been associated with curriculum:

> *Opportunity to learn* refers to equitable conditions or circumstances within the school or classroom that promote learning for all students. It includes the provision of curricula, learning materials, facilities, teachers, and instructional experiences that enable students to achieve high standards. This term also relates to the absence of barriers that prevent learning.
>
> (NCREL 2011; original italics)

But 'conditions or circumstances' are inherently relational; they involve people. Socioculturalists have argued that opportunities to learn:

> are affordances for participation, which are relations between characteristics of activity systems and characteristics of participants. Whether or not students can or do take up these opportunities, and whether they might or might not do so is an important aspect of the learning that actually occurs ...
>
> (Greeno and Gresalfi 2008: 191)

In this view, an opportunity is a possibility of participating; if and how it is taken up by the student – as a learner of language or of teaching – fulfils that possibility.

Take, for example, a role play in the language classroom. While the teacher structures it by providing the roles around a task or situation, how the students take up these prompts leads to the opportunities they have to learn from them. If students improvise and play with the new language, different learning may happen than if they use phrases by rote to get through the activity. Similarly in reflecting on a pre-service teacher education peer-teaching activity, the level of candidates' post-lesson analyses often depends on the trainer's skill in probing their reasoning. Here the trainer's questioning creates the opportunities for the candidates to learn from the teaching they have just done by extracting from that experience elements of the new professional work and identity.

The concept of learning opportunities can seem undefined, since some aspects may be intentional (created by the trainer or teacher), while others are more serendipitous and depend on what students may do. How do students get along in the class that is doing a role play? Was the teacher candidate nervous or overly confident during the peer-teaching lesson? These learning opportunities seem to sit at the intersection of skill, intention and chance. Describing this balance or connection – between what teachers do by intention and what happens in the class by luck – brings us to the next pair of concepts.

Concept pair #2: *causing* vs. *influencing learning*

There has long been a debate about what goes into teaching. On the one hand, it involves what the teacher does – the intention and planning of the lesson and the skill in enacting it. On the other hand, there is the ineffable work of 'what goes on inside and between people' in the classroom. So the debate goes: is teaching a science of skills based in researched understandings? Or is it an art, a talent for carrying out relational work in the classroom? In a way, however, the debate is less about the work of teaching per se than how it connects to learning. In terms of this analysis, it centres on what teaching has to do with achieving learning outcomes or creating learning opportunities. Thinking about this question entails somehow bridging these two broad characterizations of teaching: as a 'science' of the generalized abilities of planning and pedagogical skill on the one hand, and as an 'art' of the individual relational talent and creativity on the other. In second language education, we have used the idea of 'teaching methods' to make that bridge.

Edward Anthony's 1963 paper, 'Approach, Method, and Technique', proposed a hierarchical set of relationships to bridge the inner world of the teacher's beliefs and assumptions, which he called 'approach', with the publicly observable and participatory world of classroom activity that he called 'technique'. Anthony (1963: 64) called that space between these inner and outer worlds 'method', which he defined as: 'an overall plan for orderly presentation of language material, no part of which contradicts, and all of which is based upon, the selected approach. Approach is axiomatic; method is procedural. Within one approach, there can be many methods.'

The notion of language teaching methods as regularized ways of doing things in the classroom came into vogue throughout the 1970s with so-called innovative or designer methods (Blair 1982). Some went on to suggest modifications to the architecture that Anthony first proposed (e.g. Richards and Rodgers 1982) or to argue the hierarchy and/or the idea of method itself (e.g. Kumaravadivelu 1994; Brown 2002). But the idea of teaching methods seems to have persisted because it serves a pragmatic purpose. It gives a public place to focus on the teaching/learning relationship, even though we recognize that there was more to this connection than what we can see. As David Bell (2007: 142) concludes in a paper titled 'Do Teachers Think Methods Are Dead?':

> methods are best understood as both potential and realized resources. As potential resources they may be loosely or tightly linked to an established pattern of beliefs and procedures. As realized resources, they appear in the individual teachers as an emergent set of regular practices which may be more or less identifiable.

Whether it is phrased as the distinction between 'potential and realized resources', or between what is publicly accessible and what is situational and idiosyncratic, the idea of method serves a useful purpose. It helps to establish parameters for predictable connections between what the teacher and students do – the 'method' used – and the learning that transpires from those interactions. Thus, methods claim to predict certain efficiencies in how the prescribed student–teacher interactions lead to learning outcomes.

People argue that certain methods 'work'. That efficiency may be documented through research, or it may be asserted on the basis of belief; either way, teaching methods purport to efficiently lead to learning. In the era of the Audiolingual method (ALM), for example, proponents claimed that if the teacher drilled responses until they were automatic and corrected all errors as they occurred, students would control the new language and be able to use it independently. Like any teaching method, ALM has worked for some students and teachers, and not for others. This may be due to a variety of reasons and circumstances, some of which would be attributed to the method itself and others to how it was enacted; in essence, these become discrepancies between the ALM method as a 'potential resource' and a 'realized' one, to use Bell's terms.

At its core, however, the problem of teaching methods does not lie in how they are carried out; rather, it is a problem of expectation – no method will lead to student learning in every circumstance, all of the time. Fundamentally, this is because teaching does not *cause* learning; a particular method does not lead to specific learning outcomes under all conditions. It is more accurate to say that teaching clearly *influences* learning, but it does not make learning happen. Different methods present different resources to students, and these resources create different learning opportunities. Teaching methods persist because they predict learning outcomes; they also provide material for teacher education.

Concept pair #3: *teacher education vs. professional learning*

To recap the argument so far: methods in language teaching, as in other subjects, describe the public side of classroom activity. Their credibility and legitimacy come from the claims they assert about student learning. In this sense, teaching methods 'package' one part of the connection problem – how classroom teaching can lead to student learning (see #2 in Figure 17.1). This is what could be called the 'predictive value' of a teaching method: the claim that if you teach in this way, your students will learn. This predictive value also gives methods value in teacher preparation. Because they define what teachers should do in the classroom in order for students to learn, teaching methods (and the rationales and knowledge that underlie them) provide the general focus and substance in teacher education. Even in the so-called 'post-method' era, the same formulation continues, although the unit of prediction is now often called a 'teaching practice' (e.g. Ball and Forzani 2009).

All of which raises the central question of teacher education: how do teachers learn teaching methods? Understanding how this 'piping' works is the second part of the connection problem. One position is that teachers master this knowledge about teaching and learning through their professional preparation. Another is that the primary and enduring knowledge of teaching comes on-the-job. In professional preparation, the discussion focuses on what new teachers are taught in teacher education programmes. In on-the-job development, the examination shifts to the messier process of how and why teachers take up ideas in their daily work; this latter process is one of teacher learning.

Teacher learning focuses on how professional identities develop through practice. In this view, the knowledge teachers encounter and learn in professional education comes about through the *opportunities to learn* that they have; these opportunities *influence*, but do not cause, them to know or act in particular ways. Karen Johnson (2009: 77) captures this inherent complexity when she writes:

> If the goal of teacher education is to prepare the individual teacher to function in the professional world of teaching, then it is critical to account for how an individual's activities shape and are shaped by the social, cultural and historical macro-structures which constitute that professional world.

The view challenges the formulation that *teacher education*, which is concerned with the professional instruction side of the equation or *what* is being taught, is how new teachers are formed. Instead, the argument is that learning is primarily about taking on a new 'identity kit', so the processes of *teacher learning* are paramount. To use Gee's (2008) words about being a physicist: learning this new teacher identity entails 'special ways of acting and interacting so as to produce and use knowledge ... [and] ... special ways of seeing, valuing, and being in the world. [Teachers teach; they talk teaching] ... And when they are being [teachers], they see and value the world in a different way than do non-[teachers].'

Conceiving of teacher preparation as a process of transforming professional identity is a different way to look at the 'piping' problem. For one thing, it leads to a view of learning and change that is far less centralized, defined or expectable. Which brings us to the last two concept pairs about scalability and about sustainability.

Concept pair #4: *scalability in reform as replication vs. as generativity*

The concepts of scalability and sustainability have been the hallmarks of educational reform for more than 30 years (Fullan 2007). These ideas are based on a view of change in which the intended intervention moves the current status quo to the new situation through a series of defined steps, and success is measured by how widely the new activity is adopted and how faithfully it is implemented over time. With its roots in large-scale curricular reforms of the 1960s and 1970s in the USA and the UK, this view of learning emphasizes the fidelity with which the new activity – whether a curriculum, teaching methodology or technological innovation – is carried out (Graves 2008). In this notion of fidelity, the implementation of change brings a problem of scale: how to make what some people are doing the practice of many? In most educational reforms, the aim is to get the most effective or 'best' practices in curriculum, teaching or technology to travel or be reproduced in multiple classrooms while continuing to be faithful to the initial model. Such expansion is what reformers refer to as 'going to scale'.

This notion of 'going to scale' can be inherently problematic, however. If what the teacher does with students, his or her classroom practice, is seen primarily as a matter of teaching method, then faithfully expanding the scale from one to many classrooms has a certain logic of replication. But if, as we have argued earlier, students, teachers and classrooms differ and teaching and learning are intrinsically messy and complex, then faithfully expansive replication runs head on into the human idiosyncrasies of the people involved. In this sense, going to scale as a faithful replication is not possible or even desirable. Rather, the aim is to generate situation-specific approaches so that participating teachers and students 'infect' others (in a social sense) through their interest and excitement with the innovation.

The idea of generativity is central to change processes that adopt a systems perspective rather than one based on fidelity (the assumption that a particular method will work in all situations). Social networking, viral marketing and peer-to-peer change projects are each instances of this approach. In fact, many of the most durable educational reform efforts share this orientation to scale 'as generativity'. The US National Writing Project (NWP) is a case in point. The NWP began in 1974 as a teacher-led, peer-to-peer initiative 'to create a different form of professional development for teachers, one that made central the knowledge, leadership, and best practices of effective teachers, and that promoted the sharing of that knowledge with other teachers' (NWP 2011). By 1976, two years later, the project had 14 sites in six US states; now almost four decades later, there are over 200 sites.

This expansion was fuelled by the generativity of interest and commitment rather than fidelity or close adherence to a specific model. The NWP is described on its website as:

a network of sites anchored at colleges and universities and serving teachers across disciplines and at all levels, early childhood through university [that] provide[s] professional development, develop[s] resources, generate[s] research, and act[s] on knowledge to improve the teaching of writing and learning in schools and communities.

(NWP 2011)

The generativity of the project has been based on adaptation through this collaborative infrastructure to local circumstances. The NWP has thus created a sense of local buy-in and ownership that most large-scale reforms are often not able to achieve. This generativity is clearly articulated in the project's core principles, excerpted below (NWP 2011):

- Teachers at every level – from kindergarten through college – are the agents of reform ...
- Writing can and should be taught, not just assigned, at every grade level ...
- Knowledge about the teaching of writing comes from many sources ...
- There is no single right approach to teaching writing; however, some practices prove to be more effective than others ...
- Teachers who are well informed and effective in their practice can be successful teachers of other teachers as well as partners in educational research, development, and implementation. Collectively, teacher-leaders are our greatest resource for educational reform.

In these principles, the teacher is the source of reform, both as the one who recognizes what is needed in his or her teaching situation and also as one who supports peers in making changes in what they do. The principles capture the differences in perspective between scalability and generativity. From the scalability perspective, the NWP is measured by how many sites and teachers it reaches. From that of generativity, the concern is how the project embraces these new participants, and the difference it makes in their classroom practice.

Concept pair #5: *sustainability as reiteration* vs. *as momentum*

If scalability is about the expansion and coverage in the reform – about the space occupied by the change – then sustainability, as the other standard metric of reform, is about time, how long the new endures. Here again, reform projects have tended to frame the change process as a movement from a status quo that is stable and predictable to an equally stable new state of innovated activity. The basic assumption of sustainability is that the new state of affairs (i.e. curriculum, methodology, technology, etc.) will be faithful to the new design and will become as established as what it replaces.

This set of assumptions about the change process is as admirable as it is unfounded in experience, however. It supports an evaluative framework that attempts to measure the durability of the innovation by how it is reiterated. Reforms 'fail' in this view, because they do not continue as originally instituted; the innovation is not sustained. But if, as we have said, teaching is relational work, then it is intrinsically human and idiosyncratic. Any notion of a sustained and sustainable state of affairs that is steady and predictable is impossible. Instead of the sustainability of reiterating the new way of doing things, it is more accurate to think about the momentum that creates the change and how that momentum can carry the new practices forward. In this view, reform and innovation depend on the momentum of the new in the context of the current rather than on the degree to which the new practice stably replaces the current one.

Again the National Writing Project offers an instructive example. In the almost 40 years of operation, project participants have had to address a cascade of changing circumstances. In the 1970s, when the NWP started, there was no public Internet; digital and electronic authorship did not exist; students lived in a primarily print-based world. Although there were bilingual and second language education programmes in some US communities, most students came to school with English as the language of the home and community, so the majority were learning to write and become writers in their home or first language. Now, all of this is changing. The digital and web-based world has changed the nature of writing and the experiences and expectations that students bring to that process. And the demographics of US classrooms are quite different; in many schools and communities, students come to school with languages other than English and so are learning to write in a second language.

In the context of these evolving circumstances, the durability of the NWP depends on its capacity to adapt its practices according to its principles to meet local needs and demands. This process of adaptation depends, then, on momentum to generate possible solutions in teachers' specific circumstances, within the coherence of the project framework. It is not a matter of faithfully implementing a specified way of doing things in an increasing number of classrooms, in other words getting 'to scale', which is then continued or 'sustained' over time. Rather the question is one of the momentum that comes with generating, testing out and refining local applications of core ideas.

Conclusion

This chapter has examined how teaching can be said to 'predict' learning. Drawing on the analogy of the 'piping' problem, I have argued for reframing the teaching and learning relationship from a series of steady state concepts to the relational realm of 'what goes on inside and between people' in the classroom. The attraction of the steady state view is that it creates the illusion of predicting that specific teaching methods and classroom practices *cause* (or lead to) particular *learning*

Frameworks for meaningful language learning

outcomes. The role of *teacher education*, then, is to prepare teachers in these methods and practices. Innovation and reform aim to bring the selected practices *to scale* and assure they are *sustainable* over time.

In this calculus, prediction is a matter of generalizing solutions across situations; it is a matter of linking methods and practices to the learning outcomes they cause, and then forecasting effective expansion (*scale*) and maintenance (*sustainability*) of those ways of working across numbers of classroom settings. In this view, the relational dimensions of teaching and learning become contexts to be managed and stabilized; idiosyncrasy, specificity and localness are potential impediments to this process of generalization and prediction. The relational view recasts these shortcomings. The challenge becomes less about the concepts used to build the prediction than how those elements are framed; which is where the 'piping' analogy is helpful.

I have argued that prediction in education is firmly anchored in a view of 'piping' of change. If we shift the conceptual frame to what we have called relational work, however, these concepts align in a new logic that supports a different view of prediction. Figure 17.2 summarizes this shift in these conceptual underpinnings.

	Connections as *steady state*	Connections as *relational*
Concept #3	*Teacher education*	*Teacher learning*
Concept #2	*(trains teachers in practices that)* *causes*	*influences* *(how teachers create)*
Concept #1	*learning outcomes for students in classrooms*	*student learning opportunities*
Concepts #4 and #5	*which can be replicated as scalable and sustainable*	*which are generated under specific circumstances and together build momentum in diverse settings*

Figure 17.2 Remapping connections between teacher education, classroom teaching and student learning framed as steady state vs. as relational work

The educational statistician Lee Cronbach, who studied patterns in teaching and learning through correlational analyses, captured this dilemma. Writing about the shortcomings of an overreaching approach to generalization, he observed: 'When we give proper weight to local

284

conditions, any generalization is a working hypothesis, not a conclusion' (1975: 126). In our case, these 'working hypotheses' are predictions about the connections between teaching and learning. The redefinition of teaching and learning as relational work alters the basic metrics of prediction. What is seen as stable and scalable in a generalized prediction becomes 'a working hypothesis' under the circumstances of local relational work. This may be the reason that predicting these connections is so complex and so resistant to broad-based solutions.

References

Anthony, E. M. (1963) 'Approach, method and technique', *English Language Teaching*, 17: 63–7.

Ball, D. L. and Forzani, F. (2009) 'The work of teaching and the challenge for teacher education', *Journal of Teacher Education*, 60(5): 497–511.

Bell, D. (2007) 'Do teachers think methods are dead?', *ELT Journal*, 61(2): 135–43.

Blair, R. W. (ed.) (1982) *Innovative Approaches to Language Teaching*, Rowley, MA: Newbury House / Heinle.

Brown, H. D. (2002) 'English language teaching in the "post-method" era: toward better diagnosis, treatment, and assessment', in Richards, J. C. and Renandya, W. A. (eds.) *Methodology in Language Teaching: An Anthology of Current Practice*, Cambridge: Cambridge University Press, pp. 9–18.

Christie, F. and Martin, J. (2000) *Genre and Institutions: Social Processes in the Workplace and* School, London: Cassell.

Cohen, D. K., Raudenbush, S. W. and. Ball, D. L. (2003) 'Resources, instruction, and research', *Educational Evaluation and Policy Analysis*, 25(2): 119–42.

Cronbach, L. (1975) 'Beyond the two disciplines of scientific psychology', *The American Psychologist*, 30(2): 11–127.

Freeman, D. (1996) 'Renaming experience / reconstructing practice: developing new understandings of teaching', in Freeman, D. and Richards, J. C. (eds.) *Teacher Learning in Language Teaching*, New York: Cambridge University Press, pp. 221–41.

Freeman, D. (2006) 'Teaching and learning in the "age of reform": the problem of the verb', in Gieve, S. and Miller, I. (eds.) *Understanding the Language Classroom*, Basingstoke: Palgrave Macmillan, pp. 239–62.

Freeman, D. and Johnson, K. E. (2004) 'Towards linking teacher knowledge and student learning', in Tedick, D. (ed.) *Second Language Teacher Education: International Perspectives*, Mahwah, NJ: Lawrence Erlbaum, pp. 73–95.

Fullan, M. (2007) *The New Meaning of Educational Change*, 4th edn, New York: Teachers College Press.

Gee, J. (2008) 'A sociocultural perspective on opportunity to learn', in Moss. P., Pullin, D. C., Gee, J. P., Haertel, E. H. and Young, L. J. (eds.) *Assessment, Equity, and Opportunity to Learn*, New York: Cambridge University Press, pp. 76–108.

Graves, K. (2008) 'The language curriculum: a social contextual perspective', *Language Teaching*, 41(2): 149–83.

Greeno, J. and Gresalfi, M. S. (2008) 'Opportunities to learn in practice and identity', in Moss. P., Pullin, D. C., Gee, J. P., Haertel, E. H. and Young, L. J. (eds.) *Assessment, Equity, and Opportunity to Learn*, New York: Cambridge University Press, pp. 170–99.

Johnson, K. E. (2009) *Second Language Teacher Education: A Socio-Cultural Perspective*, Mahwah, NJ: Routledge.

Kidder, T. (1989) *Among Schoolchildren*, Boston: Houghton Mifflin.

Kumaravadivelu, B. (1994) 'The postmethod condition: emerging strategies for second/foreign language teaching', *TESOL Quarterly*, 28(1): 27–47.

Lortie, D. (1975) *Schoolteacher: A Sociological Study*, Chicago: University of Chicago Press.

National Writing Project (NWP) (2011) 'History of the National Writing Project'. Available online at http://www.nwp.org/cs/public/print/doc/about/history.csp (accessed 28 June 2011).

North Central Regional Educational Laboratory (NCREL) (2011) 'Critical issues'. Available online at http://www.ncrel.org/sdrs/areas/issues/methods/assment/as8lk18.htm (accessed 28 April 2011).

Peirce, B. N. (1995) 'Social investment, identity, and language learning', *TESOL Quarterly*, 29(1): 9–31.

Richards, J. C. and Rodgers, T. (1982) 'Methods: approach, design, and procedure', *TESOL Quarterly*, 16(2): 153–68.

Stevick, E. W. (1976) *Memory, Meaning and Method: Some Psychological Perspectives on Language Learning*, Boston: Heinle & Heinle.

Stevick, E. W. (1980) *Teaching Languages: A Way and Ways*, Rowley MA: Newbury House.

18 Individual and organizational learning: exploring the psycho-social dynamics of change

Mark A. Clarke

Introduction

Some problems in language teaching seem more than mere technical puzzles; they present us with conundrums that provide a window onto important aspects of learning and development. Earl Stevick often couched his problem-solving musings as riddles. Here is a sampling:

Riddle #1: failure and success

Why do some language students succeed, and others fail? Why do some language teachers fail and others succeed? What may the learners and teachers of foreign languages hope to succeed at, anyway? How broad, how deep, and how wide may be the measure of their failure, or their success?

(Stevick 1980: 3)

Riddle #2: methods

In the field of language teaching, Method A is the logical contradiction of Method B: if the assumptions from which A claims to be derived are correct, then B cannot work, and vice versa. Yet one colleague is getting excellent results with A, and another is getting comparable results with B. How is this possible?

(Stevick 1996: 193)

In my work as a language teacher and teacher educator, I have wrestled with these riddles and I have benefited significantly from Stevick's approach to teaching and learning – indeed, from the model his life has provided of teacher as learner. Early on in my career as a teacher educator, I was confronted by the fact that the teachers in my classes expected me to guide them in selecting from the competing claims of the dominant methods and materials even though I believed these were choices they had to make for themselves (Clarke 1982). I therefore found myself in the paradoxical position of a guru who advised young teachers to be wary of gurus (Clarke 1984).

The issue of 'success' and 'failure' applies to more than language teaching, of course, and permits us to ponder a broad continuum of possible

287

responses to life's challenges. On one extreme we have the technical issues of how we get through the day – in teaching this means attention to materials, methods and techniques – while on the other extreme we have the more philosophical domain of core values and principles – questions that in language education go beyond language competence and touch on universals of power and privilege. It seems clear that we cannot avoid this tension between the mundane pressures of teaching and the moral imperatives of theory and philosophy. Depending on one's position, practical constraints range from mandated curricula, centralized testing, skimpy budgets and bulging classes – the totality of which make it difficult to address the larger complexities of language identity, linguistic imperialism or learner autonomy.

But how do we negotiate this tension? It may be true – in fact, I take it as given – that success rests on the quality of 'what goes on inside and between people' (Stevick 1980: 4), but how do we create the physical, temporal and psychological space that permits us to productively pursue the work implied in that assertion? As I ponder that question, three more riddles spring up:

Riddle #3: students

People invest significant amounts of time and money to learn a second language so that they can pursue their academic dreams or improve their careers, yet they often resist their teachers' attempts to get them to practise the language in class, slough off their homework assignments (or treat them as assignments, rather than genuine opportunities to learn) and avoid opportunities to converse with native speakers.

Riddle #4: teachers

Dedicated and hard-working teachers attend conference workshops and pursue advanced degrees in order to improve their teaching, but they avoid taking risks in their classrooms to try out new techniques, observe other teachers or work with coaches to explore new ways of engaging students.

Riddle #5: administrators

Charter schools are created to promote learning through innovative programmes and instructional activities. Yet administrators dedicated to those innovations develop policies and procedures that virtually guarantee that the school will resemble conventional schools.

In this chapter I describe an action research project designed to explore the organizational, interactional and psychological factors that contribute to these conundrums. In the process, I examine the notion of 'transformational' learning, discuss the possibility that 'identity' is a complex phenomenon characteristic of organizations as well as individuals, and look at seminar and workshop activities we have used to promote reflection and change.

A school/university partnership for innovation

The action research project is part of a long-standing tradition in the United States of school/university partnerships designed to improve academic outcomes for students in schools serving low-income, minority and immigrant learners (Goodlad 1994; Ginsberg and Rhodes 2003).[1] Traditionally, activities led by universities have concentrated on improving instruction through professional development, while efforts led by districts have concentrated on planning and managing school change. We attempt to merge these activities into a systemic approach to school reform. Our model draws on (a) characteristics of effective schools, refined in the light of recent research on successful schools for English language learners (Goddard 2002; Goddard et al. 2004; Lezotte and Snyder 2011), (b) effective instructional practices for low-income students and for English language learners in particular (Genesee and Lindholm-Leary 2006) and (c) a change process that disrupts the historical equilibrium of low-performing schools and promotes change (Wagner et al. 2006; Kegan and Lahey 2009).

Our work has been supported by federal grants to orchestrate teacher-leadership activities aimed at school improvement (Clarke and Davis 2007a; Clarke and Davis 2007b). The goal is increased student learning and performance through improved instruction; the primary focus of our efforts has been on innovative, teacher-led seminar/workshops and classroom coaching (Brancard and Quinn Williams 2012). At the same time, widespread instructional improvement requires school-wide change so that teachers, students and parents work together in coordination towards shared goals. This requires a conceptual framework that encompasses both personal and organizational change; the three intellectual traditions on which this analysis rests are constructive developmental psychology, systems theory and cultural-historical activity theory.

[1] The Lab of Learning and Activity is a research group at the University of Colorado Denver that has functioned at the School of Education and Human Development since the early 1990s. The individuals most directly involved in the work reported here are: Ruth Brancard, Kathy Bougher, Alan Davis, Sally Nathenson-Mejia, Jennifer Quinn Williams, Mia Thomas-Ruzic, Shannon Svaldi and Barbara Vaille.

Constructive-developmental psychology is also referred to as subject/object psychology (Perry 1981; Kegan 1994), and it is based on the assertion that learning and development must be considered together. A key aspect of development is that as individuals move from one developmental level to another, they are able to analyse their worldview and to understand previously held beliefs in light of new evidence about how the world works. They are able to move concepts from the *subject* position to the *object* position; instead of being subject to an assumption, emotion or presupposition, they are able to step back from them and analyse them as objects of inspection. That is, they are able to see the assumptions on which earlier understandings rested as just that – assumptions.

Systems theory views all living organisms and stable (in the sense of 'enduring over time') collections of organisms as naturally resistant to change (Bateson 2000). From this point of view, assumptions about individuals are considered to be true for organizations as well, and vice versa. Schools which have been established to improve the academic success and life chances of low-income minority and immigrant youth will, by definition, generate counterbalancing pressures to maintain the status quo. These pressures are both external, emanating from societal structures and cultural norms, and internal, emerging from the day-to-day rhythms and routines of individuals within the organization, and proceeding from unconscious adherence to societal norms. The construct of identity is relevant to an understanding of this resistance, because it is the stable characteristics of schools and individuals that provide an ongoing sense of security and continuity.

Cultural-historical activity theory (CHAT) focuses on the fact that all of the cultural norms and societal institutions within which we live and work exercise inexorable, often imperceptible pressures that make objective decision-making and independent action difficult. Schools and the people who work in them are influenced by long-established traditions of norms and structures that are only imperfectly understood (Engeström 2008). An explicit recognition of these forces is required if patterns of failure are to be changed; school personnel need to acknowledge that they are creating their own definitions of success and working to change the way schooling is conducted.

These three traditions provide the framework required to connect individual identity and organizational identity. This is important if we are to understand how everyone in a school can be dedicated to change at the same time that they are working diligently (though unconsciously) to assure that change *does not* occur. It is also important if we are to accurately characterize the nature of the work required if significant identity adjustments are to be accomplished. In the literature, these sorts of changes are often referred to as 'transformational'.

Transformation

The word *transformational* is widely used to describe an experience that transcends the mundane, that prompts dramatic changes in the way one views the world. Transformational learning, sometimes called 'adaptive learning', is contrasted with mere 'technical' or 'informational' learning; the latter are associated with an increase in skill or understanding, while the former is seen as more profound, more fundamental, causing the individual to see the world differently (Heifetz 1994). Transformational learning, which is akin to development and therefore associated with identity development, is often seen as a prerequisite for a proposed innovation. But what does it mean and how do we know it when we see it?

Let's take an example from the classroom. Because literacy skills are central to academic success, it is expectable that teachers will focus on improving students' reading and writing skills. Conventional teaching might stress improvement in building an argument, constructing coherent paragraphs and developing skills in grammar, vocabulary selection and mechanics. An explicitly transformational approach, however, might emphasize critical reading and authentic writing activities aimed at improving the students' opportunities for academic and life success. In the former approach, it is sufficient for students to become more skilful in their use of rhetorical and grammatical conventions. If teachers have transformational aspirations, however, the expectation would be that students adopt writing as a thinking process, a way of problem-solving. And, a natural outcome of such teaching might be students taking a more active role in their own learning, pushing back against classroom and school rules and regulations, and asserting their rights as citizens. Teachers and administrators alike can be expected to chafe under such pressures from students; no matter how sincere they might have been in promoting students' independent thinking and self-advocacy, the result is likely to cause disruptions to 'business as usual'. So, for example, students who conduct surveys and interviews to discover their peers' opinions about school policies and procedures and then publish their findings in the school newspaper could reasonably expect that their voices will be heard. They will not be satisfied with positive evaluations and high marks if their demands are not met. That is, they will expect their efforts to be treated as 'real', not as mere classroom assignments, and teachers and administrators must be prepared to deal with the disruptions that result.

In other words, transformational learning will be required on everyone's part, not just on the part of the students. Morever, since such significant changes go beyond mere learning, it is expectable that fundamental adjustments in individual and organizational identity will be required. My contention is that we need to consider both together, and to understand how the two interact and mutually construct each other.

Individual and organizational identity

The fundamental assertion is this: the rhythmic, predictable activity of everyday functioning reveals the interaction between individuals and the organization. The identity of the organization and the identities of the individuals in the organization are inextricably intertwined and mutually, reciprocally, (re)produced in the activities of daily life.

The organizational meta-patterns created by policy and procedure influence the choices made by individuals on a daily basis, and these choices become ingrained in their thinking and behaviour so that, gradually, they develop powerful assumptions that govern their actions and sense of self. In the process, an organizational culture develops so that it is possible to characterize the school as having certain values – 'skills-based vs. communicative', 'traditional vs. alternative', for example. The cultural markers of a school range from the tangible (school uniforms, memos, hallway and classroom displays, etc.) to the visible (classes changing at predictable times, public prayer and classroom recitation, students lining up to pass from class to class, announcements over the public address system, etc.) to the ephemeral (an 'aura' of order or creativity or a sense of excitement or determination, etc.). Cultural norms are also evident in the behaviour and speech of students and staff, and in expressions of motivation or explanation for behaviour or non-behaviour; that is, in the reasons people give for doing or not doing certain things.

But, it is important to acknowledge that schools and the individuals who work in them are bundles of contradictions that (re)create each other every single day. The mission statement may say that the school is dedicated to the success of marginalized youth, but the drop-out rate may reveal that this goal has not yet been reached. Teachers may say that they are committed to child-centred instruction, but strict adherence to curricula and pacing guides would indicate otherwise. How do we account for these apparent contradictions? It seems especially important to answer this question in situations where people are dedicated to serious efforts at social justice, at systems change for the greater good. Why, in spite of their best efforts, do they consistently fall short of their goals? Why is change so difficult? The research we are engaged in is designed to address these questions, and the answer, in brief, is this: fundamental change in how teachers teach and schools function is difficult because it threatens the identities of individuals and schools alike. As an action research project, we have had to operationalize the construct of 'identity' so that we can work on systemic improvements at both levels; our approach is presented in Table 18.1.

Table 18.1   *Identity elements*

- <u>Policy</u>. Laws, contracts, formal agreements, etc. that govern the functioning of the organization. These are the over-arching documents that are codified and referred to as the basis for decision-making, especially when actions require official and formal justification.

- <u>Programmes</u>. Textbooks, curriculum, etc. adopted to organize instruction, address problems, etc. These always come with hidden constraints and are governed by assumptions about human nature, teaching and learning.

- <u>Organizational culture.</u> The norms, rules and regulations that people follow in their daily conduct. These are mostly invisible and difficult to change. They are the explicit and implicit rules for daily conduct, including interpersonal interaction.

- <u>Realities of time and space</u>. These are often taken as givens, rather than opportunities for change: size/character of classrooms, daily schedules, the holidays and exam periods that constitute the realities of teachers' and students' lives.

- <u>Individual rhythms and routines</u>. These are the *personal* habits and preferences that shape the day and often constitute the most important constraint for change. Whether individuals are 'early birds' or 'night owls', for example, or whether they are list makers and planners or free-flowing improvisers, the preferences people have for their daily conduct will shape their opinions about and engagement in organizational innovations.

- <u>Roles and responsibilities</u>. These are the understandings that influence how people work and how they relate to others. They have cultural, official, legal and institutional authority, which means that individuals may invoke their position or title when presenting an argument or defending a position, but they are also visible in the language they use and the prerogatives they assume as their right. The most common form of the latter is evident when an individual says, in effect, 'Do as I say because I am the boss (or teacher, director, adult, etc.).' It is also possible to catch a glimpse of this factor when an individual goes beyond the letter of his or her contract to do something that he or she considers important.

(cont.)

- <u>Epistemology</u>. The core values and authorities that govern individuals' lives, revealed both in explicit statements and in the meanings that are implicit in actions. For the observer, the relationship between explicit statements of belief and everyday behaviours is not always apparent, but individuals are generally aware of the connections, and in cases where they discern a lack of coherence, they will offer a rationale that accounts for the apparent contradiction.

Schools and individuals function towards stability by responding to internal and external stimuli in patterned, if not entirely predictable, ways. They operate according to constraints, not causes. Constraints are all of the factors that shape the behaviour and thinking of everyone in the school and that function at different levels of scale to produce the outcomes that we see every day. These outcomes are, in fact, a by-product of the daily functioning of the system, and whatever the school achieves can be said to be precisely the outcomes that it is designed to achieve. If the people associated with the school want to change those outcomes, they need to attend to the factors that produce them. And for this reason, it is important to discover how the factors interact to shape the performance of students, faculty and staff. The factors can be understood as 'identity elements', and attending to them in a change initiative is as important as attending to the fundamentals of instruction. But before returning to discuss the action research project, I would like to introduce one more riddle.

Riddle #6: context

A certain high school English teacher requires her students to participate in community service activities where they have to use English in communicative situations rather than in the comfortable routines of drills and exercises. What additional information would we need to be able to predict whether the students will:

a. Come to love or hate community service activities?
b. Love or hate English class?
c. Love or hate the English teacher?

The answer to the riddle is 'context', which we may define as 'a collective term for all those events which tell the organism among what *set* of alternatives he must make his next choice' (Bateson 2000: 289). Bateson's view is important for action researchers and educators, for two reasons. He reminds us, first, that to understand others we need to understand how they make sense of the world and what they consider to be their options for action; and second, that choices for action are not equal: we have *sets* of choices that impact system functioning at different levels of scale.

Returning to our example of emancipatory literacy attitudes and skills, the lessons are harder to teach if the only place students encounter authentic reading and writing is in the English class. But if the school has a policy of promoting student engagement and activism through critical reading and writing, and if all teachers are engaged in the same types of learning activities, the chances of success are greatly increased. In other words, if there is alignment between the identity of the school and the identities of the teachers, instructional activities of the sort I described will be more likely to succeed and greater coherence will be achieved to the benefit of all.

The seven identity elements depicted in Table 18.1 constitute the primary 'sets of alternatives' used by individuals to understand situations and make decisions. Leaders attempting to change the way teachers teach or assess their students, for example, select initiatives from among the seven elements to accomplish their goals. Similarly, teachers seeking to improve student attendance and participation identify one or more of these elements as sources of authority and rationale for action.

Exploring what goes on inside and between people: why is change so difficult?

Returning to our action research project, as participants in a school–university partnership organized around improving the academic performance and life chances of low-income, minority and immigrant students, we are committed to innovation, and yet frustrated by the contradictions depicted in riddles 3, 4 and 5.

There is really only one riddle – why do we resist change? Or perhaps we should say, 'How do we manage to resist changing even when we are earnestly engaged in promoting change?' In spite of the fact that we are sincere in our resolve to change, we nevertheless sabotage our own efforts and frustrate ourselves and others as we fall short of proclaimed goals. Significant, sustained change seems nearly impossible to achieve, and our initiatives evoke deeply embedded, very natural impulses to continue functioning the way we have always functioned. And this is true of organizations as well as individuals.

Why is change so difficult? A brief exercise will provide some insight. Please respond to the following items.

1. Think of a problem you have been working on that seems to resist all your best efforts at change and note them in column one below. The problem should concern something that ...
   a. ... is truly important to you (Do not pick a trivial 'tongue-in-cheek' difficulty.),
   b. ... is about you (Do not name another person or a situation that is 'the problem'.), and that ...
   c. ... you have the power and prerogative to change (Do not identify something outside your sphere of influence, such as racism, global warming or world peace, for example.).

It does not matter if the problems you identify are personal or professional, but it *is* important that you follow the above admonitions in your choice of problem to work on or the exercise will not work. Jot notes-to-self in the first column. Very often several separate problems are inextricably intertwined and need to be considered together. List each one separately.

I am committed to ...	... but I often do (or fail to do) the following sorts of things that prevent me from realizing my commitments ...	... so I must also be committed to ...	Apparently, I believe or assume or am afraid that ...

2. In the second column, list the things you *do* or *say* that undermine your change efforts.

This requires a measure of commitment and honesty that is sometimes difficult to muster, especially if the activity is being conducted in a group. But at the moment, it is only you and the chart, so total disclosure should be possible.

Now, take a moment to step back and ponder what you have written down in columns 1 and 2, to make sure that you have been honest with yourself, and that you have accurately uncovered contradictory tendencies between your intentions and your actions. This might take some time unless you are used to reflective soul searching. You may, in fact, want to consult with a close friend or colleague. This sort of work is generally more successful when you engage in it with trusted friends and colleagues, especially those who are able to speak frankly with you about your shortcomings.

3. In the third column, identify the reason(s) you have not actually made progress on the primary commitments you listed in column one.

This column provides an opportunity for insight, but it also gives you a chance to escape self-criticism, because you might be inclined to cloak your competing commitments in self-congratulatory motivations. It is important to avoid doing that – what you put in column 3 should evoke a sense of sheepishness. So, for example, if you have *said* that you want to cut down on credit card debt or frivolous spending, but you continue to plan extravagant vacations with friends, you might be tempted to put in column three that you do not want to hurt your friends' feelings, when in fact, if you were honest with yourself, you might admit that you do not want them to know that you cannot afford to run in the same circles.

4. In the fourth column, the task is to identify the fears and assumptions that contribute to your continued avoidance of significant change.

The payoff comes in column 4, if you are able to accurately identify heretofore unrecognized fears and assumptions that have prevented you from making progress with your change efforts, or if you are able to articulate fears that you have been aware of but not admitting even to yourself for some time.

The four-column exercise was developed by Harvard psychologists Robert Kegan and Lisa Lahey (Kegan and Lahey 2009) and is used by them and their colleagues as the basis for leadership training (Wagner et al. 2006). The activity is based on over twenty years of research in constructive developmental psychology (Kegan 1994), the key contention of which is that development is a lifelong process.

The exercise provides a framework for insights that can lead to change, but it is important to examine the conditions under which this might occur. Consider the responses of an individual teacher who is struggling to move from tightly controlled drill-based instructional techniques to a more communicative approach involving authentic interaction and critical literacy.

The following chart reveals the tensions that arise when an individual attempts to teach 'against the grain'. Societal norms, organizational rules and regulations, and the personal expectations of students and teachers make it difficult to promote student responsibility and initiative. In this case, the scripted lessons and mandated curriculum bear down on the teacher, confirming an inner sense that the free-wheeling sort of lesson that cooperative learning would promote might bring chaos to the classroom and censure from colleagues and administrators.

We were interested to see if we could promote a school-wide conversation about immunities to change, so we orchestrated a series of activities aimed at individual and collective four-column work. Teachers

I am committed to ...	... but I often do (or fail to do) the following sorts of things that prevent me from realizing my commitments ...	... so I must also be committed to ...	Apparently, I believe or assume or am afraid that ...
• ... using more cooperative group work in the classroom in which students develop critical literacy around authentic issues.	• I spend most class time explaining course concepts to the class in lecture format. • I use scripted lesson plans and textbook exercises. • I spend most class time correcting grammar, spelling and pronunciation errors.	• ... maintaining control and demonstrating my command of course concepts. • ... following the mandated curriculum, keeping up with material. • ... maintaining control through comfortable, focused activity.	• ... if I implement group work and authentic tasks, I will lose control of the class. • ... if I don't follow the curriculum guide, I'll get poor performance evaluations. • ... students are not capable of taking responsibility for their own learning.

and administrators from the school participated in an immunity-to-change workshop led by Robert Kegan. The workshop lasted all day and provided the foundation for discovering an approach to educational innovation based on the belief that organizational change requires personal change. This approach assumes that innovation requires broad participation of individuals in the organization, that everyone in the organization has leadership potential, and that effective change agents must address three important facts about people and organizations:

1. One cannot exercise unilateral control over others (indeed, we do not even exercise complete control over ourselves!). All change initiatives provoke unexpected responses and entail unintended consequences that derail even the most thoughtfully conceived change efforts. This applies to colleagues, students and subordinates.

2. People and organizations function towards stability. They are characterized by immunity systems that neutralize change initiatives and reveal that even the most committed individuals often undermine their own change efforts. That is to say, resistance to change initiatives should be viewed as a normal and healthy phenomenon, rather than as aberrant or pernicious behaviour.
3. Patterns of organizational functioning are connected in non-random ways to individuals' patterns of thinking and behaving. Significant organizational change cannot occur without significant changes by individuals.

Soon after the workshop our research team facilitated a district-wide immunity workshop involving over 50 faculty and staff. In the first half of the day, we focused on personal four-column work to uncover individuals' immunity to change. During the second half of the session, school-based groups worked separately to examine collective immunity dynamics. 'Collective immunity work' refers to collaborative exploration of the competing commitments that keep a school from realizing its goals. It is a significant step in the process of identifying how a school might change its policies, procedures and culture to support innovation.

A key element in creating synergy is the effective toggling back and forth between individual and collective four-column work. At the heart of this approach is everyone recognizing his or her own unique contributions to the problems the organization is trying to solve, and in honestly taking responsibility for personal change as well as for constructive conversations with colleagues about the process. This is not easy, as a couple of examples will illustrate.

In one of the school workshops, the group asserted that a significant column 2 behaviour was not maintaining rigorous expectations of students, but in a side bar discussion one of the teachers proclaimed that this wasn't her problem; *she* maintained high standards. The teacher has defeated the goals of the process, by agreeing with the consensus but subconsciously absolving herself of the behaviours under discussion. In order for progress to be made *as a school*, everyone has to work in collegial fashion to correct organizational norms that undermine the mission of the school.

In another conversation, there was considerable agreement that attendance problems stem from a 'pobrecito' mentality – mollycoddling or killing students with kindness – letting them off the hook so much that they don't learn to take personal responsibility for their education. But the individual speaking does not have daily contact with students, so it is unlikely that he was talking about his personal misbehaviours. By unconsciously slipping from 'we' to 'they', he moved from group problem-solving to blaming others rather than taking personal responsibility.

Only concerted effort at explicitly connecting one's own behaviour to the larger organizational functioning qualifies as immunity work. But the complications multiply when we consider the organizational pressures that make innovative teaching difficult. The chart below is an excerpt from the collective four-column work of the leadership team of the school. The leadership team recognizes that they are sending mixed messages to teachers, yet the trend of centralized control continues, with the result that teachers do not act on their creative impulses, students continue to struggle with conventional teaching methods, and the school perpetuates the process it was established to change.

We are committed to …	… but we often do (or fail to do) the following sorts of things that prevent us from realizing our commitment …	… so we must also be committed to …	Apparently, we believe or assume or are afraid that …
• … creating engaging, authentic learning experiences that will result in increased student attendance and achievement. • … nurturing our staff, to attract and foster fantastic teachers.	• We are not holding ourselves accountable. • We aren't supporting teachers to make policy achievable. • We haven't taken anything off teachers' plates so that they can focus on what's most important. Instead, we add more.	• … not taking the wrong path, to not failing. • … not re-doing curriculum. • … not admitting having used time and money poorly. • … not releasing teachers from chores, to helping them improve. • … not looking bad, of getting someone worse, of the risk of lawsuits.	• … if we fail in an initiative, we are failures (as a leader, an organization, as a school, etc.), instead of learning from it. • … we need uniform policies and procedures that apply across the board.

What do you see here? In the first column the leadership team asserts a commitment to creating structures and processes that support staff creativity and increased student learning, but they admit that they do not follow through; in the second column they identify significant actions and inactions that undermine their commitments. The third and fourth columns provide glimpses of work ahead if they decide to tackle their immunities. Taking the individual and collective four-column work together as representative of the school, I would assert the following to be true:

- There is broad support for the goal of creating a unique innovative learning environment tailored specifically for students, on the one hand, which is undermined by policies and programmes that are essentially the same as those employed by conventional schools, on the other. This might be seen as a lack of visionary leadership on the part of administrators, except for the fact that teachers also identify a strong desire to avoid being seen as a 'slacker school' (in the words of one teacher), a mere 'diploma mill' lacking academic rigour.
- School personnel operate with a strong commitment to creative problem-solving counterbalanced by a respect for authority which impedes its enactment. The source of authority may be embodied in a curriculum, a test or an individual, rather than in the personal convictions of the individual. Until individuals act with confidence on their personal values, it will be difficult for the school to achieve the coherent effort required to sustain innovation.
- The value of constructivist approaches to teaching and learning is widely acknowledged by teachers and administrators at the same time that adherence to strict rules and regulations and reverence for standardized curricula and tests legislates against them. This tension undermines innovation.
- Similarly, the importance of individualization in teaching and assessment is undermined by the conviction that curriculum and assessment must be standardized.

Conclusion

I began this chapter with a consideration of Earl Stevick's two riddles, and I would like to conclude with an elaboration on them.

With regard to Riddle #1 – conundrums of what counts as failure and success – we have to recognize that measures of success cannot be universally applied to all teachers and students. In a recent sampling of student opinion, we found that they count their school experience as a success, even though they continue to receive low grades and struggle to graduate. Their measure? They are doing better at this school than they have done at previous schools, they like their teachers and they feel 'at home' in the school. Their teachers are not content with this assessment, but it is important to recognize that their efforts have had significant impact on these young people's lives.

With regard to Riddle #2 – the apparent contradiction of the success of diametrically opposed methods – my contribution is merely to expand on Stevick's point that teaching is not merely a matter of method. Or perhaps, more accurately, what matters is authentic engagement around important content, which can occur with virtually all methods and materials.

I do not offer these comments as original insights; these are merely rephrasings of Earl Stevick's assertions. However, my recent work with teachers in urban school districts has given me an opportunity to reflect on them. Remember Stevick's advice to attend to 'what goes on inside and between people'. The advice is sound; teaching is a function of relationships, but my experience leads me to conclude that good teaching is more an organizational accomplishment than an individual *tour de force*. In order to solve the riddles he posed, we have to expand our vision of language teaching and learning. The organizational change process described above, which I believe can contribute significantly to the efforts of educational innovators, constitutes a contribution to this effort. Innovation is a collective process requiring both individual and organizational identity adjustments.

Finally, with regard to Riddle #1, Stevick asks what teachers and learners may expect to succeed at, anyway, and what might be the measure of their success? I submit that a reasonable response to the question might include individual and collective efforts at self-understanding; improvements in teaching and learning surely will follow.

References

Bateson, G. (2000) *Steps to an Ecology of Mind*, Chicago: University of Chicago Press.
Brancard, R. and Quinn Williams, J. (2012) 'Learning labs: collaborations for transformative teacher learning', *TESOL Journal*, 3: 320–49.
Clarke, M. A. (1982) 'On bandwagons, tyranny, and common sense', *TESOL Quarterly*, 16(4): 437–48.
Clarke, M. A. (1984) 'On the nature of technique: what do we owe the gurus?', *TESOL Quarterly*, 18(4): 577–94.
Clarke, M. A. and Davis, A. (2007a) ELA Leadership Academies for Secondary Teachers Denver, Colorado, United States Department of Education: National Professional Development Project CFDA #84.195N.

Clarke, M. A. and Davis, A. (2007b) Professional Development Academies for Teachers of Immigrant Students Denver, Colorado, United States Department of Education: National Professional Development Program CFDA #84.195N

Engeström, Y. (2008) *From Teams to Knots*, New York: Cambridge University Press.

Genesee, F. and Lindholm-Leary, K. (2006) *Educating English Language Learners: A Synthesis of Research Evidence*, New York: Cambridge University Press.

Ginsberg, R. and Rhodes, L. K. (2003) 'The work, support and recognition of university faculty in partner schools', *Journal of Teacher Education*, 53(6): 150–62.

Goddard, R. D. (2002) 'Collective efficacy and school organization: a multi-level analysis of teacher influence in schools', *Theory and Research in EducationalAdministration*, 1: 169–84.

Goddard, R. D., LoGerfo, L. and Hoy, W. K. (2004) 'High school accountability: the role of perceived collective efficacy', *Educational Policy*, 18(3): 403–25.

Goodlad, J. I. (1994) *Educational Renewal: Better Teachers, Better Schools*, San Francisco: Jossey-Bass Publishers.

Heifetz, R. A. (1994) *Leadership Without Easy Answers*, Cambridge, MA: Harvard University Press.

Kegan, R. (1994) *In Over Our Heads: The Mental Demands of Modern Life*, Cambridge, MA: Harvard University Press.

Kegan, R. and Lahey, L. L. (2009) *Immunity to Change: How to Overcome It and Unlock the Potential in Yourself and Your Organization*, Boston: Harvard Business Press.

Lezotte, L. W. and Snyder, K. M. (2011) *What Effective Schools Do: Re-Envisioning the Correlates*, Bloomington, IN: Solution Tree Press.

Perry, W. G. J. (1981) 'Cognitive and ethical growth: the making of meaning', in Chickering, A. W. (ed.) *The Modern American College: Responding to the New Realities of Diverse Students and Changing Society*, San Francisco: Jossey-Bass Publishers, pp. 76–116.

Stevick, E. W. (1980) *Teaching Languages: A Way and Ways*, Rowley, MA: Newbury House.

Stevick, E. W. (1996) *Memory, Meaning, and Method: A View of Language Teaching*, 2nd edn, New York: Heinle & Heinle.

Wagner, T., Kegan, R., Lahey, L. L., Lemons, R. W., Garnier, J., Helsing, D., Howell, A. and Rasmussen, H. T. (2006) *Change Leadership: A Practical Guide to Transforming Our Schools*, San Francisco: Jossey-Bass Publishers.

Epilogue: A way with words – perspectives on the contributions and influence of Earl W. Stevick

Carolyn Kristjánsson

Stevick

How does one meaningfully summarize the contributions and influence of a gifted teacher and scholar whose engagement in language education has, in one form or another, spanned six decades and several generations of language learners, educators and researchers across five continents?

When I told Earl of my task for this book, his response was to provide me with his own perspective, expressed in inimitable Stevick style:

> Most people have one or more 'talents', which is to say that they can perform various tasks more readily or satisfactorily than their average conspecifics can. Looking back over the years, I think that in comparison with most people I have known, I am a person with a single talent, namely, that I 'have a way with words'. This talent manifests itself in a number of ways: in associating new words with their meanings, in memorizing poems, in persuasion, in learning new styles of handwriting, to name a few. In other kinds of tasks – in peeling potatoes, in throwing and/or catching balls, in carrying a tune, in playing board games, and in countless more – I am simply an educable moron.
>
> (personal communication, June 2011)

A *way with words*

I begin with Earl's self-assessment for two simple reasons: first, it is not what one might expect from a distinguished expert of international renown, at least not the last part of the statement. Second, it *is* what one might expect from Earl W. Stevick: an insightful and engaging observation demonstrating clarity of thought and expression – and the unpretentious stance that has made him not just a teacher and scholar of influence, but the beloved friend and mentor of many.

Early years and prevailing methodologies

Earl was born in Iowa 'midway between the Great War and the Great Depression', as he describes it. He was first exposed to formal foreign language instruction in high school as a student of Latin 'taught by the Grammar Translation method in its dullest, most mechanical version'. It was also in this context that he got his first language teaching experience, taking on the role of tutor to a fellow student of Latin in 1940. Four years of straight 'A's in Latin contributed to his being awarded a scholarship to Harvard, where he carved out a niche on the Dean's List by taking a foreign language course each semester – German, Spanish or Russian. Persuaded by his parents and dean that 'nobody ever made a living studying foreign languages', Earl majored in Government with a minor in Foreign Affairs.

In 1947, facing the prospect of soon graduating with a major he found less than interesting, Earl learned of an opportunity to teach English in a language programme run by a church organization in Warsaw. He signed up. Preparation involved participating in an intensive training course where recruits were inducted into the principles of the Oral Approach. Although plans for work in Poland collapsed, Earl stayed on at the university that had provided the intensive training course, and in 1950 completed a Master's degree in Teaching English as a Foreign Language.

It was during his time as a graduate student that Earl first taught 'English for Foreigners' at Presbyterian Labor Temple on New York's Lower East Side. The guiding light was the most highly acclaimed methods text of the day, *Teaching and Learning English as a Foreign Language*, by Charles C. Fries (1945) of the University of Michigan. Grounded in structurally oriented descriptive linguistics and behavioural psychology, this text set forth the principles of Fries' Oral Approach, calling for a curriculum of intensive oral practice in early language learning. However, in spite of its renown and scientific pedigree, the approach was not particularly engaging for learners. Given this situation, Earl and his colleague Elizabeth Gillilan, the programme director, developed a textbook they hoped would make language learning more interesting without abandoning the principles advocated by Fries. While Earl was still a graduate student, *Practice Book for Students of English* (Gillilan and Stevick 1949) was published, and his first individually authored pedagogical publication, 'Picture-pattern Stories for Teaching English Structure', appeared a few months later (Stevick 1950).

In 1953, Earl received a teaching scholarship that enabled him to pursue doctoral studies in linguistics at Cornell University. At that time, Cornell had a contract with the US Air Force to develop courses in Soviet area languages for Air Force personnel. Earl's main faculty advisor was Charles F. Hockett, a leading figure in American structural linguistics, and as part of his teaching fellowship, Earl worked with Armenian language informants to write and supervise a full-scale two-semester course in East Armenian for Air Force captains. The methodology of choice was a precursor of audiolingualism associated with the American Council of Learned Societies. Always purposeful and creative, Earl developed and introduced into the course 'a substitution drill', which hadn't occurred to the linguists and linguistic scholars of the time.

Following the completion of a doctorate in general linguistics in 1955, Earl took a job at Scarritt College for Christian Workers, in Nashville, Tennessee. There the president of the college persuaded him to apply for a Ford Fellowship. This resulted in two years in Central Africa analysing local languages, 'thereby catapulting' him 'into the position of eleventh ranking African languages specialist in the United States', out of which, he has wryly observed, there were twelve at the time (Stevick 2000: 1).

A central part of Earl's work was at the Language School of the US State Department's Foreign Service Institute (FSI). Hired for the position of 'Scientific Linguist' in 1961, Earl's first task at FSI was to lead a small team of linguists to write basic courses in twelve of the most widely spoken indigenous languages in Africa. This work was to be done using the FSI format, believed to be the best available because of the emphasis on scientific linguistics, that is, materialistic behaviourism. These early years led to astonishing productivity in the creation of courses according to the principles of prevailing scholarly wisdom, and in 1965, the prestigious FSI title of 'Professor of Linguistics' was conferred on their chief architect. Yet the language performance of students who took these courses left something to be desired. As Earl recalls, 'The project was an almost total failure ... As far as I know, there was only one report of anyone getting any use of what had been taught, when a future ambassador, his wife, and their bloodhound named Digby were spared unkind treatment deep in a jungle somewhere' (Stevick 2006: 2).

As the African languages project began to wind down, the reach of the Peace Corps started to expand around the globe. Peace Corps volunteers had to learn and use diverse languages in a wide range of circumstances. The organization needed a language programme that could provide effective, efficient and relevant language training and a consultant who could facilitate the process and flexibly manage the inevitable challenges of such a mandate. Earl was lent to the Peace Corps as needed for the next few years, keeping a packed suitcase ready at all times so as to travel at a moment's notice. Not only did this yield rich and unparalleled experience in language instruction for the FSI consultant, it also provided opportunities to become acquainted with the principles and practices of unconventional methodologies. This, coupled with an emerging interest in memory, brought Earl to an awareness of how limited his previous understandings of learning and teaching languages had been, and a conviction, radical for the time, that 'language study is inevitably a total human experience' (Stevick 1971: viii).

The influence on language teachers: inside and between

With this shift in thinking, Earl's sphere of influence began to expand more than ever as illustrated in a performance rating for the period of 1974–1975, by James Frith, Dean of the FSI School of Language Studies:

> My earlier reports on Dr. Stevick's work reflect a performance which is characterized by initiative, innovation and professional leadership. His work during the past year has shown the same qualities and also demonstrates an ever-widening area of impact.

Dr Frith then noted 17 external engagements ranging from single events to week-long workshops of multiple sessions with a 'diverse range of audiences and professional groups'. He continued:

> I have placed my mark on Dr. Stevick's 'Productivity' in the far right-hand block, which is defined as 'phenomenal'. Phenomenal productivity is an obvious rarity and I have seldom used this block, except to describe Dr. Stevick's work.

At this point Dr Frith listed eight articles in various stages of publication, two unpublished papers and the completed manuscript for *Memory, Meaning and Method: Some Psychological Perspectives on Language Teaching* at the time being considered for publication. He went on, highlighting the significance of the recent conceptual shift that had occurred:

> As our work has evolved in recent years, the focus has shifted from what should be taught to how people learn. In this relatively new

and unnamed field of how people learn languages and interpersonal-intercultural relations, Dr. Stevick is equally as prominent, as attested by his many invitations to take part in professional gatherings on the subject … By any title, Dr. Stevick is a … major contributor of new or reinterpreted ideas in the field of foreign language instruction.

The publication of *Memory, Meaning and Method* the following year, and the response to it, resoundingly corroborated Dr Firth's view of Earl's influence as a major contributor in the field of language instruction. This book, largely a record of Earl's explorations to better understand the human experience of language learning, had a three-part focus: 'Memory is a by-product of Meaning, Method should be the servant of Meaning, and Meaning depends on what happens inside and between people' (Stevick 1976: 160). Remarks from an anonymous reviewer, forwarded to Earl by his publisher in early October of 1976, give some indication of the significance with which the contribution was viewed: 'I am in the middle of Stevick's new book. I feel it is the most important book written in over a decade. I mean that! … Stevick's work is the real thing: honest, thoughtful, human … and useful. Stevick is already making significant dents in the field … I sincerely hope you continue to promote his ideas.'

Requests from readers and Earl's own interest in the dimensions of cognitive and personal depth of language learning, originally addressed in *Memory, Meaning and Method*, led to the publication of *Teaching Languages: A Way and Ways* in 1980. In this book, Earl picked up where *Memory, Meaning and Method* had left off. 'My earlier conclusion was that success depends less on materials, techniques, and linguistic analyses, and more on what goes on inside and between the people in the classroom' (Stevick 1980: 4). And he moved forward: 'I have begun to suspect that the most important aspect of "what goes on" is the presence or absence of harmony – it is the parts working with, or against, one another. How such a thing may happen within and between the people in a language course is the subject of this book' (1980: 5). *A Way and Ways* was awarded the Modern Language Association Mildenberger Medal in recognition of its significance to the field and prompted enthusiastic responses on the part of many readers. One teacher wrote: 'This is my first fan letter ever. I've just finished *A Way and Ways* and I had to write to say "thank you" for putting down so clearly and sensitively what it is we ESL teachers have been grappling with' (personal communication, September 1981). Robert Blair, in his book *Innovative Approaches to Language Teaching* (1982), provided additional perspective on the significance attached to Earl's work by his contemporaries:

> If asked to name the persons who have contributed the most to the development of language training methodology congruent with current

views of instructional psychology and language acquisition, without
hesitation, I would put the name of Earl W. Stevick at the top ... He
is a masterful teacher of language himself and open to new ideas.
His informal experimentation with various innovative approaches to
language instruction and his insightful probings into what makes them
tick, published in many articles and books, have earned him the high
regard of the profession.

(Blair 1982: 100–1)

Earl's influence as both a master teacher and theorist of language learning continued for the next two decades, evidenced in part by the publication of additional books (Stevick 1982, 1986, 1989, 1990, 1998). In
1996, twenty years after the original publication of *Memory, Meaning
and Method*, a second, much revised, twentieth-anniversary edition
appeared. That same year, Earl was awarded the Georgetown University
Round Table Medal, honoured as a pioneer in the field and 'one of the
most widely respected writers on the theory and practice of language
teaching' (Alatis 1996: 3).

However, Earl's influence was not just a result of the insightful and
innovative ideas represented in his work. It was also due to the way in
which he communicated:

While what he says is challenging in the extreme, how he says it is
a lesson in putting a point of view over in a way that takes effect.
Stevick's gift as a writer is his ability to sustain a conversation with the
reader, which leads to a feeling of well-being ... and it makes us ready
to engage in an internal dialogue.

(Hamilton 1996: 258)

Others also noted Earl's influence, including David Nunan (1999: vi),
who expressed appreciation and gratitude:

In the late 1970s I read a book that profoundly changed the way I
thought and felt about language teaching and about myself as a teacher.
The book was by Earl Stevick, and it was called *Memory, Meaning
and Method*. In subsequent years I had the honor of meeting Earl, and
of becoming his friend ... Thank you, Earl. It is to honor your work,
and your influence on my own, that I respectfully dedicate *Second
Language Teaching and Learning* to you.

Current influence: embedded in practice

Earl's influence continues. Although the present post-method state of
affairs differs greatly from the preoccupation with methods that prevailed when he began to investigate the human dimension of language

A *way with words*

study, some things have not changed. Language learning is still, inevitably, a total human experience. What goes on inside and between people in the process continues to be of fundamental importance. And Earl's work continues to serve as a source of insight and a catalyst for seeking new understandings. His legacy has been celebrated publicly in professional circles (e.g. Arnold 1999a; Edge 2006, 2008) and has been the focus of doctoral work (Byrne 2006). He has engaged in published dialogue (Stevick with Kristjánsson 2009). His influence has been acknowledged in the dedication sections of publications by educators whose own work is a source of guidance for language teachers in many parts of the globe (e.g. Freeman with Cornwell 1993; Arnold 1999b; Nunan 1999; Edge 2002; Palmer and Christison 2007). And then there is this book. It presents readers with many more examples of the wide-ranging and ongoing influence of Earl W. Stevick and his singular talent – his way with words, words that continue to inspire.

References

Alatis, J. (1996) 'Dedication of round table proceedings to Earl W. Stevick', in Alatis, J. (ed.) *Georgetown University Round Table on Languages and Linguistics 1996*, Washington, DC: Georgetown University Press, pp. 3–4.

Arnold, J. (1999a) *Affective Learning, Effective Learning: A Tribute to Earl Stevick*, panel presented at the 33rd Annual TESOL Convention, New York 9–13 March.

Arnold, J. (ed.) (1999b) *Affect in Language Learning*, Cambridge: Cambridge University Press.

Blair, R. (1982) *Innovative Approaches to Language Teaching*, Rowley, MA: Newbury House.

Byrne, M. (2006) 'The teaching and learning of foreign languages and the influence of Earl W. Stevick', PhD thesis, National University of Ireland at Galway.

Edge, J. (ed.) (2002) *Continuing Professional Development*, Whitstable: IATEFL.

Edge. J. (2006) 'Daring not to evaluate: non-judgmental discourse', colloquium presentation at the 40th Annual TESOL Convention, *Daring to Lead*, Tampa Bay, FL, 15–19 March.

Edge, J. (2008) 'In search of depth', colloquium presentation at the 42nd Annual TESOL Convention, *TESOL's Most Creative Practices*, New York, 2–5 April.

Freeman, D. with Cornwell, S. (eds.) (1993) *New Ways in Teacher Education*, Alexandria: TESOL.

Fries, C. (1945) *Teaching and Learning English as a Foreign Language*, Ann Arbor: University of Michigan Press.

Gillilan, E. and Stevick, E. (1949) *Practice Book for Students of English*, New York: Presbyterian Institute of Industrial Relations.

Hamilton, J. (1996) *Inspiring Innovations in Language Teaching*, Clevedon: Multilingual Matters.

Nunan, D. (1999) *Second Language Teaching and Learning*, Boston: Heinle & Heinle.

Palmer, A. and Christison, M. (2007) *Seeking the Heart of Teaching*, Ann Arbor: University of Michigan Press.

Stevick, E. W. (1950) 'Picture-pattern stories for teaching English structure', *Language Learning*, 3: 34–7.

Stevick, E. W. (1971) *Adapting and Writing Language Lessons*, Washington, DC: Superintendent of Documents.

Stevick, E. W. (1976) *Memory, Meaning and Method: Some Psychological Perspectives on Language Learning*, Boston: Heinle & Heinle.

Stevick, E. W. (1980) *Teaching Languages: A Way and Ways*, Boston: Heinle & Heinle.

Stevick, E. W. (1982) *Teaching and Learning Languages*, Cambridge: Cambridge University Press.

Stevick, E. W. (1986) *Images and Options in the Language Classroom*, Cambridge: Cambridge University Press.

Stevick, E. W. (1989) *Success with Foreign Languages*, New York: Prentice Hall.

Stevick, E. W. (1990) *Humanism in Language Teaching*, Oxford: Oxford University Press.

Stevick, E. W. (1996) *Memory, Meaning and Method: A View of Language Teaching*, 2nd edn, Boston: Heinle & Heinle.

Stevick, E. W. (1998) *Working with Teaching Methods: What's at Stake?*, Boston: Heinle & Heinle.

Stevick, E. W. (2000) *Autobiographical Statement*. Available online at http://www.celea.net/sites/default/files/file/stevick/AFTERWORDS-9-AUTOBIO.pdf (accessed 21 June 2011).

Stevick, E. W. (2006) *Faith and Practices: Then & Now*, Commencement Address, Trinity Western University, Langley, Canada, 21 October.

Stevick, E. W. with Kristjánsson, C. (2009) 'Afterword: the dilemma', in Wong, M. and Canagarajah, S. (eds.) *Christian and Critical English Language Educators in Dialogue: Pedagogical and Ethical Dilemmas*, New York: Routledge, pp. 292–7.

Appendix: Words of tribute to Earl Stevick

I first met Earl when I invited him to give a workshop for teachers in Seville in the mid-1990s. For many reasons this was a very special experience for me, one from which I learned a lot. I felt very close to Earl, in part, of course, because I had read and long admired his writing in the field. But there was something else. Something I couldn't put my finger on until one day I asked him where he was from and he told me that he had grown up in Joplin, Missouri. That was it. My father and my uncle came from a town just a few miles away, and Earl's way of speaking reminded me of that of my father and uncle. And just as his speaking voice touched a deep part of me, his writing has given a clear and elegant formulation to many things I intuited were important in language teaching. His presence has been a guiding light for me throughout the years.

This volume is merely one way to say 'Thanks, Earl, for so much.'

Jane Arnold

My first meeting with Earl Stevick was in Brattleboro, Vermont, in 1973, at SIT. I had the honor of sharing a special weekend program with him in which we worked with the SIT TESOL students. I was then a fledgling assistant professor at the University of Michigan. In his first lecture, he started out by stating a seemingly random sequence of letters and numbers, e.g., 'D2K7S,' then showing how that 'syntactic' structure could be manipulated – by substitution, permutation and deletion – just like language. We of course discovered the sequence wasn't random at all, but rather ordered by a set of governing rules.

More memorable was the fact that this rather famous person was approachable, down to earth and genuinely interested in helping seminar participants to apply psychological foundations of language teaching to their own classroom practice.

And he's been doing so ever since! Earl is a person who, rightly so, will not spoon feed a student, but rather will make that student *think*. In many ways, perhaps subconsciously, I have sought to model Earl's pedagogical artistry in my own teaching. I join thousands of others in this profession who can utter a huge word of thanks to Earl Stevick, giant of a man, for all he has done to teach us all lessons we needed to learn.

Here's to you, Earl!

Doug Brown

Words of tribute to Earl Stevick

My encounters with Earl Stevick came early in my career as a graduate student and then as a young faculty member at Georgetown University. Expanding on Bakhtin, I would describe them as 'imagined dialogues at a distance', intellectual engagements with the work of someone who had taught languages and taught language teachers in so many different assignments through the Foreign Service Institute – and yet spoke with refreshing directness, practical sagacity and wonderful humanity to me who loved to teach language and was eager to learn as much as I could from 'the pros'. Over time, seeing him in the context of numerous Georgetown University Round Tables, it became possible to turn that communication at a distance into a very real sense of personal admiration for someone 'who knew what he was talking about' and had the courage to say so. I thank him for that!

Heidi Byrnes

I first met Earl Stevick in 1973 when I was at the University of Michigan, a graduate student delving into methodological debates with colleagues and participating in the workshops and seminars he offered under the auspices of the English Language Institute. His influence on my work has been significant; it is not an exaggeration to say that everything I have done in my professional career draws directly on his ideas. Stevick represents the consummate scholarly practitioner, a learner of languages who delights in pursuing linguistic nuance, a conscientious teacher and a researcher whose search for solutions to classroom conundrums has led him into explorations of pop psychology (Eric Berne's *Games People Play*, Thomas Harris's *I'm Okay, You're Okay*, Timothy Gallwey's *Inner Game of Tennis*), a detailed elaboration of the 'designer methods' (Suggestopedia, the Silent Way, Counselling-Learning) and a rigorous examination of the electrochemical changes in the brain involved in learning a language. He is not afraid to engage unconventional perspectives as he seeks answers to questions of teaching and learning. He draws on the work of cultural anthropologist Ernest Becker, philosopher and spiritual guide Krishnamurti, the poet W. H. Auden and Russian novelist Fyodor Dostoyevsky. He alarmed his editors with the proposed title for his book, *Teaching Languages: A Matter of Life and Death*. They persuaded him that *Teaching Languages: A Way and Ways* would resonate better with the intended readership. And, it is significant that the title of his revision of the text for Donald Freeman's series – *Working with Teaching Methods: What's at Stake* – permits the reader to decide for him-/herself if teaching is, in fact, a matter of life or death.

Mark Clarke

Words of tribute to Earl Stevick

In the early 1990s, when I was still living in Hungary, I started to do research on group dynamics in language learning with a friend, Angi Malderez. We decided to pool our experiences about groups and produced a comprehensive review article, which, to our dismay, was at first misunderstood by most journal reviewers. They simply did not see the point of looking at group dynamics and typically mistook 'group dynamics' for 'group work'. As a result, our paper was rejected by several journals and I was about to give up on the topic. Then one day, out of the blue, I received a letter from Earl, whom I didn't know then; as it turned out, he had been one of the (positive) reviewers of our manuscript and was upset that it had been rejected. He wrote a very kind message (as he would!) in which he encouraged us not to give up but keep trying. This encouragement finally brought fruit, and Angi and I managed to publish not one but two papers on the topic: the first one in *System*, in 1997, where the editor became very supportive after reading Earl's comments, which I copied to him; the second, in 1999, in an anthology on affect in language learning edited by Jane Arnold, to whom Earl had introduced us. Afterwards, things gathered momentum, and this initial work led to the publication of a theoretical book on group dynamics and group psychology with Madeline Ehrman, *Interpersonal Dynamics in Second Language Education* (1998), followed a few years later by a more practical book with Tim Murphey, *Group Dynamics in the Language Classroom* (2003). Thus, group dynamics has become one of my main specialization areas, but I never forget that all this goes back to Earl's message: I really don't know how things would have worked out without his initial contact and encouragement. A little kindness and caring can go a long way – thank you so much, Earl!

Zoltán Dörnyei

I closed my 1993 book, *Essentials of English Language Teaching*, with the following lines (p. 140):

> The most profound yet practical body of work on ELT is that of Earl Stevick. The first two chapters of Stevick (1980) would be a good place to start and, with great respect and thanks, that is where I should like to finish.

I haven't changed my mind. When I gave Earl a copy of the book, he asked me to sign it by those words. And he signed for me the copy of the new edition of *Memory, Meaning and Method* that I'd taken along. We talked for a couple of hours while the summer rain fell in Vermont. A strong, warm and sustaining memory.

Julian Edge

Words of tribute to Earl Stevick

It was my privilege to get to know Earl well as one of his colleagues at the US Foreign Service Institute. When I returned from my tour of duty in Thailand in 1975, I was ripe and ready for what he had to teach me, and I learned from him eagerly. He introduced me to the Silent Way and Counselling-Learning, and we collaborated in an effort to bring these approaches to FSI. Together we learned what *not* to do when attempting institutional change with an unready clientele, and yet at the same time, our effort took hold in a few language sections. Earl's broad thinking and emphasis on the whole person of the learner (cognitive, physical, emotional) were important precursors to my later turn to psychology. He might not be in full sympathy with my psychoanalytic orientation, and yet his influence still resonates for me even within that surprisingly humane approach.

One special memory is of reading and discussing the manuscript of *A Way and Ways* as he wrote it. From that experience alone, I learned an extraordinary amount about the philosophy of learning and human nature. I have never forgotten Earl's efforts to manage such dichotomies as necessary structure and needful freedom; these remain part of my own philosophical underpinnings. And for sheer fun – which was seldom lacking with Earl – I was one of the interviewees for his book on seven successful language learners. After a series of name changes, I ended up as 'Gwen'.

Thank you, Earl, for the opportunity to learn so much from you, and to enjoy your companionship as we both sought to understand the fascinating complexity we faced every day.

Madeline Ehrman

I have never had the honour of meeting Earl Stevick personally, but his work has lead to an important change in the orientation in my professional activity as a trainer of teachers of Spanish as a foreign language in Spain. From his books I have received not just information but, more importantly, inspiration. Having drawn on knowledge from many fields, he offers very useful guidelines that help us to improve our teaching practice in diverse ways.

For me Earl Stevick is a true master. Reading his books, a real educational experience, strengthens the vocation of those of us who are involved in language teaching. While he may not be an author who presents radically new, trendy issues – which may be out of date in a year or so anyway – he puts things we have always been concerned with in a new light, helping us to move towards a deeper knowledge of what teaching is really about. Reading Stevick increases our interest in humanizing teaching, in going beyond the mere acquisition of techniques.

315

Words of tribute to Earl Stevick

In Stevick's work I have found a strong visual metaphor – the creation of spaces of learning – for bringing about 'a world of meaningful action' in the classroom. This image helps me to better understand the relationship between teacher and students that facilitates the growth of both in a context where control and initiative are exercised in the most effective way. There, a harmonious conceptual structure lets the teacher organize the classroom community so learners can give the best of themselves and thus develop their potential.

José Manuel Foncubierta

My personal interaction with Earl began when, as a graduate student, I wrote to request a copy of a paper he had prepared for a panel discussion at TESOL. Not only did I receive the paper as requested, but to my amazement he expressed interest in my research and asked if he might introduce me to someone else with similar interests. That was the beginning of an enduring friendship. Since then I have come to realize the extent to which Earl has left his mark on the profession, not only through his public legacy, but also by quietly and consistently investing in people behind the scenes. At the core of this interaction is a commitment to what can best be described as self-giving, an understanding of life's activities as 'sacramental' (see *Humanism in Language Teaching*, 1990). Thank you Earl for the friendship you have shown to so many of us!

Carolyn Kristjánsson

Earl Stevick was on the MAT Board of Advisors at the School for International Training in Brattleboro, Vermont, and had a profound influence on the founding and guiding of the Masters in Teaching Languages (MAT) Program. We were fortunate to have him visit the campus every year, sometimes twice, to engage the MAT students and the faculty in thinking deeply about their teaching. He always asked to have dinner with a few students the night before the session. It was his way of getting to know what that particular class of students was thinking about, and he always found a way of addressing their issues the next day.

316

Earl's plenary at a TESOL convention was the first (and last time) that I ever saw anyone deliver a major address by standing in the middle of the stage, not in front of a lectern, and by speaking fluently and effortlessly, only occasionally consulting a handful of small cards. I am sure that it was the strength of his conviction in what he was saying that made for that most memorable talk – in style and substance.

Diane Larsen-Freeman

I first met Earl at a summer course run by ESADE in Barcelona in 1978. I found him dauntingly intense on first acquaintance, only later coming to appreciate his puckish wit and humour.

The high point of that event was a high-risk, public learning conversation he had on stage with Chris Brumfit to demonstrate the way a Counselling-Learning session might work to revive the vestigial Swahili which Brumfit had acquired in his youth. I have never forgotten the gentle yet firm way Earl scaffolded Chris through that session. It was testimony both to Earl's courage and to his skill. I salute the master!

On leaving Barcelona, he gave me a copy of his hand-produced small collection of poems (*Short Texts for Intermediate and Advanced Students of English as an Additional Language*, 1977) written in the beautiful copperplate he had taught himself. It seems appropriate to quote one of these texts.

Advice

If you try to pull a stamp

    off an envelope,

You are likely to tear it.

But if you hold the stamp,

    and pull the envelope away from it,

The stamp will not tear.

This really works.

Try it sometime!

People are like that, too.

You can take a lot away from me

If you will leave me as I am,

But if you try to pull me away

From something that I have stuck

    myself to,

It will be hard for you, and

    very hard on me.

I hope you won't forget this

    next time.

    (EWS)

Alan Maley

In the mid-1970s when I was doing my MA on situationally motivated teacher produced texts, I was much inspired by Earl's 1971 book entitled *Writing and Adapting Language Lessons*. Later, after meeting him several times at conferences and reading more of his work, I learned that Earl's experience working with the Peace Corps and with people learning 'lesser known' languages gave him an appreciation for how teachers need to adapt materials and themselves to adjust to students so they could learn. More recently this is being called the 'social turn' or 'alignment'. Earl Stevick gave me a heightened sense of what I could do to make learning easier for others, and the crucial point was that I needed to study my students. I needed to learn from them as I taught in order to adjust to them, something that Earl modelled so well. His practical books for teachers explained much of what was useful in more erudite studies in psychology, linguistics and communication and scaffolded readers gently into deeper studies. Reading his books, quite simply, makes you want to be a better person, student and teacher.

Tim Murphey

It is an intensely hot summer in 1990. I am in Barcelona as a member of the faculty at the TESOL Summer Institute at Esade Idiomas. I am delighted to find myself sharing an apartment above a noisy bar with Earl Stevick. Earl is not one for bars or restaurants, and many evenings

I spend with him sharing a simple meal made up of items garnered from the local market.

Most evenings, Earl calls his wife, to whom he is devoted. On several nights, he also makes lengthy calls to someone else. Knowing just how expensive international calls are, one night, sticking my nose in where it has no business to be, I ask him about the calls.

'Oh,' he replies, 'I'm just trying to help out a neighbour in need.'

And for me, that was Earl – quietly, modestly, unassumingly trying to help a neighbour in need.

David Nunan

Earl Stevick is one of the people whose thinking has influenced my own work deeply, to the extent that although I've never had the privilege of meeting him in person, I feel I've known him for almost all of my professional life.

I started my own career as a fairly traditional teacher of English as a foreign language in Austria. Then, just as I was beginning to notice that what I was doing in my classrooms was not at all in line with why I had initially wanted to become a teacher, I was lucky enough to come across Earl's books – and they had a very positive influence on the development of my teaching and were real eye-openers for me. And 10 years after first reading a book by Earl, I was over the moon when he, in his *Images and Options in the Language Classroom,* quoted an article I had written with my colleague Gunter Gerngross – for me as a new writer that was a fantastic experience! I felt blessed and incredibly inspired at the same time.

Herbert Puchta

In early June, 1964, my wife and I were preparing to teach English in Thailand at the Missionary Orientation Center at Stony Point, New York. I had just gotten an MA in Theoretical Linguistics at Ohio State University which had simultaneously prepared me, so I assumed, also to be a trained EFL teacher. Part of our orientation was led by an energetic young linguist who specialized in language teaching, and without him and his textbook, my three years in Thailand would have been a pedagogical disaster. I frequently relied on *Helping People Learn English.* Even back then, Earl peppered both his teaching and writing with ideas which were pragmatic, open-minded and student centered. He argued that his purpose was 'not to propagate a method or to suggest a single set of materials'. He encouraged teachers to 'start where the students are' and 'as they grow surer of themselves, you should give them greater

319

freedom'. One especially important reminder for me was his insight that 'Even in a lesson that looks perfectly simple to you, the number of new things to trouble a beginner is surprising.'

Years later, I began to meet Earl at the annual TESOL conventions, and even when we sometimes ended up with contrasting perspectives about methodology, he remained open-minded in all our dialogues and shared flashes of wry humor. Over the years, my mentor also became a valued colleague as we participated together in several public presentations and academic projects. Little did I know how fortunate I was back then in Stony Point to have had Earl Stevick as a teacher trainer, and I am blessed to call him a mentor, a colleague and a friend.

Thomas Scovel

I have never met Earl, but I feel I know him well, both through his books, and through the occasional exchanges we have had over the last 10 years, mainly by email. Not only that, a few years back I taught a semester at the School for International Training, in Vermont, and the legacy of his formative role in the MA program there was still palpable.

The first book of Earl's that I read was *A Way and Ways*. For some reason a copy came my way in Egypt, where, having taught for three or four years, I was at the point in my development as a teacher where the 'received wisdoms' of my initial training were ripe for de-stabilization. Earl's book triggered what might now be called a 'phase shift'. Until that point, I had construed language learning as a somewhat de-humanized, and at best solely cognitive process. By opening my eyes to the emotional and attitudinal dimension of learning, under the umbrella of humanistic learning theory, *A Way and Ways* marked a turning point in my professional development. I am forever grateful.

Scott Thornbury

Talking the Walk. Miami 1987 ... A large conference hotel right on the beach. There are several thousand teachers at the annual TESOL convention and it's my first visit. Marvellous organization, and I find real friendliness. Earl is one of the speakers, and of course everyone wants to talk to the stars ... usually initiated by catching them in a queue or at the end of a talk ... followed by a meeting hurriedly carried out on a convenient chair amongst the crowds. But when I speak with him, Earl immediately suggests a time and place to meet, and I feel I have a real appointment. And something else, when we meet it is not to sit at a table but rather for a walking talk, crisscrossing at a leisurely speed through the conference and the cafes, round and about the terraces and the beach, a reassuring and unusual way to focus and listen. And later I realized something else … walking around makes for a conversation that is both public and visible with no hiding, and yet private. It is clear that for that moment there is no interrupting, as it is a dialogue for two. It was a good lesson in how to have an attentive exchange of meaning within a large and distracting setting.

Adrian Underhill

Index

Index

Index

Kegan, Robert 297, 298
Kelley, Harold 112
kinesthetic image schemata 63–4
knowledge
  building on prior knowledge 47, 49–50,
    58–60
  physical aspect in the brain 46–7
knowledge integration 49–50, 51
Kohonen, Viljo 87–8, 112
Kramsch, C. 226–7
Kristjánsson, Carolyn 127

L1, use in teaching 147–8
L2 Motivational Self System 29, 36–42
Lahey, Lisa 297
languaculture concept 231
language as a semiotic system 225
language learner *see* learner
language learning methodologies 256
language learning
  role of agency 1–3
  social turn 65–9
language socialization theory 65
language teaching objectives 127–9
learner autonomy 256
learner beliefs
  changing limiting beliefs 37–9
  influence on learning 30–1
learner-centred education 3–4, 111–12, 118
learner engagement 192–4
  and ownership 50, 51–2
  and personal discovery 50
learner identity 224
  definitions 26
learner interactions
  action logs 179–80
  and adjustment 178–83
  Longitudinal Self-Evaluated Videoing
    (LSEV) 181–2
  Near Peer Role Models (NPRMs) 179,
    180–1, 182
  newsletters 179–80
  telephoning in English 179–80
  video interview of potential NPRMs
    180–1
learner narratives 95
  case studies 98
  categories 96–8
  complexity 99
  context of narrative research 95–6
  cultural issues 99–100

diaries/journals 97
emotion 99–100
flow 98–9
histories 96–7
hot cognition 98–9
identity 100–1
themes 98–101
use in educational research 112–25
with researcher/teacher interpretation
  96–7
see also learners' stories
learner narratives analysis
  accept subjectivity 102
  aesthetic interpretations 102–3
  approaches and aids 101–5
  axial-coding stage 102
  benefits for teacher development 104–5
  check and evaluate the narrative 104
  draw trajectories 104
  empathy 101
  expect complexity 103
  interpret themes through grounded
    theory 102
  look for influences 103–4
  narrative treated as a case 103
  notice triple re-storying 102
  open-coding stage 102
  selective coding stage 102
learner to learning advisor (case history)
  252–65
learners
  accommodating different learning
    rates 191–5
  agency concept 11–12, 242
  inert knowledge problem 195–9
  initiative in the classroom 25
  inner learning processes 207–17
  meaning-making inside 7–8
  relevance of the learning experience 11
  role in discursive accomplishment of
    Trust 82–7
  self-esteem 224
  sense of security in the classroom 54, 57
  viewed as 'person-in-the-world' 11
learners' stories
  Alice and Grace 115–16
  condensed narrative 119–22
  Gloria 119–22
  implications for teachers 122–4
  insights into the language learning
    process 122–4

Index

narratives
  language learner to learning advisor
    252–65
  see also learner narratives; learners' stories
National Writing Project (US) 281–2, 283
Natural Approach 152
Near Peer Role Models (NPRMs) 179,
  180–1, 182
negative emotions associated with language
  learning 45–6
neurobiology of learning processes 46–60
  building on prior knowledge 47, 49–50
  choice of texts for adult learners 52–60
  development of cognitive tools 54–8
  effects of practice 48
  knowledge is physical 46–7
  learning as brain change 47–8
  neuronal networks 46–7
  ownership 50, 51–2
  role of emotions 49–50
  teaching as an art 51–2
neuronal networks 46–7
neuroscience
  insights from 46–60
  no best method for teaching
    languages 144
newsletters, student interaction 179–80
noticing
  and learning 138
  role in high-level language learning 256
Nunan, D. 111

open-ended practice stage 167
organizational change, analysing resistance
  to 295–301
organizational identity 289–90, 292–5
Ortega, Lourdes 185–6
ownership 60, 89
  and learner engagement 50, 51–2
  of language and languages 226–32, 237
Oxford, Rebecca 257

Palmer, P. J. 4
personal competence 223, 237
  and dialogical competence 226
  goals of language teaching 224–5
  in multilingual and multicultural
    contexts 223–6
  language as a semiotic system 225
phonemic differences in sounds 190–1
phonetic differences in sounds 190–1

physical movement, influence on
  learning 64
Piaget, Jean 112, 173, 245
Pike, Kenneth 190
political geography of Discourses 237
polyphony 234
positive emotions associated with language
  learning 45
positive identity development 8
positivistic curriculum paradigm 87–92
possible selves motivation 37–42
poststructuralist view of identity 101
practice, effects of 48
presentation–practice–production (PPP) 167
primacy
  feeling in learners 34–5
  sense of 2, 4
Principled Communicative Approach
  (PCA) 165–9
  controlled practice principle 169
  corrective feedback options 166
  declarative input principle 169
  explicit options 166
  fluency and automatization 166–7
  focus on form (FonF) 165–6
  focus-on-form principle 169
  focused interaction principle 169
  form-focused instruction (FFI) 165–6
  formulaic language 167–8
  input-based options 166
  language exposure principle 169
  personal significance principle 168–9
  production options 166
  skill learning theory 167
prior knowledge, building on 47, 49–50,
  58–60
problem solving, and extended cognition
  69–72
proceduralization stage of language
  learning 133
psychological atmosphere of the teacher
  204–5
psychological factors in success and
  failure 287–9
purpose, sense of 2

question formation 197–8

random learning style 256
reading, role in language learning 255
reading aloud 147

328